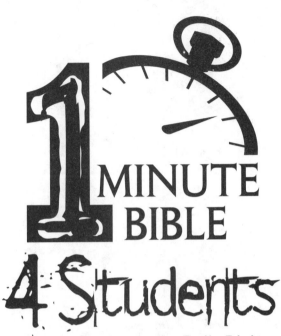

1 MINUTE BIBLE 4 Students

With 366 Devotions for Daily Living

from The New Living Translation

editor JOHN R. KOHLENBERGER III
applications by DOUG FIELDS

HOLMAN
BIBLE PUBLISHERS

Page Design by Susan Scruggs

17 08 07 06
Q

PRINTED IN THE UNITED STATES OF AMERICA

Table of Contents

Table of Contents

A General intro

The Bible is the greatest of all books. More than a book, it is in fact a collection of sixty-six books written over the span of sixteen centuries by kings and peasants, poets and prophets.

The books of the Law, Genesis through Deuteronomy, recount the early history of humanity and the great covenant at Sinai by which the living God of the universe bound Himself to the Nation of Israel. The historical books of Joshua through Ester highlight the covenant history of Israel, noting both Israel's successes and failures in keeping the covenant and God's patience and grace in enforcing its terms.

The books of poetry and wisdom, Job through Song of Songs, celebrate the God of Israel for His goodness, His holiness, and his accessibility to all who approach Him on His terms. Wisdom offers timeless principles for a successful life in relation to God and His creation.

The prophets, Isaiah through Malachi, were the preachers of old. They proclaimed to the Israelites their failure to honor covenant obligations to their God, warned them of His impending righteous judgment, and offered hope to all nations of His coming salvation.

The Gospels, Matthew through John, tell of the life and the teaching of Jesus the Messiah, the promised Savior of Israel and the nations. The book of Acts recounts the early history of the Christian church as the followers of Jesus take His message to the farthest corners of the globe.

The letters of epistles, Romans through Jude, were written by the first leaders of the church to Christian congregations and their leadership, offering encouragement, discipline, teaching, and hope. The book of Revelation tells of the end of this present world and of the establishment of the new heavens and new earth in which God will live with His people forever.

We hope The One-Minute Bible™ for Students offers you a taste of God's Word that will not be fully satisfied by our bite-sized sampling. We encourage you to read daily from a full-text Bible, perhaps even following an annual read-through-the-Bible plan.

The Editor

A Note to Students

Every day I hear students' thoughts, concerns, doubts, and **questions** about life, Christianity, God, and the Bible. In the One-Minute Bible™ for Students, I try to provide clear understandable answers—**God's answers.** The 366 daily applications in the One-Minute Bible™ for Students are intended to help you **immediately** apply God's Word to your life.

Here's one principle to remember while reading The One-Minute Bible™ for Students: **Don't give up** if you don't understand. Some parts of the Bible are **tough** to understand. **Keep reading! Ask questions!** Pray that God would make His Word **clear** to you. Keep going . . .
you can do it.

I applaud you for digging in and learning about God. **My prayer** is that your faith will grow as you take regular doses of His Word.

A Note to parents

This product was designed to meet the needs of your son or daughter. If your child has no Bible background, this book will serve as a **perfect** introductory tool! I've found that almost anyone will give a minute a day to the **greatest** book ever written. Or, if your child has grown up in the church or is a mature Christian, The One-Minute Bible™ for Students will be a **powerful** devotional resource. The content is intended to foster and encourage **spiritual** maturity.

Put this book in your child's hands, comment on the **ease** of readings, and leave him or her alone to **discover God's Word.**

My prayer is that his book will **ignite** a desire to consume more of God's love letter.

A Note to Youth Workers

As a **youth pastor** and author of twenty books, I can't think of any book, aside from the Bible itself, that I'm more **excited** for my students to read than The One-Minute Bible™ for Students. This book will not only help students understand the Bible, but it emphasizes God's **passionate** and **unconditional** love for them and will challenge them to **respond**.

Youth ministry is tough in today's world! As you know, most students are not reading the Bible. We are ministering to a **biblically illiterate** generation. They need tools to guide them through the Scriptures and **help** them understand God's Word.

My prayer is that The One-Minute Bible™ for Students will assist you in your ministry to students. I've written a 52-week teaching and small group curriculum to accompany this book and help reinforce what your students are reading. **Contact me** if you are interested.

Doug Fields
Making Young Lives Count
21612 Plano Trabuco Q-30
Trabuco Canyon, CA 92679
www.dougfields.com
www.youthworker.com

Answers to Some Common **questions**

Where do I begin?

The One-Minute Bible™ for Students offers 366 daily one-minute readings from the world's greatest literary Treasure . . . the Bible. Each day of the year, the date is indicated at the top of the page. Although this provides a one-year reading plan, you can start wherever you'd like—you don't have to limit yourself to starting in January or to reading one page a day!

Is this the entire Bible?

Although every day contains selections from the Bible, *The One-Minute Bible™ for Students* isn't a complete Bible. Reading one minute a day will allow you to survey the heart of the Bible in one year. If you want more, we've provided related texts at the end of each day to direct you to nearly 1,800 passages of Scripture that will further your understanding of the topics covered in that day's reading.

How much of the Bible is covered?

The One-Minute Bible™ for Students begins with the first verse of Genesis and ends with the last verse of Revelation. Readings follow the general flow of biblical history, interspersed with several topical series for occasions such as Easter and Mother's Day. The 700 selected Scriptures and 1,800 related texts present the key themes of the Bible and draw from all sixty-six books. Great care was taken to ensure that each text has the same meaning in *The One-Minute Bible™ for Students* as it does in its larger context in the Bible.

What happens if I don't read every day?

If you fall behind in your daily reading program, don't worry! You can make up one week in seven minutes, half a month in fifteen. But again, don't be discouraged by failing to follow our schedule. If you get behind, simply jump back in where you left off and

"Just Read It!"

A Note About the Different Daily applications

JUST a THOUGHT

issues straightforward challenge to the mind and heart

In OTHER Words

defines a theological word in everyday terms

BIG TIMe WoRd

describes a specific word or topic that is important for today

CATCH THIS

presents a short devotional reading that builds on the day's topic

Weird or What?

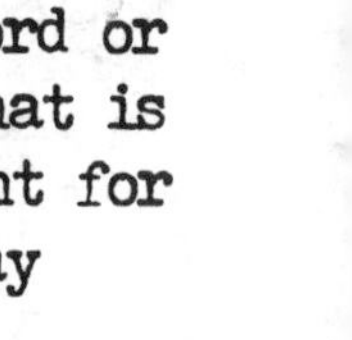

highlights an interesting, trivial, or just plain weird fact

A Note About the Different Daily applications

Personality Plus

features a short biographical sketch of a biblical character

CHECK IT OUT

directs students to other Scriptures that shed more light on the subject

What's it Mean?

clarifies the message of the text with the background information and application

One Minute Memory

extracts from the Scripture reading, a truly memorable verse

Give it a try

offers involvement with the text through written expression

Books of the Bible

Old Testament

Genesis
Exodus
Leviticus
Numbers
Deuteronomy
Joshua
Judges
Ruth
1 Samuel
2 Samuel
1 Kings
2 Kings
1 Chronicles
2 Chronicles
Ezra
Nehemiah
Esther
Job
Psalms
Proverbs
Ecclesiastes
Song of Songs
Isaiah
Jeremiah
Lamentations
Ezekiel
Daniel
Hosea
Joel
Amos
Obadiah
Jonah
Micah
Nahum
Habakkuk
Zephaniah
Haggai
Zechariah
Malachi

New Testament

Matthew
Mark
Luke
John
Acts
Romans
1 Corinthians
2 Corinthians
Galatians
Ephesians
Philippians
Colossians
1 Thessalonians
2 Thessalonians
1 Timothy
2 Timothy
Titus
Philemon
Hebrews
James
1 Peter
2 Peter
1 John
2 John
3 John
Jude
Revelation

January

Sin will keep you from this book.

This book will keep you from sin.

Dwight L. Moody
(1837–1899)
American Evangelist

In the Beginning

In the beginning God created the heavens and the earth. The earth was empty, a formless mass cloaked in darkness. And the Spirit of God was hovering over its surface.

Genesis 1:1-2

In the beginning the Word already existed. He was with God, and he was God. He was in the beginning with God. He created everything there is. Nothing exists that he didn't make. Life itself was in him, and this life gives light to everyone. The light shines through the darkness, and the darkness can never extinguish it.

John 1:1-5

Praise the LORD from the heavens!
  Praise him from the skies!
Praise him, all his angels!
  Praise him, all the armies of heaven!
Praise him, sun and moon!
  Praise him, all you twinkling stars!
Praise him, skies above!
  Praise him, vapors high above the clouds!
Let every created thing give praise to the
    LORD,
  for he issued his command, and they came
    into being.
He established them forever and forever.
  His orders will never be revoked.

Psalm 148:1-6

Related texts: Psalms 102:25-28; 139:13-18; Proverbs 8; Isaiah 40:12-31; 45:18-25; Hebrews 11:1-3

CATCH THIS

These few verses sure cause big debates in science class. Unfortunately, there are no quick or easy answers in the creation and evolution controversy. Believers in evolution claim our world suddenly exploded into existence billions of years ago—pits of slime somehow sprouted legs and started growing chest hair. It's a good story for those who don't believe in God or the Bible. The Bible informs us that God created the earth, and through Him all things were made—including us.

Actually, it takes less faith to believe God created this world and us than it does to believe our complex minds and bodies evolved from a "big bang" and a drop of ooze.

God created each of us in His image. Try thinking about that the next twenty-one times you look in the mirror. Our uniqueness is no accident!

done ☐

creation

CHECK IT OUT

The Bible uses the term "light" on many different occasions. In Matthew 5:14-16, Jesus used the illustration of light to challenge and remind Christians that their lives are open books. Jesus said, "You are the light of the world. . . . Don't hide your light. . . . Let it shine for all to see . . . so that everyone will praise your heavenly Father."

Being a light to the world is a high calling! It's pretty wild to realize that you may be the only Christian your friends will ever meet.

Are you shining brightly? If not, what are a few things you could do to become a stronger light for God?

Let There Be Light

Then God said, "Let there be light," and there was light. And God saw that it was good. Then he separated the light from the darkness. God called the light "day" and the darkness "night." Together these made up one day.

Genesis 1:3-5

O LORD, you are my light;
yes, LORD, you light up my darkness.

2 Samuel 22:29

The LORD is my light and my salvation—
so why should I be afraid?

Psalm 27:1

Jesus said to the people, "I am the light of the world. If you follow me, you won't be stumbling through the darkness, because you will have the light that leads to life."

John 8:12

No longer will anything be cursed. For the throne of God and of the Lamb will be there, and his servants will worship him. And they will see his face, and his name will be written on their foreheads. And there will be no night there—no need for lamps or sun—for the Lord God will shine on them. And they will reign forever and ever.

Revelation 22:3-5

Related texts: *Leviticus 24:1-4; Job 24:13-17; 38:8-20; John 3:19-21; 1 John 1:5-8*

Creation

And God said, "Let there be space between the waters, to separate water from water." And so it was. God made this space to separate the waters above from the waters below. And God called the space "sky." This happened on the second day.

Genesis 1:6-8

The heavens tell of the glory of God.
The skies display his marvelous craftsmanship.
Day after day they continue to speak;
night after night they make him known.
They speak without a sound or a word;
their voice is silent in the skies.

Psalm 19:1-3

I will thank you, Lord, in front of all the people.
I will sing your praises among the nations.
For your unfailing love is as high as the heavens.
Your faithfulness reaches to the clouds.
Be exalted, O God, above the highest heavens.
May your glory shine over all the earth.

Psalm 57:9-11

But God made the earth by his power,
and he preserves it by his wisdom.
He has stretched out the heavens
by his understanding.
When he speaks, there is thunder in the heavens.
He causes the clouds to rise over the earth.
He sends the lightning with the rain
and releases the wind from his storehouses.

Jeremiah 10:12-13

Related texts: 1 Chronicles 16:23-31; Job 38:22-38; Psalm 102:25-28; Acts 1:1-12

done ☑

JUST a THOUGHT

If God is powerful enough to create this huge playground we call Earth, don't you think He's mighty enough to have created you EXACTLY as He intended?

In OTHER Words

FEAR:

To fear God doesn't mean to be afraid of Him or fear some type of unknown punishment or terror.

To fear God means to respect Him, to honor Him, to be amazed by His greatness, and to admire all He has done for you and this world. When you have nothing to say but "WOW" when describing God, you're on your way to fearing Him. An attitude of fear and AWE is pleasing to God and is the first step toward gaining wisdom.

When you close this book, take a minute to say "WOW" to all God has done for you.

CREATION: Land & Seas, Plants & Trees...

And God said, "Let the waters beneath the sky be gathered into one place so dry ground may appear." And so it was. God named the dry ground "land" and the water "seas." And God saw that it was good. Then God said, "Let the land burst forth with every sort of grass and seed-bearing plant. And let there be trees that grow seed-bearing fruit. The seeds will then produce the kinds of plants and trees from which they came." And so it was. The land was filled with seed-bearing plants and trees, and their seeds produced plants and trees of like kind. And God saw that it was good. This all happened on the third day.

Genesis 1:9-13

Do you have no respect for me? Why do you not tremble in my presence? I, the LORD, am the one who defines the ocean's sandy shoreline, an everlasting boundary that the waters cannot cross. The waves may toss and roar, but they can never pass the bounds I set.

Jeremiah 5:22

You cause grass to grow for the cattle.
You cause plants to grow for people to use.
You allow them to produce food from the earth—
wine to make them glad,
olive oil as lotion for their skin,
and bread to give them strength.

Psalm 104:14-15

Related texts: Job 12:7-12; 38:8-11; Psalm 104; Revelation 20:11-21:4; 22:1-3

done ☐

CREATION

Sun, Moon, and Stars

And God said, "Let bright lights appear in the sky to separate the day from the night. They will be signs to mark off the seasons, the days, and the years. Let their light shine down upon the earth." And so it was. For God made two great lights, the sun and the moon, to shine down upon the earth. The greater one, the sun, presides during the day; the lesser one, the moon, presides through the night. He also made the stars. God set these lights in the heavens to light the earth, to govern the day and the night, and to separate the light from the darkness. And God saw that it was good. This all happened on the fourth day.

Genesis 1:14-19

No temple could be seen in the city, for the Lord God Almighty and the Lamb are its temple. And the city has no need of sun or moon, for the glory of God illuminates the city, and the Lamb is its light. The nations of the earth will walk in its light, and the rulers of the world will come and bring their glory to it. Its gates never close at the end of day because there is no night. And all the nations will bring their glory and honor into the city. Nothing evil will be allowed to enter—no one who practices shameful idolatry and dishonesty—but only those whose names are written in the Lamb's Book of Life.

Revelation 21:22-27

Related texts: Nehemiah 9:5-6; Job 9:1-9; Psalms 19:1-6; 104:19-23; Proverbs 4:18-19; Ephesians 5:8-16

Weird or What?

The word **lamb** is used in the Bible 138 times—93 of those refer to Jesus. A lamb was one of the main animals used for sacrifices. Jesus received the name "Lamb" because of His ultimate sacrifice—death on the cross. Do you understand what that means? He gave up His life so we can share eternity together—and that's a long time! His sacrifice paved the way to heaven. To get there, we have to **follow** in **His steps.**

done ☑

CHECK IT OUT

It's great to know that God not only created animals, but He cares about them as well. What's even more incredible is the truth that God cares more about us than animals. Jesus said, "Not even a sparrow . . . can fall to the ground without your Father knowing it. And the very hairs on your head are all numbered. So don't be afraid; you are more valuable to him than a whole flock of sparrows" (Matt. 10:29-31).

Next time you see an animal, let it be a reminder of how much God loves you. You are His special creation! **So special** that the number of hairs on your head is no secret to God. You might even say, "Not one hair can fall into the bathroom sink without God knowing about it."

Now, that's concern!

All Creatures

And God said, "Let the waters swarm with fish and other life. Let the skies be filled with birds of every kind." So God created great sea creatures and every sort of fish and every kind of bird. And God saw that it was good. Then God blessed them, saying, "Let the fish multiply and fill the oceans. Let the birds increase and fill the earth." This all happened on the fifth day.

Genesis 1:20-23

O LORD, what a variety of things you have made!
In wisdom you have made them all.
The earth is full of your creatures.
Here is the ocean, vast and wide,
teeming with life of every kind,
both great and small.
See the ships sailing along,
and Leviathan, which you made to play in the sea.
Every one of these depends on you
to give them their food as they need it.
When you supply it, they gather it.
You open your hand to feed them,
and they are satisfied.

Psalm 104:24-28

Related texts: Psalms 104:11-18; 148:7-12; Matthew 6:25-33; 10:29-31; Revelation 5:11-13

done ☐

CREATION:

The Cattle on a Thousand Hills

And God said, "Let the earth bring forth every kind of animal—livestock, small animals, and wildlife." And so it was. God made all sorts of wild animals, livestock, and small animals, each able to reproduce more of its own kind. And God saw that it was good.

Genesis 1:24-25

I have no complaint about your sacrifices
  or the burnt offerings you constantly
    bring to my altar.
But I want no more bulls from your barns;
  I want no more goats from your pens.
For all the animals of the forest are mine,
  and I own the cattle on a thousand hills.
Every bird of the mountains
  and all the animals of the field belong to
    me.
If I were hungry, I would not mention it to
    you,
  for all the world is mine and everything in
    it.
I don't need the bulls you sacrifice;
  I don't need the blood of goats.
What I want instead is your true thanks to
    God;
  I want you to fulfill your vows to the
    Most High.
Trust me in your times of trouble,
  and I will rescue you,
  and you will give me glory.

Psalm 50:8-15

Related texts: Genesis 9:1-3; Psalm 8; Proverbs 12:10; Isaiah 11:1-10; 65:17-25

In OTHER Words

Sacrifice:

Several types of sacrifices are mentioned throughout the Bible. People made sacrifices when they wanted to get right with God. At that time, tradition instructed a person to sacrifice (kill) an animal as a type of payment to God for sin, resulting in forgiveness. Jesus changed all that when He died on the cross. Once and for all He paid the debt for **our sin.**

done ✓

CATCH THIS

These verses are **awesome!** God created us in His image and views His creation as very good.

Not average.
Not weird.
Not ugly.
But very good!

If that truth doesn't get you excited, you'd better check your pulse; you might already be dead.

Take a minute and **thank God** for that image of yours. Rest in the truth that no matter what you think of yourself and your body, God sees it as good—

VERY GOOD.

Mankind: The Image of God

Then God said, "Let us make people in our image, to be like ourselves. They will be masters over all life—the fish in the sea, the birds in the sky, and all the livestock, wild animals, and small animals."
So God created people in his own image;
God patterned them after himself;
male and female he created them.
God blessed them and told them, "Multiply and fill the earth and subdue it. Be masters over the fish and birds and all the animals." And God said, "Look! I have given you the seed-bearing plants throughout the earth and all the fruit trees for your food. And I have given all the grasses and other green plants to the animals and birds for their food." And so it was. Then God looked over all he had made, and he saw that it was excellent in every way. This all happened on the sixth day.

Genesis 1:26-31

Related texts: Genesis 2:4-25; 9:6-7; Psalm 8; 1 Corinthians 6:1-4; 2 Corinthians 4:4-6; Colossians 1:9-20; 3:5-10

God Rests

So the creation of the heavens and the earth and everything in them was completed. On the seventh day, having finished his task, God rested from all his work. And God blessed the seventh day and declared it holy, because it was the day when he rested from his work of creation.

Genesis 2:1-3

Remember to observe the Sabbath day by keeping it holy. . . . For in six days the LORD made the heavens, the earth, the sea, and everything in them; then he rested on the seventh day. That is why the LORD blessed the Sabbath day and set it apart as holy.

Exodus 20:8,11

One Sabbath day as Jesus was walking through some grainfields, his disciples began breaking off heads of wheat. But the Pharisees said to Jesus, "They shouldn't be doing that! It's against the law to work by harvesting grain on the Sabbath."

But Jesus replied, "Haven't you ever read in the Scriptures what King David did when he and his companions were hungry? He went into the house of God (during the days when Abiathar was high priest), ate the special bread reserved for the priests alone, and then gave some to his companions. That was breaking the law, too." Then he said to them, "The Sabbath was made to benefit people, and not people to benefit the Sabbath. And I, the Son of Man, am master even of the Sabbath!"

Mark 2:23-28

Related texts: Exodus 16:11-30; Psalm 62:1-5; Matthew 11:25-30; Mark 6:30-32; Hebrews 4:1-4

JUST a THOUGHT

Don't you think that if **God found the time to rest** after all He did, **you can spend some time** enjoying **His good work?**

done ☑

Adam and Eve

BIG TIMe WoRd

United is an important word to understand because it's a very graphic description of sex. That's right—SEX! Sex wasn't invented by a group of scientists. Sex was God's idea. He created it. But from the very beginning, God has set a standard for sex by informing us that sex unites husband and wife into "one flesh." It's sort of reverse arithmetic: two become one. God wants us to become one flesh with only one other person. Just like Adam and Eve, that one other person is to be our spouse. What a beautiful gift from God! It's worth the wait!

The First Man and Woman

And the LORD God formed a man's body from the dust of the ground and breathed into it the breath of life. And the man became a living person. . . .

The LORD God placed the man in the Garden of Eden to tend and care for it. But the LORD God gave him this warning: "You may freely eat any fruit in the garden except fruit from the tree of the knowledge of good and evil. If you eat of its fruit, you will surely die."

And the LORD God said, "It is not good for the man to be alone. I will make a companion who will help him."

So the LORD God caused Adam to fall into a deep sleep. He took one of Adam's ribs and closed up the place from which he had taken it. Then the LORD God made a woman from the rib and brought her to Adam.

"At last!" Adam exclaimed. "She is part of my own flesh and bone! She will be called 'woman,' because she was taken out of a man." This explains why a man leaves his father and mother and is joined to his wife, and the two are united into one. Now, although Adam and his wife were both naked, neither of them felt any shame.

Genesis 2:7,15-18,21-25

Related texts: *Genesis* 1:26-29; Matthew 19:1-12; Mark 10:1-12; 1 Corinthians 6:15-7:40

done ☐

JANUARY 11

Rulers of God's Creation

O LORD, our Lord, the majesty of your name fills the earth!
  Your glory is higher than the heavens. thats pretty high.
You have taught children and nursing infants
  to give you praise.
They silence your enemies
  who were seeking revenge.
When I look at the night sky and see the work of your fingers—
  the moon and the stars you have set in place—
what are mortals that you should think of us,
  mere humans that you should care for us? I'm feeling more
For you made us only a little lower than God, special every second.
  and you crowned us with glory and honor.
You put us in charge of everything you made,
  giving us authority over all things—
the sheep and the cattle
  and all the wild animals,
the birds in the sky, the fish in the sea,
  and everything that swims the ocean currents.
O LORD, our Lord, the majesty of your name fills the earth!

Psalm 8

Related texts: *Genesis 1-2; Matthew 21:16; Hebrews 2:5-9*

Give it a try

This psalm was written to express thankfulness for all God has done. What are three things for which you are thankful?

1. God.

2. My family

3. The world and all that inhabits it.

done ☑

What's it Mean?

Satan

is not a make-believe character created to scare us.

Satan is real.

The Bible refers to Satan many times and gives him several names: Evil One, Serpent or Snake, Murderer, Roaring Lion, Liar, Tempter, Dragon, and the Devil. These aren't great names to have.

Satan's role started when he tempted Adam and Eve to disobey God. Their act of rebellion is known as the "first" or "original" sin. This sin led our entire world into more sin and disobedience.

Since then, this world has gotten pretty bad. Death, violence, pain, and wickedness are everywhere.

But there's hope in the midst of this mess!

If you read to the end of this book, you'll see how God has His way with Satan.

THE FIRST SIN

Now the serpent was the shrewdest of all the creatures the LORD God had made. "Really?" he asked the woman. "Did God really say you must not eat any of the fruit in the garden?"

"Of course we may eat it," the woman told him. "It's only the fruit from the tree at the center of the garden that we are not allowed to eat. God says we must not eat it or even touch it, or we will die."

"You won't die!" the serpent hissed. "God knows that your eyes will be opened when you eat it. You will become just like God, knowing everything, both good and evil."

The woman was convinced. The fruit looked so fresh and delicious, and it would make her so wise! So she ate some of the fruit. She also gave some to her husband, who was with her. Then he ate it, too. At that moment, their eyes were opened, and they suddenly felt shame at their nakedness. So they strung fig leaves together around their hips to cover themselves.

Toward evening they heard the LORD God walking about in the garden, so they hid themselves among the trees.

Genesis 3:1-8

Related texts: Ezekiel 28:13-19; Romans 5:12-19; 1 Timothy 2:11-15; James 1:12-15

done ☐

God Judges the First Sin

The LORD God called to Adam, "Where are you?"

He replied, "I heard you, so I hid. I was afraid because I was naked."

"Who told you that you were naked?" the LORD God asked. "Have you eaten the fruit I commanded you not to eat?"

"Yes," Adam admitted, "but it was the woman you gave me who brought me the fruit, and I ate it."

Then the LORD God asked the woman, "How could you do such a thing?"

"The serpent tricked me," she replied. "That's why I ate it."

So the LORD God said to the serpent, "Because you have done this, you will be punished. You are singled out from all the domestic and wild animals of the whole earth to be cursed. You will grovel in the dust as long as you live, crawling along on your belly. From now on, you and the woman will be enemies, and your offspring and her offspring will be enemies. He will crush your head, and you will strike his heel."

Then he said to the woman, "You will bear children with intense pain and suffering. And though your desire will be for your husband, he will be your master."

Genesis 3:9-16

So now there is no condemnation for those who belong to Christ Jesus.

Romans 8:1

Related texts: Deuteronomy 32:1-6; Romans 3:9-18; Revelation 12:9; 20:1-3, 7-15; 22:1-3

One Minute Memory

So now there is no condemnation for those who belong to Christ Jesus.

Romans 8:1

done ☐

CHECK IT OUT

It sounds depressing to read that we will die because of our disobedience. You may even be thinking, What did I do wrong? The answer is, "Just like the rest of us, you were born into a sinful world where death goes along with living."

It's good news to know that our future is in God's hands and it's one filled with hope. One day God will get rid of sin and death. The Bible informs us in Romans 8:21, "All creation anticipates the day when it will join God's children in glorious freedom from death and decay."

If you are one of God's children, get ready to party! If not . . .

YIKES.

God Exiles Adam and Eve from the Garden

And to Adam he said, "Because you listened to your wife and ate the fruit I told you not to eat, I have placed a curse on the ground. All your life you will struggle to scratch a living from it. It will grow thorns and thistles for you, though you will eat of its grains. All your life you will sweat to produce food, until your dying day. Then you will return to the ground from which you came. For you were made from dust, and to the dust you will return."

Then Adam named his wife Eve, because she would be the mother of all people everywhere. And the Lord God made clothing from animal skins for Adam and his wife.

Then the LORD God said, "The people have become as we are, knowing everything, both good and evil. What if they eat the fruit of the tree of life? Then they will live forever!" So the LORD God banished Adam and his wife from the Garden of Eden, and he sent Adam out to cultivate the ground from which he had been made. After banishing them from the garden, the LORD God stationed mighty angelic beings to the east of Eden. And a flaming sword flashed back and forth, guarding the way to the tree of life.

Genesis 3:17-24

Everyone dies because all of us are related to Adam, the first man. But all who are related to Christ, the other man, will be given new life.

1 Corinthians 15:22

Related texts: Genesis18:16-33; Psalm 50; Romans 8:18-25; Revelation 22

Death in Adam, Life in Christ

One Minute Memory

When Adam sinned, sin entered the entire human race. Adam's sin brought death, so death spread to everyone, for everyone sinned. Yes, people sinned even before the law was given. And though there was no law to break, since it had not yet been given, they all died anyway—even though they did not disobey an explicit commandment of God, as Adam did. What a contrast between Adam and Christ, who was yet to come! And what a difference between our sin and God's generous gift of forgiveness. For this one man, Adam, brought death to many through his sin. But this other man, Jesus Christ, brought forgiveness to many through God's bountiful gift. And the result of God's gracious gift is very different from the result of that one man's sin. For Adam's sin led to condemnation, but we have the free gift of being accepted by God, even though we are guilty of many sins. The sin of this one man, Adam, caused death to rule over us, but all who receive God's wonderful, gracious gift of righteousness will live in triumph over sin and death through this one man, Jesus Christ.

Romans 5:12-17

For the wages of sin is death, but the free gift of God is eternal life through Christ Jesus our Lord.

Romans 6:23

Related texts: Genesis 3; Romans 5:18–6:23; Ephesians 2:1-10; Colossians 3:1-17

For the wages of sin is death, but the free gift of God is eternal life through Christ Jesus our Lord.

Romans 6:23

done ☑

CATCH THIS

It doesn't take the IQ of a brain surgeon to recognize Cain's jealousy. He compared his gift with Abel's and he lost. Instead of attacking his own problem of jealousy, he attacked his brother and killed him. Not exactly a fairy-tale ending, right?

Jealous people are typically not happy with who they are. They spend too much time comparing themselves to others and trying to conform to another's style, personality, or look. This comparison game leaves us feeling like losers because we'll always find someone stronger, smarter, more athletic, or better looking than we are.

Fortunately, God doesn't play the comparison game with us. He doesn't care if we are tan, fat, thin, athletic, or smart. God is interested in our hearts. If you can understand this truth, you'll find no reason for jealousy. He loves you just the way you are; so thank Him and celebrate your creation.

Cain and Abel: The First Murder

Now Adam slept with his wife, Eve, and she became pregnant. When the time came, she gave birth to Cain, and she said, "With the LORD's help, I have brought forth a man!" Later she gave birth to a second son and named him Abel.

When they grew up, Abel became a shepherd, while Cain was a farmer. At harvest-time Cain brought to the LORD a gift of his farm produce, while Abel brought several choice lambs from the best of his flock. The LORD accepted Abel and his offering, but he did not accept Cain and his offering. This made Cain very angry and dejected.

"Why are you so angry?" the LORD asked him. "Why do you look so dejected? You will be accepted if you respond in the right way. But if you refuse to respond correctly, then watch out! Sin is waiting to attack and destroy you, and you must subdue it."

Later Cain suggested to his brother, Abel, "Let's go out into the fields." And while they were there, Cain attacked and killed his brother.

Afterward the LORD asked Cain, "Where is your brother? Where is Abel?"

"I don't know!" Cain retorted. "Am I supposed to keep track of him wherever he goes?"

But the LORD said, "What have you done? Listen—your brother's blood cries out to me from the ground! You are hereby banished from the ground you have defiled with your brother's blood. No longer will it yield abundant crops for you, no matter how hard you work! From now on you will be a homeless fugitive on the earth, constantly wandering from place to place."

Genesis 4:1-12

Related texts: Exodus 20:13; Matthew 5:21-26; Hebrews 11:4; 1 John 3:11-12

JANUARY 17

Noah

This is the history of Noah and his family. Noah was a righteous man, the only blameless man living on earth at the time. He consistently followed God's will and enjoyed a close relationship with him. Noah had three sons: Shem, Ham, and Japheth.

Now the earth had become corrupt in God's sight, and it was filled with violence. God observed all this corruption in the world, and he saw violence and depravity everywhere. So God said to Noah, "I have decided to destroy all living creatures, for the earth is filled with violence because of them. Yes, I will wipe them all from the face of the earth!

"Make a boat from resinous wood and seal it with tar, inside and out. Then construct decks and stalls throughout its interior. . . .

"Look! I am about to cover the earth with a flood that will destroy every living thing. Everything on earth will die! But I solemnly swear to keep you safe in the boat, with your wife and your sons and their wives. Bring a pair of every kind of animal—a male and a female—into the boat with you to keep them alive during the flood. . . . And remember, take enough food for your family and for all the animals."

So Noah did everything exactly as God had commanded him.

Genesis 6:9-14,17-19,21-22

Related texts: Psalms 29; 36; Hebrews 11:1-7; 1 Peter 3:18-22

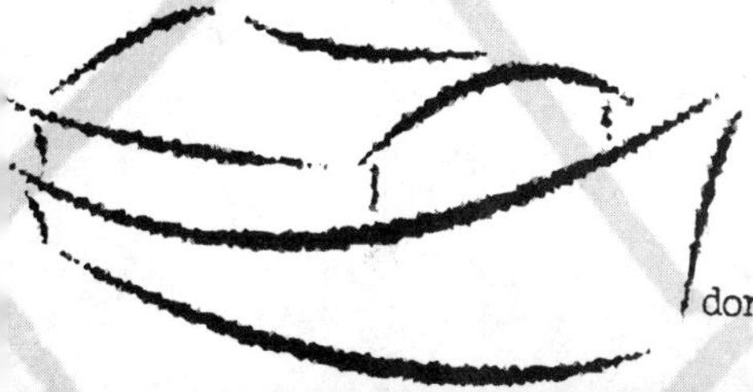

done

Personality Plus

Noah

Rarely related with the story of Noah and the Ark is the fact that Noah was a man who walked with God. Noah lived during a difficult time period when sin was everywhere, people were wicked, and the world was losing control to evil. Noah is a hero because he remained faithful to God, and God was faithful to him and honored him by choosing him and his family to repopulate the world.

Are you open to God's using you to do great things? Prepare yourself by remaining faithful during difficult times. You never know how or when God may choose to use you.

The Great FLOOD

Weird or What?

It's not clear what the ark looked like. All we can do is guess. But we do know its dimensions. **It was 300 cubits in length, 50 cubits in width, and 30 cubits in height.** If that doesn't help you any, you can figure out the size of the boat by multiplying 21 inches per cubit. If you don't want the math challenge but want to use the answers to stump a friend, turn this book upside down for the dimensions.

[Noah] was 600 years old when the flood came, and he went aboard the boat to escape—he and his wife and his sons and their wives. With them were all the various kinds of animals—those approved for eating and sacrifice and those that were not—along with all the birds and other small animals. They came into the boat in pairs, male and female, just as God had commanded Noah. One week later, the flood came and covered the earth.

When Noah was 600 years old, on the seventeenth day of the second month, the underground waters burst forth on the earth, and the rain fell in mighty torrents from the sky. The rain continued to fall for forty days and forty nights. . . .

For forty days the floods prevailed, covering the ground and lifting the boat high above the earth. As the waters rose higher and higher above the ground, the boat floated safely on the surface. Finally, the water covered even the highest mountains on the earth. . . . Every living thing on the earth was wiped out—people, animals both large and small, and birds. They were all destroyed, and only Noah was left alive, along with those who were with him in the boat.

Genesis 7:6-12,17-19,23

It was by faith that Noah built an ark to save his family from the flood. He obeyed God, who warned him about something that had never happened before. By his faith he condemned the rest of the world and was made right in God's sight.

Hebrews 11:7

Related texts: Psalm 93; Nahum 1:1-8; Matthew 24:36-42; Luke 17:26-36; 2 Peter 2:4-9

done ☐

[It's 525 feet long, 87 feet 6 inches wide, and 52 feet 6 inches high.]

AFTER THE FLOOD

But God remembered Noah and all the animals in the boat. He sent a wind to blow across the waters, and the floods began to disappear. . . .

After another forty days, Noah opened the window he had made in the boat and released a raven that flew back and forth until the earth was dry. Then he sent out a dove to see if it could find dry ground. But the dove found no place to land because the water was still too high. So it returned to the boat, and Noah held out his hand and drew the dove back inside.

Seven days later, Noah released the dove again. This time, toward evening, the bird returned to him with a fresh olive leaf in its beak. Noah now knew that the water was almost gone. . . .

So Noah, his wife, and his sons and their wives left the boat. . . .

And the LORD was pleased with the sacrifice and said to himself, "I will never again curse the earth, destroying all living things, even though people's thoughts and actions are bent toward evil from childhood."

Genesis 8:1,6-11,18,21

Related texts: Genesis 9; 2 Peter 3:1-14; Revelation 21:1-4

What's it Mean?

These last two verses are referred to as the **Noahic covenant. A covenant is an oath or a promise made by God.** The Noahic covenant is the promise God made to Noah—and to all of us who would be alive in the future—that **He will never again destroy the earth by flooding.** That's good news!

As you read the Bible, you can always look to God's covenants with confidence that He will keep His promises. Take a minute to thank God for His promises.

done ☑

Personality Plus

Abraham is one of the most popular people in the Bible. He is known as the **"Father of the faithful."** Like Noah, Abraham was a faithful person who put God first. His first test of faith was to leave his country and family and travel to an unknown land. He left this security because he was confident in God's vision. He trusted God so much that he was willing to offer his only child, Isaac, as a sacrifice to prove this faithfulness.

God rewarded Abraham's faithfulness. As you read about Abraham, think about how you can show God your faithfulness. He has a vision for your life. Are you ready? available? faithful? willing? How about today? **Let Him know.**

Abraham

Then the LORD told Abram, "Leave your country, your relatives, and your father's house, and go to the land that I will show you. I will cause you to become the father of a great nation. I will bless you and make you famous, and I will make you a blessing to others. I will bless those who bless you and curse those who curse you. All the families of the earth will be blessed through you."

So Abram departed as the LORD had instructed him, and Lot went with him. Abram was seventy-five years old when he left Haran. He took his wife, Sarai, his nephew Lot, and all his wealth—his livestock and all the people who had joined his household at Haran—and finally arrived in Canaan. Traveling through Canaan, they came to a place near Shechem and set up camp beside the oak at Moreh. At that time, the area was inhabited by Canaanites.

Then the LORD appeared to Abram and said, "I am going to give this land to your offspring." And Abram built an altar there to commemorate the LORD's visit.

Genesis 12:1-7

Related texts: Psalm 67: Acts 7:2-5; Hebrews 6:13-16; 11:8-10

done ☑

JANUARY 21

GOD Promises Abraham a Son

Afterward the LORD spoke to Abram in a vision and said to him, "Do not be afraid, Abram, for I will protect you, and your reward will be great."

But Abram replied, "O Sovereign LORD, what good are all your blessings when I don't even have a son? Since I don't have a son, Eliezer of Damascus, a servant in my household, will inherit all my wealth. You have given me no children, so one of my servants will have to be my heir."

Then the LORD said to him, "No, your servant will not be your heir, for you will have a son of your own to inherit everything I am giving you." Then the LORD brought Abram outside beneath the night sky and told him, "Look up into the heavens and count the stars if you can. Your descendants will be like that—too many to count!"

Genesis 15:1-6

Now this wonderful truth—that God declared him to be righteous—wasn't just for Abraham's benefit. It was for us, too, assuring us that God will also declare us to be righteous if we believe in God, who brought Jesus our Lord back from the dead. He was handed over to die because of our sins, and he was raised from the dead to make us right with God.

Romans 4:23-25

Related texts: Genesis 21:1-5; Romans 4; Galatians 3:1-9

In OTHER Words

Righteous

The words *righteous* and *righteousness* are used many times in the Bible. A "righteous person" is someone who has an intimate relationship with God and constantly lives to please Him and do what's right.

In the Old Testament a "righteous" person is someone who "fears" God and lives his life by keeping God's commandments.

In the New Testament, Jesus went beyond the definition of doing and focused more on being. He placed higher priority on a person's heart (being) than his behavior (doing). A person with a good heart automatically wants to do what's right. How's your heart today?

done ☑

JUST a THOUGHT

God's ability to perform miracles in your life and **answer** your **prayers** doesn't depend on how **young** or **old** **you are.**

Fortunately, God isn't confined to **OUR** limited way of thinking—remember, He's God!

Ishmael and Isaac: Abraham's Sons

But Sarai, Abram's wife, had no children. So Sarai took her servant, an Egyptian woman named Hagar, and gave her to Abram so she could bear his children. "The LORD has kept me from having any children," Sarai said to Abram. "Go and sleep with my servant. Perhaps I can have children through her." And Abram agreed. So Sarai, Abram's wife, took Hagar the Egyptian servant and gave her to Abram as a wife. (This happened ten years after Abram first arrived in the land of Canaan.)

So Abram slept with Hagar, and she became pregnant. When Hagar knew she was pregnant, she began to treat her mistress Sarai with contempt. . . . So Hagar gave Abram a son, and Abram named him Ishmael. Abram was eighty-six years old at that time. . . .

Then the LORD did exactly what he had promised. Sarah became pregnant, and she gave a son to Abraham in his old age. It all happened at the time God had said it would. And Abraham named his son Isaac. Eight days after Isaac was born, Abraham circumcised him as God had commanded. Abraham was one hundred years old at the time.

Genesis 16:1-4,15-16; 21:1-5

It was by faith that Abraham obeyed when God called him to leave home and go to another land that God would give him as his inheritance. . . . It was by faith that Sarah together with Abraham was able to have a child, even though they were too old and Sarah was barren. Abraham believed that God would keep his promise.

Hebrews 11:8,11

Related texts: Genesis 21:6-21; Acts 7:1-8; Romans 4; Galatians 4:22-31

done ☑

Abraham Offers Isaac as a Sacrifice

Later on God tested Abraham's faith and obedience. "Abraham!" God called.

"Yes," he replied. "Here I am."

"Take your son, your only son—yes, Isaac, whom you love so much—and go to the land of Moriah. Sacrifice him there as a burnt offering on one of the mountains, which I will point out to you. . . ."

When they arrived at the place where God had told Abraham to go, he built an altar and placed the wood on it. Then he tied Isaac up and laid him on the altar over the wood. And Abraham took the knife and lifted it up to kill his son as a sacrifice to the LORD. At that moment the angel of the LORD shouted to him from heaven, "Abraham! Abraham!"

"Yes," he answered. "I'm listening."

"Lay down the knife," the angel said. "Do not hurt the boy in any way, for now I know that you truly fear God. You have not withheld even your beloved son from me."

Then Abraham looked up and saw a ram caught by its horns in a bush. So he took the ram and sacrificed it as a burnt offering on the altar in place of his son. Abraham named the place "The LORD Will Provide." This name has now become a proverb: "On the mountain of the LORD it will be provided."

Genesis 22:1-2,9-14

This is real love. It is not that we loved God, but that he loved us and sent his Son as a sacrifice to take away our sins.

1 John 4:10

Related texts: Genesis 22:15-19; John 3:16; Romans 8:31-39; Hebrews 11:17-19

Give it a try

God tested Abraham's faith by seeing whether he loved his son more than Him. What is it that you love more than anything else? Write your answer in the blank space below.

"For I know that God is first in your life-you have not withheld even your Mother from me."

Is this true? ______________________

If your answer is no, what do you need to do to make God the greatest love in your life? I dunno.

____

done ☑

JUST a THOUGHT

Everyone is a favorite creation to God! God's love for you has **nothing** to do with your **background, skin color, financial situation, IQ, neighborhood,** or even your **grades.** Take a look at yourself- **you're one of God's favorite creations.**

Esau and Jacob: Isaac's Sons

This is the history of the family of Isaac, the son of Abraham. When Isaac was forty years old, he married Rebekah, the daughter of Bethuel the Aramean from Paddan-aram and the sister of Laban. Isaac pleaded with the LORD to give Rebekah a child because she was childless. So the LORD answered Isaac's prayer, and his wife became pregnant with twins. But the two children struggled with each other in her womb. So she went to ask the LORD about it. "Why is this happening to me?" she asked.

And the LORD told her, "The sons in your womb will become two rival nations. One nation will be stronger than the other; the descendants of your older son will serve the descendants of your younger son."

And when the time came, the twins were born. The first was very red at birth. He was covered with so much hair that one would think he was wearing a piece of clothing. So they called him Esau. Then the other twin was born with his hand grasping Esau's heel. So they called him Jacob. Isaac was sixty years old when the twins were born.

As the boys grew up, Esau became a skillful hunter, a man of the open fields, while Jacob was the kind of person who liked to stay at home. Isaac loved Esau in particular because of the wild game he brought home, but Rebekah favored Jacob.

Genesis 25:19-28

Related texts: 1 Samuel 1; Malachi 1:1-5; Romans 9

done ☑

ESAU SELLS OUT

One day when Jacob was cooking some stew, Esau arrived home exhausted and hungry from a hunt. Esau said to Jacob, "I'm starved! Give me some of that red stew you've made." (This was how Esau got his other name, Edom—"Red.")

Jacob replied, "All right, but trade me your birthright for it."

"Look, I'm dying of starvation!" said Esau. "What good is my birthright to me now?"

So Jacob insisted, "Well then, swear to me right now that it is mine." So Esau swore an oath, thereby selling all his rights as the firstborn to his younger brother. Then Jacob gave Esau some bread and lentil stew. Esau ate and drank and went on about his business, indifferent to the fact that he had given up his birthright.

Genesis 25:29-34

"I have loved you deeply," says the LORD.

But you retort, "Really? How have you loved us?"

And the LORD replies, "I showed my love for you by loving your ancestor Jacob. Yet Esau was Jacob's brother, and I rejected Esau and devastated his hill country. I turned Esau's inheritance into a desert for jackals."

Malachi 1:2-3

Make sure that no one is immoral or godless like Esau. He traded his birthright as the oldest son for a single meal. And afterward, when he wanted his father's blessing, he was rejected. It was too late for repentance, even though he wept bitter tears.

Hebrews 12:16-17

Related texts: Genesis 27-36; Psalm 60; Obadiah

What's it Mean?

Birthright

A *birthright* was a special privilege given to the oldest son. The one with the birthright received the blessing of the father and all the father had built and accomplished. In the case of Esau and Jacob, it was about more than gaining their dad's money: it was about receiving special blessings from God.

Today we have the opportunity to receive the birthright that God intended for Jesus. Jesus is both the only Son of God and the firstborn of God. By having a relationship with Jesus, we can share in the blessings intended for Him. The Bible says: "All who are led by the Spirit of God are children of God. . . . And since we are his children, we will share his treasures-for everything God gives to his Son, Christ, is ours, too" (Rom. 8:14,17).

Congratulations!

done ☑

Joseph

Personality Plus

Joseph is another example of good things happening to a faithful man. Joseph was abducted by his brothers and sold into slavery. But God was with him and took care of him. Joseph's life illustrates this truth: When you are obedient to God, you can conquer any obstacle put in your way. Joseph's statement supports this. "Don't be angry with yourselves that you did this to me, for God did it. He sent me here ahead of you to preserve your lives" (Gen. 45:5). Joseph believed that no matter what harm his enemies might inflict upon him, God would remain faithful and come through.

Be faithful today and see if any good happens to you.

When Joseph was seventeen years old, he often tended his father's flocks with his half brothers, the sons of his father's wives Bilhah and Zilpah. But Joseph reported to his father some of the bad things his brothers were doing. Now Jacob loved Joseph more than any of his other children because Joseph had been born to him in his old age. So one day he gave Joseph a special gift—a beautiful robe. But his brothers hated Joseph because of their father's partiality. They couldn't say a kind word to him.

One night Joseph had a dream and promptly reported the details to his brothers, causing them to hate him even more. "Listen to this dream," he announced. "We were out in the field tying up bundles of grain. My bundle stood up, and then your bundles all gathered around and bowed low before it!"

Then Joseph had another dream and told his brothers about it. "Listen to this dream," he said. "The sun, moon, and eleven stars bowed low before me!"

This time he told his father as well as his brothers, and his father rebuked him. "What do you mean?" his father asked. "Will your mother, your brothers, and I actually come and bow before you?" But while his brothers were jealous of Joseph, his father gave it some thought and wondered what it all meant.

Genesis 37:2b-7,9-11

Related texts: Genesis 28:10-19; 41:1-45; Joel 2:28-32; Matthew 1:18–2:22

done

JANUARY 27

Jacob Moves His Family to Egypt

God also gave Abraham the covenant of circumcision at that time. And so Isaac, Abraham's son, was circumcised when he was eight days old. Isaac became the father of Jacob, and Jacob was the father of the twelve patriarchs of the Jewish nation.

These sons of Jacob were very jealous of their brother Joseph, and they sold him to be a slave in Egypt. But God was with him and delivered him from his anguish. And God gave him favor before Pharaoh, king of Egypt. God also gave Joseph unusual wisdom, so that Pharaoh appointed him governor over all of Egypt and put him in charge of all the affairs of the palace.

But a famine came upon Egypt and Canaan. There was great misery for our ancestors, as they ran out of food. Jacob heard that there was still grain in Egypt, so he sent his sons to buy some. The second time they went, Joseph revealed his identity to his brothers, and they were introduced to Pharaoh. Then Joseph sent for his father, Jacob, and all his relatives to come to Egypt, seventy-five persons in all. So Jacob went to Egypt. He died there, as did all his sons.

Acts 7:8-15

Jacob lived for seventeen years after his arrival in Egypt, so he was 147 years old when he died.

Genesis 47:28

Related texts: Genesis 37–50; Psalm 46; Matthew 8:5-13; Mark 12:24-27

BIG TIMe WoRd

Delivered

Joseph is one of many examples of God delivering someone from evil, pain, or a specific situation. Other words that could be used to help define "delivered" are "rescued," "saved," or "escaped." God's deliverance can give you hope for daily living. Jesus taught His followers to pray using words like these: "Don't bring us into temptation, but "delive us from the evil one."

What's an area in your life from which you need to be rescued?

Ask God to deliver you. He's done it millions of times. He can do it for YOU.

done ☑

One Minute Memory

And we know **God causes** everything to **work together** for the **good** of those who **love God** and are called according to his purposes for them.

Romans 8:28

JOSEPH: God Intended It for Good

But now that their father was dead, Joseph's brothers became afraid. "Now Joseph will pay us back for all the evil we did to him," they said. So they sent this message to Joseph: "Before your father died, he instructed us to say to you: 'Forgive your brothers for the great evil they did to you.' So we, the servants of the God of your father, beg you to forgive us." When Joseph received the message, he broke down and wept. Then his brothers came and bowed low before him. "We are your slaves," they said.

But Joseph told them, "Don't be afraid of me. Am I God, to judge and punish you? As far as I am concerned, God turned into good what you meant for evil. He brought me to the high position I have today so I could save the lives of many people. No, don't be afraid. Indeed, I myself will take care of you and your families." And he spoke very kindly to them, reassuring them. . . .

"Soon I will die," Joseph told his brothers, "but God will surely come for you, to lead you out of this land of Egypt. He will bring you back to the land he vowed to give to the descendants of Abraham, Isaac, and Jacob."

Genesis 50:15-21,24

And we know that God causes everything to work together for the good of those who love God and are called according to his purpose for them.

Romans 8:2

Related texts: Genesis 37–50; Exodus 1; 12:17-19, Joshua 24:32; Psalm 105:7-25; Hebrews 11:21-22

done ☑

Job: Blameless and Blessed

There was a man named Job who lived in the land of Uz. He was blameless, a man of complete integrity. He feared God and stayed away from evil. He had seven sons and three daughters. He owned seven thousand sheep, three thousand camels, five hundred teams of oxen, and five hundred female donkeys, and he employed many servants. He was, in fact, the richest person in that entire area. . . .

One day the angels came to present themselves before the LORD, and Satan the Accuser came with them. "Where have you come from?" the LORD asked Satan.

And Satan answered the LORD, "I have been going back and forth across the earth, watching everything that's going on."

Then the LORD asked Satan, "Have you noticed my servant Job? He is the finest man in all the earth—a man of complete integrity. He fears God and will have nothing to do with evil."

Satan replied to the LORD, "Yes, Job fears God, but not without good reason! You have always protected him and his home and his property from harm. You have made him prosperous in everything he does. Look how rich he is! But take away everything he has, and he will surely curse you to your face!"

"All right, you may test him," the LORD said to Satan. "Do whatever you want with everything he possesses, but don't harm him physically." So Satan left the LORD's presence.

Job 1:1-3,6-12

Related texts: Job 28; Proverbs 1:7; 8:13; 9:10; Philippians 2:14-15; 1 Peter 5:8-11

Personality Plus

Job

was one of the richest, most righteous, most well-known, most respected people in his world. There was no wrong found in him. But unlike the other characters we've already looked at, Job suffered tragically. It's an unbelievable story!

No matter how incredible the pain, Job was able to keep his faith. He never blamed God. Job is proof that one can endure incredible pain and still remain confident in God.

Job's life reminds us that God remains God no matter how happy and wealthy or sad and poor we might be. His statement sums this up: "The Lord gave me everything I had, and the Lord has taken it away. Blessed be the name of the Lord!" (Job 1:21).

done ☑

CATCH THIS

No one wakes up in the morning and hopes for a lousy day. Crummy days just seem to happen without any warning. It would be great if someone called ahead to warn us about potentially dreadful days. We wouldn't even have to get out of bed. Dream on, right? The truth is, bad days happen!

Next time you have a terrible day, realize you're not alone. People have been having them for thousands of years, and you're going to record several more onto your life scroll before it's over.

Consider yourself lucky you weren't created to be Job. Talk about a lousy day-it doesn't get any worse. What's interesting about Job is that he didn't blame God for his pain. This is amazing! It's so easy to blame God. But Job chose a different response.

If today or tomorrow screams "lousy," remember Job's example.

Job Loses BIG

One day when Job's sons and daughters were dining at the oldest brother's house, a messenger arrived at Job's home with this news: "Your oxen were plowing, with the donkeys feeding beside them, when the Sabeans raided us. They stole all the animals and killed all the farmhands. I am the only one who escaped to tell you."

While he was still speaking, another messenger arrived with this news: "The fire of God has fallen from heaven and burned up your sheep and all the shepherds. I am the only one who escaped to tell you."

While he was still speaking, a third messenger arrived with this news: "Three bands of Chaldean raiders have stolen your camels and killed your servants. I am the only one who escaped to tell you."

While he was still speaking, another messenger arrived with this news: "Your sons and daughters were feasting in their oldest brother's home. Suddenly, a powerful wind swept in from the desert and hit the house on all sides. The house collapsed, and all your children are dead. I am the only one who escaped to tell you."

Job stood up and tore his robe in grief. Then he shaved his head and fell to the ground before God. He said,

"I came naked from my mother's womb,
and I will be stripped of everything
when I die.
The LORD gave me everything I had,
and the LORD has taken it away.
Praise the name of the LORD!"

In all of this, Job did not sin by blaming God.

Job 1:13-22

Related texts: Habakkuk 3:17-19; 1 Thessalonians 5:16-18; Revelation 7:13-17

lose it!

 done ☐

Job Loses His Health

One day the angels came again to present themselves before the LORD, and Satan the Accuser came with them. . . .

Then the LORD asked Satan, "Have you noticed my servant Job? He is the finest man in all the earth—a man of complete integrity. He fears God and will have nothing to do with evil. And he has maintained his integrity, even though you persuaded me to harm him without cause."

Satan replied to the LORD, "Skin for skin—he blesses you only because you bless him. A man will give up everything he has to save his life. But take away his health, and he will surely curse you to your face!"

"All right, do with him as you please," the LORD said to Satan. "But spare his life." So Satan left the LORD's presence, and he struck Job with a terrible case of boils from head to foot.

Then Job scraped his skin with a piece of broken pottery as he sat among the ashes. His wife said to him, "Are you still trying to maintain your integrity? Curse God and die."

But Job replied, "You talk like a godless woman. Should we accept only good things from the hand of God and never anything bad?" So in all this, Job said nothing wrong.

Job 2:1,3-10

Related texts: Job 19:25-27; Proverbs 11:2-6; Philippians 3:7-11

Give it a try

Even when life is going well, it's easier to focus on the negative than the positive. In the midst of pain it's even more difficult to recognize anything good about life.

Write down two good things that happened to you this month:

1.

2.

Write down three good things you want to do next month:

1.

2.

3.

done ☑

February

It ain't those parts of the Bible that I can't understand that bother me, it is the parts that I do understand.

Mark Twain
(1835–1910)
American Author

Is Suffering Always Punishment?

Three of Job's friends were Eliphaz the Temanite, Bildad the Shuhite, and Zophar the Naamathite. When they heard of the tragedy he had suffered, they got together and traveled from their homes to comfort and console him. When they saw Job from a distance, they scarcely recognized him. Wailing loudly, they tore their robes and threw dust into the air over their heads to demonstrate their grief. Then they sat on the ground with him for seven days and nights. And no one said a word, for they saw that his suffering was too great for words. . . .

Then Eliphaz the Temanite replied to Job . . . "Stop and think! Does the innocent person perish? When has the upright person been destroyed? My experience shows that those who plant trouble and cultivate evil will harvest the same. They perish by a breath from God. They vanish in a blast of his anger.

"My advice to you is this: Go to God and present your case to him. . . . But consider the joy of those corrected by God! Do not despise the chastening of the Almighty when you sin. For though he wounds, he also bandages. He strikes, but his hands also heal. . . . We have found from experience that all this is true. Listen to my counsel, and apply it to yourself."

Job 2:11-13; 4:1,7-9; 5:8,17-18,27

Related texts: Job 4–5; 8; 11; 15; 18; 20; 22; 25; 32–37; Hebrews 12:5-11

BIG TIME WORD

Comfort + Console =

EMPATHY

Empathy is possessing and showing genuine interest and concern in what is happening. With empathy you can actually feel the pain of others. If you express empathy you don't need to know what to say, how to act, or what Bible verse to quote.

People around you are experiencing tragedies on a daily basis. Your empathy for their situation will reveal God's love. Where there is empathy, there is support; where there is support, there is encouragement; and where there is encouragement, there is love.

Next time a friend is in pain and you don't know what to say, don't worry. Your empathy will communicate the right words:

"I care!"

done ☑

2 FEBRUARY

CHECK IT OUT

God heard the prayers of Job thousands of years ago and He hears our prayers today! God doesn't always choose to answer them when WE want them answered, but He ALWAYS hears them. We can be confident that God is not hard of hearing!

In Luke 18:1-11, Jesus explained our need to pray consistently and to keep praying until an answer comes. I verses 7-8 Jesus said, "Don't you think God will surely give justice to his chosen people who plead with him day and night? He will grant justice to them quickly!"

Next time you get the urge to worry, try replacing your worry with a prayer. Worrying won't help you at all, but your prayers will be heard by the One who can make things happen.

Keep praying!

Job Protests His Innocence

Then Job spoke again:

"How long will you torture me? How long will you try to break me with your words? Ten times now you have meant to insult me. You should be ashamed of dealing with me so harshly. And even if I have sinned, that is my concern, not yours. You are trying to overcome me, using my humiliation as evidence of my sin, but it is God who has wronged me. I cannot defend myself, for I am like a city under siege.

"I cry out for help, but no one hears me. I protest, but there is no justice."

Job 19:1-7

Job continued speaking:

"I make this vow by the living God, who has taken away my rights, by the Almighty who has embittered my soul. As long as I live, while I have breath from God, my lips will speak no evil, and my tongue will speak no lies. I will never concede that you are right; until I die, I will defend my innocence. I will maintain my innocence without wavering. My conscience is clear for as long as I live."

Job 27:1-6

Related texts: Job 3; 6–7; 9–10; 12–14; 16–17; 19; 21; 23–24; 26–31; Psalm 7; Luke 18:1-8

done ☐

God Answers Job

Then the LORD answered Job from the whirlwind:

"Who is this that questions my wisdom with such ignorant words? Brace yourself, because I have some questions for you, and you must answer them.

"Where were you when I laid the foundations of the earth? Tell me, if you know so much. Do you know how its dimensions were determined and who did the surveying? What supports its foundations, and who laid its cornerstone as the morning stars sang together and all the angels shouted for joy?"

Job 38:1-7

Then the LORD said to Job, "Do you still want to argue with the Almighty? You are God's critic, but do you have the answers?"

Then Job replied to the LORD, "I am nothing—how could I ever find the answers? I will put my hand over my mouth in silence. I have said too much already. I have nothing more to say."

Then the LORD answered Job from the whirlwind:

"Brace yourself, because I have some questions for you, and you must answer them. Are you going to discredit my justice and condemn me so you can say you are right?"

Job 40:1-8

Related texts: Psalm 30; Job 38–41; Habakkuk 1:1–2:1; Romans 9–10

Weird or What?

Job screamed out because of his pain, anguish, and torment. Do you blame him? What's totally unexpected is God's response to Job. Instead of answering Job's cry and explaining why a good person can suffer, God instead reminded Job of His greatness. God pointed to the fact that He is awesome. Job listened and did the only thing he could do in God's presence—he shut his mouth.

Be reminded today that God is bigger than your ability to understand Him. Just take a survey of His incredible creations, and **you may end up speechless—too!**

JUST a THOUGHT

"God doesn't promise to give the faithful **twice as much as they had before,** but He has a way of **rewarding faith-fulness** in terms that can't be **measured.**

God Vindicates and Restores Job

Then Job replied to the LORD:

"I know that you can do anything, and no one can stop you. You ask, 'Who is this that questions my wisdom with such ignorance?' It is I. And I was talking about things I did not understand, things far too wonderful for me.

"You said, 'Listen and I will speak! I have some questions for you, and you must answer them.'

"I had heard about you before, but now I have seen you with my own eyes. I take back everything I said, and I sit in dust and ashes to show my repentance."

After the LORD had finished speaking to Job, he said to Eliphaz the Temanite: "I am angry with you and with your two friends, for you have not been right in what you said about me, as my servant Job was. Now take seven young bulls and seven rams and go to my servant Job and offer a burnt offering for yourselves. My servant Job will pray for you, and I will accept his prayer on your behalf. I will not treat you as you deserve, for you have not been right in what you said about me, as my servant Job was."

So Eliphaz the Temanite, Bildad the Shuhite, and Zophar the Naamathite did as the LORD commanded them, and the LORD accepted Job's prayer.

When Job prayed for his friends, the LORD restored his fortunes. In fact, the LORD gave him twice as much as before!

Job 42:1-10

Related texts: Psalms 17; 37; Matthew 5:1-6; James 5:11

done √

The Beatitudes: Poor in Spirit

One day as the crowds were gathering, Jesus went up the mountainside with his disciples and sat down to teach them.

This is what he taught them:

"God blesses those who realize their need for him,
for the Kingdom of Heaven is given to them."

Matthew 5:1-3

The sacrifice you want is a broken spirit.
A broken and repentant heart, O God,
you will not despise. *Psalm 51:17*

The high and lofty one who inhabits eternity, the Holy One, says this: "I live in that high and holy place with those whose spirits are contrite and humble. I refresh the humble and give new courage to those with repentant hearts." *Isaiah 57:15*

My dear brothers and sisters, how can you claim that you have faith in our glorious LORD Jesus Christ if you favor some people more than others?

For instance, suppose someone comes into your meeting dressed in fancy clothes and expensive jewelry, and another comes in who is poor and dressed in shabby clothes. If you give special attention and a good seat to the rich person, but you say to the poor one, "You can stand over there, or else sit on the floor"—well, doesn't this discrimination show that you are guided by wrong motives?

Listen to me, dear brothers and sisters. Hasn't God chosen the poor in this world to be rich in faith? Aren't they the ones who will inherit the kingdom God promised to those who love him?

James 2:1-5

Related texts: Job 34:17-19; Isaiah 57:15-19; 66:2; Luke 6:20; Acts 10:34-35; Ephesians 6:5-9

What's it Mean?

"Beatitudes" is a name given to a special sermon from Jesus. Jesus introduced a new way of thinking that was radically different from the way the world thought. Here's what He said:

Mourn and you'll be COMFORTED.
Be meek and you'll be HAPPY.
Do what is right and you'll be SATISFIED.
Show mercy and MERCY will be shown to you.
Have a pure heart and you'll SEE God.
Bring peace to others and you'll be God's CHILD.
Be treated badly for doing good and you'll be REWARDED.

If you can follow these teachings, you will definitely stand out—there's no question about it. But look at the promised outcomes—seem too good to be true?

Give it a try and find out!

done ☑

JUST a THOUGHT

Next time you worry about **your future,** remember that God has already taken care of the ultimate future and wants you to know it. When you know it, you'll experience **a new peace and hope for living today.**

The Beatitudes: Those Who Mourn

God blesses those who mourn,
for they will be comforted.

Matthew 5:4

The Spirit of the Sovereign LORD is upon me, because the LORD has appointed me to bring good news to the poor. He has sent me to comfort the brokenhearted and to announce that captives will be released and prisoners will be freed. He has sent me to tell those who mourn that the time of the LORD's favor has come, and with it, the day of God's anger against their enemies. To all who mourn in Israel, he will give beauty for ashes, joy instead of mourning, praise instead of despair. For the LORD has planted them like strong and graceful oaks for his own glory.

Isaiah 61:1-3

I heard a loud shout from the throne, saying, "Look, the home of God is now among his people! He will live with them, and they will be his people. God himself will be with them. He will remove all of their sorrows, and there will be no more death or sorrow or crying or pain. For the old world and its evils are gone forever."

Revelation 21:3-4

Related texts: Nehemiah 8:1-12; Ecclesiastes 3:1-8; Psalm 119:49-50; Luke 6:21; 2 Corinthians 10:1-5; 1 Peter 3:8-9

 done ☑

The Beatitudes: THE MEEK

God blesses those who are gentle and lowly,
for the whole earth will belong to them.

Matthew 5:5

Don't worry about the wicked.
Don't envy those who do wrong.
For like grass, they soon fade away.
Like springtime flowers, they soon wither.
Trust in the LORD and do good.
Then you will live safely in the land and prosper.
Take delight in the LORD,
and he will give you your heart's desires.
Commit everything you do to the LORD.
Trust him, and he will help you.
He will make your innocence as clear as the dawn,
and the justice of your cause will shine like the noonday sun.
Be still in the presence of the LORD,
and wait patiently for him to act.
Don't worry about evil people who prosper
or fret about their wicked schemes.
Stop your anger!
Turn from your rage!
Do not envy others—
it only leads to harm.
For the wicked will be destroyed,
but those who trust in the LORD will possess the land.
In a little while, the wicked will disappear.
Though you look for them, they will be gone.
Those who are gentle and lowly will possess the and;
they will live in prosperous security.

Psalm 37:1-11

Related texts: Psalms 25:12-13; 37:12-40; Matthew 11:25-30; Galatians 5:19-23; 2 Corinthians 10:1-5; 1 Peter 3:8-9

One Minute Memory

Those who are **gentle** and lowly will **possess** the land; they will live in **prosperous security.**

Psalm 37:11

done ☑

CATCH THIS

These are good Scriptures to recall next time you swing open the refrigerator and exclaim, "I'm starving!" If you're like most people, you'll spend a few minutes checking out all the food and then say, "There's nothing to eat." So you slam the door, frustrated, hungry, and in search of some munchies.

Though Jesus doesn't promise we'll have a lifetime supply of pizza, ice cream, and potato chips, He does guarantee that we'll never go hungry or thirsty if we believe in Him. Jesus isn't talking about how to make sure our stomachs never growl. He's referring to our spiritual needs and how He can completely satisfy them. Picture Jesus' promise as being like living next door to a grocery store that's open twenty-four hours every day, filled with free all-you-can-eat food. Jesus' assurance is even better than that because you never have to leave your home, and His "food" is completely healthy.

How can you eat from the "Bread of Life" today?

The Beatitudes: Hungry for Righteousness

God blesses those who are hungry and
thirsty for justice,
for they will receive it in full.

Matthew 5:6

As the deer pants for streams of water,
so I long for you, O God.
I thirst for God, the living God.
When can I come and stand before him?

Psalm 42:1-2

Jesus replied, "People soon become thirsty again after drinking this water. But the water I give them takes away thirst altogether. It becomes a perpetual spring within them, giving them eternal life."

Jesus replied, "I am the bread of life. No one who comes to me will ever be hungry again. Those who believe in me will never thirst."

On the last day, the climax of the festival, Jesus stood and shouted to the crowds, "If you are thirsty, come to me! If you believe in me, come and drink! For the Scriptures declare that rivers of living water will flow out from within." (When he said "living water," he was speaking of the Spirit, who would be given to everyone believing in him.)

John 4:13-14; 6:35; 7:37-39a

The Spirit and the bride say, "Come." Let each one who hears them say, "Come." Let the thirsty ones come—anyone who wants to. Let them come and drink the water of life without charge.

Revelation 22:17

Related texts: Psalms 107:1-9; 146; Isaiah 55:1-2; Luke 6:21; Revelation 7:16-17

done ☑

The Beatitudes: The Merciful

God blesses those who are merciful,
for they will be shown mercy.

Matthew 5:7

For the LORD your God is merciful—he will not abandon you or destroy you or forget the solemn covenant he made with your ancestors.

Deuteronomy 4:31

I lift my eyes to you,
O God, enthroned in heaven.
We look to the LORD our God for his mercy,
just as servants keep their eyes on their master,
as a slave girl watches her mistress for the slightest signal.
Have mercy on us, LORD, have mercy,
for we have had our fill of contempt.
We have had our fill of the scoffing of the proud
and the contempt of the arrogant.

Psalm 123:1-4

I want you to be merciful; I don't want your sacrifices. I want you to know God; that's more important than burnt offerings.

Hosea 6:6

No, O people, the LORD has already told you what is good, and this is what he requires: to do what is right, to love mercy, and to walk humbly with your God.

Micah 6:8

So whenever you speak, or whatever you do, remember that you will be judged by the law of love, the law that set you free. For there will be no mercy for you if you have not been merciful to others. But if you have been merciful, then God's mercy toward you will win out over his judgment against you.

James 2:12-13

Related texts: Psalm 6; Micah 7:18-19; Zechariah 7:9-10; Luke 6:27-38; 10:25-37; Jude 1:20-23

done ☐

In OTHER Words

MERCY

Mercy is showing compassion or empathy. It's given by God to meet the needs of His people and to care for them.

Mercy starts with God. God shows mercy to us as His followers because He has compassion and cares for us. But mercy doesn't stop with God! We can also express mercy to others in need.

Can you think of one person who is in need of your mercy? How can you show this person mercy **TODAY?**

The Beatitudes: The Pure in Heart

God blesses those whose hearts are pure,
for they will see God. *Matthew 5:8*

Who may climb the mountain of the LORD?
Who may stand in his holy place?
Only those whose hands and hearts are pure,
who do not worship idols and never tell lies.
They will receive the LORD's blessing
and have right standing with God their savior. . . .
Create in me a clean heart, O God.
Renew a right spirit within me. *Psalms 24:3-5; 51:10*

Run from anything that stimulates youthful lust. Follow anything that makes you want to do right. Pursue faith and love and peace, and enjoy the companionship of those who call on the LORD with pure hearts. *2 Timothy 2:22*

And so, dear brothers and sisters, we can boldly enter heaven's Most Holy Place because of the blood of Jesus. This is the new, life-giving way that Christ has opened up for us through the sacred curtain, by means of his death for us.

And since we have a great High Priest who rules over God's people, let us go right into the presence of God, with true hearts fully trusting him. For our evil consciences have been sprinkled with Christ's blood to make us clean, and our bodies have been washed with pure water. *Hebrews 10:19-22*

Related texts: 2 Chronicles 30:13-20; Proverbs 20:5-11; Mark 7:1-23; Hebrews 3; 12:14-29

Give it a try

Second Timothy 2:22 gives you an action plan on how to remain pure in heart. Here it is:

1. Run from the things that give you evil thoughts.
2. Stay close to anything that makes you do right.
3. Have faith and love.
4. Enjoy the company of others who love God and live by this plan. Do you have at least one friend who could help you meet number 4?

Write three qualities you admire about this friend.

Sometime real soon, let this friend know how important he or she is to you and your faith.

done ☑

The Beatitudes: The Peacemakers

God blesses those who work for peace,
for they will be called the children of God.

Matthew 5:9

Come, my children, and listen to me,
and I will teach you to fear the LORD.
Do any of you want to live
a life that is long and good?
Then watch your tongue!
Keep your lips from telling lies!
Turn away from evil and do good.
Work hard at living in peace with others. . . .

Look at those who are honest and good,
for a wonderful future lies before those who love peace.
But the wicked will be destroyed;
they have no future.

Psalms 34:11-14; 37:37-38

"But there is no peace for the wicked," says the LORD.

Isaiah 48:22

Do your part to live in peace with everyone, as much as possible.

Romans 12:18

But the wisdom that comes from heaven is first of all pure. It is also peace loving, gentle at all times, and willing to yield to others. It is full of mercy and good deeds. It shows no partiality and is always sincere.

James 3:17

Related texts: Isaiah 9:6-7; John 1:1-13; Romans 8:9-23; Galatians 3:26–4:7; 1 John 3:1-11

JUST a THOUGHT

In a world filled with **violence, war, racism,** and **hatred,** it would be great if others could count on **YOU** as one of our **world's peace-makers!** Can you start **today?**

done ☑

12 FEBRUARY

One Minute Memory

When I am weak, then I am strong.

2 Corinthians 12:10b

The **less** I have, the **more** I **depend** on **Him.**

The Beatitudes: The Persecuted Righteous

God blesses those who are persecuted
because they live for God,
for the Kingdom of Heaven is theirs.

"God blesses you when you are mocked and persecuted and lied about because you are my followers. Be happy about it! Be very glad! For a great reward awaits you in heaven. And remember, the ancient prophets were persecuted, too."

Matthew 5:10-12

But the LORD stands beside me like a great warrior. Before him they will stumble. They cannot defeat me. They will be shamed and thoroughly humiliated. Their dishonor will never be forgotten.

Jeremiah 20:11

For God is pleased with you when, for the sake of your conscience, you patiently endure unfair treatment. Of course, you get no credit for being patient if you are beaten for doing wrong. But if you suffer for doing right and are patient beneath the blows, God is pleased with you.

This suffering is all part of what God has called you to. Christ, who suffered for you, is your example. Follow in his steps.

1 Peter 2:19-21

Since I know it is all for Christ's good, I am quite content with my weaknesses and with insults, hardships, persecutions, and calamities. For when I am weak, then I am strong.

2 Corinthians 12:10

Related texts: Job 36:15-17; Isaiah 53; 1 Peter 1:3-9; 4:12-19

done ☑

That's a lot of love!

Unconditional LOVE

Can anything ever separate us from Christ's love? Does it mean he no longer loves us if we have trouble or calamity, or are persecuted, or are hungry or cold or in danger or threatened with death? . . .

And I am convinced that nothing can ever separate us from his love. Death can't, and life can't. The angels can't, and the demons can't. Our fears for today, our worries about tomorrow, and even the powers of hell can't keep God's love away. Whether we are high above the sky or in the deepest ocean, nothing in all creation will ever be able to separate us from the love of God that is revealed in Christ Jesus our Lord.

Romans 8:35,38-39

We know how much God loves us, and we have put our trust in him.

God is love, and all who live in love live in God, and God lives in them. And as we live in God, our love grows more perfect. So we will not be afraid on the day of judgment, but we can face him with confidence because we are like Christ here in this world.

Such love has no fear because perfect love expels all fear. . . .

We love each other as a result of his loving us first.

1 John 4:16-18a,19

Related texts: Deuteronomy 7:7-11; 10:14-15; John 3:16-19; Romans 5:8-11; Ephesians 2:4-10

CATCH THIS

Unconditional love is the way God loves you. God's love for you isn't based on your grades, your looks, your athletic performance, your friendships, your personality, or your past. If God loved you for what you did, that would be called conditional love. But God's love is unconditional because His love has no strings attached. There are some things you do that God doesn't like, but He never stops loving you.

Nothing you do will distance you from God's love. Believe it or not, there's no sin that's too gross, no language that's too bad, no action that's too evil to stop God from loving you. Doesn't it seem crazy not to love God in response to His love for you?

Thank Him for His love for you today.

done ✓

14 FEBRUARY

The Greatest Love

If I could speak in any language in heaven or on earth but didn't love others, I would only be making meaningless noise like a loud gong or a clanging cymbal. If I had the gift of prophecy, and if I knew all the mysteries of the future and knew everything about everything, but didn't love others, what good would I be? And if I had the gift of faith so that I could speak to a mountain and make it move, without love I would be no good to anybody. If I gave everything I have to the poor and even sacrificed my body, I could boast about it; but if I didn't love others, I would be of no value whatsoever.

Love is patient and kind. Love is not jealous or boastful or proud or rude. Love does not demand its own way. Love is not irritable, and it keeps no record of when it has been wronged. It is never glad about injustice but rejoices whenever the truth wins out. Love never gives up, never loses faith, is always hopeful, and endures through every circumstance.

Love will last forever. . . .

There are three things that will endure—faith, hope, and love—and the greatest of these is love.

1 Corinthians 13:1-8a,13

Related texts: Deuteronomy 6:1-15; Psalm 136; John 15:9-17; 1 John 3

love is very nice

I'll say

Give it a try

Listed below you will find several qualities of love. Grade yourself on how you live out each of these qualities (A–F). Next to your lowest grades write a few ideas on how you might improve your "love life" with that specific quality.

______________ (Replace "love" with your name)

A is patient
B is kind
C rejoices when truth wins
F doesn't notice when others do wrong
D is loyal
E believes in others
X expects the best of others

Don't let today be the only day of the year when you celebrate love. Work toward being a "lover" every day!

done ☑

Israelites Oppressed in Egypt

These are the sons of Jacob who went with their father to Egypt, each with his family: Reuben, Simeon, Levi, Judah, Issachar, Zebulun, Benjamin, Dan, Naphtali, Gad, and Asher. Joseph was already down in Egypt. In all, Jacob had seventy direct descendants.

In time, Joseph and each of his brothers died, ending that generation. But their descendants had many children and grandchildren. In fact, they multiplied so quickly that they soon filled the land. Then a new king came to the throne of Egypt who knew nothing about Joseph or what he had done. He told his people, "These Israelites are becoming a threat to us because there are so many of them. We must find a way to put an end to this. If we don't and if war breaks out, they will join our enemies and fight against us. Then they will escape from the country."

So the Egyptians made the Israelites their slaves and put brutal slave drivers over them, hoping to wear them down under heavy burdens. They forced them to build the cities of Pithom and Rameses as supply centers for the king. But the more the Egyptians oppressed them, the more quickly the Israelites multiplied! The Egyptians soon became alarmed and decided to make their slavery more bitter still. . . .

Then Pharaoh gave this order to all his people: "Throw all the newborn Israelite boys into the Nile River. But you may spare the baby girls."

Exodus 1:1-13,22

Related texts: Psalm 105:23-25; Acts 7:9-34: 1 Corinthians 7:21-23; Galatians 3:26-28

Weird or What?

A **taskmaster's** job description included **torturing** the Jewish people (Hebrews) with slave labor.

Taskmasters tormented from **morning until night,** so the Hebrews wouldn't have time or strength to have children who might grow up and challenge Pharaoh's leadership.

It was not uncommon for a taskmaster to **beat, even to the point of death,** a Hebrew who wasn't working hard.

These people became slaves, with no rights, under these cruel taskmasters.

Today, those with faith in Jesus are called "children of God" and are no longer slaves of Pharaoh or slaves to sin. You have freedom from these "masters" through Jesus.

Today, thank God for your freedom.

done ☑

16 FEBRUARY

Personality Plus

MOSES

Moses is famous for many accomplishments: He delivered the Israelites from captivity, with God's power he opened the Red Sea so the Israelites could escape the Egyptians, and he received God's Ten Commandments.

One interesting truth about Moses is how God protected him as a newborn baby. After Moses' birth, the Pharaoh ordered all newborn Hebrew boys to be killed. Moses' mother created a floatable basket and sent him down the Nile River hoping he'd remain alive. Pharaoh's daughter found baby Moses floating and adopted him—even though she knew he was a Hebrew baby. An amazing story!

When God wants to get something done, He doesn't mess around! God also has a special purpose for your life. Today, trust in Him and watch what happens.

The Birth of Moses

During this time, a man and woman from the tribe of Levi got married. The woman became pregnant and gave birth to a son. She saw what a beautiful baby he was and kept him hidden for three months. But when she could no longer hide him, she got a little basket made of papyrus reeds and waterproofed it with tar and pitch. She put the baby in the basket and laid it among the reeds along the edge of the Nile River. The baby's sister then stood at a distance, watching to see what would happen to him.

Soon after this, one of Pharaoh's daughters came down to bathe in the river, and her servant girls walked along the riverbank. When the princess saw the little basket among the reeds, she told one of her servant girls to get it for her. As the princess opened it, she found the baby boy. His helpless cries touched her heart. "He must be one of the Hebrew children," she said.

Then the baby's sister approached the princess. "Should I go and find one of the Hebrew women to nurse the baby for you?" she asked.

"Yes, do!" the princess replied. So the girl rushed home and called the baby's mother.

"Take this child home and nurse him for me," the princess told her. "I will pay you for your help." So the baby's mother took her baby home and nursed him.

Later, when he was older, the child's mother brought him back to the princess, who adopted him as her son. The princess named him Moses, for she said, "I drew him out of the water."

Exodus 2:1-10

Related texts: Isaiah 49:13-19; Acts 7:20-22; Hebrews 11:23

done ☑

Moses Flees from Egypt

Many years later, when Moses had grown up, he went out to visit his people, the Israelites, and he saw how hard they were forced to work. During his visit, he saw an Egyptian beating one of the Hebrew slaves. After looking around to make sure no one was watching, Moses killed the Egyptian and buried him in the sand.

The next day, as Moses was out visiting his people again, he saw two Hebrew men fighting. "What are you doing, hitting your neighbor like that?" Moses said to the one in the wrong.

"Who do you think you are?" the man replied. "Who appointed you to be our prince and judge? Do you plan to kill me as you killed that Egyptian yesterday?"

Moses was badly frightened because he realized that everyone knew what he had done. And sure enough, when Pharaoh heard about it, he gave orders to have Moses arrested and killed. . . .

Years passed, and the king of Egypt died. But the Israelites still groaned beneath their burden of slavery. They cried out for help, and their pleas for deliverance rose up to God. God heard their cries and remembered his covenant promise to Abraham, Isaac, and Jacob. He looked down on the Israelites and felt deep concern for their welfare.

Exodus 2:11-15a,23-25

He has paid a full ransom for his people.
He has guaranteed his covenant with them forever.
What a holy, awe-inspiring name he has!

Psalm 111:9

Related texts: Deuteronomy 7:7-11; 10:14-15; John 3:16-19; Romans 5:8-11; Ephesians 2:4-10

done ☐

BIG TIME WORD

FRIGHTENED

Fright is a natural and common reaction. Everyone has a few quirks that trigger fear: spiders, the dark, speaking to a crowd, nuclear war, AIDS, etc. Fright causes physical as well as emotional reactions. It's an uncomfortable sensation that puts your entire body on the defense. To constantly live with fear would do terrible damage to your body.

Some people allow fears to control their lives and keep them from living and taking risks. Some Christians allow fears to keep them from being all God wants them to be. Do you have any fears holding you back?

If your fears are stronger than your faith, you'll be in trouble. Faith counteracts fear because God is stronger than the object of your fear. If you have any fears keeping you from living a vital Christian life, ask God to take away those fears today.

18 FEBRUARY

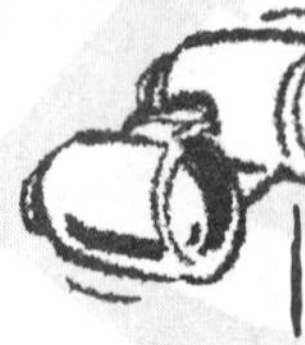

CHECK IT OUT

Moses was in the presence of God and on holy territory. Being in God's presence was not to be taken lightly. It still isn't! This same principle of holiness and respect also applies to Jesus. Unlike many people's beliefs, Jesus is more than JUST a nice man and a good teacher. Jesus is God and worthy of **AWE.**

The Bible informs us that there will be a day when just the "name" of Jesus will cause respect. Check out Philippians 2:10-11: "At the name of Jesus every knee will bow, in heaven and on earth and under the earth, and every tongue will confess that **Jesus Christ is Lord,** to the glory of God the Father."

That's a powerful name! How do **you** respond when you hear it?

The Lord Appears to Moses

One day Moses was tending the flock of his father-in-law, Jethro, the priest of Midian, and he went deep into the wilderness near Sinai, the mountain of God. Suddenly, the angel of the LORD appeared to him as a blazing fire in a bush. Moses was amazed because the bush was engulfed in flames, but it didn't burn up. "Amazing!" Moses said to himself. "Why isn't that bush burning up? I must go over to see this."

When the LORD saw that he had caught Moses' attention, God called to him from the bush, "Moses! Moses!"

"Here I am!" Moses replied.

"Do not come any closer," God told him. "Take off your sandals, for you are standing on holy ground." Then he said, "I am the God of your ancestors—the God of Abraham, the God of Isaac, and the God of Jacob." When Moses heard this, he hid his face in his hands because he was afraid to look at God.

Then the LORD told him, "You can be sure I have seen the misery of my people in Egypt. I have heard their cries for deliverance from their harsh slave drivers. Yes, I am aware of their suffering. So I have come to rescue them from the Egyptians and lead them out of Egypt into their own good and spacious land. . . . Now go, for I am sending you to Pharaoh. You will lead my people, the Israelites, out of Egypt."

Exodus 3:1-8a,10

Related texts: Isaiah 6; Acts 7:30-35; Revelation 15:2-4

done ☐

THE LORD REVEALS HIS NAME TO MOSES

"But who am I to appear before Pharaoh?" Moses asked God. "How can you expect me to lead the Israelites out of Egypt?"

Then God told him, "I will be with you. And this will serve as proof that I have sent you: When you have brought the Israelites out of Egypt, you will return here to worship God at this very mountain."

But Moses protested, "If I go to the people of Israel and tell them, 'The God of your ancestors has sent me to you,' they won't believe me. They will ask, 'Which god are you talking about? What is his name?' Then what should I tell them?"

God replied, "I AM THE ONE WHO ALWAYS IS. Just tell them, 'I AM has sent me to you.'"

God also said, "Tell them, 'The LORD, the God of your ancestors—the God of Abraham, the God of Isaac, and the God of Jacob—has sent me to you.' This will be my name forever; it has always been my name, and it will be used throughout all generations." . . .

And God continued, "I am the LORD. I appeared to Abraham, to Isaac, and to Jacob as God Almighty, though I did not reveal my name, the LORD, to them."

Exodus 3:11-15; 6:2-3

Related texts: Exodus 20:7; John 6:35; 8:12,58; 10:7,11; 11:25; 14:6; 15:1; Revelation 1:8

What's it Mean?

Ever wondered if God has a name? God has several different names. In this passage God tells Moses His name is **"i am."**

Seems like an odd name, doesn't it? **i am** is the name God chose for himself. Many believe this name says it all. "Who's in charge?" i am. "Who's the greatest?" **i am.** This name—**i am**—shows that God is all. There is nothing else but God.

Jesus also said this about Himself in John 8:58. He did not say "I was" or "I will be," but He said **"i am."**

What does all this mean to you today? It means the same thing to you as it did to Moses:

God is everything you need.

done ☐

Personality Plus

LORD

"Lord" is a title and a name for God. It's also a name that gives us better insight into the nature of God.

A traditional definition of "a lord" is someone who owned land and ruled over people. If you have a relationship with God, God is the Lord and Master of your life. He owns you and has authority over you. This means God watches over you and takes care of you. You are His creation and His property.

It's a comforting way to think of yourself—as the Lord's.

You are God's personal possession. ENJOY that truth today!

The Names of God: The Lord

The LORD is a shelter for the oppressed,
a refuge in times of trouble.
Those who know your name trust in you,
for you, O LORD, have never abandoned
anyone who searches for you.

Psalm 9:9-10

Do not misuse the name of the LORD your God. The LORD will not let you go unpunished if you misuse his name.

Exodus 20:7

I will proclaim the name of the LORD;
how glorious is our God!
He is the Rock; his work is perfect.
Everything he does is just and fair.
He is a faithful God who does no wrong;
how just and upright he is!

Deuteronomy 32:3-4

Give thanks to the LORD and proclaim his greatness.
Let the whole world know what he has done.
Sing to him; yes, sing his praises.
Tell everyone about his miracles.
Exult in his holy name;
O worshipers of the LORD, rejoice!

1 Chronicles 16:8-10

The name of the LORD is a strong fortress;
the godly run to him and are safe.

Proverbs 18:10

LORD, there is no one like you! For you are great, and your name is full of power.

Jeremiah 10:6

Related texts: Exodus 15:1-3; Isaiah 42:5-9; Colossians 3:16-17; Hebrews 13:15

done ☐

The Names of God: The Sovereign Lord

How great you are, O Sovereign LORD! There is no one like you—there is no other God. We have never even heard of another god like you! What other nation on earth is like Israel? What other nation, O God, have you redeemed from slavery to be your own people? You made a great name for yourself when you rescued your people from Egypt. You performed awesome miracles and drove out the nations and gods that stood in their way. You made Israel your people forever, and you, O LORD, became their God.

2 Samuel 7:22-24

Our God is a God who saves!
The Sovereign LORD rescues us from death. . . .

O LORD, you alone are my hope.
I've trusted you, O LORD, from childhood. . . .

But those who desert him will perish,
for you destroy those who abandon you.
But as for me, how good it is to be near God!
I have made the Sovereign LORD my shelter,
and I will tell everyone about the wonderful things you do.

Psalms 68:20; 71:5; 73:27-28

Related texts: Isaiah 50:4-11; Acts 4:23-35; Ephesians 5:19-20

In OTHER Words

SOVEREIGN

The word "sovereign" usually is used to describe God. The dictionary defines sovereign as "above" or "superior to all others." It also uses the words "chief" and "one in authority". Although these descriptive words may help us understand "sovereign", a dictionary doesn't explain why God is sovereign.

God is the one who created all, knows all, controls all, is above all, and is everywhere. There is nothing bigger or greater than God. That's why God gets the title Sovereign.

Today, think about God being superior and in complete control of your life. Because God IS sovereign, He's definitely capable of caring for you today.

done ☑

22 FEBRUARY

The Names of God:
The Lord Almighty

Open up, ancient gates!
  Open up, ancient doors,
  and let the King of glory enter.
Who is the King of glory?
  The LORD, strong and mighty,
  the LORD, invincible in battle.
Open up, ancient gates!
  Open up, ancient doors,
  and let the King of glory enter.
Who is the King of glory?
  The LORD Almighty—
  he is the King of glory.

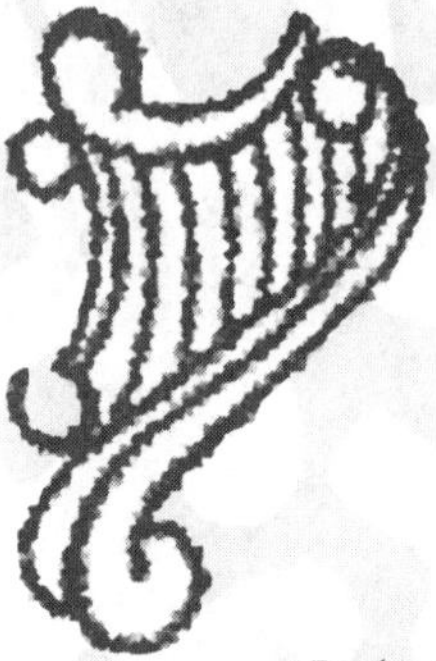

Psalm 24:7-10

I saw before me what seemed to be a crystal sea mixed with fire. And on it stood all the people who had been victorious over the beast and his statue and the number representing his name. They were all holding harps that God had given them. And they were singing the song of Moses, the servant of God, and the song of the Lamb:
"Great and marvelous are your actions,
  Lord God Almighty.
Just and true are your ways,
  O King of the nations.
Who will not fear, O Lord, and glorify your name?
  For you alone are holy.
All nations will come and worship before you,
  for your righteous deeds have been revealed."

Revelation 15:2-4

Related texts: 1 Samuel 17:39-51; Isaiah 54:5; Revelation 4:1-8

Give it a try

What are a few qualities that a king is traditionally known for?

Do these words also describe God as you understand Him?

Why do you think "King" is a good title for God?

 done ☑

NAMES OF GOD: THE ALMIGHTY

"Listen to me, you who have understanding. Everyone knows that God doesn't sin! The Almighty can do no wrong. He repays people according to their deeds. He treats people according to their ways. There is no truer statement than this: God will not do wrong. The Almighty cannot twist justice. . . .

"We cannot imagine the power of the Almighty, yet he is so just and merciful that he does not oppress us. No wonder people everywhere fear him. People who are truly wise show him reverence."

Job 34:10-12; 37:23-24

Those who live in the shelter of the Most High
will find rest in the shadow of the Almighty.
This I declare of the LORD:
He alone is my refuge, my place of safety;
he is my God, and I am trusting him.
For he will rescue you from every trap
and protect you from the fatal plague.
He will shield you with his wings.
He will shelter you with his feathers.
His faithful promises are your armor and protection.

Psalm 91:1-4

"I am the Alpha and the Omega—the beginning and the end," says the Lord God. "I am the one who is, who always was, and who is still to come, the Almighty One."

Revelation 1:8

Related texts: Genesis 17:1; 28:3; 35:11; 43:14; 48:3; 49:25; Exodus 6:2-4; Revelation 21:22-27

What's it Mean?

God uses the alphabet to better describe another of His many qualities—"I am the A and the Z." With this analogy, God is reminding us that He is the beginning (A) and the end (Z).

God was around before the earth, before the stars, before your grandparents, and WAY before you. God is also the end of everything, which means you are somewhere in the middle of His big plan—maybe around the letter J—nobody knows.

The only thing we do know is His promise to come back to us. When that happens, you'll need to know more than just the alphabet. You'll need to know Jesus.

Are you ready for His return?

done ☐

Names of God: The LORD

One Minute Memory

Let your **roots grow** down into him and draw up **nourishment** from him, so you will **grow in faith**, strong and **vigorous in the truth** you were taught. Let your lives overflow with **thanksgiving** for all he has done.

Colossians 2:7

The LORD your God is the God of gods and Lord of lords. He is the great God, mighty and awesome, who shows no partiality and takes no bribes. He gives justice to orphans and widows. He shows love to the foreigners living among you and gives them food and clothing.

Deuteronomy 10:17-18

O LORD, our Lord, the majesty of your name fills the earth! . . .

Lord, through all the generations
 you have been our home!
Before the mountains were created,
 before you made the earth and the world,
 you are God, without beginning or end.

Psalms 8:9; 90:1-2

For if you confess with your mouth that Jesus is Lord and believe in your heart that God raised him from the dead, you will be saved. For it is by believing in your heart that you are made right with God, and it is by confessing with your mouth that you are saved. As the Scriptures tell us, "Anyone who believes in him will not be disappointed." Jew and Gentile are the same in this respect. They all have the same Lord, who generously gives his riches to all who ask for them. For "Anyone who calls on the name of the LORD will be saved."

Romans 10:9-13

And now, just as you accepted Christ Jesus as your Lord, you must continue to live in obedience to him. Let your roots grow down into him and draw up nourishment from him, so you will grow in faith, strong and vigorous in the truth you were taught. Let your lives overflow with thanksgiving for all he has done.

Colossians 2:6-7

Related texts: Job 28; Psalms 8; 86; 110; Daniel 9:1-19; Philippians 2:5-11

done ☐

Names of God: The Most High

God is my shield,
saving those whose hearts are true and right. . . .
God is our refuge and strength,
always ready to help in times of trouble.
So we will not fear, even if earthquakes come
and the mountains crumble into the sea.
Let the oceans roar and foam.
Let the mountains tremble as the waters surge!
A river brings joy to the city of our God,
the sacred home of the Most High.
God himself lives in that city; it cannot be destroyed.
God will protect it at the break of day.
The nations are in an uproar,
and kingdoms crumble!
God thunders,
and the earth melts!
The LORD Almighty is here among us;
the God of Israel is our fortress. . . .
Come, everyone, and clap your hands for joy!
Shout to God with joyful praise!
For the LORD Most High is awesome.
He is the great King of all the earth. . . .
It is good to give thanks to the LORD,
to sing praises to the Most High.
It is good to proclaim your unfailing love in the morning,
your faithfulness in the evening,
accompanied by the harp and lute
and the harmony of the lyre.
You thrill me, LORD, with all you have done for me!
I sing for joy because of what you have done.
O LORD, what great miracles you do!
And how deep are your thoughts.

Psalms 7:10; 46:1-7; 47:1-2; 92:1-5

Related texts: Genesis 14:18-24; Psalms 7; 9:1-2; 91; Luke 1:26-38

JUST a THOUGHT

If God is known to save and protect the faithful, don't you think it's worth putting Him to the test with your life?

done

CHECK IT OUT

You've probably heard it said, "Time flies when you're having fun!" Well, time flies even if you aren't having fun. Time and life move very quickly. It's easy to waste time and move through life being bored when you don't have the big picture of why you're on this crazy playground we call Earth. You're here to love God, celebrate life, love others, and do good things that will make a difference in the world.

Check out the advice from the psalmist regarding our time: "Teach us to make the most of our time, so that we may grow in wisdom."

Spend a minute today asking God for His direction on how you spend today's time.

If God is a part of the day, it's never wasted.

Names of God: The Creator

Don't let the excitement of youth cause you to forget your Creator. Honor him in your youth before you grow old and no longer enjoy living. It will be too late then to remember him, when the light of the sun and moon and stars is dim to your old eyes, and there is no silver lining left among the clouds. Your limbs will tremble with age, and your strong legs will grow weak. Your teeth will be too few to do their work, and you will be blind, too. And when your teeth are gone, keep your lips tightly closed when you eat! Even the chirping of birds will wake you up. But you yourself will be deaf and tuneless, with a quavering voice. You will be afraid of heights and of falling, white-haired and withered, dragging along without any sexual desire. You will be standing at death's door. And as you near your everlasting home, the mourners will walk along the streets.

Yes, remember your Creator now while you are young, before the silver cord of life snaps and the golden bowl is broken. Don't wait until the water jar is smashed at the spring and the pulley is broken at the well. For then the dust will return to the earth, and the spirit will return to God who gave it.

Ecclesiastes 12:1-7

Related texts: Genesis 1; 14:18-24; Ecclesiastes 12:9-14; Isaiah 40:27-31; Revelation 4:11

done ☑

The Names of God: Everlasting God, King Eternal

O Israel, how can you say the LORD does not see your troubles? How can you say God refuses to hear your case? Have you never heard or understood? Don't you know that the LORD is the everlasting God, the Creator of all the earth? He never grows faint or weary. No one can measure the depths of his understanding. He gives power to those who are tired and worn out; he offers strength to the weak. Even youths will become exhausted, and young men will give up. But those who wait on the LORD will find new strength. They will fly high on wings like eagles. They will run and not grow weary. They will walk and not faint.

Isaiah 40:27-31

This is a true saying, and everyone should believe it: Christ Jesus came into the world to save sinners—and I was the worst of them all. But that is why God had mercy on me, so that Christ Jesus could use me as a prime example of his great patience with even the worst sinners. Then others will realize that they, too, can believe in him and receive eternal life. Glory and honor to God forever and ever. He is the eternal King, the unseen one who never dies; he alone is God. Amen.

1 Timothy 1:15-17

Related texts: Deuteronomy 33:27; Psalm 90:1-2; Romans 16:25-27; Hebrews 9:14

Give it a try

Record your feelings in the space provided after reading the following verse:
"Those who wait on the Lord will find new strength. They will fly high on wings like eagles. They will run and not grow weary. They will walk and not faint" (Isa. 40:31).

done ☐

BIG TIMe WoRd

HOLY

Holy is a famous religious term given to things associated with God. Something that is holy is SET APART from sin. Holy or holiness is rare and in a league of its own.

Holiness starts with God because God is holy. God then calls us and encourages us to be holy—to be SET APART from sin.

Since God has given us His Son to redeem us, holiness is a goal for those wanting to mature and grow in their faith. Make it a goal–aim at it. Remember the old proverb: If you aim at nothing, you'll hit it every time.

Take aim at holiness today.

Names of God: The Holy One

Yet you are holy.
  The praises of Israel surround your throne.
Our ancestors trusted in you,
  and you rescued them.
You heard their cries for help and saved them.
  They put their trust in you and were never disappointed.

Psalm 22:3-5

Fear of the LORD is the beginning of wisdom. Knowledge of the Holy One results in understanding.

Wisdom will multiply your days and add years to your life. If you become wise, you will be the one to benefit. If you scorn wisdom, you will be the one to suffer.

Proverbs 9:10-12

Our Redeemer, whose name is the LORD Almighty, is the Holy One of Israel.

Isaiah 47:4

Once when he was in the synagogue, a man possessed by a demon began shouting at Jesus, "Go away! Why are you bothering us, Jesus of Nazareth? Have you come to destroy us? I know who you are—the Holy One sent from God."

Jesus cut him short. "Be silent!" he told the demon. "Come out of the man!" The demon threw the man to the floor as the crowd watched; then it left him without hurting him further.

Amazed, the people exclaimed, "What authority and power this man's words possess! Even evil spirits obey him and flee at his command!"

Luke 4:33-36

Related texts: Psalm 16; Isaiah 40:25-31; 54:5; Acts 2:22-39

done ☐

FEBRUARY 29

Names of God: Judge

But the LORD reigns forever,
executing judgment from his throne.
He will judge the world with justice
and rule the nations with fairness. . . .

LORD, the God to whom vengeance
belongs,
O God of vengeance, let your glorious
justice be seen!
Arise, O judge of the earth.
Sentence the proud to the penalties
they deserve.

Psalms 9:7-8; 94:1-2

Out of the stump of David's family will grow a shoot—yes, a new Branch bearing fruit from the old root. And the Spirit of the LORD will rest on him—the Spirit of wisdom and understanding, the Spirit of counsel and might, the Spirit of knowledge and the fear of the LORD. He will delight in obeying the LORD. He will never judge by appearance, false evidence, or hearsay. He will defend the poor and the exploited. He will rule against the wicked and destroy them with the breath of his mouth. He will be clothed with fairness and truth. . . .

For the LORD is our judge, our lawgiver, and our king. He will care for us and save us.

Isaiah 11:1-5; 33:22

Related texts: Judges 11:27; Psalms 7; 82; 96; John 5:25-30; Acts 10:34-43; James 4:11-12; Revelation 19:11-16

CHECK IT OUT

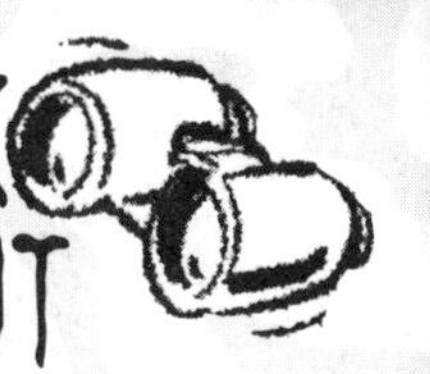

In the Old Testament God is seen as the judge. In the New Testament Jesus is given the responsibility of judgment. But since God and Jesus are one, we can assume they will work together and decide the details of judgment. Judgment Day is a mystery day; no one knows when except God. Check out how you can be prepared for that day.

He is the one all the prophets testified about, saying everyone who believes in him (Jesus) will have their sins forgiven through his name (Acts 10:43).

It's not always an easy decision to completely trust Jesus, but it's sure an easy choice between eternal life in heaven or eternal life in hell.

What's your choice?

done ☐

March

No sciences are better attested than the religion of the Bible

Sir Isaac Newton
(1642–1727)
English Scientist

Names of God: KING

The LORD rules over the floodwaters.
The LORD reigns as king forever.
The LORD gives his people strength.

Psalm 29:10-11a

I am the LORD, your Holy One, Israel's Creator and King.

Isaiah 43:15

So Pilate asked him, "Are you the King of the Jews?"

Jesus replied, "Yes, it is as you say."

Luke 23:3

Then I saw heaven opened, and a white horse was standing there. And the one sitting on the horse was named Faithful and True. For he judges fairly and then goes to war. His eyes were bright like flames of fire, and on his head were many crowns. A name was written on him, and only he knew what it meant. He was clothed with a robe dipped in blood, and his title was the Word of God. The armies of heaven, dressed in pure white linen, followed him on white horses. From his mouth came a sharp sword, and with it he struck down the nations. He ruled them with an iron rod, and he trod the winepress of the fierce wrath of almighty God. On his robe and thigh was written this title: King of kings and Lord of lords.

Revelation 19:11-16

Related texts: Psalms 47; 95:1-7; Isaiah 44:6-8; Jeremiah 10:6-10; Matthew 21:1-5; 1 Timothy 1:17; 6:15

JUST a THOUGHT

God showed His awesome power in creating this world, and He displayed His great love for people long before you. The good news is that **His power** AND **love** are available for you TODAY!

done ☐

2 MARCH

The Names of God:
The Mighty One

"Though you were once despised and hated and rebuffed by all, you will be beautiful forever. You will be a joy to all generations, for I will make you so. Powerful kings and mighty nations will bring the best of their goods to satisfy your every need. You will know at last that I, the LORD, am your Savior and Redeemer, the Mighty One of Israel."

Isaiah 60:15-16

Mary responded,
"Oh, how I praise the Lord.
How I rejoice in God my Savior!
For he took notice of his lowly servant girl,
and now generation after generation will call me blessed.
For he, the Mighty One, is holy,
and he has done great things for me.
His mercy goes on from generation to generation,
to all who fear him.
His mighty arm does tremendous things!
How he scatters the proud and haughty ones!
He has taken princes from their thrones
and exalted the lowly.
He has satisfied the hungry with good things
and sent the rich away with empty hands.
And how he has helped his servant Israel!
He has not forgotten his promise to be merciful.
For he promised our ancestors—Abraham and his children—
to be merciful to them forever."

Luke 1:46-55

Related texts: Joshua 22:22; Psalms 50; 132; Isaiah 49:24-26; Mark 14:60-62

Give it a try

In Mary's joy she said, "(God) has done great things for me." What are four great things God has done for you?

1.
2.
3.
4.

Take a minute to thank Him and give Him praise for the great things He has done in your life.

done ☐

Names of God: Redeemer

But as for me, I know that my Redeemer lives, and that he will stand upon the earth at last. And after my body has decayed, yet in my body I will see God! I will see him for myself. Yes, I will see him with my own eyes. I am overwhelmed at the thought!

Job 19:25-27

How can I know all the sins lurking in my
    heart?
  Cleanse me from these hidden faults.
Keep me from deliberate sins!
  Don't let them control me.
Then I will be free of guilt
  and innocent of great sin.
May the words of my mouth and the
    thoughts of my heart
  be pleasing to you,
  O LORD, my rock and my redeemer.

Psalm 19:12-14

This is what the LORD, Israel's King and Redeemer, the LORD Almighty, says: I am the First and the Last; there is no other God. Who else can tell you what is going to happen in the days ahead? Let them tell you if they can and thus prove their power. Let them do as I have done since ancient times. Do not tremble; do not be afraid. Have I not proclaimed from ages past what my purposes are for you? You are my witnesses—is there any other God? No! There is no other Rock—not one!

Isaiah 44:6-8

Related texts: Isaiah 44:24-28; 54; Luke 24:13-36; Galatians 4:4-5; Titus 2:11-14

In OTHER Words

REDEEMER

God is called a redeemer because He saves people from being prisoners to sin. Since God cannot tolerate sin, we have to be brought out, saved, or REDEEMED from being captive to sin. God redeems us through Jesus' death on the cross.

Jesus has paid for our sins! He bought us back by dying for our sins and rescued us (or those who believe) from the penalty of sin: death. When you believe in Him, you are saved from being a prisoner to sin, and you experience salvation.

Be sure to ask questions if you need help understanding this word—**it's very important!**

done ☑

CATCH THIS

These verses are great to return to when you feel lonely, hurt, or scared. It's exciting to know that God promises to comfort you during times of trouble.

A typical move during tough times is to run to friends. This can be both good and bad. Friends can provide comfort and direction. But friends can also turn their backs or even make things worse (remember Job's friends?).

God is different from a friend. He's more consistent, for one thing. But He's also stronger, wiser, more powerful, and able to provide you with hope and strength for your specific hurt.

Allow today's verses to remind you not to overlook God as the source of comfort. If you don't think He's strong enough, just wait until tomorrow's reading—you'll see.

Names of God: REFUGE

The LORD is a shelter for the oppressed,
a refuge in times of trouble.
Those who know your name trust in you,
for you, O LORD, have never abandoned
anyone who searches for you. . . .

O God, listen to my cry!
Hear my prayer!
From the ends of the earth,
I will cry to you for help,
for my heart is overwhelmed.
Lead me to the towering rock of safety,
for you are my safe refuge,
a fortress where my enemies cannot
reach me.
Let me live forever in your sanctuary,
safe beneath the shelter of your wings!. . .

You are my refuge and my shield;
your word is my only source of hope.

Psalms 9:9-10; 61:1-4; 119:114

LORD, you are my strength and fortress, my refuge in the day of trouble! Nations from around the world will come to you and say, "Our ancestors were foolish, for they worshiped worthless idols. Can people make their own god? The gods they make are not real gods at all!"

"So now I will show them my power and might," says the LORD. "At last they will know that I am the LORD."

Jeremiah 16:19-21

Related texts: 2 Samuel 22:3; 31; Psalms 46; 59:16-17; 71; 91; Isaiah 25:1-5

done ☐

Names of God: ROCK

"Listen, O heavens, and I will speak!
 Hear, O earth, the words that I say!
My teaching will fall on you like rain;
 my speech will settle like dew.
My words will fall like rain on tender grass,
 like gentle showers on young plants.
I will proclaim the name of the LORD;
 how glorious is our God!
He is the Rock; his work is perfect.
 Everything he does is just and fair.
He is a faithful God who does no wrong;
 how just and upright he is!"

Deuteronomy 32:1-4

Then Hannah prayed:
"My heart rejoices in the LORD!
 Oh, how the LORD has blessed me!
Now I have an answer for my enemies,
 as I delight in your deliverance.
No one is holy like the LORD!
 There is no one besides you;
 there is no Rock like our God."

1 Samuel 2:1-2

The LORD is my rock, my fortress, and my savior;
 my God is my rock, in whom I find protection.
 He is my shield, the strength of my salvation, and my stronghold.
I will call on the LORD, who is worthy of praise,
 for he saves me from my enemies.

Psalm 18:2-3

Related texts: Deuteronomy 32; 2 Samuel 22; Psalm 62; Romans 9:30-33; 1 Corinthians 10:1-4; 1 Peter 2:1-8

CHECK IT OUT

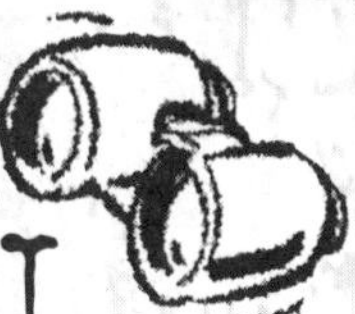

In the New Testament, Jesus is also referred to as the Rock. Check out 1 Peter 2:4-6, where, in addition to Jesus' being named the "Rock," you also receive two names or identities—"the living stones" and "holy priests." Read the following passage and underline your given identity.

"Come to Christ, who is the living cornerstone of God's temple. He was rejected by the people, but he is precious to God who chose him. And now God is building you, as living stones, into his spiritual temple. What's more, you are God's holy priests, who offer the spiritual sacrifices that please him because of Jesus Christ."

Try to live up to your new identity today!

done ☐

In OTHER Words

SALVATION

This word represents one of the main messages throughout the Bible. When someone says, "I've been saved," he is saying he has been saved from sin's death and returned to God.

The only way to experience salvation is by accepting Jesus' death as the payment for your sin. There's no other way to be saved or no other plan or method to get to God. The Bible says in Acts 4:12, "There is salvation in no one else (but Jesus)! **There is no other name in all of heaven for people to call on to save them."**

Names of God: SAVIOR

Why am I discouraged?
Why so sad?
I will put my hope in God!
I will praise him again—
my Savior and my God!

Psalm 42:11

"But you are my witnesses, O Israel!" says the LORD. "And you are my servant. You have been chosen to know me, believe in me, and understand that I alone am God. There is no other God; there never has been and never will be. I am the LORD, and there is no other Savior. First I predicted your deliverance; I declared what I would do, and then I did it—I saved you. No foreign god has ever done this before. You are witnesses that I am the only God," says the LORD. "From eternity to eternity I am God. No one can oppose what I do. No one can reverse my actions."

Isaiah 43:10-13

For the grace of God has been revealed, bringing salvation to all people. And we are instructed to turn from godless living and sinful pleasures. We should live in this evil world with self-control, right conduct, and devotion to God, while we look forward to that wonderful event when the glory of our great God and Savior, Jesus Christ, will be revealed. He gave his life to free us from every kind of sin, to cleanse us, and to make us his very own people, totally committed to doing what is right.

Titus 2:11-14

Related texts: Psalm 68:19-20; Micah 7:1-7; Habakkuk 3:16-19; Luke 1:47-55; 2:8-20; John 4:40-42; Acts 5:29-32

done ☐

MARCH 7

The Names of God: Shepherd

The LORD is my shepherd;
  I have everything I need.

Psalm 23:1

Yes, the Sovereign LORD is coming in all his glorious power. He will rule with awesome strength. See, he brings his reward with him as he comes. He will feed his flock like a shepherd. He will carry the lambs in his arms, holding them close to his heart. He will gently lead the mother sheep with their young.

Isaiah 40:10-11

And now, may the God of peace, who brought again from the dead our Lord Jesus, equip you with all you need for doing his will. May he produce in you, through the power of Jesus Christ, all that is pleasing to him. Jesus is the great Shepherd of the sheep by an everlasting covenant, signed with his blood. To him be glory forever and ever. Amen.

Hebrews 13:20-21

That is why they are standing in front of the throne of God, serving him day and night in his Temple. And he who sits on the throne will live among them and shelter them. They will never again be hungry or thirsty, and they will be fully protected from the scorching noontime heat. For the Lamb who stands in front of the throne will be their Shepherd. He will lead them to the springs of life-giving water. And God will wipe away all their tears.

Revelation 7:15-17

Related texts: Psalms 23; 80:1-7; Ezekiel 34; Micah 5:2-5; John 10:11-15; 1 Peter 2:21-25; 5:1-4

Give it a try

A shepherd's responsibility is to care for his sheep. In the left column you'll find a few qualities that describe a shepherd. Next to those qualities, in the right column, write how God is like a shepherd in your life.

A Shepherd:	God
1. Knows his sheep.	1.
2. Keeps the sheep from danger.	2.
3. Makes sure his sheep are fed.	3.

Take a minute to thank God for the role He plays as your Shepherd.

done ☐

THE FRUIT OF THE SPIRIT

What's it Mean?

The fruits of the Spirit are:

- love
- joy
- peace
- patience
- kindness
- goodness
- faithfulness
- gentleness
- self-control

The challenge in these verses is for these fruits to reside in your life. To help you better understand this concept, replace the word "fruit" with the word "actions." Think of them as "actions of the spirit."

Look at the three key words just before the listing of the fruits in today's passage: "controls our lives." When you live your life in faithfulness and obedience to God, His Spirit will energize you to produce these actions in how you think, feel, and act.

Read again the listing of bad fruit—it's pretty ugly. Today, ask God to begin or continue controlling your life so you'll become a person of "good fruit."

When you follow the desires of your sinful nature, your lives will produce these evil results: sexual immorality, impure thoughts, eagerness for lustful pleasure, idolatry, participation in demonic activities, hostility, quarreling, jealousy, outbursts of anger, selfish ambition, divisions, the feeling that everyone is wrong except those in your own little group, envy, drunkenness, wild parties, and other kinds of sin. Let me tell you again, as I have before, that anyone living that sort of life will not inherit the Kingdom of God.

But when the Holy Spirit controls our lives, he will produce this kind of fruit in us: love, joy, peace, patience, kindness, goodness, faithfulness, gentleness, and self-control. Here there is no conflict with the law.

Galatians 5:19-23

For though your hearts were once full of darkness, now you are full of light from the Lord, and your behavior should show it! For this light within you produces only what is good and right and true.

Try to find out what is pleasing to the Lord. Take no part in the worthless deeds of evil and darkness; instead, rebuke and expose them.

Ephesians 5:8-11

A good person produces good deeds from a good heart, and an evil person produces evil deeds from an evil heart. Whatever is in your heart determines what you say.

Luke 6:45

Related texts: Psalms 1; 112; Isaiah 27:2-3; John 15:1-16; Romans 7:1-6

done ☐

The Fruit of the Spirit: LOVE

Jesus replied, "The most important commandment is this: 'Hear, O Israel! The Lord our God is the one and only Lord. And you must love the Lord your God with all your heart, all your soul, all your mind, and all your strength.' The second is equally important: 'Love your neighbor as yourself.' No other commandment is greater than these." *Mark 12:29-31*

"So now I am giving you a new commandment: Love each other. Just as I have loved you, you should love each other. Your love for one another will prove to the world that you are my disciples." *John 13:34-35*

"You have heard that the law of Moses says, 'Love your neighbor' and hate your enemy. But I say, love your enemies! Pray for those who persecute you! In that way, you will be acting as true children of your Father in heaven. For he gives his sunlight to both the evil and the good, and he sends rain on the just and on the unjust, too. If you love only those who love you, what good is that? Even corrupt tax collectors do that much." *Matthew 5:43-46*

Since God chose you to be the holy people whom he loves, you must clothe yourselves with tenderhearted mercy, kindness, humility, gentleness, and patience. You must make allowance for each other's faults and forgive the person who offends you. Remember, the Lord forgave you, so you must forgive others. And the most important piece of clothing you must wear is love. Love is what binds us all together in perfect harmony. *Colossians 3:12-14*

Related texts: Deuteronomy 6:4-6; John 14-15; 21:15-17; 1 Corinthians 13; 1 John 4:17-21; 1 Peter 4:7-8

JUST A THOUGHT

The secret to changing enemies, friends, parents, teachers, or even **little brothers** or **sisters** is to **love them as Jesus loves you. People can't stay the same** when they're **drenched** with the type of **love Jesus displays.**

done ☐

10 MARCH

God Is Love

One Minute Memory

For God so loved the world that he gave his **only Son,** so that **everyone** who believes in him will **not perish but have eternal life.**

John 3:16

If you already have this verse memorized, try the next one.

But **God showed his great love for us** by **sending Christ to die for us** while **we were still sinners.**

Romans 5:8

Then the LORD came down in a pillar of cloud and called out his own name, "the LORD," as Moses stood there in his presence. He passed in front of Moses and said, "I am the LORD, I am the LORD, the merciful and gracious God. I am slow to anger and rich in unfailing love and faithfulness. I show this unfailing love to many thousands by forgiving every kind of sin and rebellion. Even so I do not leave sin unpunished, but I punish the children for the sins of their parents to the third and fourth generations."

Exodus 34:5-7

He loves whatever is just and good,
and his unfailing love fills the earth.

Psalm 33:5

For God so loved the world that he gave his only Son, so that everyone who believes in him will not perish but have eternal life.

John 3:16

But God showed his great love for us by sending Christ to die for us while we were still sinners. . . .

And I am convinced that nothing can ever separate us from his love. Death can't, and life can't. The angels can't, and the demons can't. Our fears for today, our worries about tomorrow, and even the powers of hell can't keep God's love away. Whether we are high above the sky or in the deepest ocean, nothing in all creation will ever be able to separate us from the love of God that is revealed in Christ Jesus our LORD.

Romans 5:8; 8:38-39

We know how much God loves us, and we have put our trust in him.

God is love, and all who live in love live in God, and God lives in them.

1 John 4:16

Related texts: Psalms 1; 112; Isaiah 27:2-3; John 15:1-16; Romans 7:1-6

done ☐

The Fruit of the Spirit: JOY

Let the godly sing with joy to the LORD,
for it is fitting to praise him.
Praise the LORD with melodies on the lyre;
make music for him on the ten-stringed harp.
Sing new songs of praise to him;
play skillfully on the harp and sing with joy.
For the word of the LORD holds true,
and everything he does is worthy of our trust.

Psalm 33:1-4

Even though the fig trees have no blossoms, and there are no grapes on the vine; even though the olive crop fails, and the fields lie empty and barren; even though the flocks die in the fields, and the cattle barns are empty, yet I will rejoice in the LORD! I will be joyful in the God of my salvation.

Habakkuk 3:17-18

So I pray that God, who gives you hope, will keep you happy and full of peace as you believe in him. May you overflow with hope through the power of the Holy Spirit.

Romans 15:13

Always be full of joy in the Lord. I say it again—rejoice!

Philippians 4:4

Dear friends, don't be surprised at the fiery trials you are going through, as if something strange were happening to you. Instead, be very glad—because these trials will make you partners with Christ in his suffering, and afterward you will have the wonderful joy of sharing his glory when it is displayed to all the world.

1 Peter 4:12-13

Related texts: Nehemiah 8:1-12; Psalms 28:6-9; 30:4-5; Isaiah 61

JUST a THOUGHT

When you wake up tomorrow morning, try the joyful phrase "GOOD MORNING, GOD!" It may jump-start your day with a joyful attitude.

done ☐

BIG TIMe WoRd

JOY

Did you know that the word JOY is different from the word HAPPINESS? Happiness is based on some thing or circumstantial happening.

Joy is different. True joy isn't dependent on anything. Joy is an attitude that lives within you. Joy doesn't change when situations change.

Even though it may seem impossible, joy can exist in the midst of difficulty. In the Bible, Christians are encouraged to be joyful when they encounter problems and to have joy during difficult times because Jesus has overcome the world.

Pain is unavoidable, and being happy is conditional, but joy is a fruit of the Spirit that becomes available when you depend on God.

God Is Joyful

May the glory of the LORD last forever!
The LORD rejoices in all he has made!
The earth trembles at his glance;
the mountains burst into flame at his touch.
I will sing to the LORD as long as I live.
I will praise my God to my last breath!
May he be pleased by all these thoughts about him,
for I rejoice in the LORD.

Psalm 104:31-34

On that day the announcement to Jerusalem will be, "Cheer up, Zion! Don't be afraid! For the LORD your God has arrived to live among you. He is a mighty savior. He will rejoice over you with great gladness. With his love, he will calm all your fears. He will exult over you by singing a happy song."

Zephaniah 3:16-17

We do this by keeping our eyes on Jesus, on whom our faith depends from start to finish. He was willing to die a shameful death on the cross because of the joy he knew would be his afterward. Now he is seated in the place of highest honor beside God's throne in heaven. Think about all he endured when sinful people did such terrible things to him, so that you don't become weary and give up.

Hebrews 12:2-3

Related texts: 1 Chronicles 16:23-33; Nehemiah 8:1-12; Psalm 21:1-7; Isaiah 62:4-7

done ☐

The Fruit of the Spirit: PEACE

May the LORD bless you
and protect you.
May the LORD smile on you
and be gracious to you.
May the LORD show you his favor
and give you his peace.

Numbers 6:24-26

Those who love your law have great peace
and do not stumble.

Psalm 119:165

You will keep in perfect peace all who trust
in you,
whose thoughts are fixed on you!
Trust in the LORD always,
for the LORD GOD is the eternal Rock.

Isaiah 26:3-4

"I am leaving you with a gift—peace of mind and heart. And the peace I give isn't like the peace the world gives. So don't be troubled or afraid."

John 14:27

Don't worry about anything; instead, pray about everything. Tell God what you need, and thank him for all he has done. If you do this, you will experience God's peace, which is far more wonderful than the human mind can understand. His peace will guard your hearts and minds as you live in Christ Jesus.

Philippians 4:6-7

And let the peace that comes from Christ rule in your hearts. For as members of one body you are all called to live in peace. And always be thankful.

Colossians 3:15

Related texts: Proverbs 12:20; Isaiah 32:17; 57:21; Micah 4:1-5; Luke 2:13-14; Romans 8:1-6

One Minute Memory

Don't worry about anything; instead, pray about everything. Tell God what you need, and thank him for all he has done.

Philippians 4:6

done ☐

Weird or What?

God Is Peaceful

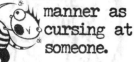

In the Old Testament the Hebrew word for "peace" is **shalom.** This is the same word you might hear as a greeting or closing remark in many present-day Jewish temples. **Shalom is used to communicate a blessing to another person.** The meaning of the blessing has its source in God. **To withhold shalom is to withhold the blessing and might be interpreted in a similar manner as cursing at someone.**

The LORD gives his people strength.
The LORD blesses them with peace.

Psalm 29:11

For a child is born to us, a son is given to us. And the government will rest on his shoulders. These will be his royal titles: Wonderful Counselor, Mighty God, Everlasting Father, Prince of Peace. His ever expanding, peaceful government will never end. He will rule forever with fairness and justice from the throne of his ancestor David. The passionate commitment of the LORD Almighty will guarantee this!

Isaiah 9:6-7

Therefore, since we have been made right in God's sight by faith, we have peace with God because of what Jesus Christ our Lord has done for us. Because of our faith, Christ has brought us into this place of highest privilege where we now stand, and we confidently and joyfully look forward to sharing God's glory.

Romans 5:1-2

Now may the God of peace make you holy in every way, and may your whole spirit and soul and body be kept blameless until that day when our LORD Jesus Christ comes again.

1 Thessalonians 5:23

May the Lord of peace himself always give you his peace no matter what happens. The LORD be with you all.

2 Thessalonians 3:16

Related texts: Ecclesiastes 3:1-8; Romans 15:33; 16:20; 2 Corinthians 13:11; Philippians 4:6-9

done ☐

The Fruit of the Spirit: PEACE

Be still in the presence of the LORD,
and wait patiently for him to act.
Don't worry about evil people who prosper
or fret about their wicked schemes.
Stop your anger!
Turn from your rage!
Do not envy others—
it only leads to harm.
For the wicked will be destroyed,
but those who trust in the LORD will
possess the land. . . .

I waited patiently for the LORD to help me,
and he turned to me and heard my cry.
He lifted me out of the pit of despair,
out of the mud and the mire.
He set my feet on solid ground
and steadied me as I walked along.
He has given me a new song to sing,
a hymn of praise to our God.
Many will see what he has done and be
astounded.
They will put their trust in the LORD.

Psalms 37:7-9; 40:1-3

Those who control their anger have great understanding; those with a hasty temper will make mistakes. *Proverbs 14:29*

Love is patient and kind. Love is not jealous or boastful or proud or rude.

1 Corinthians 13:4-5a

Dear brothers and sisters, you must be patient as you wait for the Lord's return. Consider the farmers who eagerly look for the rains in the fall and in the spring. They patiently wait for the precious harvest to ripen. You, too, must be patient. And take courage, for the coming of the Lord is near.

James 5:7-8

Related texts: Proverbs 15:18; 16:32; 19:11; 25:15; Ecclesiastes 7:8; Romans 12:9-12

done ☐

CATCH THIS

Having patience in today's world is tough! We live in a time-oriented society where "quick serve," getting "in and out," fast food, and not waiting in lines have become important values for survival.

Have you ever noticed that having patience is really tough when you desperately want something to happen? What's even tougher is being patient with God's timing. Most of us want God to answer our prayers NOW. But whether or not we like it, God answers them WHEN He wants to, and His timing is always better than ours—because He's God.

Try being patient today. Next time you ask God for something, accept His timing. Be confident that He hears your prayers.

JUST a THOUGHT

The greatest news any of your friends could ever hear is that God loves them more than they love themselves and He wants them to have everlasting life.

Can you do anything to let them know this good news today?

God Is Patient

This is a true saying, and everyone should believe it: Christ Jesus came into the world to save sinners—and I was the worst of them all. But that is why God had mercy on me, so that Christ Jesus could use me as a prime example of his great patience with even the worst sinners. Then others will realize that they, too, can believe in him and receive eternal life.

1 Timothy 1:15-16

The Lord isn't really being slow about his promise to return, as some people think. No, he is being patient for your sake. He does not want anyone to perish, so he is giving more time for everyone to repent. But the day of the LORD will come as unexpectedly as a thief. Then the heavens will pass away with a terrible noise, and everything in them will disappear in fire, and the earth and everything on it will be exposed to judgment. . . .

And remember, the Lord is waiting so that people have time to be saved. This is just as our beloved brother Paul wrote to you with the wisdom God gave him.

2 Peter 3:9-10,15

Related texts: Isaiah 7:13; 65:17-25; Romans 2:1-4; 3:21-28; 1 Peter 3:18-20; Revelation 21:1-8

done ☐

The Fruit of the Spirit

Kindness

Beautiful women obtain wealth, and violent men get rich.
Your own soul is nourished when you are kind, but you destroy yourself when you are cruel. . . .

Those who oppress the poor insult their Maker, but those who help the poor honor him. . . .

If you help the poor, you are lending to the LORD—and he will repay you! *Proverbs 11:16-17; 14:31; 19:17*

Instead, be kind to each other, tenderhearted, forgiving one another, just as God through Christ has forgiven you. *Ephesians 4:32*

Since God chose you to be the holy people whom he loves, you must clothe yourselves with tenderhearted mercy, kindness, humility, gentleness, and patience. You must make allowance for each other's faults and forgive the person who offends you. Remember, the LORD forgave you, so you must forgive others. And the most important piece of clothing you must wear is love. Love is what binds us all together in perfect harmony. *Colossians 3:12-14*

Related texts: Ruth 1:1-3:10; Proverbs 14:21; 1 Thessalonians 5:15

Give it a try

When you help the poor, you are lending to the Lord—and he pays wonderful interest on your loan.

This is unbelievable!

Try to list five specific ways you can help the poor, both in your community and around the world.

1.

2.

3.

4.

5.

Circle your best idea and get started in God's interest-bearing program today.

done ☐

CHECK IT OUT

Prophets

foretold God's ultimate act of kindness prior to the birth of Jesus. Check out what was written in Isaiah 53:4-6 about God's plan for Jesus and YOU thousands of years ago:

Yet it was our weaknesses he carried; it was our sorrows that weighed him down. And we thought his troubles were a punishment from God for his own sins! But he was wounded and crushed for our sins. He was beaten that we might have peace. He was whipped, and we were healed! We have left God's paths to follow our own. Yet the Lord laid on him the guilt and sins of us all.

Go back through the passage and circle the words **our** and **we** and then thank God that His ultimate plan included **YOU.**

God Is KIND

I will tell of the LORD's unfailing love. I will praise the LORD for all he has done. I will rejoice in his great goodness to Israel, which he has granted according to his mercy and love.

Isaiah 63:7

This is what the LORD says: "Let not the wise man gloat in his wisdom, or the mighty man in his might, or the rich man in his riches. Let them boast in this alone: that they truly know me and understand that I am the LORD who is just and righteous, whose love is unfailing, and that I delight in these things. I, the LORD, have spoken!"

Jeremiah 9:23-24

Once we, too, were foolish and disobedient. We were misled by others and became slaves to many wicked desires and evil pleasures. Our lives were full of evil and envy. We hated others, and they hated us.

But then God our Savior showed us his kindness and love. He saved us, not because of the good things we did, but because of his mercy.

Titus 3:3-5a

Related texts: Isaiah 53:1-8; Romans 2:
1-8; 11:11-24

done ☐

The Fruit of the Spirit Goodness

The LORD approves of those who are good, but he condemns those who plan wickedness.

Proverbs 12:2

So I concluded that there is nothing better for people than to be happy and to enjoy themselves as long as they can. And people should eat and drink and enjoy the fruits of their labor, for these are gifts from God.

Ecclesiastes 3:12-13

So don't get tired of doing what is good. Don't get discouraged and give up, for we will reap a harvest of blessing at the appropriate time. Whenever we have the opportunity, we should do good to everyone, especially to our Christian brothers and sisters.

Galatians 6:9-10

For we are God's masterpiece. He has created us anew in Christ Jesus, so that we can do the good things he planned for us long ago.

Ephesians 2:10

Dear friend, don't let this bad example influence you. Follow only what is good. Remember that those who do good prove that they are God's children, and those who do evil prove that they do not know God.

3 John 11

Related texts: Psalm 34:8-14; Proverbs 3:27; 11:27; 1 Peter 2:12-15

One Minute Memory

For we are **God's masterpiece.** He has **created us anew** in **Christ Jesus,** so that we can do the **good things** he **planned for us** long ago.

Ephesians 2:10

done ☐

Good Stuff

CATCH THIS

God IS good!
You can see His goodness; you can hear it; you can touch His goodness and even smell it every single day. See for yourself! **Experience His goodness with any one of these ideas:**

Watch a sunset
Smell a flower
Examine the legs of a centipede
Listen to the waves break on the beach
Ask a Christian to tell you how he or she was saved
Listen to the sounds of nature in a quiet location
Watch a caterpillar turn into a butterfly
Look at the stars on a clear night
Kiss a baby

Look out a window and see God's playground—called Earth.

God Is Good

Taste and see that the LORD is good.
Oh, the joys of those who trust in him! . . .

I will praise you forever, O God,
for what you have done.
I will wait for your mercies
in the presence of your people. . . .

Truly God is good to Israel,
to those whose hearts are pure. . . .

For the LORD is good.
His unfailing love continues forever,
and his faithfulness continues to each generation. . . .

Give thanks to the LORD, for he is good!
His faithful love endures forever. . . .

You are good and do only good;
teach me your principles. . . .

Praise the LORD, for the LORD is good;
celebrate his wonderful name with music. . . .

The LORD is good to everyone.
He showers compassion on all his creation.

Psalms 34:8; 52:9; 73:1; 100:5; 118:29; 119:68; 135:3; 145:9

Related texts: 2 Chronicles 6:41; Psalm 84:9-12; Mark 10:17-18; Romans 8:18-28; 3 John 11

done ☑

The Fruit of the Spirit: Faithfulness

But be sure to fear the LORD and sincerely worship him. Think of all the wonderful things he has done for you.

1 Samuel 12:24

To the faithful you show yourself faithful;
to those with integrity you show integrity.
To the pure you show yourself pure,
but to the wicked you show yourself hostile.
You rescue those who are humble,
but your eyes are on the proud to humiliate them.

2 Samuel 22:26-28

Love the LORD, all you faithful ones!
For the LORD protects those who are loyal to him,
but he harshly punishes all who are arrogant.
So be strong and take courage,
all you who put your hope in the LORD!

Psalm 31:23-24

This is a true saying:
If we die with him,
we will also live with him.
If we endure hardship,
we will reign with him.
If we deny him,
he will deny us.
If we are unfaithful,
he remains faithful,
for he cannot deny himself.

2 Timothy 2:11-13

Related texts: Psalm 101; Proverbs 3:1-4; Matthew 24:45-51; 25:14-30

BIG TIMe WoRd

FAITHFUL

"Faith" is believing that an unseen God is big enough to know everything about you, to care intimately for you, and to provide for all your needs. Being "faithful" is living like you believe in that definition of faith.

It's easy to be faithful when everything is going well. It's a lot tougher to be faithful when you live with difficult times. Trusting that God is going to be God and you're going to be okay is a process you'll be working on for years.

Practice being faithful today and don't worry about tomorrow until it gets here.

done ☑

One Minute Memory

But if we confess our sins to him, he is faithful and just to forgive us and to cleanse us from every wrong.

1 John 1:9

God Is Faithful

Understand, therefore, that the LORD your God is indeed God. He is the faithful God who keeps his covenant for a thousand generations and constantly loves those who love him and obey his commands. But he does not hesitate to punish and destroy those who hate him.

Deuteronomy 7:9-10

I will sing of the tender mercies of the LORD
forever!
Young and old will hear of your faithfulness.
Your unfailing love will last forever.
Your faithfulness is as enduring as the
heavens.

Psalm 89:1-2

Yet I still dare to hope when I remember this: The unfailing love of the LORD never ends! By his mercies we have been kept from complete destruction. Great is his faithfulness; his mercies begin afresh each day.

Lamentations 3:21-23

If you think you are standing strong, be careful, for you, too, may fall into the same sin. But remember that the temptations that come into your life are no different from what others experience. And God is faithful. He will keep the temptation from becoming so strong that you can't stand up against it. When you are tempted, he will show you a way out so that you will not give in to it.

1 Corinthians 10:12-13

But if we confess our sins to him, he is faithful and just to forgive us and to cleanse us from every wrong.

1 John 1:9

Related texts: Deuteronomy 31:30–32:4; 2 Thessalonians 3:3; 2 Timothy 2:11-13; Revelation 19:11-16

done ☑

The Fruit of the Spirit: Gentleness

A gentle answer turns away wrath, but harsh words stir up anger. . . .

Patience can persuade a prince, and soft speech can crush strong opposition.

Proverbs 15:1; 25:15

Be humble and gentle. Be patient with each other, making allowance for each other's faults because of your love. Always keep yourselves united in the Holy Spirit, and bind yourselves together with peace.

Ephesians 4:2-3

Always be full of joy in the Lord. I say it again—rejoice! Let everyone see that you are considerate in all you do. Remember, the Lord is coming soon.

Don't worry about anything; instead, pray about everything. Tell God what you need, and thank him for all he has done. If you do this, you will experience God's peace, which is far more wonderful than the human mind can understand. His peace will guard your hearts and minds as you live in Christ Jesus.

Philippians 4:4-7

Now, who will want to harm you if you are eager to do good? But even if you suffer for doing what is right, God will reward you for it. So don't be afraid and don't worry. Instead, you must worship Christ as Lord of your life. And if you are asked about your Christian hope, always be ready to explain it. But you must do this in a gentle and respectful way. Keep your conscience clear. Then if people speak evil against you, they will be ashamed when they see what a good life you live because you belong to Christ.

1 Peter 3:13-16

Related texts: Isaiah 8:12-15; 1 Timothy 6:3-11; 2 Timothy 2:24-25; 1 Peter 3:1-6

BIG TIME WORD

GENTLE

Being gentle is a rare quality in today's world. Unfortunately, people who are loud, wild, and obnoxious tend to get most of the attention, while gentle people are often overlooked. But the truth is, gentleness is an important quality.

Being gentle is often associated with weakness, femininity, or being soft. But it's actually just the opposite. Gentleness is a character quality associated with strength. People who display gentleness have a quiet, controlled confidence about themselves and their faith in God.

Pray for gentleness today and be confident in the person God has planned for you to become.

done ☑

God Is Gentle

Yes, the Sovereign LORD is coming in all his glorious power. He will rule with awesome strength. See, he brings his reward with him as he comes. He will feed his flock like a shepherd. He will carry the lambs in his arms, holding them close to his heart. He will gently lead the mother sheep with their young.

Isaiah 40:10-11

Rejoice greatly, O people of Zion! Shout in triumph, O people of Jerusalem! Look, your king is coming to you. He is righteous and victorious, yet he is humble, riding on a donkey—even on a donkey's colt.

Zechariah 9:9

Then Jesus said, "Come to me, all of you who are weary and carry heavy burdens, and I will give you rest. Take my yoke upon you. Let me teach you, because I am humble and gentle, and you will find rest for your souls. For my yoke fits perfectly, and the burden I give you is light."

Matthew 11:28-30

Related texts: 1 Kings 19:9-12; 2 Corinthians 10:1; Matthew 21:1-12

Give it a try

A yoke or a "burden" is something that troubles you or creates hard times in your life.

What burdens or problems are heavy and need to be lightened in your life today?

1.

2.

3.

Ask God for His gentleness to comfort these burdens. He wants to make your burdens light.

done ☑

The Fruit of the Spirit: Self-control

A person without self-control is as defenseless as a city with broken-down walls.

Proverbs 25:28

But as for you, promote the kind of living that reflects right teaching. Teach the older men to exercise self-control, to be worthy of respect, and to live wisely. They must have strong faith and be filled with love and patience.

Similarly, teach the older women to live in a way that is appropriate for someone serving the Lord. They must not go around speaking evil of others and must not be heavy drinkers. Instead, they should teach others what is good. These older women must train the younger women to love their husbands and their children, to live wisely and be pure, to take care of their homes, to do good, and to be submissive to their husbands. Then they will not bring shame on the word of God.

In the same way, encourage the young men to live wisely in all they do.

Titus 2:1-6

So make every effort to apply the benefits of these promises to your life. Then your faith will produce a life of moral excellence. A life of moral excellence leads to knowing God better. Knowing God leads to self-control. Self-control leads to patient endurance, and patient endurance leads to godliness. Godliness leads to love for other Christians, and finally you will grow to have genuine love for everyone. The more you grow like this, the more you will become productive and useful in your knowledge of our Lord Jesus Christ.

2 Peter 1:5-8

Related texts: Proverbs 1:1-17; 23:23; 1 Thessalonians 5:5-10; 2 Timothy 1:7; Titus 2:11-14; 1 Peter 4:7

BIG TIMe WoRd

SELF-CONTROL

The term "self-control" has to do with having power over yourself. Self-control expresses the power not to do something that might seem natural. For instance, keeping our mouth closed when we want to yell at our little brother for putting hair ointment on our toothbrush. Or, controlling our sexual urges that tell us to "go all the way"!

Having self-control doesn't mean we will express complete control in all situations. Self-control comes with maturity, practice, and prayer. It's learned on a daily basis through trial and error. It's worth having. If you don't have it, ask God for it and begin trusting in His power today for self-control.

done ☐

26 MARCH

CHECK IT OUT

God may be slow to anger, but He does give us indication that He will return, in His own time, and express His anger and judgment on those who don't know Jesus. Check out what is written in 2 Peter 3:8-10: "But you must not forget, dear friends, that a day is like a thousand years to the Lord, and a thousand years is like a day."

The Lord isn't really being slow about His promise to return, as some people think. No, He is being patient for your sake. He does not want anyone to perish, so He is giving more time for everyone to repent.

But the day of the Lord will come as unexpectedly as a thief. Then the heavens will pass away with a terrible noise, and everything in them will disappear in fire, and the earth and everything on it will be exposed to judgment.

Are you ready for God to return and show His anger?

God Is Slow to Anger

The LORD is merciful and gracious;
he is slow to get angry and full of unfailing love.
He will not constantly accuse us,
nor remain angry forever.
He has not punished us for all our sins,
nor does he deal with us as we deserve.
For his unfailing love toward those who fear him
is as great as the height of the heavens above the earth.
He has removed our rebellious acts
as far away from us as the east is from the west. . . .

The LORD is kind and merciful,
slow to get angry, full of unfailing love.
The LORD is good to everyone.
He showers compassion on all his creation.

Psalms 103:8-12; 145:8-9

The LORD is a jealous God, filled with vengeance and wrath. He takes revenge on all who oppose him and furiously destroys his enemies! The LORD is slow to get angry, but his power is great, and he never lets the guilty go unpunished. He displays his power in the whirlwind and the storm. The billowing clouds are the dust beneath his feet.

Nahum 1:2-3

Related texts: Exodus 34:5-7; Psalm 86:15-17; Joel 2:12-14; Jonah 3–4; 2 Peter 3:8-15

done ☐

GOD SENDS MOSES TO EGYPT

God also said, "Tell them, 'The LORD, the God of your ancestors—the God of Abraham, the God of Isaac, and the God of Jacob—has sent me to you.' This will be my name forever; it has always been my name, and it will be used throughout all generations.

"Now go and call together all the leaders of Israel. Tell them, 'The LORD, the God of your ancestors—the God of Abraham, Isaac, and Jacob—appeared to me in a burning bush. He said, "You can be sure that I am watching over you and have seen what is happening to you in Egypt. I promise to rescue you from the oppression of the Egyptians. I will lead you to the land now occupied by the Canaanites, Hittites, Amorites, Perizzites, Hivites, and Jebusites—a land flowing with milk and honey."'

"The leaders of the people of Israel will accept your message. Then all of you must go straight to the king of Egypt and tell him, 'The LORD, the God of the Hebrews, has met with us. Let us go on a three-day journey into the wilderness to offer sacrifices to the LORD our God.'

"But I know that the king of Egypt will not let you go except under heavy pressure. So I will reach out and strike at the heart of Egypt with all kinds of miracles. Then at last he will let you go. And I will see to it that the Egyptians treat you well. They will load you down with gifts so you will not leave empty-handed. The Israelite women will ask for silver and gold jewelry and fine clothing from their Egyptian neighbors and their neighbors' guests. With this clothing, you will dress your sons and daughters. In this way, you will plunder the Egyptians!"

Exodus 3:15-22

Related texts: Genesis 13:12-17; 15:12-16; Haggai 2:4-8; Acts 7:30-36

What's it Mean?

Over several hundred years, the Israelites immigrated to Egypt. There they became slaves to the Egyptian people. They had no freedom of their own. For four hundred years they suffered hardship and torture and were robbed of their freedom.

God wanted Moses to return to Egypt and free the Israelites because they had suffered long enough. God wanted to deliver them and move them into the Promised Land. This Promised Land was a place for the Israelites to raise their families, prosper, and enjoy their intimate relationship with God. It's a long story, but they eventually get there. Keep reading and you'll see several illustrations of God's amazing power.

done ☐

Personality Plus

AARON

Aaron was Moses' oldest brother and his spokesperson. God spoke mainly to Moses, but Aaron told others what God said to Moses.

As the people of Israel left Egypt and wandered through the wilderness, Moses became the headmaster and Aaron became the "priest." This was the first "priesthood" of Israel. In this position Aaron represented the people of Israel to Moses and God.

Directions for Aaron's service came straight from God. Aaron is another example of a faithful and normal person whom God used to do great things. Are you ready to be used by God? He uses ordinary people to do extraordinary things. **You never know what He has planned for you today!**

Moses Confronts Pharaoh

Then the LORD reminded him, "When you arrive back in Egypt, go to Pharaoh and perform the miracles I have empowered you to do. But I will make him stubborn so he will not let the people go. Then you will tell him, 'This is what the LORD says: Israel is my firstborn son. I commanded you to let him go, so he could worship me. But since you have refused, be warned! I will kill your firstborn son!' ". . .

Now the LORD had said to Aaron, "Go out into the wilderness to meet Moses." So Aaron traveled to the mountain of God, where he found Moses and greeted him warmly. Moses then told Aaron everything the LORD had commanded them to do and say. And he told him about the miraculous signs they were to perform.

So Moses and Aaron returned to Egypt and called the leaders of Israel to a meeting. Aaron told them everything the LORD had told Moses, and Moses performed the miraculous signs as they watched. The leaders were soon convinced that the LORD had sent Moses and Aaron. And when they realized that the LORD had seen their misery and was deeply concerned for them, they all bowed their heads and worshiped.

After this presentation to Israel's leaders, Moses and Aaron went to see Pharaoh. They told him, "This is what the LORD, the God of Israel, says: 'Let my people go, for they must go out into the wilderness to hold a religious festival in my honor.' "

"Is that so?" retorted Pharaoh. "And who is the LORD that I should listen to him and let Israel go? I don't know the LORD, and I will not let Israel go."

Exodus 4:21-23,27-31; 5:1-2

Related texts: Exodus 1:8-13; 9:13-16; Proverbs 29:1-2; John 10:33-38

done ☐

God Hardens Pharaoh's Heart

Then the LORD said to Moses, "Pay close attention to this. I will make you seem like God to Pharaoh. Your brother, Aaron, will be your prophet; he will speak for you. Tell Aaron everything I say to you and have him announce it to Pharaoh. He will demand that the people of Israel be allowed to leave Egypt. But I will cause Pharaoh to be stubborn so I can multiply my miraculous signs and wonders in the land of Egypt. Even then Pharaoh will refuse to listen to you. So I will crush Egypt with a series of disasters, after which I will lead the forces of Israel out with great acts of judgment. When I show the Egyptians my power and force them to let the Israelites go, they will realize that I am the LORD."...

Then the LORD said to Moses and Aaron, "Pharaoh will demand that you show him a miracle to prove that God has sent you. When he makes this demand, say to Aaron, 'Throw down your shepherd's staff,' and it will become a snake."

So Moses and Aaron went to see Pharaoh, and they performed the miracle just as the LORD had told them. Aaron threw down his staff before Pharaoh and his court, and it became a snake. Then Pharaoh called in his wise men and magicians, and they did the same thing with their secret arts. Their staffs became snakes, too! But then Aaron's snake swallowed up their snakes. Pharaoh's heart, however, remained hard and stubborn. He still refused to listen, just as the LORD had predicted.

Exodus 7:1-5,8-13

Related texts: Exodus 8:7,18-19; Romans 9:14-21; 2 Timothy 3:8-9

Weird or What?

Pharaoh's magicians were most likely from a group of Egyptian priests or wise men called "snake charmers." The actual illusion of the sticks turning into snakes appears to be quite amazing. The wise men were schooled in magic, and the snake charmers were able to put the serpents into a rigid or stiff position, which gave the illusion of snakes being transformed into sticks.

The fact that Moses' staff ate the other two snakes demonstrated God's supernatural power over the natural or man-made illusion of Pharaoh's snake charmers.

Today, look for God's supernatural power displayed in some event or person's life.

THE PLAGUES AGAINST EGYPT

What's it Mean?

One of the common securities of the Egyptian people was the power of their gods. The Pharaohs believed their magicians or wise men were a powerful advantage to their kingdom because their gods could perform miracles, or the appearance of miracles.

Every time Moses did a miracle, the Pharaoh would summon his magicians to do the same. Because the Pharaoh's magicians performed similar miracles to those of Moses, Pharaoh's heart hardened, and he questioned the power of God.

As you'll read in two days, God's plague of death upon the firstborn was something Pharaoh's magicians could not duplicate or stop. Once again God showed Himself to be the one true God. This truth is the same today as it was in the days of Moses.

O my people, listen to my teaching.
Open your ears to what I am saying,
for I will speak to you in a parable.
I will teach you hidden lessons from our past—
stories we have heard and know,
stories our ancestors handed down to us.
We will not hide these truths from our children
but will tell the next generation about the glorious deeds of the LORD.
We will tell of his power and the mighty miracles he did. . . .

They forgot his miraculous signs in Egypt,
his wonders on the plain of Zoan.
For he turned their rivers into blood,
so no one could drink from the streams.
He sent vast swarms of flies to consume them
and hordes of frogs to ruin them.
He gave their crops to caterpillars;
their harvest was consumed by locusts.
He destroyed their grapevines with hail
and shattered their sycamores with sleet.
He abandoned their cattle to the hail,
their livestock to bolts of lightning.
He loosed on them his fierce anger—
all his fury, rage, and hostility.
He dispatched against them
a band of destroying angels.
He turned his anger against them;
he did not spare the Egyptians' lives
but handed them over to the plague.
He killed the oldest son in each Egyptian family,
the flower of youth throughout the land of Egypt.

Psalm 78:1-4,43-51

Related texts: Exodus 7:15–10:29; Deuteronomy 4:32-38; 1 Samuel 4:2-8; Acts 7:30-36

done ☐

God Kills the Firstborn in Egypt

Then the LORD said to Moses, "I will send just one more disaster on Pharaoh and the land of Egypt. After that, Pharaoh will let you go. In fact, he will be so anxious to get rid of you that he will practically force you to leave the country." . . .

So Moses announced to Pharaoh, "This is what the LORD says: About midnight I will pass through Egypt. All the firstborn sons will die in every family in Egypt, from the oldest son of Pharaoh, who sits on the throne, to the oldest son of his lowliest slave. Even the firstborn of the animals will die. Then a loud wail will be heard throughout the land of Egypt; there has never been such wailing before, and there never will be again. But among the Israelites it will be so peaceful that not even a dog will bark. Then you will know that the LORD makes a distinction between the Egyptians and the Israelites. All the officials of Egypt will come running to me, bowing low. 'Please leave!' they will beg. 'Hurry! And take all your followers with you.' Only then will I go!" Then, burning with anger, Moses left Pharaoh's presence.

Now the LORD had told Moses, "Pharaoh will not listen to you. But this will give me the opportunity to do even more mighty miracles in the land of Egypt." Although Moses and Aaron did these miracles in Pharaoh's presence, the LORD hardened his heart so he wouldn't let the Israelites leave the country.

Exodus 11:1,4-10

Related texts: Exodus 4:22-23; Psalms 105:23-38; 135:8-9; 136:10-12; Romans 9:14-21; Hebrews 11:28

Personality Plus

PHARAOH

"Pharaoh" is more of a title than a person. A Pharaoh is equivalent to a "King" in many countries or similar to the President in the United States.

One difference of a Pharaoh from other leaders is that a Pharaoh was considered a god. He was thought to be a son of the great sun god. Many believed that once a Pharaoh died he would become the sun-god Osisris. The followers believed that after the Pharaoh died, he became part of the divine gods of the afterworld.

done ☐

April

A thorough **knowledge** of the **Bible** is worth **more** than a **college** education.

Theodore Roosevelt
(1858–1919)
United States President

THE FIRST PASSOVER

Then Moses called for the leaders of Israel and said, "Tell each of your families to slaughter the lamb they have set apart for the Passover. Drain each lamb's blood into a basin. Then take a cluster of hyssop branches and dip it into the lamb's blood. Strike the hyssop against the top and sides of the doorframe, staining it with the blood. And remember, no one is allowed to leave the house until morning. For the LORD will pass through the land and strike down the Egyptians. But when he sees the blood on the top and sides of the doorframe, the LORD will pass over your home. He will not permit the Destroyer to enter and strike down your firstborn.

"Remember, these instructions are permanent and must be observed by you and your descendants forever. When you arrive in the land the LORD has promised to give you, you will continue to celebrate this festival. Then your children will ask, 'What does all this mean? What is this ceremony about?' And you will reply, 'It is the celebration of the LORD's Passover, for he passed over the homes of the Israelites in Egypt. And though he killed the Egyptians, he spared our families and did not destroy us.'"

Then all the people bowed their heads and worshiped.

Exodus 12:21-27

Related Texts: Numbers 9:1-14; Deuteronomy 16:1-8; 2 Chronicles 30; 1 Corinthians 5:6-8

What's it Mean?

Passover

The history of Passover starts with the tenth plague God sent to the people of Egypt—death to the firstborn. The Israelites were given special instructions to save their firstborn from death. They were told to smear blood from a lamb over their front door. This blood was a sign to the "Destroyer," or the "Angel of Death," to pass over those homes. Those who didn't put blood over their doors, mostly Egyptians, experienced a massive death throughout the "Passover night."

Passover is a tragic story of death but a beautiful story of God's saving power and promise to save the Israelite people from Egyptian captivity.

God keeps His promises!

done ☐

One Minute Memory

The Prophecy of the Suffering Servant

All of us have strayed away like sheep.
We have left God's paths to follow our own.
Yet the Lord laid on him the guilt and
sins of us all.

Isaiah 53:6

See, my servant will prosper; he will be highly exalted. . . .

He was despised and rejected—a man of sorrows, acquainted with bitterest grief. We turned our backs on him and looked the other way when he went by. He was despised, and we did not care.

Yet it was our weaknesses he carried; it was our sorrows that weighed him down. And we thought his troubles were a punishment from God for his own sins! But he was wounded and crushed for our sins. He was beaten that we might have peace. He was whipped, and we were healed! All of us have strayed away like sheep. We have left God's paths to follow our own. Yet the LORD laid on him the guilt and sins of us all.

He was oppressed and treated harshly, yet he never said a word. He was led as a lamb to the slaughter. And as a sheep is silent before the shearers, he did not open his mouth. . . .

But it was the LORD's good plan to crush him and fill him with grief. Yet when his life is made an offering for sin, he will have a multitude of children, many heirs. He will enjoy a long life, and the LORD's plan will prosper in his hands.

Isaiah 52:13; 53:3-7,10

Related Texts: Psalm 22; Mark 10:45; Acts 8:26-39; 1 Peter 2:21-25

done ☐

John the Baptist

The next day John saw Jesus coming toward him and said, "Look! There is the Lamb of God who takes away the sin of the world! He is the one I was talking about when I said, 'Soon a man is coming who is far greater than I am, for he existed long before I did.' I didn't know he was the one, but I have been baptizing with water in order to point him out to Israel."

Then John said, "I saw the Holy Spirit descending like a dove from heaven and resting upon him. I didn't know he was the one, but when God sent me to baptize with water, he told me, 'When you see the Holy Spirit descending and resting upon someone, he is the one you are looking for. He is the one who baptizes with the Holy Spirit.' I saw this happen to Jesus, so I testify that he is the Son of God."

John 1:29-34

Then I looked again, and I heard the singing of thousands and millions of angels around the throne and the living beings and the elders. And they sang in a mighty chorus:

"The Lamb is worthy—the Lamb who
was killed.
He is worthy to receive power and riches
and wisdom and strength
and honor and glory and blessing."

Revelation 5:11-12

Related Texts: Genesis 22:1-19; Hebrews 9:11-28; 1 Peter 1:18-20; Revelation 5-7; 21:9-22:4

Personality Plus

John the Baptist

John the Baptist wasn't a representative from the Baptist church. He was a preacher who spoke of forgiveness and salvation. While preaching one day, John spotted Jesus and said, "This is the one (referring to the person of Jesus) I was talking about when I said, 'Someone is coming who is greater by far than I am—for he existed long before I did' " (John 1:15). God used John the Baptist to "roll out the carpet" for Jesus to begin His public ministry.

Sounds as if we have something in common with John the Baptist—**to prepare people for the coming of Jesus. How can you do this today?**

done ☐

JUST a THOUGHT

"The greatest person ever to live (Jesus) flipped the world upside down when He claimed that the journey to GREATNESS can only be reached by following the road of servanthood.

Jesus Predicts His Resurrection

So Jesus called them together and said, "You know that in this world kings are tyrants, and officials lord it over the people beneath them. But among you it should be quite different. Whoever wants to be a leader among you must be your servant, and whoever wants to be first must be the slave of all. For even I, the Son of Man, came here not to be served but to serve others, and to give my life as a ransom for many."

Mark 10:42-45

One day as Jesus was alone, praying, he came over to his disciples and asked them, "Who do people say I am?"

"Well," they replied, "some say John the Baptist, some say Elijah, and others say you are one of the other ancient prophets risen from the dead."

Then he asked them, "Who do you say I am?"

Peter replied, "You are the Messiah sent from God!"

Jesus warned them not to tell anyone about this. "For I, the Son of Man, must suffer many terrible things," he said. "I will be rejected by the leaders, the leading priests, and the teachers of religious law. I will be killed, but three days later I will be raised from the dead."

Luke 9:18-22

Related Texts: Psalm 16; Matthew 12:38-41; Mark 10:32-34; Luke 24:13-32; Acts 2:14-40

done ☐

Jesus' Triumphal Entry

As Jesus and the disciples approached Jerusalem, they came to the town of Bethphage on the Mount of Olives. Jesus sent two of them on ahead. "Go into the village over there," he said, "and you will see a donkey tied there, with its colt beside it. Untie them and bring them here. If anyone asks what you are doing, just say, 'The Lord needs them,' and he will immediately send them." This was done to fulfill the prophecy,

"Tell the people of Israel,
'Look, your King is coming to you.
He is humble, riding on a donkey—
even on a donkey's colt.' "

The two disciples did as Jesus said. They brought the animals to him and threw their garments over the colt, and he sat on it.

Most of the crowd spread their coats on the road ahead of Jesus, and others cut branches from the trees and spread them on the road. He was in the center of the procession, and the crowds all around him were shouting,

"Praise God for the Son of David!
Bless the one who comes in the name of the Lord!
Praise God in highest heaven!"

The entire city of Jerusalem was stirred as he entered. "Who is this?" they asked.

And the crowds replied, "It's Jesus, the prophet from Nazareth in Galilee."

Matthew 21:1-11

Related Texts: Psalm 118; Zechariah 9:9; Mark 11:1-11; Luke 19:28-40; John 12:12-16

CATCH THIS

When you learn about the person of Jesus, you'll see how different He was from the rest in the world. For one thing, He wasn't selfish; He was a servant. His entire life modeled this truth. He was born in a barn instead of a palace. He entered Jerusalem on a donkey instead of a large horse, and He washed His followers' feet, saying, "I have given you an example to follow: do as I have done to you." Jesus gave us a model to follow.

The model is called servanthood. It's not about being first, the biggest, or the best. Servanthood is about serving others. Jesus said, "Whoever wants to be great among you must be your servant." It's as easy or as tough as this: if you want to be great in God's eyes, you need to serve.

Think about how you might be a servant today. Give it a try and see if you find God's reward of greatness.

done ☐

What's it Mean?

You can get a feel for the anger of Jesus by reading this story.

He was mad!

His anger was directed at the people who had turned the temple into a market for profit. These people were more concerned about selling their overpriced doves and other sacrificial animals than they were concerned for the house of God.

Jesus continually expresses concern for our motives and heart. The merchants and moneychangers around the temple didn't have the motive to please God with their business. They intended to make a quick buck by cheating the worshipers into buying unfit animals at high prices.

This is a great illustration to keep in mind today. What would Jesus clean out of your life if you gave Him the chance?

Keep checking those inner motives!

JESUS CLEANSES THE TEMPLE

But as they came closer to Jerusalem and Jesus saw the city ahead, he began to cry. "I wish that even today you would find the way of peace. But now it is too late, and peace is hidden from you. Before long your enemies will build ramparts against your walls and encircle you and close in on you. They will crush you to the ground, and your children with you. Your enemies will not leave a single stone in place, because you have rejected the opportunity God offered you."

Luke 19:41-44

Jesus entered the Temple and began to drive out the merchants and their customers. He knocked over the tables of the money changers and the stalls of those selling doves. He said, "The Scriptures declare, 'My Temple will be called a place of prayer,' but you have turned it into a den of thieves!"

The blind and the lame came to him, and he healed them there in the Temple. The leading priests and the teachers of religious law saw these wonderful miracles and heard even the little children in the Temple shouting, "Praise God for the Son of David." But they were indignant and asked Jesus, "Do you hear what these children are saying?"

"Yes," Jesus replied. "Haven't you ever read the Scriptures? For they say, 'You have taught children and infants to give you praise.'"

Matthew 21:12-16

Related Texts: Psalm 8; Isaiah 56; Jeremiah 7:9-11; Mark 11:15-18; John 2:13-17

done ☐

Whose Son Is the Messiah?

Then, surrounded by the Pharisees, Jesus asked them a question: "What do you think about the Messiah? Whose son is he?"

They replied, "He is the son of David."

Jesus responded, "Then why does David, speaking under the inspiration of the Holy Spirit, call him Lord? For David said,

'The LORD said to my Lord,
Sit in honor at my right hand until I humble your enemies beneath your feet.'

"Since David called him Lord, how can he be his son at the same time?"

No one could answer him. And after that, no one dared to ask him any more questions.

Matthew 22:41-46

Six days later Jesus took Peter, James, and John to the top of a mountain. No one else was there. As the men watched, Jesus' appearance changed, and his clothing became dazzling white, far whiter than any earthly process could ever make it.

Then a cloud came over them, and a voice from the cloud said, "This is my beloved Son. Listen to him."

Mark 9:2,3,7

Related Texts: Psalm 110; Matthew 27:45-54; Mark 1:9-11; Luke 9:28-36; Acts 2

In OTHER Words

TRANSFIGURATION

This is a big word to describe the bodily change that happened to Jesus on the day you just read. On the top of the mountain, Jesus' appearance was transformed or changed into a likeness of God's presence. It was evident to Peter, James, and John that when Jesus was transfigured, His presence became like a radiant light that they believed to be God. For a brief moment Jesus' radiant deity was allowed to shine through in the presence of His Father.

Unlike Jesus, you can't be transfigured into God. **But with His power you can change your ways to become more like the person God wants you to become.**

done ☐

The Last SUPPER

In OTHER Words

LAST SUPPER

Since the death of Jesus, Christians have followed a model He left us, called the Lord's Supper or communion. It's intended to remind us of Jesus' death on the cross. The cracker or bread used during communion represents the body of Jesus that was broken on the cross, while the wine or grape juice represents Jesus' blood shed on the cross for us.

Communion helps us remember what Jesus did on the cross two thousand years ago. He died for us. More specifically,

His death was for YOU!

Remember Jesus' death and celebrate your new life!

Now the Festival of Unleavened Bread arrived, when the Passover lambs were sacrificed. Jesus sent Peter and John ahead and said, "Go and prepare the Passover meal, so we can eat it together."...

Then at the proper time Jesus and the twelve apostles sat down together at the table. Jesus said, "I have looked forward to this hour with deep longing, anxious to eat this Passover meal with you before my suffering begins. For I tell you now that I won't eat it again until it comes to fulfillment in the Kingdom of God."

Then he took a cup of wine, and when he had given thanks for it, he said, "Take this and share it among yourselves. For I will not drink wine again until the Kingdom of God has come."

Then he took a loaf of bread; and when he had thanked God for it, he broke it in pieces and gave it to the disciples, saying, "This is my body, given for you. Do this in remembrance of me." After supper he took another cup of wine and said, "This wine is the token of God's new covenant to save you—an agreement sealed with the blood I will pour out for you.

"But here at this table, sitting among us as a friend, is the man who will betray me. For I, the Son of Man, must die since it is part of God's plan. But how terrible it will be for my betrayer!"

Luke 22:7-8,14-22

Related Texts: Jeremiah 31:31-36; Matthew 26:17-30; Mark 14:12-26; Revelation 19:4-9

Jesus is Betrayed

After saying these things, Jesus crossed the Kidron Valley with his disciples and entered a grove of olive trees. Judas, the betrayer, knew this place, because Jesus had gone there many times with his disciples. The leading priests and Pharisees had given Judas a battalion of Roman soldiers and Temple guards to accompany him. Now with blazing torches, lanterns, and weapons, they arrived at the olive grove.

Jesus fully realized all that was going to happen to him. Stepping forward to meet them, he asked, "Whom are you looking for?"

"Jesus of Nazareth," they replied.

"I am he," Jesus said. Judas was standing there with them when Jesus identified himself. And as he said, "I am he," they all fell backward to the ground! Once more he asked them, "Whom are you searching for?"

And again they replied, "Jesus of Nazareth."

"I told you that I am he," Jesus said. "And since I am the one you want, let these others go." He did this to fulfill his own statement: "I have not lost a single one of those you gave me."

John 18:1-9

Related Texts:
Genesis 37; Matthew 26:47-56; Mark 14:43-50; Luke 22:47-54; John 6:35-40; 17:1-12

Personality Plus

JUDAS

Judas (also known as Judas Iscariot) was one of the main disciples of Jesus. His job was to oversee the money, but he's best known for his deception and betrayal of Jesus.

He was a greedy man who deserted his commitment to Jesus. Judas led a crowd of officers to arrest Jesus for thirty pieces of silver. After Jesus was crucified, Judas repented and gave back all the money, but later hung himself.

Unfortunately, even those closest to Jesus didn't completely follow Him and change their ways.

Watch yourself so you don't get "bribed" into betraying Jesus in your life.

done ☐

In OTHER Words

Blasphemy

Blasphemy is a word used to describe an abusive comment or action directed at something sacred or holy. Blasphemy is more than cussing with God's name; it's total disrespect for God or godliness in general.

The high priest shouted "blasphemy" because Jesus claimed to be God's Son. They thought Jesus was crazy because of this claim.

The priests said Jesus' claim to be God's Son was blasphemous, so they charged Him with a religious crime.

Because Jesus proved who He claimed to be, His words weren't blasphemous.

Take a minute to thank God for this truth.

Jesus Is Condemned to Death

Inside, the leading priests and the entire high council were trying to find witnesses who would lie about Jesus, so they could put him to death. But even though they found many who agreed to give false witness, there was no testimony they could use. Finally, two men were found who declared, "This man said, 'I am able to destroy the Temple of God and rebuild it in three days.' "

Then the high priest stood up and said to Jesus, "Well, aren't you going to answer these charges? What do you have to say for yourself?" But Jesus remained silent. Then the high priest said to him, "I demand in the name of the living God that you tell us whether you are the Messiah, the Son of God."

Jesus replied, "Yes, it is as you say. And in the future you will see me, the Son of Man, sitting at God's right hand in the place of power and coming back on the clouds of heaven."

Then the high priest tore his clothing to show his horror, shouting, "Blasphemy! Why do we need other witnesses? You have all heard his blasphemy. What is your verdict?"

"Guilty!" they shouted. "He must die!"

Then they spit in Jesus' face and hit him with their fists. And some slapped him, saying, "Prophesy to us, you Messiah! Who hit you that time?"

Matthew 26:59-68

Related Texts: Leviticus 24:13-16; Daniel 7:13-14; Mark 14:55-65; Luke 23:63-71

APRIL 11

Jesus Is Crucified

It was nine o'clock in the morning when the crucifixion took place. A signboard was fastened to the cross above Jesus' head, announcing the charge against him. It read: "The King of the Jews." Two criminals were crucified with him, their crosses on either side of his. And the people passing by shouted abuse, shaking their heads in mockery. "Ha! Look at you now!" they yelled at him. "You can destroy the Temple and rebuild it in three days, can you? Well then, save yourself and come down from the cross!"

The leading priests and teachers of religious law also mocked Jesus. "He saved others," they scoffed, "but he can't save himself! Let this Messiah, this king of Israel, come down from the cross so we can see it and believe him!" Even the two criminals who were being crucified with Jesus ridiculed him. . . .

Then Jesus uttered another loud cry and breathed his last. And the curtain in the Temple was torn in two, from top to bottom. When the Roman officer who stood facing him saw how he had died, he exclaimed, "Truly, this was the Son of God!"

Mark 15:25-32,37-39

Related Texts: Psalm 22; Isaiah 53; Matthew 27:33-56; Luke 23:26-48; John 3:13-16; 19:16-37

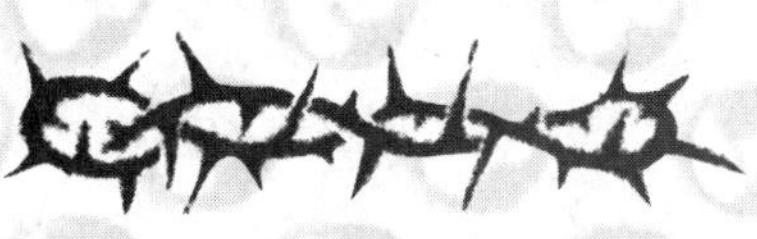

Weird or What?

Crucifying someone on a cross was one of the most abusive punishments ever devised because of its slow, torturous death of suffocation.

The inscription that was put over Jesus' head was not unusual. These inscriptions informed visitors of the crimes worthy of this brutal death. Typically, criminals were crucified immediately outside the city gates so everyone could see the consequences of their crime. Jesus was crucified for being "King of the Jews."

Jesus died a real and painful death. He died so that you might have new life today.

done ☐

JUST a THOUGHT

He's ALIVE! He has risen from the dead! He's alive! Shout it out ... "He's alive!" Celebrate this Easter with Jesus alive in your life ...tell a friend... He's alive!

Alive Again!

Early on Sunday morning, as the new day was dawning, Mary Magdalene and the other Mary went out to see the tomb. Suddenly there was a great earthquake, because an angel of the Lord came down from heaven and rolled aside the stone and sat on it. His face shone like lightning, and his clothing was as white as snow. The guards shook with fear when they saw him, and they fell into a dead faint.

Then the angel spoke to the women. "Don't be afraid!" he said. "I know you are looking for Jesus, who was crucified. He isn't here! He has been raised from the dead, just as he said would happen. Come, see where his body was lying. And now, go quickly and tell his disciples he has been raised from the dead, and he is going ahead of you to Galilee. You will see him there. Remember, I have told you."

The women ran quickly from the tomb. They were very frightened but also filled with great joy, and they rushed to find the disciples to give them the angel's message. And as they went, Jesus met them. "Greetings!" he said. And they ran to him, held his feet, and worshiped him. Then Jesus said to them, "Don't be afraid! Go tell my brothers to leave for Galilee, and they will see me there."

Matthew 28:1-10

Related Texts: Psalm 16:8-11; Mark 16:1-8; Luke 24:1-10; John 20:1-18; 1 Corinthians 15

done ☐

The All-Importance of the Resurrection

But tell me this—since we preach that Christ rose from the dead, why are some of you saying there will be no resurrection of the dead? For if there is no resurrection of the dead, then Christ has not been raised either. And if Christ was not raised, then all our preaching is useless, and your trust in God is useless. And we apostles would all be lying about God, for we have said that God raised Christ from the grave, but that can't be true if there is no resurrection of the dead. If there is no resurrection of the dead, then Christ has not been raised. And if Christ has not been raised, then your faith is useless, and you are still under condemnation for your sins. In that case, all who have died believing in Christ have perished! And if we have hope in Christ only for this life, we are the most miserable people in the world.

But the fact is that Christ has been raised from the dead. He has become the first of a great harvest of those who will be raised to life again.

So you see, just as death came into the world through a man, Adam, now the resurrection from the dead has begun through another man, Christ. Everyone dies because all of us are related to Adam, the first man. But all who are related to Christ, the other man, will be given new life.

1 Corinthians 15:12-22

Related Texts: Job 19:23-27; 1 Corinthians 15:23-58; Romans 6:1-11; Acts 2:22-36

JUST a THOUGHT

Belief in the resurrection of Jesus is the backbone of the Christian faith. If Jesus didn't rise from the dead, then He'd be a liar and just another man in a grave. Who would worship a dead guy?

done

CHECK IT OUT

Not only did Jesus die in our place and save us from eternal death, but He also brought us into a NEW family. Check out Hebrews 2:11: "So now Jesus and the ones he makes holy have the same Father. That is why Jesus is not ashamed to call them his brothers and sisters."

You're part of God's family. Congratulations, and don't forget to talk to your Heavenly Father today.

Jesus Christ: Our Passover

How terrible that you should boast about your spirituality, and yet you let this sort of thing go on. Don't you realize that if even one person is allowed to go on sinning, soon all will be affected? Remove this wicked person from among you so that you can stay pure. Christ, our Passover Lamb, has been sacrificed for us. So let us celebrate the festival, not by eating the old bread of wickedness and evil, but by eating the new bread of purity and truth.

1 Corinthians 5:6-8

And remember that the heavenly Father to whom you pray has no favorites when he judges. He will judge or reward you according to what you do. So you must live in reverent fear of him during your time as foreigners here on earth. For you know that God paid a ransom to save you from the empty life you inherited from your ancestors. And the ransom he paid was not mere gold or silver. He paid for you with the precious lifeblood of Christ, the sinless, spotless Lamb of God. God chose him for this purpose long before the world began, but now in these final days, he was sent to the earth for all to see. And he did this for you.

1 Peter 1:17-20

Related Texts: Exodus 12-13; John 1:19-36; Hebrews 2:11-18; Revelation 13:8

done ☐

THE ISRAELITES LEAVE EGYPT

And at midnight the LORD killed all the firstborn sons in the land of Egypt, from the firstborn son of Pharaoh, who sat on the throne, to the firstborn son of the captive in the dungeon. Even the firstborn of their livestock were killed. Pharaoh and his officials and all the people of Egypt woke up during the night, and loud wailing was heard throughout the land of Egypt. There was not a single house where someone had not died.

Pharaoh sent for Moses and Aaron during the night. "Leave us!" he cried. "Go away, all of you! Go and serve the LORD as you have requested. Take your flocks and herds, and be gone. Go, but give me a blessing as you leave." All the Egyptians urged the people of Israel to get out of the land as quickly as possible, for they thought, "We will all die!"

The Israelites took with them their bread dough made without yeast. They wrapped their kneading bowls in their spare clothing and carried them on their shoulders. And the people of Israel did as Moses had instructed and asked the Egyptians for clothing and articles of silver and gold. The LORD caused the Egyptians to look favorably on the Israelites, and they gave the Israelites whatever they asked for. So, like a victorious army, they plundered the Egyptians!

Exodus 12:29-36

Related Texts: Deuteronomy 16:1-8; Psalm 78:41-52; 105:26-38; 2 Thessalonians 1:5-10

What's it Mean?

The release of the Israelites is another example of how God remains faithful to His promises! No doubt the Israelites wanted God's help a lot earlier. They screamed, cried, and prayed like crazy. But God had His own plans and demonstrated His goodness by protecting the Israelites' release from Egypt. He proved that He is God and that His timing is perfect.

These same principles can be applied today. Most of us want God to move faster than He does. BUT He is God, He is faithful, and His timing is always perfect.

That's plenty of reason to trust Him and give Him your praise today—don't you think?

done ☐

16 APRIL

Pharaoh Pursues the Israelites

All the forces in Pharaoh's army—all his horses, chariots, and charioteers—were used in the chase. The Egyptians caught up with the people of Israel as they were camped beside the shore near Pi-hahiroth, across from Baal-zephon.

As Pharaoh and his army approached, the people of Israel could see them in the distance, marching toward them. The people began to panic, and they cried out to the LORD for help.

Then they turned against Moses and complained, "Why did you bring us out here to die in the wilderness? Weren't there enough graves for us in Egypt? Why did you make us leave? Didn't we tell you to leave us alone while we were still in Egypt? Our Egyptian slavery was far better than dying out here in the wilderness!"

But Moses told the people, "Don't be afraid. Just stand where you are and watch the LORD rescue you. The Egyptians that you see today will never be seen again. The LORD himself will fight for you. You won't have to lift a finger in your defense!"

Then the LORD said to Moses, "Why are you crying out to me? Tell the people to get moving! Use your shepherd's staff—hold it out over the water, and a path will open up before you through the sea. Then all the people of Israel will walk through on dry ground. Yet I will harden the hearts of the Egyptians, and they will follow the Israelites into the sea. Then I will receive great glory at the expense of Pharaoh and his armies, chariots, and charioteers. When I am finished with Pharaoh and his army, all Egypt will know that I am the LORD!"

Exodus 14:9-18

Related Texts: Psalms 37:7; 46:10; Isaiah 59:1; Romans 9:14-24; Hebrews 11:1-2

Give it a try

God saved the Israelites from captivity and they still complained. Write down three complaints you have about your life. Next to each complaint list what you can do to change each complaint. Next, express your thankfulness to God for saving you from the bondage of sin.

1.
2.
3.

done ☐

Crossing the Red Sea

Then Moses raised his hand over the sea, and the LORD opened up a path through the water with a strong east wind. The wind blew all that night, turning the seabed into dry land. So the people of Israel walked through the sea on dry ground, with walls of water on each side! Then the Egyptians—all of Pharaoh's horses, chariots, and charioteers—followed them across the bottom of the sea. But early in the morning, the LORD looked down on the Egyptian army from the pillar of fire and cloud, and he threw them into confusion. Their chariot wheels began to come off, making their chariots impossible to drive. "Let's get out of here!" the Egyptians shouted. "The LORD is fighting for Israel against us!"

When all the Israelites were on the other side, the LORD said to Moses, "Raise your hand over the sea again. Then the waters will rush back over the Egyptian chariots and charioteers." So as the sun began to rise, Moses raised his hand over the sea. The water roared back into its usual place, and the LORD swept the terrified Egyptians into the surging currents. The waters covered all the chariots and charioteers—the entire army of Pharaoh. Of all the Egyptians who had chased the Israelites into the sea, not a single one survived.

Exodus 14:21-28

Related Texts: Psalms 114; 136:13-15; Deuteronomy 11:1-4; Joshua 24:5-7; Hebrews 11:23-29

Weird or What?

Today the Red Sea is known to have a total length of **1,200 miles** and to range between **230 miles wide** in the south and **130 miles wide** in the north. The greatest depth of the Red Sea is about 7,200 feet. This doesn't describe a little puddle! God performed a major miracle when He opened the sea for the Israelites to cross.

God loves you so much that He's willing to part seas and open mountains to express His love and fulfill His promises.

Count on that today!

18 APRIL

The Lord Is a Warrior

This was how the LORD rescued Israel from the Egyptians that day. And the Israelites could see the bodies of the Egyptians washed up on the shore. When the people of Israel saw the mighty power that the LORD had displayed against the Egyptians, they feared the LORD and put their faith in him and his servant Moses.

Then Moses and the people of Israel sang this song to the LORD:
"I will sing to the LORD, for he has triumphed gloriously;
he has thrown both horse and rider into the sea.
The LORD is my strength and my song;
he has become my victory.
He is my God, and I will praise him;
he is my father's God, and I will exalt him!
The LORD is a warrior;
yes, the LORD is his name!
Pharaoh's chariots and armies,
he has thrown into the sea.
The very best of Pharaoh's officers
have been drowned in the Red Sea. . . .

"Who else among the gods is like you, O LORD?
Who is glorious in holiness like you—
so awesome in splendor,
performing such wonders? . . .

"With unfailing love you will lead
this people whom you have ransomed.
You will guide them in your strength
to the place where your holiness dwells. . . .

The LORD will reign forever and ever!"

Exodus 14:30-31; 15:1-4,11,13,18

Related Texts: Psalm 136; Ephesians 5:19-20; Revelation 15:2-4

Give it a try

Try writing a song or poem of praise describing the incredible saving power of God. (If you need help getting started, use some of the words from today's reading.)

done ☐

APRIL 19

God's Care in the Desert

Give thanks to the LORD and proclaim his greatness.
  Let the whole world know what he has done.
Sing to him; yes, sing his praises.
  Tell everyone about his miracles.
Exult in his holy name;
  O worshipers of the LORD, rejoice!
Search for the LORD and for his strength,
  and keep on searching.
Think of the wonderful works he has done,
  the miracles and the judgments he handed down,
O children of Abraham, God's servant,
  O descendants of Jacob, God's chosen one. . . .

But he brought his people safely out of
    Egypt, loaded with silver and gold;
  there were no sick or feeble people among them.
Egypt was glad when they were gone,
  for the dread of them was great.
The Lord spread out a cloud above them as a covering
  and gave them a great fire to light the darkness.
They asked for meat, and he sent them quail;
  he gave them manna—bread from heaven.
He opened up a rock, and water gushed out
  to form a river through the dry and barren land.
For he remembered his sacred promise
  to Abraham his servant.
So he brought his people out of Egypt with joy,
  his chosen ones with rejoicing.
He gave his people the lands of pagan nations,
  and they harvested crops that others had planted.
All this happened so they would follow his principles
  and obey his laws.
Praise the LORD!

Psalm 105:1-6,37-45

Related Texts: Genesis 15; Exodus 15:19-18:27; John 6; Acts 7:36-38; 1 Corinthians 10:1-4

Give it a try

Yesterday you wrote a song or poem of praise describing God's power. Today list one specific area in your life where you need God's saving power.

____

How can God provide for this need? ______________

"Search for the Lord and his strength, and keep on searching" (Ps. 105:4).

done ☐

What's it Mean?

On this mountain Moses received from God what we know as the **Ten Commandments.** Over the next ten days you will read these commandments. It's important for you to notice that the first **four** commandments give us **directions about loving God.** The next **six** commandments provide us with **instructions on how to live with and relate to one another.**

This is why Jesus summed up the Ten Commandments by saying, **"Love God with all your heart, soul, and mind** (1-4). **And love your neighbor as you love yourself"** (5-10).

Look for opportunities you have **today** to **love God, your friends (neighbors), and yourself.**

GOD MAKES A COVENANT WITH ISRAEL

The Israelites arrived in the wilderness of Sinai exactly two months after they left Egypt. After breaking camp at Rephidim, they came to the base of Mount Sinai and set up camp there.

Then Moses climbed the mountain to appear before God. The LORD called out to him from the mountain and said, "Give these instructions to the descendants of Jacob, the people of Israel: 'You have seen what I did to the Egyptians. You know how I brought you to myself and carried you on eagle's wings. Now if you will obey me and keep my covenant, you will be my own special treasure from among all the nations of the earth; for all the earth belongs to me. And you will be to me a kingdom of priests, my holy nation.' Give this message to the Israelites."

Moses returned from the mountain and called together the leaders of the people and told them what the LORD had said. They all responded together, "We will certainly do everything the LORD asks of us." So Moses brought the people's answer back to the LORD.

Then the LORD said to Moses, "I am going to come to you in a thick cloud so the people themselves can hear me as I speak to you. Then they will always have confidence in you."

Moses told the LORD what the people had said.

Exodus 19:1-9

Related Texts: Deuteronomy 4:1-20; Jeremiah 31:31-34; Hebrews 8

done ☐

APRIL 21

The Ten Commandments: No Other Gods

I am the LORD your God, who rescued you from slavery in Egypt.
Do not worship any other gods besides me.

Exodus 20:2-3

Let the whole earth sing to the LORD!
Each day proclaim the good news that he saves.
Publish his glorious deeds among the nations.
Tell everyone about the amazing things he does.
Great is the LORD! He is most worthy of praise!
He is to be revered above all gods.
The gods of other nations are merely idols,
but the LORD made the heavens!
Honor and majesty surround him;
strength and beauty are in his dwelling.
O nations of the world, recognize the LORD,
recognize that the LORD is glorious and strong.
Give to the LORD the glory he deserves!
Bring your offering and come to worship him.
Worship the LORD in all his holy splendor.
Let all the earth tremble before him.
The world is firmly established and cannot be shaken.
Let the heavens be glad, and let the earth rejoice!
Tell all the nations that the LORD is king.

1 Chronicles 16:23-31

Related Texts: Exodus 18:8-10; Deuteronomy 4:32-39; 5:1-21; 13:1-16; Isaiah 37:15-20; Ephesians 4:4-6

Idols were viewed as having **godlike power.** People believed the power of gods could be contained in an idol. This is one reason why **God refused to allow any images to be made of Him.**

God cannot be limited to an idol. Idols have no power and can be stolen or destroyed. God can't be captured in any man-made image. **He is a God who is living: One who can't be bound by a church, a temple, a golden calf, or even the Bible.**

You'd **search forever** to find any book, person, or crystal that has anything like God's power. **Today tell a friend this truth.**

done ☐

BIG TIMe WoRd

IDOL

During biblical times an idol was a handmade item that became the object of worship. People may have worshiped a wooden pigeon, a golden calf, or a ceramic armadillo. The important thing wasn't what they worshiped but that they worshiped something other than the true God.

Is idol worship even an issue today? No and yes. No, because you probably don't have friends bowing before foreign objects. But yes, it's an issue when you see the different things people value and worship that take their eyes off God.

How about you? Do you have any modern-day idols? Television? Clothes? Music? Boyfriend or girlfriend? Do you have other "gods" that are more important than God? If so, you may want to reread the last sentence in today's reading!

The Ten Commandments: No Idols

Do not make idols of any kind, whether in the shape of birds or animals or fish. You must never worship or bow down to them, for I, the LORD your God, am a jealous God who will not share your affection with any other god! I do not leave unpunished the sins of those who hate me, but I punish the children for the sins of their parents to the third and fourth generations. But I lavish my love on those who love me and obey my commands, even for a thousand generations.

Exodus 20:4-6

Not to us, O LORD, but to you goes all the glory
for your unfailing love and faithfulness.
Why let the nations say,
"Where is their God?"
For our God is in the heavens,
and he does as he wishes.
Their idols are merely things of silver and gold,
shaped by human hands.
They cannot talk, though they have mouths,
or see, though they have eyes!
They cannot hear with their ears,
or smell with their noses,
or feel with their hands,
or walk with their feet,
or utter sounds with their throats!
And those who make them are just like them,
as are all who trust in them.

Psalm 115:1-8

Related Texts: Deuteronomy 7; Isaiah 44:6-19; Jeremiah 10:1-16; 16:19-21; Matthew 6:19-24; 1 John 5:21

 done ☐

The Ten Commandments: God's Name

Do not misuse the name of the LORD your God. The LORD will not let you go unpunished if you misuse his name.

Exodus 20:7

One day a man who had an Israelite mother and an Egyptian father got into a fight with one of the Israelite men. During the fight, this son of an Israelite woman blasphemed the LORD's name. So the man was brought to Moses for judgment. His mother's name was Shelomith. She was the daughter of Dibri of the tribe of Dan. They put the man in custody until the LORD's will in the matter should become clear.

Then the LORD said to Moses, "Take the blasphemer outside the camp, and tell all those who heard him to lay their hands on his head. Then let the entire community stone him to death. Say to the people of Israel: Those who blaspheme God will suffer the consequences of their guilt and be punished. Anyone who blasphemes the LORD's name must be stoned to death by the whole community of Israel. Any Israelite or foreigner among you who blasphemes the LORD's name will surely die.

Leviticus 24:10-16

The name of the Lord is a strong fortress; the godly run to him and are safe.

Proverbs 18:10

Related Texts: Exodus 3:13-15; Psalms 20; 86:5-12; Acts 4:5-12

One Minute Memory

The name of the **Lord** is a strong fortress; the godly run to him and are **safe.**

Proverbs 18:10

done ☐

24 APRIL

Weird or What?

For those faithful to Judaism, the Sabbath is a day when all work stops. During Old Testament times if someone broke Sabbath rules, that person was judged and put to death (see Num. 15:32-36).

Today there is a problem with the rule prohibiting anyone from making a fire. Turning on a light switch in a modern home is a noncombustive type of burning that is labeled by some as starting a fire. Those faithful to Judaism are prohibited from turning on any electrical outlet. **The only electrical appliance that can be left on is the refrigerator.**

The Ten Commandments: The Sabbath

Remember to observe the Sabbath day by keeping it holy. Six days a week are set apart for your daily duties and regular work, but the seventh day is a day of rest dedicated to the LORD your God. On that day no one in your household may do any kind of work. This includes you, your sons and daughters, your male and female servants, your livestock, and any foreigners living among you. For in six days the LORD made the heavens, the earth, the sea, and everything in them; then he rested on the seventh day. That is why the LORD blessed the Sabbath day and set it apart as holy.

Exodus 20:8-11

Then he went over to the synagogue, where he noticed a man with a deformed hand. The Pharisees asked Jesus, "Is it legal to work by healing on the Sabbath day?" (They were, of course, hoping he would say yes, so they could bring charges against him.)

And he answered, "If you had one sheep, and it fell into a well on the Sabbath, wouldn't you get to work and pull it out? Of course you would. And how much more valuable is a person than a sheep! Yes, it is right to do good on the Sabbath." Then he said to the man, "Reach out your hand." The man reached out his hand, and it became normal, just like the other one.

Matthew 12:9-13

Related Texts: Genesis 2:1-3; Exodus 16:11-30; Psalm 62:1-5; Mark 2:23-28; Hebrews 4:1-4

done ☐

The Ten Commandments: PARENTS

Honor your father and mother. Then you will live a long, full life in the land the LORD your God will give you. . . .

Anyone who strikes father or mother must be put to death.

Exodus 20:12; 21:15

All who curse their father or mother must be put to death. They are guilty of a capital offense.

Leviticus 20:9

A wise child brings joy to a father; a foolish child brings grief to a mother. . . .

Listen to your father, who gave you life, and don't despise your mother's experience when she is old. Get the truth and don't ever sell it; also get wisdom, discipline, and discernment. The father of godly children has cause for joy. What a pleasure it is to have wise children. So give your parents joy! May she who gave you birth be happy.

Proverbs 10:1; 23:22-25

Children, obey your parents because you belong to the Lord, for this is the right thing to do. "Honor your father and mother." This is the first of the Ten Commandments that ends with a promise. And this is the promise: If you honor your father and mother, "you will live a long life, full of blessing."

Ephesians 6:1-3

Related Texts: Malachi 4:5-6; Colossians 3:20-21; 2 Timothy 3:1-5; Titus 1:6-9

CATCH THIS

There is no perfect family, and there are no perfect parents. Parents don't have an easy job; it's one of the toughest responsibilities ever created. Parents didn't receive a college degree in parenting, and there's no such thing as a professional parent. Parents live with a lot of pressure to care for their children, their careers, and their own personal lives. In case you've forgotten, parents are also human, which means they've got real feelings and pain just like us.

One of the ways in which you can HONOR your parents is to allow them the freedom to fail. Like you, they're not perfect; they need your love, forgiveness, and acceptance. Many parents are so accustomed to their child's greed—always wanting something—that they'll be shocked when greed is replaced with caring behavior. Give it a try. Honor your parents and watch for God's blessing on your life.

done ☐

BIG TIMe WoRd

ANGER

Murder is bad. Anger isn't bad. Resentment is bad. Anger isn't bad. Hate is bad. Anger isn't bad. Revenge is bad. Anger isn't bad. Bitterness is bad. Anger isn't bad. Get the point?

Anger comes and goes as a quick and natural emotion. Anger becomes negative when we allow it to stay in our lives, our thoughts, and our hearts. When anger remains, it transforms into resentment, which then can lead to bitterness, hate, and revenge.

Be careful your anger doesn't lead to sin. The Bible instructs us to deal with our anger before the sun goes down. Deal with your anger today so it doesn't become resentment—you'll sleep a lot better.

The Ten Commandments: MURDER

Do not murder. *Exodus 20:13*

Yes, you must execute anyone who murders another person, for to kill a person is to kill a living being made in God's image. *Genesis 9:6*

You have heard that the law of Moses says, "Do not murder. If you commit murder, you are subject to judgment." But I say, if you are angry with someone, you are subject to judgment! If you call someone an idiot, you are in danger of being brought before the high council. And if you curse someone, you are in danger of the fires of hell. *Matthew 5:21-22*

This is the message we have heard from the beginning: We should love one another. We must not be like Cain, who belonged to the evil one and killed his brother. And why did he kill him? Because Cain had been doing what was evil, and his brother had been doing what was right. So don't be surprised, dear brothers and sisters, if the world hates you.

If we love our Christian brothers and sisters, it proves that we have passed from death to eternal life. But a person who has no love is still dead. Anyone who hates another Christian is really a murderer at heart. And you know that murderers don't have eternal life within them. We know what real love is because Christ gave up his life for us. And so we also ought to give up our lives for our Christian brothers and sisters. *1 John 3:11-16*

Related Texts: Genesis 4:1-16; Numbers 35:9-34; Matthew 15:10-20; John 8:42-44; Romans 1:28-32

done ☐

The Ten Commandments:

ADULTERY

Do not commit adultery.

Exodus 20:14

Why be captivated, my son, with an immoral woman, or embrace the breasts of an adulterous woman?
For the LORD sees clearly what a man does, examining every path he takes.

Proverbs 5:20-21

You have heard that the law of Moses says, "Do not commit adultery." But I say, anyone who even looks at a woman with lust in his eye has already committed adultery with her in his heart.

Matthew 5:27-28

Don't you know that those who do wrong will have no share in the Kingdom of God? Don't fool yourselves. Those who indulge in sexual sin, who are idol worshipers, adulterers, male prostitutes, homosexuals, thieves, greedy people, drunkards, abusers, and swindlers—none of these will have a share in the Kingdom of God. There was a time when some of you were just like that, but now your sins have been washed away, and you have been set apart for God. You have been made right with God because of what the Lord Jesus Christ and the Spirit of our God have done for you.

1 Corinthians 6:9-11

Give honor to marriage, and remain faithful to one another in marriage. God will surely judge people who are immoral and those who commit adultery.

Hebrews 13:4

Related Texts: Proverbs 5:1-19; 6:20-35; Romans 1:18-27; Ephesians 4:17-24; Colossians 3:1-7; 1 Thessalonians 4:3-8

done ☐

CATCH THIS

God wasn't big on setting up rules to frustrate people. A lot of people believe God is a "cosmic kill-joy" who lives in heaven trying to discover ways to quench our joy. This couldn't be further from the truth! God created rules and guidelines to help us live life to its fullest.

When it comes to adultery or sex outside of marriage, God established this rule for our own good. God isn't down on sex. He created it. GOD IS DOWN ON PAIN! And the pain from adultery is intense. Adultery usually ends up with broken families, destroyed lives, and terrible lifelong memories.

God wants His people to be sexually pure for the health, happiness, and goodness of His children. Sex is a beautiful gift from God, and He created it to be shared and experienced between a husband and wife. God gets really excited when life is lived as He created it to be lived. Keep following Him and you'll continue to discover how rich and full life was intended to be.

28 APRIL

The Ten Commandments:
Stealing

Do not steal. *Exodus 20:15*

Don't try to get rich
by extortion or robbery.
And if your wealth increases,
don't make it the center of your life.
God has spoken plainly,
and I have heard it many times:
Power, O God, belongs to you;
unfailing love, O Lord, is yours.
Surely you judge all people
according to what they have done.

Psalm 62:10-12

Tell those who are rich in this world not to be proud and not to trust in their money, which will soon be gone. But their trust should be in the living God, who richly gives us all we need for our enjoyment. Tell them to use their money to do good. They should be rich in good works and should give generously to those in need, always being ready to share with others whatever God has given them. By doing this they will be storing up their treasure as a good foundation for the future so that they may take hold of real life.

1 Timothy 6:17-19

If you are a thief, stop stealing. Begin using your hands for honest work, and then give generously to others in need.

Ephesians 4:28

Related Texts: Proverbs 1:10-19; 10:2; Isaiah 10:1-4; Malachi 3:6-12; Titus 2:9-10

Give it a try

What would you say to your very best friend if you caught him or her stealing?

 done ☐

The Ten Commandments: False Testimony

Do not testify falsely against your neighbor.
Exodus 20:16

If a malicious witness comes forward and accuses someone of a crime, then both the accuser and accused must appear before the priests and judges who are on duty before the LORD. They must be closely questioned, and if the accuser is found to be lying, the accuser will receive the punishment intended for the accused. In this way, you will cleanse such evil from among you. Those who hear about it will be afraid to do such an evil thing again.

Deuteronomy 19:16-20

Who may worship in your sanctuary, LORD?
Who may enter your presence on your holy hill?
Those who lead blameless lives
and do what is right,
speaking the truth from sincere hearts.
Those who refuse to slander others
or harm their neighbors
or speak evil of their friends.
Those who despise persistent sinners,
and honor the faithful followers of the LORD
and keep their promises even when it hurts.
Those who do not charge interest on the money they lend,
and who refuse to accept bribes to testify against the innocent.
Such people will stand firm forever.

Psalm 15

Related Texts: Proverbs 12:17-18; 25:18; Isaiah 29:19-21; Matthew 15:10-20; Mark 14:53-64

CHECK IT OUT

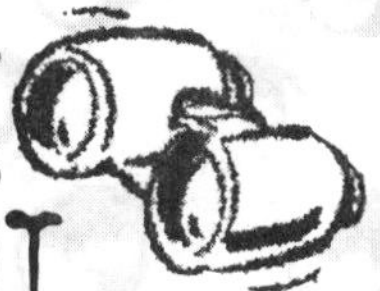

The Book of Proverbs is an incredible book filled with wisdom, common sense, and good, old-fashioned values. Here are a few verses on telling the truth:

"The wicked are trapped by their own words, but the godly bear their own fruit" (Prov. 12:13).

"An honest witness tells the truth; a false witness tells lies" (Prov. 12:17).

"Telling lies about others is as harmful as hitting them with an ax, wounding them with a sword, or shooting them with a sharp arrow" (Prov. 25:18).

If you want truth to be a part of your life, memorize these words of Jesus: "I came to bring truth to the world. All who love the truth recognize that what I say is true" (John 18:37).

See that truth comes from your lips today!

The Ten Commandments: Coveting

One Minute Memory

Stay away from the love of money; be satisfied with what you have. For God has said, "I will never fail you; I will never forsake you."

Hebrews 13:5

Do not covet your neighbor's house. Do not covet your neighbor's wife, male or female servant, ox or donkey, or anything else your neighbor owns.

Exodus 20:17

Pay all your debts, except the debt of love for others. You can never finish paying that! If you love your neighbor, you will fulfill all the requirements of God's law. For the commandments against adultery and murder and stealing and coveting—and any other commandment—are all summed up in this one commandment: "Love your neighbor as yourself." Love does no wrong to anyone, so love satisfies all of God's requirements.

Romans 13:8-10

Yet true religion with contentment is great wealth. After all, we didn't bring anything with us when we came into the world, and we certainly cannot carry anything with us when we die. So if we have enough food and clothing, let us be content.

1 Timothy 6:6-8

Stay away from the love of money; be satisfied with what you have. For God has said,
"I will never fail you.
I will never forsake you."

Hebrews 13:5

Related Texts: Deuteronomy 31:6; Proverbs 1:10-19; Philippians 4:11-12; 1 Timothy 6:9-11; James 4:1-3; 1 John 2:15-17

done ☐

The **Bible** is the greatest benefit which the human race has ever experienced. A **single line** in the **Bible** has **consoled me more** than **all the books** I ever read besides.

Immanuel Kant
(1724–1804)
German Philosopher

Key

The Greatest Commandment

Hear, O Israel! The LORD is our God, the LORD alone. And you must love the LORD your God with all your heart, all your soul, and all your strength. And you must commit yourselves wholeheartedly to these commands I am giving you today. Repeat them again and again to your children. Talk about them when you are at home and when you are away on a journey, when you are lying down and when you are getting up again. Tie them to your hands as a reminder, and wear them on your forehead. Write them on the doorposts of your house and on your gates.

Deuteronomy 6:4-9

"Teacher, which is the most important commandment in the law of Moses?"

Jesus replied, " 'You must love the Lord your God with all your heart, all your soul, and all your mind.' This is the first and greatest commandment. A second is equally important: 'Love your neighbor as yourself.' All the other commandments and all the demands of the prophets are based on these two commandments."

Matthew 22:36-40

Related Texts: Leviticus 19:18,33-34; Micah 6:8; Mark 12:28-31; Luke 10:25-37; Acts 4:32-35; Romans 13:8-10; 2 Corinthians 8:13-15

Give it a try

What does the sentence "Love your neighbor as yourself" mean to you?

____

____

____

What can you do today to bring the second greatest commandment into action?

done ☐

JUST a THOUGHT

God's presence will be evident in your life when you go out of your way to care for orphans and widows. Do you know someone like this? Delight God by loving that person today.

The Law:
Widows, Orphans, and Foreigners

Do not exploit widows or orphans. If you do and they cry out to me, then I will surely help them. My anger will blaze forth against you, and I will kill you with the sword. Your wives will become widows, and your children will become fatherless.

Exodus 22:22-24

True justice must be given to foreigners living among you and to orphans, and you must never accept a widow's garment in pledge of her debt. Always remember that you were slaves in Egypt and that the LORD your God redeemed you. That is why I have given you this command.

When you are harvesting your crops and forget to bring in a bundle of grain from your field, don't go back to get it. Leave it for the foreigners, orphans, and widows. Then the LORD your God will bless you in all you do. When you beat the olives from your olive trees, don't go over the boughs twice. Leave some of the olives for the foreigners, orphans, and widows. This also applies to the grapes in your vineyard. Do not glean the vines after they are picked, but leave any remaining grapes for the foreigners, orphans, and widows. Remember that you were slaves in the land of Egypt. That is why I am giving you this command.

Deuteronomy 24:17-22

Pure and lasting religion in the sight of God our Father means that we must care for orphans and widows in their troubles and refuse to let the world corrupt us.

James 1:27

Related Texts: Deuteronomy 10:17-20; Psalms 68:5; 146:9; 1 Timothy 5:3-16

done ☐

The Law: Restitution

A fine must be paid by anyone who steals an ox or sheep and then kills or sells it. For oxen the fine is five oxen for each one stolen. For sheep the fine is four sheep for each one stolen. . . .

But if it happens in daylight, the one who killed the thief is guilty of murder.

A thief who is caught must pay in full for everything that was stolen. If payment is not made, the thief must be sold as a slave to pay the debt. If someone steals an ox or a donkey or a sheep and it is recovered alive, then the thief must pay double the value.

If an animal is grazing in a field or vineyard and the owner lets it stray into someone else's field to graze, then the animal's owner must pay damages in the form of high-quality grain or grapes. . . .

Suppose there is a dispute between two people as to who owns a particular ox, donkey, sheep, article of clothing, or anything else. Both parties must come before God for a decision, and the person whom God declares guilty must pay double to the other.

Exodus 22:1,3-5,9

Related Texts: Numbers 5:5-8; Matthew 5:23-24; Luke 19:1-10; 1 Corinthians 6:1-11

In OTHER Words. . . . . .

Restitution

Restitution means to pay back or to make equal. For example, if you stole something, you would need to pay the person you stole from in order to restore his or her property and the relationship.

The theme of restoration, or bringing people back together, is biblical. Jesus taught His followers to restore relationships. He told them to leave church if they must and find the friend who has something against them and apologize in order to be reconciled.

The Bible doesn't give instructions so that our joy might be stolen. The opposite is true; instructions help us live right and enjoy the friendships God has given us. Do you have any friends you need to forgive or be forgiven by today? Reconcile with them, and you'll find yourself a happier person.

done ☐

The Law: Eye for Eye

BIG TIMe WoRd

REVENGE

During Old Testament times, controlled revenge was apparent—you smack Tom in the face, and he gets to hit you back. But in the New Testament, Jesus explains the essential meaning of the Law. He tells us not to strike back. He wants us to live without seeking revenge. He said: "Love your enemies! Pray for those who persecute you! If you love only those who love you, what good is that? Even corrupt tax collectors do that much. If you are kind only to your friends, how are you different from anyone else?" (Matt. 5:44,46-47).

Jesus wants us to be different! Next time you pass someone you don't like, pray for that person—see what happens.

Now suppose two people are fighting, and in the process, they hurt a pregnant woman so her child is born prematurely. If no further harm results, then the person responsible must pay damages in the amount the woman's husband demands and the judges approve. But if any harm results, then the offender must be punished according to the injury. If the result is death, the offender must be executed. If an eye is injured, injure the eye of the person who did it. If a tooth gets knocked out, knock out the tooth of the person who did it. Similarly, the payment must be hand for hand, foot for foot, burn for burn, wound for wound, bruise for bruise. *Exodus 21:22-25*

Anyone who takes another person's life must be put to death.

Anyone who kills another person's animal must pay it back in full—a live animal for the animal that was killed.

Anyone who injures another person must be dealt with according to the injury inflicted—fracture for fracture, eye for eye, tooth for tooth. Whatever anyone does to hurt another person must be paid back in kind.

Whoever kills an animal must make full restitution, but whoever kills another person must be put to death.

These same regulations apply to Israelites by birth and foreigners who live among you. I, the LORD, am your God. *Leviticus 24:17-22*

You have heard that the law of Moses says, "If an eye is injured, injure the eye of the person who did it. If a tooth gets knocked out, knock out the tooth of the person who did it." But I say, don't resist an evil person! If you are slapped on the right cheek, turn the other, too. *Matthew 5:38-39*

Related Texts: Exodus 21:22-25; Deuteronomy 19:16-21; Psalm 103:8-12; Matthew 5:38-42

done ☐

The Law: Capital Punishment

Anyone who hits a person hard enough to cause death must be put to death. . . .

Anyone who strikes father or mother must be put to death.

Kidnappers must be killed, whether they are caught in possession of their victims or have already sold them as slaves. . . .

A sorceress must not be allowed to live.

Anyone who has sexual relations with an animal must be executed.

Anyone who sacrifices to any god other than the LORD must be destroyed. . . .

Yes, keep the Sabbath day, for it is holy. Anyone who desecrates it must die; anyone who works on that day will be cut off from the community.

Exodus 21:12,15-16; 22:18-20; 31:14

All who curse their father or mother must be put to death. They are guilty of a capital offense.

If a man commits adultery with another man's wife, both the man and the woman must be put to death. If a man has intercourse with his father's wife, both the man and the woman must die, for they are guilty of a capital offense. If a man has intercourse with his daughter-in-law, both must be put to death. They have acted contrary to nature and are guilty of a capital offense.

The penalty for homosexual acts is death to both parties. They have committed a detestable act and are guilty of a capital offense.

Leviticus 20:9-13

Related Texts: Genesis 9:6; Leviticus 24:17-22; Deuteronomy 24:16; Matthew 21:33-44

done ☐

BIG TIME WoRd

CAPITAL PUNISHMENT

It's fairly clear from these Old Testament passages that there was a stronger cultural view of the death penalty than we have today. Now capital punishment is more a political issue than a religious one.

Though the death penalty isn't always enforced for killing someone, there usually is a "price" for crime. This price is better defined by the word ***consequence.***

The decisions you make today probably won't result in the death penalty, but the consequences may result in pain, broken relations, negative memories, and other difficulties. All decisions have consequences, and it's important to think through the potential consequences prior to decisions. Life was created to be lived. Today, think through your decisions and their consequences and stay alive for another day.

Personality Plus

Israelites

The Israelites were descendants of Abraham and called God's chosen people. They were His special group because of God's promise to Abraham. Because of Abraham's faithfulness, God promised Abraham that his descendants would be blessed.

The Israelites' journey was an up-and-down one. They lived in slavery for four hundred years before God delivered them from Egyptian bondage. God promised them a new home. But before they got there, they rebelled against God. God punished them by allowing them to wander in the desert for forty years before fulfilling His promise to Abraham and allowing them to enter into the Promised Land.

Through the Israelites' journey we can learn a lot about God's character. (1) God is faithful to His promise. (2) God loves His people. (3) God hates sin. (4) God wants us to be faithful in our relationship with Him. Which of these four truths do you need to learn today?

done ☐

The Law: Clean and Unclean

Then the LORD said to Moses and Aaron, "Give the following instructions to the Israelites: The animals you may use for food include those that have completely divided hooves and chew the cud. . . .

"As for marine animals, you may eat whatever has both fins and scales, whether taken from fresh water or salt water. You may not, however, eat marine animals that do not have both fins and scales. You are to detest them, and they will always be forbidden to you. You must never eat their meat or even touch their dead bodies. . . .

"You are to consider detestable all swarming insects that walk along the ground. However, there are some exceptions that you may eat. These include insects that jump with their hind legs. . . .

After all, I, the LORD, am your God. You must be holy because I am holy. So do not defile yourselves by touching any of these animals that scurry along the ground. I, the LORD, am the one who brought you up from the land of Egypt to be your God. You must therefore be holy because I am holy."

Leviticus 11:1-3,9-11,20-21,44-45

Related Texts: Genesis 7:1-4; Matthew 15:1-20; Mark 7:1-23; Acts 10; Romans 14

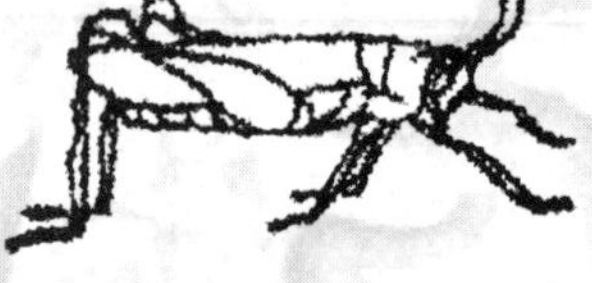

done

The Law: The Festivals

In honor of the LORD your God, always celebrate the Passover at the proper time in early spring, for that was when the LORD your God brought you out of Egypt by night. Your Passover sacrifice may be from either the flock or the herd, and it must be sacrificed to the LORD your God at the place he chooses for his name to be honored. . . .

For the next six days you may not eat bread made with yeast. On the seventh day the people must assemble before the LORD your God, and no work may be done on that day.

Count off seven weeks from the beginning of your grain harvest. Then you must celebrate the Festival of Harvest to honor the LORD your God. Bring him a freewill offering in proportion to the blessings you have received from him. . . .

Another celebration, the Festival of Shelters, must be observed for seven days at the end of the harvest season, after the grain has been threshed and the grapes have been pressed. . . . For seven days celebrate this festival to honor the LORD your God at the place he chooses, for it is the LORD your God who gives you bountiful harvests and blesses all your work. This festival will be a time of great joy for all. Each year every man in Israel must celebrate these three festivals: the Festival of Unleavened Bread, the Festival of Harvest, and the Festival of Shelters. They must appear before the LORD your God at the place he chooses on each of these occasions, and they must bring a gift to the LORD. All must give as they are able, according to the blessings given to them by the LORD your God.

Deuteronomy 16:1-2,8-10,13,15-17

Related Texts: Exodus 12; 23:14-17; Leviticus 23; Colossians 2:16-23

done ☐

CATCH THIS

The names of these festivals might seem a bit bizarre to us, but they were very important to the people of Israel. The word festival is taken from a Hebrew word that means "to celebrate." These festivals were commanded by God for the Israelites to take time from their busy schedules and give thanks to Him.

Unfortunately, we have an absence of celebration in our world today. We have lots of parties, but not true celebration. Most of today's parties don't honor God; they honor the god of alcohol. They're celebrations in disguise—they give momentary happiness. Once the party is over and the buzz wears off, the people start to look for a new high the next day.

We can celebrate in a new way. Celebration is giving thanks for all God has done in your life. Create your own festivals and wake up each morning thanking God for all He is and all He has done in your life. You'll be a different person if you learn how to celebrate at the party that never ends.

Honor Your Mother

Honor your father and mother, as the LORD your God commanded you. Then you will live a long, full life in the land the LORD your God will give you.

Deuteronomy 5:16

Some Pharisees and teachers of religious law now arrived from Jerusalem to interview Jesus. "Why do your disciples disobey our age-old traditions?" they demanded. "They ignore our tradition of ceremonial hand washing before they eat."

Jesus replied, "And why do you, by your traditions, violate the direct commandments of God? For instance, God says, 'Honor your father and mother,' and 'Anyone who speaks evil of father or mother must be put to death.' But you say, 'You don't need to honor your parents by caring for their needs if you give the money to God instead.' And so, by your own tradition, you nullify the direct commandment of God. You hypocrites! Isaiah was prophesying about you when he said,

'These people honor me with their lips,
  but their hearts are far away.
Their worship is a farce,
  for they replace God's commands with their own man-made teachings.' "

Matthew 15:1-9

Related Texts: Exodus 20:12; 21:15; Leviticus 20:9; Ephesians 6:1-2

Give it a try

What are four qualities you like about your mother?

____

____

____

____

You can show her great honor by taking the time to let her know what you like about her. Through words or a letter you can give her a better gift than money could buy.

done ☐

The Lord Has a Mother's Compassion

Sing for joy, O heavens! Rejoice, O earth! Burst into song, O mountains! For the LORD has comforted his people and will have compassion on them in their sorrow.

Yet Jerusalem says, "The LORD has deserted us; the LORD has forgotten us."

"Never! Can a mother forget her nursing child? Can she feel no love for a child she has borne? But even if that were possible, I would not forget you! See, I have written your name on my hand. Ever before me is a picture of Jerusalem's walls in ruins. Soon your descendants will come back, and all who are trying to destroy you will go away. Look and see, for all your children will come back to you. As surely as I live," says the LORD, "they will be like jewels or bridal ornaments for you to display.

"Even the most desolate parts of your abandoned land will soon be crowded with your people. Your enemies who enslaved you will be far away."

Isaiah 49:13-19

Related Texts: Psalms 51:1-9; 77:1-8; 103:1-18; Isaiah 66:12-14; Lamentations 3:22-33; Colossians 3:12-14

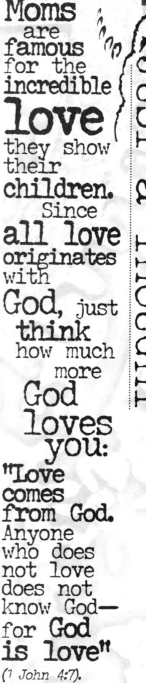

JUST a THOUGHT

Moms are **famous** for the **incredible** **love** they show their **children.** Since **all love originates** with **God,** just **think** how much more **God loves you:** **"Love comes from God.** Anyone who does not love does not know God—for **God is love"** *(1 John 4:7).*

done ☐

10 MAY

Weird or What?

Did you know that the Psalms were written to be sung?

Music was both popular and powerful during biblical times. Moses sang and taught his followers to sing. The Israelites sang on their way to the Promised Land. Jesus sang with His disciples. Paul sang in jail. And you can just imagine how great the singing will be in heaven.

Since God isn't concerned about the quality of your voice, **try singing a song of thanksgiving to God for giving you another day to enjoy His love.**

A Happy Mother

Praise the LORD!
Yes, give praise, O servants of the LORD.
  Praise the name of the LORD!
Blessed be the name of the LORD
  forever and ever.
Everywhere—from east to west—
  praise the name of the LORD.
For the LORD is high above the nations;
  his glory is far greater than the heavens.
Who can be compared with the LORD our God,
  who is enthroned on high?
Far below him are the heavens and the earth.
  He stoops to look,
and he lifts the poor from the dirt
  and the needy from the garbage dump.
He sets them among princes,
  even the princes of his own people!
He gives the barren woman a home,
  so that she becomes a happy mother.
Praise the LORD!

Psalm 113

Related Texts: 1 Samuel 2:1-10; Job 42:12-16; Psalm 127:3-5; Proverbs 17:6; Isaiah 54:1-8; Luke 1

done ☐

A Mother's Teaching

Listen, my child, to what your father teaches you. Don't neglect your mother's teaching. What you learn from them will crown you with grace and clothe you with honor. . . .

These are the sayings of King Lemuel, an oracle that his mother taught him.

O my son, O son of my womb, O son of my promises, do not spend your strength on women, on those who ruin kings.

And it is not for kings, O Lemuel, to guzzle wine. Rulers should not crave liquor. For if they drink, they may forget their duties and be unable to give justice to those who are oppressed. Liquor is for the dying, and wine for those in deep depression. Let them drink to forget their poverty and remember their troubles no more.

Speak up for those who cannot speak for themselves; ensure justice for those who are perishing. Yes, speak up for the poor and helpless, and see that they get justice.

Proverbs 1:8-9; 31:1-9

Related Texts: Exodus 2:1-9; Proverbs 6:20-24; 2 Timothy 1:5; 3:14-17

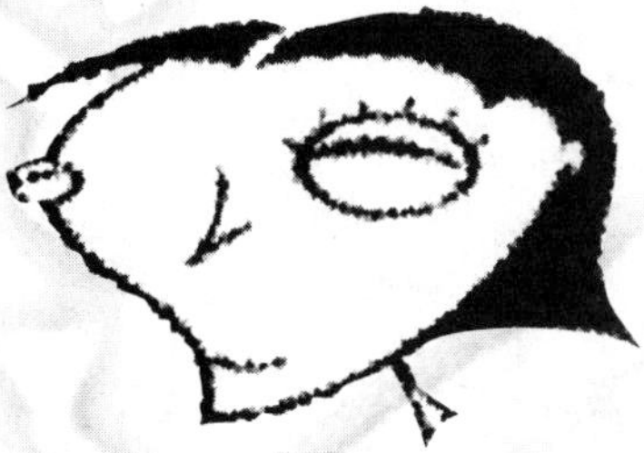

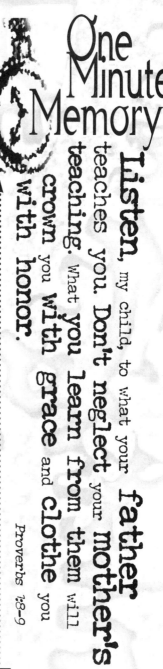

One Minute Memory

Listen, my child, to what your **father** teaches **you. Don't neglect** your **mother's teaching.** What **you learn from them** will **crown** you **with grace** and **clothe** you **with honor.**

Proverbs 1:8-9

done ☐

JUST a THOUGHT

A beautiful woman is easy to find, but a woman who loves God and celebrates life is a remarkable discovery.

The Noble Wife: Part 1

A worthy wife is her husband's joy and crown; a shameful wife saps his strength. . . .

Who can find a virtuous and capable wife? She is worth more than precious rubies. Her husband can trust her, and she will greatly enrich his life. She will not hinder him but help him all her life.

She finds wool and flax and busily spins it. She is like a merchant's ship; she brings her food from afar. She gets up before dawn to prepare breakfast for her household and plan the day's work for her servant girls. She goes out to inspect a field and buys it; with her earnings she plants a vineyard.

She is energetic and strong, a hard worker. She watches for bargains; her lights burn late into the night. Her hands are busy spinning thread, her fingers twisting fiber.

She extends a helping hand to the poor and opens her arms to the needy.

Proverbs 12:4; 31:10-20

Related Texts: Genesis 24; Acts 18:23-26; Romans 16:1-6

The Noble Wife: Part 2

Who can find a virtuous and capable wife? She is worth more than precious rubies. . . . She has no fear of winter for her household because all of them have warm clothes. She quilts her own bed-spreads. She dresses like royalty in gowns of finest cloth.

Her husband is well known, for he sits in the council meeting with the other civic leaders.

She makes belted linen garments and sashes to sell to the merchants.

She is clothed with strength and dignity, and she laughs with no fear of the future. When she speaks, her words are wise, and kindness is the rule when she gives instructions. She carefully watches all that goes on in her household and does not have to bear the consequences of laziness.

Her children stand and bless her. Her husband praises her: "There are many virtuous and capable women in the world, but you surpass them all!" Charm is deceptive, and beauty does not last; but a woman who fears the LORD will be greatly praised. Reward her for all she has done. Let her deeds publicly declare her praise. . . . The man who finds a wife finds a treasure and receives favor from the LORD.

Proverbs 31:10,21-31; 18:22

Related Texts: 1 Samuel 25:1-42; Proverbs 19:14; Luke 1:26-55; Ephesians 5:21-24; 1 Peter 3:1-6

Give it a try

These verses describe a woman who possesses godly qualities that make her shine with a new type of beauty.

If you are a female, write down three qualities from the passage that you would like to own in your life. Next to each quality write one goal that will help you develop that quality.

female	Qualities	Goals
	1.	1.
	2.	2.
	3.	3.

If you are a male, write down three qualities you would like to see in the woman you marry. Then ask God to prepare you to be the kind of man who will bring out the inner beauty in your future wife.

male	Qualities	Goals
	1.	1.
	2.	2.
	3.	3.

done ☐

CHECK IT OUT

While we are alive, we will experience times of pain, emptiness, and sadness—everyone does. In the midst of pain there is hope for those who have been promised eternal life. Check out the description of heaven from Revelation 21:2-4:

"And I saw the holy city, the new Jerusalem, coming down from God out of heaven like a beautiful bride prepared for her husband.

"I heard a loud shout from the throne, saying, "'Look, the home of God is now among his people! He will live with them, and they will be his people. God himself will be with them. He will remove all of their sorrows, and there will be no more death or sorrow or crying or pain. For the old world and its evils are gone forever.'"

God will be your husband, your wife, your everything. May this give you hope to keep living every day with the faith that

you'll be in God's presence someday!

Your Maker Is Your Husband

"Sing, O childless woman! Break forth into loud and joyful song, O Jerusalem, even though you never gave birth to a child. For the woman who could bear no children now has more than all the other women," says the LORD. "Enlarge your house; build an addition; spread out your home! . . .

"Fear not; you will no longer live in shame. The shame of your youth and the sorrows of widowhood will be remembered no more, for your Creator will be your husband. The LORD Almighty is his name! He is your Redeemer, the Holy One of Israel, the God of all the earth. For the LORD has called you back from your grief—as though you were a young wife abandoned by her husband," says your God. "For a brief moment I abandoned you, but with great compassion I will take you back. In a moment of anger I turned my face away for a little while. But with everlasting love I will have compassion on you," says the LORD, your Redeemer.

Isaiah 54:1-2,4-8

Related Texts: Psalm 45; Song of Songs 4; Isaiah 62:1-7; Revelation 19:5-9; 21:1-4

done ☐

THE LAW: WOMEN'S RIGHTS

When a man sells his daughter as a slave, she will not be freed at the end of six years as the men are. If she does not please the man who bought her, he may allow her to be bought back again. But he is not allowed to sell her to foreigners, since he is the one who broke the contract with her. And if the slave girl's owner arranges for her to marry his son, he may no longer treat her as a slave girl, but he must treat her as his daughter. If he himself marries her and then takes another wife, he may not reduce her food or clothing or fail to sleep with her as his wife. If he fails in any of these three ways, she may leave as a free woman without making any payment.

Exodus 21:7-11

Do not defile your daughter by making her a prostitute, or the land will be filled with promiscuity and detestable wickedness.

Leviticus 19:29

If two brothers are living together on the same property and one of them dies without a son, his widow must not marry outside the family. Instead, her husband's brother must marry her and fulfill the duties of a brother-in-law. The first son she bears to him will be counted as the son of the dead brother, so that his name will not be forgotten in Israel.

Deuteronomy 25:5-6

Related Texts: Exodus 22:16-17; Numbers 27; 30; 36; Deuteronomy 21:10-17; 22:13-30; 25:7-10; Ruth 3-4; 1 Timothy 3:2,12

What's it Mean?

Women throughout the Bible are found in many different roles and situations. During Old Testament times women weren't considered as important as men, so God made laws to protect women that sound very strange today. Both culture and family models were very male-centered. The woman's place was in the fields and home working long and hard hours cooking, grinding grain, and drawing water. The Law shielded women from the abuse ancient society often subjected them to.

The Old Testament law is not the Bible's final word on women. Within the Bible we are blessed with some incredible exceptions to the ancient world's stereotype of women. Exceptional women such as Miriam, Deborah, Huldah, and Esther were political and religious leaders who led, served, and guided the nation as well as any man.

done ☐

In OTHER Words

High Priest

In the Old Testament the high priest was the greatest of all priests and performed sacrifices to God on behalf of the people. In the New Testament, Jesus is given the title High Priest because He sacrificed his life on behalf of all people.

By understanding the meaning of this title, you can better appreciate that Jesus destroyed the power of sin in your life by dying on the cross.

You can never thank God too many times for that ultimate sacrifice on your behalf. Go ahead and thank Him one more time.

The Law: The Tabernacle

Now in that first covenant between God and Israel, there were regulations for worship and a sacred tent here on earth. There were two rooms in this tent. In the first room were a lampstand, a table, and loaves of holy bread on the table. This was called the Holy Place. Then there was a curtain, and behind the curtain was the second room called the Most Holy Place. In that room were a gold incense altar and a wooden chest called the Ark of the Covenant, which was covered with gold on all sides. . . .

When these things were all in place, the priests went in and out of the first room regularly as they performed their religious duties. But only the high priest goes into the Most Holy Place, and only once a year, and always with blood, which he offers to God to cover his own sins and the sins the people have committed in ignorance. . . .

So Christ has now become the High Priest over all the good things that have come. He has entered that great, perfect sanctuary in heaven, not made by human hands and not part of this created world. Once for all time he took blood into that Most Holy Place, but not the blood of goats and calves. He took his own blood, and with it he secured our salvation forever.

Hebrews 9:1-4a,6-7,11-12

Related Texts: Exodus 25-27; 35-40; Mark 15:37,38; Hebrews 9:13-28; 10:19-23

done ☐

The Law: The Priesthood

The LORD now said to Aaron: "You, your sons, and your relatives from the tribe of Levi will be held responsible for any offenses related to the sanctuary. But you and your sons alone will be held liable for violations connected with the priesthood.

"Bring your relatives of the tribe of Levi to assist you and your sons as you perform the sacred duties in front of the Tabernacle of the Covenant. . . .

"You yourselves must perform the sacred duties within the sanctuary and at the altar. If you follow these instructions, the LORD's anger will never again blaze against the people of Israel. I myself have chosen your fellow Levites from among the Israelites to be your special assistants. They are dedicated to the LORD for service in the Tabernacle. But you and your sons, the priests, must personally handle all the sacred service associated with the altar and everything within the inner curtain. I am giving you the priesthood as your special gift of service. Any other person who comes too near the sanctuary will be put to death." . . .

"Yes, I am giving you all these holy offerings that the people of Israel bring to the LORD. They are for you and your sons and daughters, to be eaten as your regular share. This is an unbreakable covenant between the LORD and you and your descendants."

And the LORD said to Aaron, "You priests will receive no inheritance of land or share of property among the people of Israel. I am your inheritance and your share."

Numbers 18:1-2,5-7,19-20

Related Texts: Leviticus 1-7; 21-22; Numbers 3; Hebrews 7-9; 1 Peter 2:4-10

CHECK IT OUT

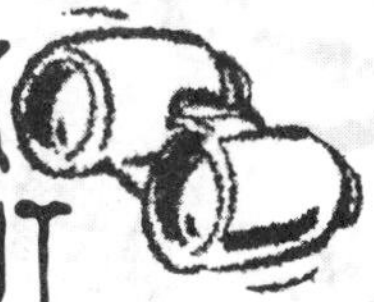

One of the duties of the high priest was to present sacrifices. Today Christians are called priests because we also present sacrifices. Christians are called to give their lives as LIVING sacrifices. Check out Romans 12:1: "I plead with you to give your bodies to God. Let them be a living and holy sacrifice—the kind he will accept."

This type of sacrifice requires us to present to God all that we are, into all that we know about God. This type of living sacrifice shows God that He is top priority in our lives. It's not the easiest sacrifice to make, but it sure pleases God.

Today, think about what a living sacrifice would mean with your life.

done ☐

THE LAW: DRIVING OUT THE NATIONS

What's it Mean?

When you read these types of Bible passages, it's hard to imagine God possessing mercy, compassion, and love. But consider this: other nations served other gods—just as today (for example, China serves Buddha; Palestine serves Allah, etc.).

Israel traveled through nations that served other gods. When one nation conquered another, it was proof their nation's god was more powerful. War was common, and if Israel didn't kill other nations, they would have been killed or taken as slaves.

Today those of us who believe in Jesus are a nation. There will come a day when we will be raised to heaven and made like Jesus. We are God's children; we are God's army. God is a God of love, mercy, and compassion, but there will come a time when He will destroy all who are not His nation. **What nation are you a citizen of?**

"When the LORD your God brings you into the land you are about to enter and occupy, he will clear away many nations ahead of you: the Hittites, Girgashites, Amorites, Canaanites, Perizzites, Hivites, and Jebusites. These seven nations are all more powerful than you. When the LORD your God hands these nations over to you and you conquer them, you must completely destroy them. Make no treaties with them and show them no mercy. Do not intermarry with them, and don't let your daughters and sons marry their sons and daughters. They will lead your young people away from me to worship other gods. Then the anger of the LORD will burn against you, and he will destroy you. Instead, you must break down their pagan altars and shatter their sacred pillars. Cut down their Asherah poles and burn their idols. For you are a holy people, who belong to the LORD your God. Of all the people on earth, the LORD your God has chosen you to be his own special treasure.

"The LORD did not choose you and lavish his love on you because you were larger or greater than other nations, for you were the smallest of all nations! It was simply because the LORD loves you, and because he was keeping the oath he had sworn to your ancestors. That is why the LORD rescued you with such amazing power from your slavery under Pharaoh in Egypt."

Deuteronomy 7:1-8

Related Texts: Deuteronomy 8:18–9:5; Judges 2:10-23; 2 Corinthians 6:14–7:1; Colossians 4:4-6; 1 Peter 2:1-12

done ☐

The Law: Not Too Difficult

"This command I am giving you today is not too difficult for you to understand or perform. It is not up in heaven, so distant that you must ask, 'Who will go to heaven and bring it down so we can hear and obey it?' It is not beyond the sea, so far away that you must ask, 'Who will cross the sea to bring it to us so we can hear and obey it?' The message is very close at hand; it is on your lips and in your heart so that you can obey it.

"Now listen! Today I am giving you a choice between prosperity and disaster, between life and death. I have commanded you today to love the LORD your God and to keep his commands, laws, and regulations by walking in his ways. If you do this, you will live and become a great nation, and the LORD your God will bless you and the land you are about to enter and occupy. But if your heart turns away and you refuse to listen, and if you are drawn away to serve and worship other gods, then I warn you now that you will certainly be destroyed. You will not live a long, good life in the land you are crossing the Jordan to occupy.

"Today I have given you the choice between life and death, between blessings and curses. I call on heaven and earth to witness the choice you make. Oh, that you would choose life, that you and your descendants might live! Choose to love the LORD your God and to obey him and commit yourself to him, for he is your life. Then you will live long in the land the LORD swore to give your ancestors Abraham, Isaac, and Jacob." *Deuteronomy 30:11-20*

Related Texts: Deuteronomy 7:9-15; 10:12-13; Micah 6:6-8; John 14:15; Romans 10:5-13; 1 John 5:3

One Minute Memory

Choose to love the LORD your God and to obey him and to commit yourself to him, for he is your life.

Deuteronomy 30:20a

done ☐

BIG TIMe WoRd

HUMBLE

A humble person has a proper perspective of himself before God and other people. A humble person is secure in who he was created to be and doesn't need to bring attention to himself. Unfortunately, a living example of humility is difficult to find.

The Bible says humble people are fortunate. They are fortunate because they're secure with themselves, and they understand the true greatness of God and don't NEED attention from others.

You'll never hear humble people tell you they're humble, but you would give them a great compliment if you appreciated their humility. Do this today and keep watching for humble examples and be ready to learn from them.

Sermon on the Mount: The Beatitudes

One day as the crowds were gathering, Jesus went up the mountainside with his disciples and sat down to teach them.

This is what he taught them:

"God blesses those who realize their need for him,
for the Kingdom of Heaven is given to them.
God blesses those who mourn,
for they will be comforted.
God blesses those who are gentle and lowly,
for the whole earth will belong to them.
God blesses those who are hungry and thirsty for justice,
for they will receive it in full.
God blesses those who are merciful,
for they will be shown mercy.
God blesses those whose hearts are pure,
for they will see God.
God blesses those who work for peace,
for they will be called the children of God.
God blesses those who are persecuted because they live for God,
for the Kingdom of Heaven is theirs."

Matthew 5:1-10

Related Texts: Genesis 12:1-3; Psalms 1; 84; Luke 6:17-26; 11:27-28; John 20:24-29

done ☐

Sermon on the Mount: Salt and Light

"God blesses you when you are mocked and persecuted and lied about because you are my followers. Be happy about it! Be very glad! For a great reward awaits you in heaven. And remember, the ancient prophets were persecuted, too.

"You are the salt of the earth. But what good is salt if it has lost its flavor? Can you make it useful again? It will be thrown out and trampled underfoot as worthless. You are the light of the world—like a city on a mountain, glowing in the night for all to see. Don't hide your light under a basket! Instead, put it on a stand and let it shine for all. In the same way, let your good deeds shine out for all to see, so that everyone will praise your heavenly Father."

Matthew 5:11-16

For though your hearts were once full of darkness, now you are full of light from the Lord, and your behavior should show it! For this light within you produces only what is good and right and true.

Try to find out what is pleasing to the Lord.

Ephesians 5:8-10

Related Texts:
Proverbs 13:9; Mark 9:50; Luke 14:34-35; 1 Peter 4:12-19

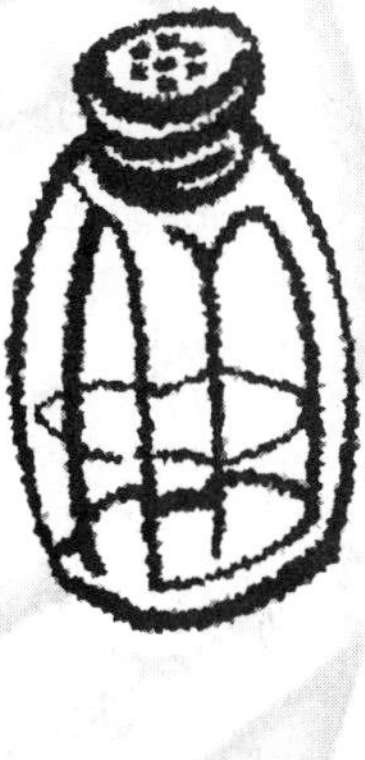

JUST a THOUGHT

Don't hide it! Let your life shine! The world is filled with darkness and needs you to be a bright light today.

done ☐

Personality Plus

Pharisee

The Pharisees were a very respected and influential group of religious men. They were known for their strict commitment to following the Law exactly as it was written.

They focused so much on right behavior that they missed the Scripture's revealing of Jesus as the Messiah. They started with good intentions, but they became blind to what Jesus had to say. Jesus focused on the heart, and they focused on actions. Jesus constantly battled with them and even called them "painted tombs" because they looked good on the outside (by doing the right actions), but they were dead on the inside (heart in the wrong place).

You can fool anyone with your spirituality—anyone except God. God knows your heart, and He knows the real you. If you're a modern-day Pharisee, take off your mask, get your heart right with God, and start living.

Sermon on the Mount: Fulfilling the Law

"Don't misunderstand why I have come. I did not come to abolish the law of Moses or the writings of the prophets. No, I came to fulfill them. I assure you, until heaven and earth disappear, even the smallest detail of God's law will remain until its purpose is achieved. So if you break the smallest commandment and teach others to do the same, you will be the least in the Kingdom of Heaven. But anyone who obeys God's laws and teaches them will be great in the Kingdom of Heaven.

"But I warn you—unless you obey God better than the teachers of religious law and the Pharisees do, you can't enter the Kingdom of Heaven at all!"

Matthew 5:17-20

So now there is no condemnation for those who belong to Christ Jesus. For the power of the life-giving Spirit has freed you through Christ Jesus from the power of sin that leads to death. The law of Moses could not save us, because of our sinful nature. But God put into effect a different plan to save us. He sent his own Son in a human body like ours, except that ours are sinful. God destroyed sin's control over us by giving his Son as a sacrifice for our sins. He did this so that the requirement of the law would be fully accomplished for us who no longer follow our sinful nature but instead follow the Spirit.

Romans 8:1-4

Related Texts: Psalm 119:161-176; Matthew 22:34-40; Romans 3:21-31; 7–8

done ☐

Sermon on the Mount:

Murder and Hate

"You have heard that the law of Moses says, 'Do not murder. If you commit murder, you are subject to judgment.' But I say, if you are angry with someone, you are subject to judgment! If you call someone an idiot, you are in danger of being brought before the high council. And if you curse someone, you are in danger of the fires of hell.

"So if you are standing before the altar in the Temple, offering a sacrifice to God, and you suddenly remember that someone has something against you, leave your sacrifice there beside the altar. Go and be reconciled to that person. Then come and offer your sacrifice to God. Come to terms quickly with your enemy before it is too late and you are dragged into court, handed over to an officer, and thrown in jail. I assure you that you won't be free again until you have paid the last penny."

Matthew 5:21-26

If anyone says, "I am living in the light," but hates a Christian brother or sister, that person is still living in darkness. Anyone who loves other Christians is living in the light and does not cause anyone to stumble. Anyone who hates a Christian brother or sister is living and walking in darkness. Such a person is lost, having been blinded by the darkness.

1 John 2:9-11

Related Texts: Exodus 20:13; Proverbs 8:12-13; Matthew 5:38-48; Luke 6:22-36

Give it a try

If you were to try to follow the teachings in today's reading, what should you do with your enemies or those you don't like?

What are the results of disliking another person according to 1 John 2:9-11?

done ☐

24 MAY

Sermon on the Mount:
Adultery

You have heard that the law of Moses says, "Do not commit adultery." But I say, anyone who even looks at a woman with lust in his eye has already committed adultery with her in his heart. So if your eye—even if it is your good eye—causes you to lust, gouge it out and throw it away. It is better for you to lose one part of your body than for your whole body to be thrown into hell. And if your hand—even if it is your stronger hand—causes you to sin, cut it off and throw it away. It is better for you to lose one part of your body than for your whole body to be thrown into hell.

You have heard that the law of Moses says, "A man can divorce his wife by merely giving her a letter of divorce." But I say that a man who divorces his wife, unless she has been unfaithful, causes her to commit adultery. And anyone who marries a divorced woman commits adultery.

Matthew 5:27-32

God wants you to be holy, so you should keep clear of all sexual sin. Then each of you will control your body and live in holiness and honor— not in lustful passion as the pagans do, in their ignorance of God and his ways.

Never cheat a Christian brother in this matter by taking his wife, for the Lord avenges all such sins, as we have solemnly warned you before. God has called us to be holy, not to live impure lives. Anyone who refuses to live by these rules is not disobeying human rules but is rejecting God, who gives his Holy Spirit to you.

1 Thessalonians 4:3-8

Related Texts: Deuteronomy 24:1-4; Proverbs 5; Malachi 2:10-16; Matthew 19:3-12; 1 Corinthians 7

Weird or What?

The Old Testament was written in the Hebrew language. The Hebrew word used to describe sex outside of the marriage relationship (fornication) is *Zanah*. This word is used ninety-three times in the Old Testament. In the New Testament that same word is translated in the Greek language as *porneia*, which is the root word for pornography.

The Bible has a lot to say about sex. Whether it's in Hebrew, Greek, or translated to English, it still says God created it, He sees it as good, and it's intended for marriage.

Love in any language says the same thing: wait until you're married.

done ☐

SERMON ON THE MOUNT: LOVE, NOT REVENGE

You have heard that the law of Moses says, "If an eye is injured, injure the eye of the person who did it. If a tooth gets knocked out, knock out the tooth of the person who did it." But I say, don't resist an evil person! If you are slapped on the right cheek, turn the other, too. If you are ordered to court and your shirt is taken from you, give your coat, too. If a soldier demands that you carry his gear for a mile, carry it two miles. Give to those who ask, and don't turn away from those who want to borrow.

You have heard that the law of Moses says, "Love your neighbor" and hate your enemy. But I say, love your enemies! Pray for those who persecute you! In that way, you will be acting as true children of your Father in heaven. For he gives his sunlight to both the evil and the good, and he sends rain on the just and on the unjust, too. If you love only those who love you, what good is that? Even corrupt tax collectors do that much. If you are kind only to your friends, how are you different from anyone else? Even pagans do that. But you are to be perfect, even as your Father in heaven is perfect.

Matthew 5:38-48

Dear friends, let us continue to love one another, for love comes from God. Anyone who loves is born of God and knows God. But anyone who does not love does not know God—for God is love.

1 John 4:7-8

Related Texts: Genesis 12:1-3; Leviticus 24:17-20; Luke 6:27-37; Romans 12:14-18

What's it Mean?

During the Sermon on the Mount, Jesus brings some additions to the Old Testament Law. He challenges people to take the Law one step further. These steps are no baby steps; they are huge jumps! Jesus does this six times in Matthew 5. Here are two examples in addition to the two in today's reading:

Old Law #1: If you kill, you die (v. 21).

New Law #1: But I say: if you are angry, you are in danger of judgment (v. 22).

Old Law #2: You shall not commit adultery (v. 27).

New Law #2: But I say: anyone who lusts has already committed adultery in his heart (v. 28).

Jesus is concerned about your heart. Actions without proper motives in the heart are empty actions. Check yourself today, and if you need a little help, ask God to perform "heart surgery" on you.

done ☐

CATCH THIS

Churches, various ministries, and Christian service organizations wouldn't have to waste their time raising money if God's people would give. These ministries could spend their fund-raising time trying to change the world. But the world is filled with more takers than givers, and, unfortunately, not all Christians are free from this selfish attitude.

During Old Testament times people were required by law to give a portion (called a tithe) of their money to God's work. But in the New Testament, Jesus is more concerned about the attitude of our hearts when we give than He is with the amount. The Bible teaches that the cheerful givers are the ones God appreciates (2 Cor. 9:7).

Giving demonstrates obedience to God. Be guaranteed that God will honor your giving, your faithfulness, and your heart. He will take care of you; put Him to the test.

Sermon on the Mount: Treasure in Heaven

Take care! Don't do your good deeds publicly, to be admired, because then you will lose the reward from your Father in heaven. When you give a gift to someone in need, don't shout about it as the hypocrites do—blowing trumpets in the synagogues and streets to call attention to their acts of charity! I assure you, they have received all the reward they will ever get. But when you give to someone, don't tell your left hand what your right hand is doing. Give your gifts in secret, and your Father, who knows all secrets, will reward you. . . .

Don't store up treasures here on earth, where they can be eaten by moths and get rusty, and where thieves break in and steal. Store your treasures in heaven, where they will never become moth-eaten or rusty and where they will be safe from thieves. Wherever your treasure is, there your heart and thoughts will also be.

Your eye is a lamp for your body. A pure eye lets sunshine into your soul. But an evil eye shuts out the light and plunges you into darkness. If the light you think you have is really darkness, how deep that darkness will be!

No one can serve two masters. For you will hate one and love the other, or be devoted to one and despise the other. You cannot serve both God and money.

Matthew 6:1-4,19-24

Related Texts: Proverbs 11:24-25; Mark 10:17-31; Luke 6:38; 12:32-34; Acts 20:32-35; 2 Corinthians 9:6-15

done ☐

Sermon on the Mount: Prayer

And now about prayer. When you pray, don't be like the hypocrites who love to pray publicly on street corners and in the synagogues where everyone can see them. I assure you, that is all the reward they will ever get. But when you pray, go away by yourself, shut the door behind you, and pray to your Father secretly. Then your Father, who knows all secrets, will reward you.

When you pray, don't babble on and on as people of other religions do. They think their prayers are answered only by repeating their words again and again. Don't be like them, because your Father knows exactly what you need even before you ask him! Pray like this:

Our Father in heaven,
  may your name be honored.
May your Kingdom come soon.
May your will be done here on earth,
  just as it is in heaven.
Give us our food for today,
and forgive us our sins,
  just as we have forgiven those who have sinned against us.
And don't let us yield to temptation,
  but deliver us from the evil one.

If you forgive those who sin against you, your heavenly Father will forgive you. But if you refuse to forgive others, your Father will not forgive your sins.

Matthew 6:5-15

Related Texts: Psalm 5; Mark 11:22-26; Luke 11:1-13; 18:1-14; James 5:13-20

JUST a THOUGHT

If you don't know what to say or how to pray, don't worry. Talk to God like a friend. He hears your prayers, and He doesn't give you a grade on how "good" it is. Your words directed toward God will always make sense to Him.

done ☐

What's it Mean?

Fasting is going without food or drink for a period of time. During biblical times fasting was done for a variety of reasons. Today the most common description of fasting is related to a spiritual discipline. The discipline is to spend extra time focusing on God and giving Him priority over food. People who fast may spend time in prayer during the times they would normally eat.

Before you try to fast, discuss it further with your parents or pastor to better understand the spiritual reasoning as well as the health precautions. Whether or not you fast, be reminded that Jesus is focusing on the motives of your heart. **He knows your heart. He knows the real you!**

SERMON ON THE MOUNT: FASTING

And when you fast, don't make it obvious, as the hypocrites do, who try to look pale and disheveled so people will admire them for their fasting. I assure you, that is the only reward they will ever get. But when you fast, comb your hair and wash your face. Then no one will suspect you are fasting, except your Father, who knows what you do in secret. And your Father, who knows all secrets, will reward you.

Matthew 6:16-18

John's disciples and the Pharisees sometimes fasted. One day some people came to Jesus and asked, "Why do John's disciples and the Pharisees fast, but your disciples don't fast?"

Jesus replied, "Do wedding guests fast while celebrating with the groom? Of course not. They can't fast while they are with the groom. But someday he will be taken away from them, and then they will fast. And who would patch an old garment with unshrunk cloth? For the new patch shrinks and pulls away from the old cloth, leaving an even bigger hole than before. And no one puts new wine into old wineskins. The wine would burst the wineskins, spilling the wine and ruining the skins. New wine needs new wineskins."

Mark 2:18-22

Related Texts: Esther 3-4; Isaiah 58; Jonah 3; Zechariah 7-8; Acts 14:21-23

done ☐

Sermon on the Mount: Why Worry?

"So I tell you, don't worry about everyday life—whether you have enough food, drink, and clothes. Doesn't life consist of more than food and clothing? Look at the birds. They don't need to plant or harvest or put food in barns because your heavenly Father feeds them. And you are far more valuable to him than they are. Can all your worries add a single moment to your life? Of course not.

"And why worry about your clothes? Look at the lilies and how they grow. They don't work or make their clothing, yet Solomon in all his glory was not dressed as beautifully as they are. And if God cares so wonderfully for flowers that are here today and gone tomorrow, won't he more surely care for you? You have so little faith!

"So don't worry about having enough food or drink or clothing. Why be like the pagans who are so deeply concerned about these things? Your heavenly Father already knows all your needs, and he will give you all you need from day to day if you live for him and make the Kingdom of God your primary concern.

"So don't worry about tomorrow, for tomorrow will bring its own worries. Today's trouble is enough for today."

Matthew 6:25-34

Related Texts: Proverbs 12:25; Mark 13:11; Luke 12:11-34; Philippians 4:6-7

One Minute Memory

So **don't worry** about **tomorrow,** for tomorrow will bring its own worries. Today's trouble is enough for **today.**

Matthew 6:34

done ☐

30 MAY

Weird or What?

The word hypocrite means to "act out the part of a character in a play."

In ancient times actors covered their faces with masks, representing the characters they were playing.

In today's world a hypocrite is one who covers his real self and "acts out" as a different person. This person is better known as a fake.

You can always fool an "audience," but God wrote the script, created the characters, and knows everything about the play. God created you just as He wants you to be. If you're wearing a mask, try taking it off.

You'll enjoy life a lot better when you show the real you.

Sermon on the Mount: Judging and Asking

Stop judging others, and you will not be judged. For others will treat you as you treat them. Whatever measure you use in judging others, it will be used to measure how you are judged. And why worry about a speck in your friend's eye when you have a log in your own? How can you think of saying, 'Let me help you get rid of that speck in your eye,' when you can't see past the log in your own eye? Hypocrite! First get rid of the log from your own eye; then perhaps you will see well enough to deal with the speck in your friend's eye.

Don't give what is holy to unholy people. Don't give pearls to swine! They will trample the pearls, then turn and attack you.

Keep on asking, and you will be given what you ask for. Keep on looking, and you will find. Keep on knocking, and the door will be opened. For everyone who asks, receives. Everyone who seeks, finds. And the door is opened to everyone who knocks. You parents—if your children ask for a loaf of bread, do you give them a stone instead? Or if they ask for a fish, do you give them a snake? Of course not! If you sinful people know how to give good gifts to your children, how much more will your heavenly Father give good gifts to those who ask him.

Do for others what you would like them to do for you. This is a summary of all that is taught in the law and the prophets.

Matthew 7:1-12

Related Texts: Romans 14:1-13; John 16:24; 1 Corinthians 5; James 4:1-3; 1 John 3:21-22

done ☐

Sermon on the Mount: The Two Ways

"You can enter God's Kingdom only through the narrow gate. The highway to hell is broad, and its gate is wide for the many who choose the easy way. But the gateway to life is small, and the road is narrow, and only a few ever find it. …

"Not all people who sound religious are really godly. They may refer to me as 'Lord,' but they still won't enter the Kingdom of Heaven. The decisive issue is whether they obey my Father in heaven. On judgment day many will tell me, 'Lord, Lord, we prophesied in your name and cast out demons in your name and performed many miracles in your name.' But I will reply, 'I never knew you. Go away; the things you did were unauthorized.'

"Anyone who listens to my teaching and obeys me is wise, like a person who builds a house on solid rock. Though the rain comes in torrents and the floodwaters rise and the winds beat against that house, it won't collapse, because it is built on rock. But anyone who hears my teaching and ignores it is foolish, like a person who builds a house on sand. When the rains and floods come and the winds beat against that house, it will fall with a mighty crash."

After Jesus finished speaking, the crowds were amazed at his teaching, for he taught as one who had real authority—quite unlike the teachers of religious law.

Matthew 7:13-14,21-29

Related Texts: Proverbs 14:11-12; Luke 13:22-30; John 10:1-10; Ephesians 2:13-22

JUST a THOUGHT

When Jesus finished speaking, the crowds were amazed! People came from everywhere to hear Him speak, and He continually amazed them. Now, as God, He amazes those of us who remain on earth.

done ☐

When you read God's word, you must constantly be saying to yourself, "It is talking to me, and about me."

Soren Kierkegaard
(1813–1855)
Danish Philosopher

The Golden Calf

When Moses failed to come back down the mountain right away, the people went to Aaron. "Look," they said, "make us some gods who can lead us. This man Moses, who brought us here from Egypt, has disappeared. We don't know what has happened to him."

So Aaron said, "Tell your wives and sons and daughters to take off their gold earrings, and then bring them to me."

All the people obeyed Aaron and brought him their gold earrings. Then Aaron took the gold, melted it down, and molded and tooled it into the shape of a calf. The people exclaimed, "O Israel, these are the gods who brought you out of Egypt!"

When Aaron saw how excited the people were about it, he built an altar in front of the calf and announced, "Tomorrow there will be a festival to the LORD!"

So the people got up early the next morning to sacrifice burnt offerings and peace offerings. After this, they celebrated with feasting and drinking, and indulged themselves in pagan revelry.

Then the LORD told Moses, "Quick! Go down the mountain! The people you brought from Egypt have defiled themselves. They have already turned from the way I commanded them to live. They have made an idol shaped like a calf, and they have worshiped and sacrificed to it. They are saying, 'These are your gods, O Israel, who brought you out of Egypt.' "

Then the LORD said, "I have seen how stubborn and rebellious these people are. Now leave me alone so my anger can blaze against them and destroy them all. Then I will make you, Moses, into a great nation instead of them." *Exodus 32:1-10*

Related Texts: Deuteronomy 9:7-15; Nehemiah 9:16-19; Psalm 106:19-22; Acts 7:37-41

CATCH THIS

Moses was a great leader! He accomplished amazing things with a group of people who weren't good at following a leader.

Today our world is in desperate need of quality leaders, but, unfortunately, we have a misunderstanding about leadership. It's accepted that effective leaders must have charisma to lead people. This description only describes one type of leader.

You can be a leader and stay completely behind the scenes. There are leaders in your church you may not recognize because their leadership isn't in public view. They may set up chairs, straighten the church building, or cut out paper figures for the Sunday School class. These people are leaders because they're used by God to do His work.

Jesus gave us a new standard for leadership when He came into the world. He showed us the true heart of leadership. True leadership is servanthood. When you serve others, you are displaying leadership gifts. God's work needs all kinds of leaders, especially servant-leaders. One of those leaders looks just like you.

done ☐

BIG TIMe WoRd

INTERCESSORY PRAYER

When Moses begged God on behalf of the Israelites, he was praying or pleading for their own good. Today this type of prayer is called intercessory prayer. You perform intercessory prayer when you pray for someone else. Also the Holy Spirit intercedes on your behalf. Check it out: "The Holy Spirit prays for us with groanings that cannot be expressed in words. And the Father who knows all hearts knows what the Spirit is saying, for the Spirit pleads for us believers in harmony with God's own will" (Rom. 8:26b-27).

God hears your prayers on behalf of the people you pray for, and God hears the prayers of the Holy Spirit, who pleads for you. Put God's ears to the test today on behalf of someone you know and care for.

Moses Pleads for the Israelites

But Moses pleaded with the LORD his God not to do it. "O LORD!" he exclaimed. "Why are you so angry with your own people whom you brought from the land of Egypt with such great power and mighty acts? The Egyptians will say, 'God tricked them into coming to the mountains so he could kill them and wipe them from the face of the earth.' Turn away from your fierce anger. Change your mind about this terrible disaster you are planning against your people! Remember your covenant with your servants—Abraham, Isaac, and Jacob. You swore by your own self, 'I will make your descendants as numerous as the stars of heaven. Yes, I will give them all of this land that I have promised to your descendants, and they will possess it forever.' "

So the LORD withdrew his threat and didn't bring against his people the disaster he had threatened.

Then Moses turned and went down the mountain. He held in his hands the two stone tablets inscribed with the terms of the covenant. They were inscribed on both sides, front and back. These stone tablets were God's work; the words on them were written by God himself. . . .

When they came near the camp, Moses saw the calf and the dancing. In terrible anger, he threw the stone tablets to the ground, smashing them at the foot of the mountain. He took the calf they had made and melted it in the fire. And when the metal had cooled, he ground it into powder and mixed it with water. Then he made the people drink it. *Exodus 32:11-16,19-20*

Related Texts: Genesis 15:1-5; 22:15-18; 26:2-4; Deuteronomy 9:16-21; Psalm 106:23; Jonah 3; Acts 7:40-42

done ☐

Israel's History Is Our Warning

I don't want you to forget, dear brothers and sisters, what happened to our ancestors in the wilderness long ago. God guided all of them by sending a cloud that moved along ahead of them, and he brought them all safely through the waters of the sea on dry ground. . . .

And all of them ate the same miraculous food, and all of them drank the same miraculous water. For they all drank from the miraculous rock that traveled with them, and that rock was Christ. Yet after all this, God was not pleased with most of them, and he destroyed them in the wilderness. . . .

All these events happened to them as examples for us. They were written down to warn us, who live at the time when this age is drawing to a close.

If you think you are standing strong, be careful, for you, too, may fall into the same sin. But remember that the temptations that come into your life are no different from what others experience. And God is faithful. He will keep the temptation from becoming so strong that you can't stand up against it. When you are tempted, he will show you a way out so that you will not give in to it.

1 Corinthians 10:1,3-5,11-13

Related Texts: Exodus 14; 17:1-7; 32; John 6; Hebrews 2:9-18; James 1:12-15

One Minute Memory

God is faithful. He will keep the temptation from becoming so strong that you can't stand up against it. When you are tempted, he will show you a way out so that you will not give in to it.

1 Corinthians 10:13b

done ☐

In OTHER Words ••••••

Repent

The word repent means to confess to God that you've sinned and then change your mind so you won't do that sin again. Repentance is more than confession; it means changing the direction of your life and STOPPING the sins you've confessed.

Jesus forgave a woman who was caught in adultery. As she left His presence, Jesus said to her, "Go and sin no more." Her repentance required more than simply receiving forgiveness; it also included a radical change in her life.

Do you have an area of your life where you need to repent? Remember, it's "confess" and "change."

Be sorry enough about your sin to stop sinning!

God Forgives Those Who Repent

The LORD told Moses, "Prepare two stone tablets like the first ones. I will write on them the same words that were on the tablets you smashed....

So Moses cut two tablets of stone like the first ones. Early in the morning he climbed Mount Sinai as the LORD had told him, carrying the two stone tablets in his hands.

Then the LORD came down in a pillar of cloud and called out his own name, "the LORD," as Moses stood there in his presence. He passed in front of Moses and said, "I am the LORD, I am the LORD, the merciful and gracious God. I am slow to anger and rich in unfailing love and faithfulness. I show this unfailing love to many thousands by forgiving every kind of sin and rebellion. Even so I do not leave sin unpunished, but I punish the children for the sins of their parents to the third and fourth generations."

Moses immediately fell to the ground and worshiped. And he said, "If it is true that I have found favor in your sight, O LORD, then please go with us. Yes, this is an unruly and stubborn people, but please pardon our iniquity and our sins. Accept us as your own special possession."

The LORD replied, "All right. This is the covenant I am going to make with you. I will perform wonders that have never been done before anywhere in all the earth or in any nation. And all the people around you will see the power of the LORD—the awesome power I will display through you."

Exodus 34:1,4-10

Related Texts: Psalms 86:15; 103:8; 145:8; John 3:16-21; 1 John 1:9

done ☐

God Is Compassionate

Do not be like your ancestors and relatives who abandoned the LORD, the God of their ancestors, and became an object of derision, as you yourselves can see. Do not be stubborn, as they were, but submit yourselves to the LORD. Come to his Temple which he has set apart as holy forever. Worship the LORD your God so that his fierce anger will turn away from you. For if you return to the LORD, your relatives and your children will be treated mercifully by their captors, and they will be able to return to this land.

For the LORD your God is gracious and merciful. If you return to him, he will not continue to turn his face from you.

2 Chronicles 30:7-9

The LORD is kind and merciful,
slow to get angry, full of unfailing love.
The LORD is good to everyone.
He showers compassion on all his creation.

Psalm 145:8-9

All praise to the God and Father of our Lord Jesus Christ. He is the source of every mercy and the God who comforts us. He comforts us in all our troubles so that we can comfort others. When others are troubled, we will be able to give them the same comfort God has given us. You can be sure that the more we suffer for Christ, the more God will shower us with his comfort through Christ.

2 Corinthians 1:3-5

Related Texts: Exodus 33:19; 2 Chronicles 30:7-9; Nehemiah 9:16-19; Psalm 103; Lamentations 3:19-23; Colossians 3:12-14

JUST A THOUGHT

God won't allow more to be put "on you" than He puts "in you" to deal with the temptation that comes your way.

done ☐

God Is Forgiving

CATCH THIS

There are few things more mind-blowing than God's forgiveness. God forgives us over and over. Do you ever wonder why He doesn't get tired of forgiving just you? Well, add the times He's forgiven you to the times He's forgiven forty billion other people—that's a lot of forgiveness.

In addition to God's forgiveness, He instructs us to forgive and keep forgiving. We can't expect God to forgive us if we aren't willing to forgive others. Jesus said, "Your heavenly Father will forgive you if you forgive those who sin against you; but if you refuse to forgive them, he will not forgive you." It's clear cut! If we want to be forgiven, we must forgive others.

After you've confessed your sins to God, rest in the truth that He delights in forgiving and forgetting your sins. He's absent-minded when it comes to your confessed sins. There's great freedom and hope in that truth—as long as you've forgiven others. Do you have any forgiving you need to do today?

Where is another God like you, who pardons the sins of the survivors among his people? You cannot stay angry with your people forever, because you delight in showing mercy. Once again you will have compassion on us. You will trample our sins under your feet and throw them into the depths of the ocean! You will show us your faithfulness and unfailing love as you promised with an oath to our ancestors Abraham and Jacob long ago.

Micah 7:18-20

This is the message he has given us to announce to you: God is light and there is no darkness in him at all. So we are lying if we say we have fellowship with God but go on living in spiritual darkness. We are not living in the truth. But if we are living in the light of God's presence, just as Christ is, then we have fellowship with each other, and the blood of Jesus, his Son, cleanses us from every sin.

If we say we have no sin, we are only fooling ourselves and refusing to accept the truth. But if we confess our sins to him, he is faithful and just to forgive us and to cleanse us from every wrong. If we claim we have not sinned, we are calling God a liar and showing that his word has no place in our hearts.

1 John 1:5-10

Related Texts: Numbers 14:1-35; 1 Kings 8:27-53; Psalm 32:1-5; Daniel 9:1-19; Matthew 6:14-15; 18:21-35

done ☐

God Is Gracious

How kind the LORD is! How good he is!
So merciful, this God of ours!
The LORD protects those of childlike faith;
I was facing death, and then he saved me.
Now I can rest again,
for the LORD has been so good to me.

Psalm 116:5-7

But God is so rich in mercy, and he loved us so very much, that even while we were dead because of our sins, he gave us life when he raised Christ from the dead. (It is only by God's special favor that you have been saved!) For he raised us from the dead along with Christ, and we are seated with him in the heavenly realms—all because we are one with Christ Jesus. And so God can always point to us as examples of the incredible wealth of his favor and kindness toward us, as shown in all he has done for us through Christ Jesus.

God saved you by his special favor when you believed. And you can't take credit for this; it is a gift from God. Salvation is not a reward for the good things we have done, so none of us can boast about it.

Ephesians 2:4-9

Related Texts: Numbers 6:24-26; Proverbs 3:33-35; Romans 5:12-21

In OTHER Words

Grace

The word grace is one of the greatest words you could ever learn within the Christian faith. Grace is best defined by the words *undeserved gift*. The gift is God's love. His love never stops! This gift keeps giving.

There is nothing you have done or can do to deserve God's grace. You can't work for it, earn it, achieve it, or buy it. All you can do is receive it. It's free! What a gift!

When you sense God's love today, stop for a moment and thank Him for His free gift of grace.

done ☐

GOD IS HOLY

What's it Mean?

It's heavy duty to think God wants us to be holy as He is holy. It's a good thing He has promised us His Holy Spirit to help us!

God calls us to be holy or "set apart." Being "set apart" means to be "different" from the world. For example, if your friends plan to do something bad and you're trying to be holy, you wouldn't be a part of their bad plans. You would set yourself apart from them, and you would be different.

Holiness is hating that which is evil and trying to live a life pleasing to God.

Ask God to help you live a life that is set apart today.

I, the LORD, am the one who brought you up from the land of Egypt to be your God. You must therefore be holy because I am holy.

Leviticus 11:45

In the year King Uzziah died, I saw the LORD. He was sitting on a lofty throne, and the train of his robe filled the Temple. Hovering around him were mighty seraphim, each with six wings. With two wings they covered their faces, with two they covered their feet, and with the remaining two they flew. In a great chorus they sang, "Holy, holy, holy is the LORD Almighty! The whole earth is filled with his glory!" . . .

The high and lofty one who inhabits eternity, the Holy One, says this: "I live in that high and holy place with those whose spirits are contrite and humble. I refresh the humble and give new courage to those with repentant hearts. For I will not fight against you forever; I will not always show my anger. If I did, all people would pass away—all the souls I have made.

Isaiah 6:1-3; 57:15-16

Obey God because you are his children. Don't slip back into your old ways of doing evil; you didn't know any better then. But now you must be holy in everything you do, just as God—who chose you to be his children—is holy. For he himself has said, "You must be holy because I am holy."

1 Peter 1:14-16

Related Texts: Exodus 15:11; Leviticus 22:31-33; Psalm 99; Revelation 4; 15:2-4

done ☐

God Is Merciful

I lift my eyes to you,
O God, enthroned in heaven.
We look to the LORD our God for his mercy,
just as servants keep their eyes on their master,
as a slave girl watches her mistress for the slightest signal.
Have mercy on us, LORD, have mercy,
for we have had our fill of contempt.
We have had our fill of the scoffing of the proud
and the contempt of the arrogant.

Psalm 123:1-4

Once you were dead, doomed forever because of your many sins. You used to live just like the rest of the world, full of sin, obeying Satan, the mighty prince of the power of the air. He is the spirit at work in the hearts of those who refuse to obey God. All of us used to live that way, following the passions and desires of our evil nature. We were born with an evil nature, and we were under God's anger just like everyone else.

But God is so rich in mercy, and he loved us so very much, that even while we were dead because of our sins, he gave us life when he raised Christ from the dead. (It is only by God's special favor that you have been saved!)

Ephesians 2:1-5

Related Texts: Exodus 33:19; Deuteronomy 4:31; Nehemiah 9:29-31; Micah 7:18-20; Romans 9:11-18

Personality Plus

Jehovah

Jehovah was one of the common names for God during Old Testament times. Jehovah was most commonly referred to as God's personal name. The name Jehovah is really an English word used to translate and pronounce God's Hebrew name: JHWH. The word JHWH has no vowels and probably could be better enunciated as Yahweh rather than Jehovah.

God is given several different names throughout the Bible. Though His names may have changed, His character, His abilities, and the way in which He loves His creation has stayed consistent.

That's news worthy of your celebration today!

done ☐

God Is All-Powerful

Then Job replied to the LORD:
"I know that you can do anything, and no one can stop you."

Job 42:1-2

Tell everyone about God's power.
His majesty shines down on Israel;
his strength is mighty in the heavens.
God is awesome in his sanctuary.
The God of Israel gives power and strength to his people.
Praise be to God!

Psalm 68:34-35

"O Sovereign LORD! You have made the heavens and earth by your great power. Nothing is too hard for you! You are loving and kind to thousands, though children suffer for their parents' sins. You are the great and powerful God, the Lord Almighty. You have all wisdom and do great and mighty miracles. You are very aware of the conduct of all people, and you reward them according to their deeds."

Jeremiah 32:17-19

"You are worthy, O Lord our God,
to receive glory and honor and power.
For you created everything,
and it is for your pleasure that they exist and were created."

Revelation 4:11

Related Texts: Genesis 18:14; Exodus 15:1-18; Psalm 29; Mark 4:35-41

Give it a try

God is worthy of your honor and praise. List five creations of God that you are thankful for.

1.
2.
3.
4.
5.

done ☐

God Is Everywhere

I can never escape from your spirit!
  I can never get away from your presence!
If I go up to heaven, you are there;
  if I go down to the place of the dead, you are there.
If I ride the wings of the morning,
  if I dwell by the farthest oceans,
even there your hand will guide me,
  and your strength will support me.
I could ask the darkness to hide me
  and the light around me to become night—
  but even in darkness I cannot hide from you.
To you the night shines as bright as day.
  Darkness and light are both alike to you.

Psalm 139:7-12

"Am I a God who is only in one place?" asks the LORD. "Do they think I cannot see what they are doing? Can anyone hide from me? Am I not everywhere in all the heavens and earth?" asks the LORD.

Jeremiah 23:23-24

Jesus came and told his disciples, "I have been given complete authority in heaven and on earth. Therefore, go and make disciples of all the nations, baptizing them in the name of the Father and the Son and the Holy Spirit. Teach these new disciples to obey all the commands I have given you. And be sure of this: I am with you always, even to the end of the age."

Matthew 28:18-20

Related Texts: Deuteronomy 4:7; 1 Kings 8:27; John 1:45-49; 14:16-17

JUST a THOUGHT

Have you ever played **hide-and-seek** and **hidden so well** that your **friends gave up looking for you?** Well, there is **nowhere** you could go to **hide** from the **love of God.**

done ☐

God Knows Everything

O LORD, you have examined my heart
and know everything about me.
You know when I sit down or stand up.
You know my every thought when far away.
You chart the path ahead of me
and tell me where to stop and rest.
Every moment you know where I am.
You know what I am going to say
even before I say it, LORD.
You both precede and follow me.
You place your hand of blessing on my head.
Such knowledge is too wonderful for me,
too great for me to know!

Psalm 139:1-6

Oh, what a wonderful God we have! How great are his riches and wisdom and knowledge! How impossible it is for us to understand his decisions and his methods! For who can know what the Lord is thinking?... Everything exists by his power and is intended for his glory. To him be glory evermore. Amen.

Romans 11:33-34a,36b

For the word of God is full of living power. It is sharper than the sharpest knife, cutting deep into our innermost thoughts and desires. It exposes us for what we really are. Nothing in all creation can hide from him. Everything is naked and exposed before his eyes. This is the God to whom we must explain all that we have done.

Hebrews 4:12-13

Related Texts: Psalm 94:1-11; Proverbs 5:21; 2 Chronicles 16:9; 1 Corinthians 1:18-25; John 3:19-20

One Minute Memory

For the word of God is **full of living power.** It is **sharper** than the sharpest **knife, cutting deep** into our **innermost thoughts** and **desires.** It **exposes us** for what we **really are.**

Hebrews 4:12

done ☐

God Is One

"Hear, O Israel! The LORD is our God, the LORD alone."

Deuteronomy 6:4

And the LORD will be king over all the earth. On that day there will be one LORD—his name alone will be worshiped.

Zechariah 14:9

After all, God is not the God of the Jews only, is he? Isn't he also the God of the Gentiles? Of course he is. There is only one God, and there is only one way of being accepted by him. He makes people right with himself only by faith, whether they are Jews or Gentiles.

Romans 3:29-30

According to some people, there are many so-called gods and many lords, both in heaven and on earth. But we know that there is only one God, the Father, who created everything, and we exist for him. And there is only one Lord, Jesus Christ, through whom God made everything and through whom we have been given life.

1 Corinthians 8:5-6

We are all one body, we have the same Spirit, and we have all been called to the same glorious future. There is only one Lord, one faith, one baptism, and there is only one God and Father, who is over us all and in us all and living through us all.

Ephesians 4:4-6

Related Texts: Isaiah 44:6-8; Malachi 2:10; Matthew 19:16-17; 23:1-10; Mark 12:28-34

CHECK IT OUT

When Jesus was asked which of the Ten Commandments was the most important, He said, "The most important commandment is this: 'Hear, O Israel! The Lord our God is the one and only Lord. And you must love the Lord your God with all your heart, all your soul, all your mind, and all your strength' " (Mark 12:29-30).

There's no question about the importance of loving God and God only. This truth may come in opposition to friends from other religions who worship other gods. The Bible is clear about loving only God. Check out Isaiah 44:6,8: "I am the First and the Last; there is no other God. . . . You are my witnesses—is there any other God? No! There is no other Rock—not one!"

This is an important truth for our faith. Talk to God today as your only God.

done ☐

14 JUNE

Personality Plus

King David

David was a man with great strengths who made some serious mistakes.

David's strengths were numerous: he was used by God to kill Goliath and claim victory for Israel; he displayed great acts of friendship with Jonathan; he was the most loved king of Israel, and he wrote many of the psalms in the Bible.

Opposing David's strengths is a weakness that involved obvious disobedience to God. David had sex with Bathsheba—the wife of one of his soldiers. Afterward he arranged her husband's death so Bathsheba could become his own.

Though David's life was not perfect, God chose to use David's family line, through which Jesus would be born. When you hear about Jesus being born from the Davidic line, you will now know that David was an ancestor of Jesus.

God Is Righteous

Wake up, my God, and bring justice!
Gather the nations before you.
Sit on your throne high above them.
The LORD passes judgment on the
nations.
Declare me righteous, O LORD,
for I am innocent, O Most High!
End the wickedness of the ungodly,
but help all those who obey you.
For you look deep within the mind and
heart,
O righteous God.

Psalm 7:6b-9

"For the time is coming," says the LORD, "when I will place a righteous Branch on King David's throne. He will be a King who rules with wisdom. He will do what is just and right throughout the land. And this is his name: 'The LORD Is Our Righteousness.' In that day Judah will be saved, and Israel will live in safety."

Jeremiah 23:5-6

My dear children, I am writing this to you so that you will not sin. But if you do sin, there is someone to plead for you before the Father. He is Jesus Christ, the one who pleases God completely. He is the sacrifice for our sins. He takes away not only our sins but the sins of all the world.

1 John 2:1-2

Related Texts: Ezra 9; Psalms 36:5-10; 71; Daniel 9:1-19; Matthew 6:28-33; Acts 3:12-16

done ☐

Our Heavenly Father

So you are all children of God through faith in Christ Jesus. And all who have been united with Christ in baptism have been made like him. There is no longer Jew or Gentile, slave or free, male or female. For you are all Christians—you are one in Christ Jesus. And now that you belong to Christ, you are the true children of Abraham. You are his heirs, and now all the promises God gave to him belong to you. . . .

They have to obey their guardians until they reach whatever age their father set. . . .

And that's the way it was with us before Christ came. We were slaves to the spiritual powers of this world. But when the right time came, God sent his Son, born of a woman, subject to the law. God sent him to buy freedom for us who were slaves to the law, so that he could adopt us as his very own children. And because you Gentiles have become his children, God has sent the Spirit of his Son into your hearts, and now you can call God your dear Father. Now you are no longer a slave but God's own child. And since you are his child, everything he has belongs to you.

Galatians 3:26-29; 4:2-7

See how very much our heavenly Father loves us, for he allows us to be called his children, and we really are! But the people who belong to this world don't know God, so they don't understand that we are his children. Yes, dear friends, we are already God's children, and we can't even imagine what we will be like when Christ returns.

1 John 3:1-2a

Related Texts: Deuteronomy 32:6; Psalm 2; Isaiah 9:1-7; John 1:12-13; Romans 8; Hebrews 12:1-14

JUST a THOUGHT

Every day can be Father's Day when you focus on God as your Heavenly Father and rejoice over the fact that He loves you and accepts you just as you are.

done ☐

CATCH THIS

There is a way to celebrate Father's Day every day. It's a different type of celebration, for it doesn't celebrate our earthly fathers but rather God our Father.

We can . . .

1. CELEBRATE God the Father as our CREATOR. God made the delicate, inner parts of our body and knit us together in our mother's womb.

2. CELEBRATE God the Father as our COMFORTER. God will never let us down. People will always let us down, but God promises to comfort and care for us in every situation.

3. CELEBRATE God the Father as our CHALLENGER. God doesn't want us to "get stuck." He wants us to grow, change, and mature.

We can do this every day—

1. REJOICE in our CREATION by thanking God for our unique design and accepting ourselves as He created us.

2. RELAX in God's COMFORT. God loves us more than we love ourselves.

3. RUN with the CHALLENGE by taking "baby steps" toward maturity.

Celebrate this week by rejoicing, relaxing, and running. You'll get there!

Honor Your Father

Honor your father and mother. Then you will live a long, full life in the land the LORD your God will give you.

Exodus 20:12

It is painful to be the parent of a fool; there is no joy for the father of a rebel. . . .

My child, how I will rejoice if you become wise. Yes, my heart will thrill when you speak what is right and just. . . .

My child, listen and be wise. Keep your heart on the right course.

Proverbs 17:21; 23:15-16,19

Let the words of Christ, in all their richness, live in your hearts and make you wise. Use his words to teach and counsel each other. Sing psalms and hymns and spiritual songs to God with thankful hearts. And whatever you do or say, let it be as a representative of the Lord Jesus, all the while giving thanks through him to God the Father.

You wives must submit to your husbands, as is fitting for those who belong to the Lord. And you husbands must love your wives and never treat them harshly.

You children must always obey your parents, for this is what pleases the Lord. Fathers, don't aggravate your children. If you do, they will become discouraged and quit trying.

Colossians 3:16-21

Related Texts: Exodus 21:15; Leviticus 19:3; Proverbs 10:1; 23:22-25; Ephesians 6:1-3

done ☐

A Father's Instruction

My children, listen to me. Listen to your father's instruction. Pay attention and grow wise, for I am giving you good guidance. Don't turn away from my teaching. For I, too, was once my father's son, tenderly loved by my mother as an only child.

My father told me, "Take my words to heart. Follow my instructions and you will live. Learn to be wise, and develop good judgment. Don't forget or turn away from my words. Don't turn your back on wisdom, for she will protect you. Love her, and she will guard you. Getting wisdom is the most important thing you can do! And whatever else you do, get good judgment. If you prize wisdom, she will exalt you. Embrace her and she will honor you. She will place a lovely wreath on your head; she will present you with a beautiful crown."

My child, listen to me and do as I say, and you will have a long, good life. I will teach you wisdom's ways and lead you in straight paths. If you live a life guided by wisdom, you won't limp or stumble as you run.

Proverbs 4:1-12

Related Texts: Deuteronomy 6:1-9; Proverbs 1:8; 6:20-24; 31:1-9; 2 Timothy 1:2-3

CHECK IT OUT

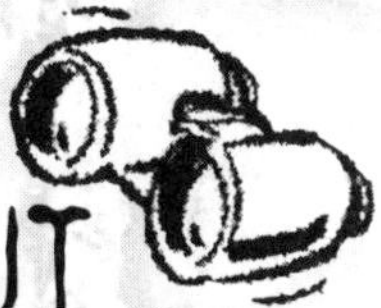

The Proverbs are filled with common-sense wisdom. The following two selections from Proverbs have to do with the wisdom your parents will bring you:

"Listen, my child, to what your father teaches you. Don't neglect your mother's teaching. What you learn from them will crown you with grace and clothe you with honor" (1:8-9).

"Obey your father's commands, and don't neglect your mother's teaching. Keep their words always in your heart. Tie them around your neck. Wherever you walk, their counsel can lead you. When you sleep, they will protect you. When you wake up in the morning, they will advise you" (6:20-22).

You may not like to hear this, but God gave you parents to guide and direct you. They'll never be perfect, but you'll please God and honor your parents when you hear their wisdom.

Keep listening.

done ☐

BIG TIMe WoRd

DISCIPLINE

The word used in today's selection is punish. Another word commonly used in this context is correct. God corrects or disciplines those He loves. Discipline means **CORRECTION.**

God's discipline is to move us toward maturity, to correct us so we might be holier. Proverbs 10:17 says, "People who accept correction are on the pathway to life, but those who ignore it will lead others astray."

God loves us so much that He wants us to gain understanding and celebrate life. Be open to God's correction through reading the Bible, listening to the Holy Spirit, and learning from other Christians. Don't turn your back on correction. Here's why: "If you ignore criticism, you will end in poverty and disgrace; if you accept criticism, you will be honored" (Prov. 13:18).

A Father's Discipline

After all, you have not yet given your lives in your struggle against sin.

And have you entirely forgotten the encouraging words God spoke to you, his children? He said,

"My child, don't ignore it when the
Lord disciplines you,
and don't be discouraged when he
corrects you.
For the Lord disciplines those he loves,
and he punishes those he accepts as
his children."

As you endure this divine discipline, remember that God is treating you as his own children. Whoever heard of a child who was never disciplined? If God doesn't discipline you as he does all of his children, it means that you are illegitimate and are not really his children after all. Since we respect our earthly fathers who disciplined us, should we not all the more cheerfully submit to the discipline of our heavenly Father and live forever?

For our earthly fathers disciplined us for a few years, doing the best they knew how. But God's discipline is always right and good for us because it means we will share in his holiness. No discipline is enjoyable while it is happening—it is painful! But afterward there will be a quiet harvest of right living for those who are trained in this way.

Hebrews 12:4-11

Related Texts: Deuteronomy 8:5; 1 Samuel 2:12-36; Proverbs 3:11-12; 15:5; Revelation 3:14-20

done ☐

JUNE 19

A Faithful Husband

My son, pay attention to my wisdom; listen carefully to my wise counsel. Then you will learn to be discreet and will store up knowledge.

The lips of an immoral woman are as sweet as honey, and her mouth is smoother than oil. But the result is as bitter as poison, sharp as a double-edged sword. . . .

Drink water from your own well—share your love only with your wife. Why spill the water of your springs in public, having sex with just anyone? You should reserve it for yourselves. Don't share it with strangers.

Let your wife be a fountain of blessing for you. Rejoice in the wife of your youth. She is a loving doe, a graceful deer. Let her breasts satisfy you always. May you always be captivated by her love. Why be captivated, my son, with an immoral woman, or embrace the breasts of an adulterous woman?

For the LORD sees clearly what a man does, examining every path he takes. An evil man is held captive by his own sins; they are ropes that catch and hold him. He will die for lack of self-control; he will be lost because of his incredible folly.

Proverbs 5:1-4,15-23

Related Texts: Exodus 20:14; Leviticus 20:10; Proverbs 2:16-22; 6:23-35; 7; Ephesians 5:1-3

Give it a try

These verses include a father's wisdom to his son. The father advises his son to be careful and faithful in his relationship to his wife.

If you are a male, write down three qualities you would like to have in your life before you are a husband. Next to each quality write one goal that will help you develop that quality.

Male	Qualities	Goals
	1.	1.
	2.	2.
	3.	3.

If you are a female, write down three qualities you would like to see in the man you marry. Then ask God to prepare you to be the kind of woman who will love and be faithful to her future husband.

Female Qualities
1.
2.
3.

done ☐

Weird or What?

Song of Songs is one of the most confusing and widely interpreted books in the Bible. It contains sexual lyrics, a mysterious religious meaning, and an intriguing plot.

Song of Songs illustrates the power of human love. This love is a special gift from God. The book is filled with a lot of sexual allegories that will definitely grab your attention. Read it with an open mind and a heart to experience God's radical yet tender love.

Love Song to a Husband

"And compared to other youths, my lover is like the finest apple tree in the orchard. I am seated in his delightful shade, and his fruit is delicious to eat. He brings me to the banquet hall, so everyone can see how much he loves me. Oh, feed me with your love—your 'raisins' and your 'apples'—for I am utterly lovesick! His left hand is under my head, and his right hand embraces me. . . .

"Ah, I hear him—my lover! Here he comes, leaping on the mountains and bounding over the hills. My lover is like a swift gazelle or a young deer. Look, there he is behind the wall! Now he is looking in through the window, gazing into the room.

"My lover said to me, 'Rise up, my beloved, my fair one, and come away. For the winter is past, and the rain is over and gone. The flowers are springing up, and the time of singing birds has come, even the cooing of turtledoves. The fig trees are budding, and the grapevines are in blossom. How delicious they smell! Yes, spring is here! Arise, my beloved, my fair one, and come away.' "

Song of Songs 2:3-6,8-13

Related Texts: Psalm 45; Song of Songs 1–8; 2 Corinthians 11:2-3; 1 Peter 3:1-6

done ☐

Husbands, Love Your Wives

And you husbands must love your wives with the same love Christ showed the church. He gave up his life for her to make her holy and clean, washed by baptism and God's word. He did this to present her to himself as a glorious church without a spot or wrinkle or any other blemish. Instead, she will be holy and without fault. In the same way, husbands ought to love their wives as they love their own bodies. For a man is actually loving himself when he loves his wife. No one hates his own body but lovingly cares for it, just as Christ cares for his body, which is the church. And we are his body. . . .

So again I say, each man must love his wife as he loves himself, and the wife must respect her husband.

Ephesians 5:25-30, 33

In the same way, you husbands must give honor to your wives. Treat her with understanding as you live together. She may be weaker than you are, but she is your equal partner in God's gift of new life. If you don't treat her as you should, your prayers will not be heard.

1 Peter 3:7

Related Texts: Genesis 2:18-25; Hosea 3:1-3; Malachi 2:13-16; Colossians 3:19; Revelation 21:1-4

JUST A THOUGHT

Imagine what families would be like if husbands and wives loved each other as much as Jesus loves His children.

done ☐

What's it Mean?

The tabernacle was a portable sanctuary. Its purpose was to serve as a place where the Israelites could worship God, make sacrifices, and store the ark containing the Ten Commandments.

In Exodus 25:8 God said, "I want the people of Israel to make me a sacred residence where I can live among them." The tabernacle became a visual symbol of God's presence for the Israelites. The cloud and fire described in today's reading were a physical testimony to the Israelites that God was with them.

Today God has given us His Holy Spirit to express His presence in our lives. The clouds and fire aren't used these days, but God's presence is available in a portable sanctuary—your body.

Spend time today thinking about yourself as God's temple.

GOD'S DAILY GUIDANCE FOR ISRAEL

The Tabernacle was set up, and on that day the cloud covered it. Then from evening until morning the cloud over the Tabernacle appeared to be a pillar of fire. This was the regular pattern—at night the cloud changed to the appearance of fire. When the cloud lifted from over the sacred tent, the people of Israel followed it. And wherever the cloud settled, the people of Israel camped. In this way, they traveled at the LORD's command and stopped wherever he told them to. Then they remained where they were as long as the cloud stayed over the Tabernacle. If the cloud remained over the Tabernacle for a long time, the Israelites stayed for a long time, just as the LORD commanded. Sometimes the cloud would stay over the Tabernacle for only a few days, so the people would stay for only a few days. Then at the LORD's command they would break camp. Sometimes the cloud stayed only overnight and moved on the next morning. But day or night, when the cloud lifted, the people broke camp and followed. Whether the cloud stayed above the Tabernacle for two days, a month, or a year, the people of Israel stayed in camp and did not move on. But as soon as it lifted, they broke camp and moved on. So they camped or traveled at the LORD's command, and they did whatever the LORD told them through Moses.

Numbers 9:15-23

Related Texts: Exodus 13:22,33; 40:34-38; Numbers 14:11-14; 1 Corinthians 10:1-2

done ☐

JUNE 23

Israel Puts God to the Test

They willfully tested God in their hearts,
demanding the foods they craved.
They even spoke against God himself, saying,
"God can't give us food in the desert.
Yes, he can strike a rock so water gushes out,
but he can't give his people bread and meat."
When the LORD heard them, he was angry.
The fire of his wrath burned against Jacob.
Yes, his anger rose against Israel,
for they did not believe God
or trust him to care for them.
But he commanded the skies to open—
he opened the doors of heaven—
and rained down manna for them to eat.
He gave them bread from heaven.
They ate the food of angels!
God gave them all they could hold.
He released the east wind in the heavens
and guided the south wind by his mighty power.
He rained down meat as thick as dust—
birds as plentiful as the sands along the seashore!
He caused the birds to fall within their camp
and all around their tents.
The people ate their fill.
He gave them what they wanted.
But before they finished eating this food they had craved,
while the meat was yet in their mouths,
the anger of God rose against them,
and he killed their strongest men;
he struck down the finest of Israel's young men.
But in spite of this, the people kept on sinning.
They refused to believe in his miracles.

Psalm 78:18-32

Related Texts: Numbers 11; Psalm 106:1-15; Luke 4:1-13; James 4:1-4

CHECK IT OUT

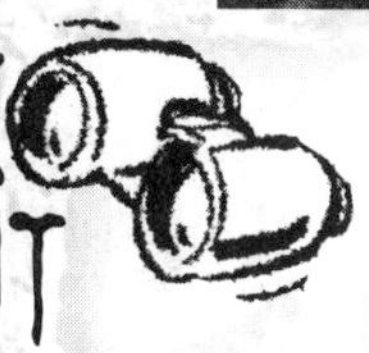

This attitude of unthankfulness, unfaithfulness, and complaining wasn't only an Israelite problem. Thousands of years later James wrote to Christians about the same type of problem. Check out James 4:2-4:

"You want what you don't have, so you scheme and kill to get it. You are jealous for what others have, and you can't possess it, so you fight and quarrel to take it away from them. And yet the reason you don't have what you want is that you don't ask God for it.

"And even when you do ask, you don't get it because your whole motive is wrong—you want only what will give you pleasure. You adulterers!

"Don't you realize that friendship with this world makes you an enemy of God? I say it again, that if your aim is to enjoy this world, you can't be a friend of God."

Today, a few thousand years later, this type of attitude is still a problem. Though God continues to show himself faithful, we complain about things we don't have.

If you had to choose between being God's friend or enemy, you'd better run from the evil pleasures of the world and be thankful God has given you what you have; it's more than most of the world will ever have.

done ☐

CATCH THIS

God gave the Israelites a leader—Moses. God saved them from slavery—in Egypt. God directed them to a new place to live—the Promised Land. With all of God's provisions, you wouldn't think that the Israelites would whine and complain. How quickly they forgot His blessings.

Can you relate to the Israelites' feelings? We can sit back and read about the Israelites and make fun of how unfaithful they were, but in reality, we're a lot like them. God has provided for us over and over, and yet we still complain when we don't get what we want.

Being faithful is tough, but it's not impossible! Spend time today thinking of all the different ways God has shown himself faithful to you. **Then promise to trust Him a little more today than you did yesterday.**

Israel Rejects the Promised Land

The LORD now said to Moses, "Send men to explore the land of Canaan, the land I am giving to Israel. Send one leader from each of the twelve ancestral tribes."...

After exploring the land for forty days, the men returned to Moses, Aaron, and the people of Israel at Kadesh in the wilderness of Paran. They reported to the whole community what they had seen and showed them the fruit they had taken from the land. This was their report to Moses: "We arrived in the land you sent us to see, and it is indeed a magnificent country—a land flowing with milk and honey. Here is some of its fruit as proof. But the people living there are powerful, and their cities and towns are fortified and very large."...

But Caleb tried to encourage the people as they stood before Moses. "Let's go at once to take the land," he said. "We can certainly conquer it!"

But the other men who had explored the land with him answered, "We can't go up against them! They are stronger than we are!"...

Then all the people began weeping aloud, and they cried all night. Their voices rose in a great chorus of complaint against Moses and Aaron. "We wish we had died in Egypt, or even here in the wilderness!" they wailed. "Why is the LORD taking us to this country only to have us die in battle? Our wives and little ones will be carried off as slaves! Let's get out of here and return to Egypt!" Then they plotted among themselves, "Let's choose a leader and go back to Egypt!"

Numbers 13:1-2,25-28a,30-31; 14:1-4

Related Texts: Deuteronomy 1:19-33; Psalm 106:24-27; Proverbs 29:25; Philippians 2:12-16

done ☐

Forty Years in the Desert

Then Moses and Aaron fell face down on the ground before the people of Israel. Two of the men who had explored the land, Joshua son of Nun and Caleb son of Jephunneh, tore their clothing. They said to the community of Israel, "The land we explored is a wonderful land! And if the LORD is pleased with us, he will bring us safely into that land and give it to us. It is a rich land flowing with milk and honey, and he will give it to us! Do not rebel against the LORD, and don't be afraid of the people of the land. They are only helpless prey to us! They have no protection, but the LORD is with us! Don't be afraid of them!"...

Then the LORD said to Moses and Aaron, "How long will this wicked nation complain about me? I have heard everything the Israelites have been saying. Now tell them this: 'As surely as I live, I will do to you the very things I heard you say. I, the LORD, have spoken! You will all die here in this wilderness! Because you complained against me, none of you who are twenty years old or older and were counted in the census will enter the land I swore to give you. The only exceptions will be Caleb son of Jephunneh and Joshua son of Nun.

" 'Because the men who explored the land were there for forty days, you must wander in the wilderness for forty years—a year for each day, suffering the consequences of your sins. You will discover what it is like to have me for an enemy.' "

Numbers 14:5-9,26-30,34

What can we say about such wonderful things as these? If God is for us, who can ever be against us?

Romans 8:31

Related Texts: Joshua 5:1-6; John 6:48-51; 1 Corinthians 10:1-6; Hebrews 3:7-4:7

One Minute Memory

If **God** is for us, who can ever be **against** us?

Romans 8:31b

done ☐

Listen to God's Voice

That is why the Holy Spirit says,
"Today you must listen to his voice.
Don't harden your hearts against him
as Israel did when they rebelled,
when they tested God's patience in the wilderness.
There your ancestors tried my patience,
even though they saw my miracles for forty years.
So I was angry with them, and I said,
'Their hearts always turn away from me.
They refuse to do what I tell them.'
So in my anger I made a vow:
'They will never enter my place of rest.' "

Be careful then, dear friends. Make sure that your own hearts are not evil and unbelieving, turning you away from the living God. You must warn each other every day, as long as it is called "today," so that none of you will be deceived by sin and hardened against God. For if we are faithful to the end, trusting God just as firmly as when we first believed, we will share in all that belongs to Christ. But never forget the warning:
"Today you must listen to his voice.
Don't harden your hearts against him
as Israel did when they rebelled."

Hebrews 3:7-15

Related Texts: Psalm 95; Matthew 17:1-5; John 14:15-24; Acts 3:19-23; Hebrews 4

Give it a try

A person with a hardened heart has become closed to the truth, teachings, and ways of God. What are three things you can do today to ensure that your heart doesn't become hardened and that you continue to grow?

1.
2.
3.

done ☐

God Crushes Rebellion

One day Korah son of Izhar, a descendant of Kohath son of Levi, conspired with Dathan and Abiram, the sons of Eliab, and On son of Peleth, from the tribe of Reuben. They incited a rebellion against Moses, involving 250 other prominent leaders, all members of the assembly. They went to Moses and Aaron and said, "You have gone too far! Everyone in Israel has been set apart by the LORD, and he is with all of us. What right do you have to act as though you are greater than anyone else among all these people of the LORD?"

When Moses heard what they were saying, he threw himself down with his face to the ground. Then he said to Korah and his followers, "Tomorrow morning the LORD will show us who belongs to him and who is holy. The LORD will allow those who are chosen to enter his holy presence." . . .

Meanwhile, Korah had stirred up the entire community against Moses and Aaron, and they all assembled at the Tabernacle entrance. Then the glorious presence of the LORD appeared to the whole community. . . .

The earth opened up and swallowed the men, along with their households and the followers who were standing with them, and everything they owned. So they went down alive into the grave, along with their belongings. The earth closed over them, and they all vanished.

Numbers 16:1-5,19,32-33

Related Texts: Psalm 106:16-17; Hebrews 10:26-31; 12:23-29; 2 Peter 1:16-2:22; Jude 1:11

JUST a THOUGHT

Anytime you take a position of leadership, you can be confident there will be someone who doesn't like or appreciate you; just ask Moses and Aaron.

done ☐

Weird or What?

Moses Disobeys God

In early spring the people of Israel arrived in the wilderness of Zin and camped at Kadesh. . . .

There was no water for the people to drink at that place, so they rebelled against Moses and Aaron. . . . Did you bring the LORD's people into this wilderness to die, along with all our livestock? Why did you make us leave Egypt and bring us here to this terrible place?" . . .

Moses and Aaron turned away from the people and went to the entrance of the Tabernacle, where they fell face down on the ground. Then the glorious presence of the LORD appeared to them, and the LORD said to Moses, "You and Aaron must take the staff and assemble the entire community. As the people watch, command the rock over there to pour out its water. You will get enough water from the rock to satisfy all the people and their livestock."

So Moses did as he was told. He took the staff from the place where it was kept before the LORD. Then he and Aaron summoned the people to come and gather at the rock. "Listen, you rebels!" he shouted. "Must we bring you water from this rock?" Then Moses raised his hand and struck the rock twice with the staff, and water gushed out. So all the people and their livestock drank their fill.

But the LORD said to Moses and Aaron, "Because you did not trust me enough to demonstrate my holiness to the people of Israel, you will not lead them into the land I am giving them!"

Numbers 20:1a,2,4-5a,6-12

Related Texts: Exodus 7:19-21; 8:16-17; 17:1-6; Deuteronomy 4:20-22; Acts 5:1-11

It seems strange that after all Moses and Aaron had done, they wouldn't be allowed to enter and enjoy the Promised Land. But when Moses and Aaron brought water from the rock by striking it, they tried to improve on God's unimprovable plan. God could not reward them for failing to believe in and honor Him. Moses and Aaron learned a hard lesson that day: No one is exempt from obeying God.

Being faithful is an ongoing, everyday battle.

Try to win that battle today, and God will be pleased with your victory.

done

Look Up and Live

Then the people of Israel set out from Mount Hor, taking the road to the Red Sea to go around the land of Edom. But the people grew impatient along the way, and they began to murmur against God and Moses. "Why have you brought us out of Egypt to die here in the wilderness?" they complained. "There is nothing to eat here and nothing to drink. And we hate this wretched manna!"

So the LORD sent poisonous snakes among them, and many of them were bitten and died. Then the people came to Moses and cried out, "We have sinned by speaking against the LORD and against you. Pray that the LORD will take away the snakes." So Moses prayed for the people.

Then the LORD told him, "Make a replica of a poisonous snake and attach it to the top of a pole. Those who are bitten will live if they simply look at it!" So Moses made a snake out of bronze and attached it to the top of a pole. Whenever those who were bitten looked at the bronze snake, they recovered! *Numbers 21:4-9*

And as Moses lifted up the bronze snake on a pole in the wilderness, so I, the Son of Man, must be lifted up on a pole, so that everyone who believes in me will have eternal life.

"For God so loved the world that he gave his only Son, so that everyone who believes in him will not perish but have eternal life. God did not send his Son into the world to condemn it, but to save it."

John 3:14-17

Related Texts: Exodus 16:6-12; Numbers 14:26-37; 2 Kings 18:1-4; Lamentations 3:25-40; 1 Corinthians 10:1-11

One Minute Memory

God did not send his Son **into** the **world** to **condemn** it, but to **save it.**

John 3:17

done ☐

30 JUNE

Personality Plus

Balaam

Balaam is an interesting character because of the strange way God got his attention.

One day Balaam was riding a donkey, and an angel appeared before them. Balaam didn't see the angel, but the donkey went crazy. Three times the donkey went wild, and all three times Balaam beat the animal. God then caused the donkey to speak, saying, "What have I done that deserves your beating me these three times?" Now Balaam went crazy.

God was trying to stop Balaam's direction by speaking through a donkey. Balaam responded with repentance.

Does God have your full attention? Today ask Him if you're going in the right direction.

Balaam Hired to Curse Israel

Then the people of Israel traveled to the plains of Moab and camped east of the Jordan River, across from Jericho. Balak son of Zippor, the Moabite king, knew what the Israelites had done to the Amorites. And when they saw how many Israelites there were, he and his people were terrified. The king of Moab said to the leaders of Midian, "This mob will devour everything in sight, like an ox devours grass!"

So Balak, king of Moab, sent messengers to Balaam son of Beor, who was living in his native land of Pethor near the Euphrates River. He sent this message to request that Balaam come to help him:

"A vast horde of people has arrived from Egypt. They cover the face of the earth and are threatening me. Please come and curse them for me because they are so numerous. Then perhaps I will be able to conquer them and drive them from the land. I know that blessings fall on the people you bless. I also know that the people you curse are doomed."

Numbers 22:1-6

"No Ammonites or Moabites, or any of their descendants for ten generations, may be included in the assembly of the LORD. These nations did not welcome you with food and water when you came out of Egypt. Instead, they tried to hire Balaam son of Beor from Pethor in Aram-naharaim to curse you. (But the LORD your God would not listen to Balaam. He turned the intended curse into a blessing because the LORD your God loves you.)

Deuteronomy 23:3-5

Related Texts: Genesis 12:1-3; Numbers 22-24; Joshua 24:8-10; 2 Peter 2:15-16

done ☐

July

After
more than
sixty years
of almost
daily
reading of
the **Bible,**
I never fail
to find it
always new
and
marvelously
in tune
with the
changing needs
of **every**
day.

Cecil B. DeMille
(1881–1959)
American Movie Producer

Balaam Blesses Israel

By now Balaam realized that the LORD intended to bless Israel, so he did not resort to divination as he often did. Instead, he turned and looked out toward the wilderness, where he saw the people of Israel camped, tribe by tribe. Then the Spirit of God came upon him, and this is the prophecy he delivered:

"This is the prophecy of Balaam son of Beor,
the prophecy of the man whose eyes see clearly,
who hears the words of God,
who sees a vision from the Almighty,
who falls down with eyes wide open:
How beautiful are your tents, O Jacob;
how lovely are your homes, O Israel!
They spread before me like groves of palms,
like fruitful gardens by the riverside.
They are like aloes planted by the LORD,
like cedars beside the waters.
Water will gush out in buckets;
their offspring are supplied with all they need.
Their king will be greater than Agag;
their kingdom will be exalted.
God brought them up from Egypt,
drawing them along like a wild ox.
He devours all the nations that oppose him,
breaking their bones in pieces,
shooting them with arrows.
Like a lion, Israel crouches and lies down;
like a lioness, who dares to arouse her?
Blessed is everyone who blesses you, O Israel,
and cursed is everyone who curses you."

Numbers 24:1-9

Related Texts: Genesis 12:1-3; 22:15-18; 27:26-29; Deuteronomy 23:3-5; Joshua 13:22; 24:8-10; Revelation 2:12-14

In OTHER Words

Prophecy

Prophecy is a word used to describe a vision, a truth, a burden, or a word from God spoken by a person called a prophet. Prophets were messengers who were authorized to speak for God.

The prophecies in the Bible have been coming true for thousands of years. One book in the Bible filled with prophecy is Revelation. If you read those prophecies, you can be confident God is unfolding history in His timing. God will fulfill all prophecies! This is good news for those who believe. Go ahead and **thank God for your future that He already knows.**

done ☐

One Minute Memory

God bought you with a high price. So you must honor God with your body.

1 Corinthians 6:20

Judgment for Immorality

While the Israelites were camped at Acacia, some of the men defiled themselves by sleeping with the local Moabite women. These women invited them to attend sacrifices to their gods, and soon the Israelites were feasting with them and worshiping the gods of Moab. Before long Israel was joining in the worship of Baal of Peor, causing the LORD's anger to blaze against his people.

The LORD issued the following command to Moses: "Seize all the ringleaders and execute them before the LORD in broad daylight, so his fierce anger will turn away from the people of Israel." So Moses ordered Israel's judges to execute everyone who had joined in worshiping Baal of Peor.

Numbers 25:1-5

Run away from sexual sin! No other sin so clearly affects the body as this one does. For sexual immorality is a sin against your own body. Or don't you know that your body is the temple of the Holy Spirit, who lives in you and was given to you by God? You do not belong to yourself, for God bought you with a high price. So you must honor God with your body.

1 Corinthians 6:18-20

Related Texts: Deuteronomy 4:1-4; Joshua 22:16-20; Psalm 106:28-31; Hosea 9:10; 1 Corinthians 10:1-8

done

Vengeance against Midian

Then the LORD said to Moses, "Take vengeance on the Midianites for leading the Israelites into idolatry. After that, you will die and join your ancestors."

So Moses said to the people, "Choose some men to fight the LORD's war of vengeance against Midian. From each tribe of Israel, send one thousand men into battle." So they chose one thousand men from each tribe of Israel, a total of twelve thousand men armed for battle. . . .

They attacked Midian just as the LORD had commanded Moses, and they killed all the men. All five of the Midianite kings—Evi, Rekem, Zur, Hur, and Reba—died in the battle. They also killed Balaam son of Beor with the sword.

Then the Israelite army captured the Midianite women and children and seized their cattle and flocks and all their wealth as plunder. They burned all the towns and villages where the Midianites had lived. . . .

Moses, Eleazar the priest, and all the leaders of the people went to meet them outside the camp. But Moses was furious with all the military commanders who had returned from the battle.

"Why have you let all the women live?" he demanded. "These are the very ones who followed Balaam's advice and caused the people of Israel to rebel against the LORD at Mount Peor. They are the ones who caused the plague to strike the LORD's people."

Numbers 31:1-5,7-10,13-16

Related Texts: Numbers 25; Deuteronomy 21:10-14; Joshua 13:16-22; Judges 6-8; Romans 12:16-21

CHECK IT OUT

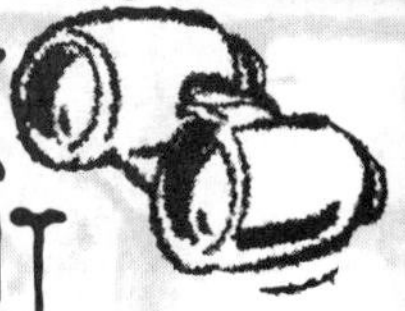

As we've already learned, the battling between the nations was a necessary task in order for the Israelites to occupy the Promised Land. The victorious battles proved God was the only God.

The New Testament teaches us to take a different position on killing and revenge. Check out the teaching in Romans 12:17-18: "Never pay back evil for evil to anyone. Do things in such a way that everyone can see you are honorable. Do your part to live in peace with everyone, as much as possible."

The key words are "as much as possible."

It's tough not to fight and quarrel, but try doing less of it today than you did yesterday. Then celebrate your progress.

done ☐

CATCH THIS

If you've been reading this book for a while, you've noticed that God is serious when He asks us to love Him and follow His instructions. Today's passage gives the results of doing this: "You will enjoy a long life." That's worth underlining! God gave us instructions so we might live better and longer. The Bible is God's instruction book.

Think about this: if you built a house, you would know everything about it. You'd know the location of all the wires, the minor flaws, the strong areas, the depth of the foundation. You'd know it all! With this knowledge you could inform the potential homeowners how best to live in it. This same principle works with God and His creations. God built us. He knows His creations best. He knows our hearts, thoughts, and plans. If we follow His instructions, we'll live life to its fullest. These instructions are in God's love letter to us—the Bible.

It's your choice; you can either live the way you want and risk damaging your life, or live how God wants you to and celebrate life. Which way do you plan to go?

Love the Lord Your God

These are all the commands, laws, and regulations that the LORD your God told me to teach you so you may obey them in the land you are about to enter and occupy, and so you and your children and grandchildren might fear the LORD your God as long as you live. If you obey all his laws and commands, you will enjoy a long life. Listen closely, Israel, to everything I say. Be careful to obey. Then all will go well with you, and you will have many children in the land flowing with milk and honey, just as the LORD, the God of your ancestors, promised you.

Hear, O Israel! The LORD is our God, the LORD alone. And you must love the LORD your God with all your heart, all your soul, and all your strength. And you must commit yourselves wholeheartedly to these commands I am giving you today. Repeat them again and again to your children. Talk about them when you are at home and when you are away on a journey, when you are lying down and when you are getting up again. Tie them to your hands as a reminder, and wear them on your forehead. Write them on the doorposts of your house and on your gates.

Deuteronomy 6:1-9

Even perfection has its limits,
but your commands have no limit.
Oh, how I love your law!
I think about it all day long.

Psalm 119:96-97

Related Texts: Deuteronomy 10:12-16; 11:18-21; Psalms 1; 119; Proverbs 22:6; Mark 12:28-34; Luke 10:25-28; 1 John 5:1-4

done ☐

Joshua Succeeds Moses

When Moses had finished saying these things to all the people of Israel, he said, "I am now 120 years old and am no longer able to lead you. The LORD has told me that I will not cross the Jordan River. But the LORD your God himself will cross over ahead of you. He will destroy the nations living there, and you will take possession of their land. Joshua is your new leader, and he will go with you, just as the LORD promised. The LORD will destroy the nations living in the land, just as he destroyed Sihon and Og, the kings of the Amorites. The LORD will hand over to you the people who live there, and you will deal with them as I have commanded you. Be strong and courageous! Do not be afraid of them! The LORD your God will go ahead of you. He will neither fail you nor forsake you."

Then Moses called for Joshua, and as all Israel watched he said to him, "Be strong and courageous! For you will lead these people into the land that the LORD swore to give their ancestors. You are the one who will deliver it to them as their inheritance. Do not be afraid or discouraged, for the LORD is the one who goes before you. He will be with you; he will neither fail you nor forsake you."

So Moses wrote down this law and gave it to the priests, who carried the Ark of the LORD's covenant, and to the leaders of Israel.

Deuteronomy 31:1-9

Related Texts: Numbers 21:21-35; Deuteronomy 2:24–3:17; 1 Kings 8:54-57; Hebrews 13:5-6

Personality Plus

Joshua

Moses sent twelve spies into the Promised Land to evaluate the land's occupants. Joshua was one of the two who returned with a positive outlook and faith that God would lead the Israelites into the Promised Land.

In addition to Joshua's confidence in God, he was a leader. He was such a strong leader that God appointed him to replace Moses. His leadership proved capable as he conquered the enemies and led the Israelites into their inheritance.

Joshua's faithfulness allowed him to be used to fulfill God's prophecy and promise. There's that word again: faithfulness.

Does the word faithful belong next to your name?

done ☐

BIG TIMe WoRd

COURAGEOUS

Being courageous is tough! It's easy to be a coward and hide your feelings and beliefs and go along with the crowd. But courageous people "stand their ground" and accept comments directed at them. Courageous people are willing to tell someone no even when their friends are saying yes.

Courageous people aren't afraid of the jeers, laughter, or put-downs they might receive. Being courageous doesn't mean they enjoy the attacks; rather, they aren't AFRAID of receiving them.

It takes courage to be a Christian in today's world. Try being courageous for God today and be willing to stand up for what you believe is right.

Be Strong and Courageous

After the death of Moses the LORD's servant, the LORD spoke to Joshua son of Nun, Moses' assistant. He said, "Now that my servant Moses is dead, you must lead my people across the Jordan River into the land I am giving them. I promise you what I promised Moses: 'Everywhere you go, you will be on land I have given you— from the Negev Desert in the south to the Lebanon mountains in the north, from the Euphrates River on the east to the Mediterranean Sea on the west, and all the land of the Hittites.' No one will be able to stand their ground against you as long as you live. For I will be with you as I was with Moses. I will not fail you or abandon you.

"Be strong and courageous, for you will lead my people to possess all the land I swore to give their ancestors. Be strong and very courageous. Obey all the laws Moses gave you. Do not turn away from them, and you will be successful in everything you do. Study this Book of the Law continually. Meditate on it day and night so you may be sure to obey all that is written in it. Only then will you succeed. I command you—be strong and courageous! Do not be afraid or discouraged. For the LORD your God is with you wherever you go."

Joshua 1:1-9

Related Texts: Deuteronomy 11:22-25; Psalms 1; 19; 119; 1 Corinthians 16:13-14; Hebrews 3:1-6

done ☐

Rahab Hides the Israelite Spies

Then Joshua secretly sent out two spies from the Israelite camp at Acacia. He instructed them, "Spy out the land on the other side of the Jordan River, especially around Jericho." So the two men set out and came to the house of a prostitute named Rahab and stayed there that night. But someone told the king of Jericho, "Some Israelites have come here tonight to spy out the land." So the king of Jericho sent orders to Rahab: "Bring out the men who have come into your house. They are spies sent here to discover the best way to attack us."

Rahab, who had hidden the two men, replied, "The men were here earlier, but I didn't know where they were from. They left the city at dusk, as the city gates were about to close, and I don't know where they went. If you hurry, you can probably catch up with them." (But she had taken them up to the roof and hidden them beneath piles of flax.)...

The spies went up into the hill country and stayed there three days. The men who were chasing them had searched everywhere along the road, but they finally returned to the city without success. Then the two spies came down from the hill country, crossed the Jordan River, and reported to Joshua all that had happened to them. "The LORD will certainly give us the whole land," they said, "for all the people in the land are terrified of us."

Joshua 2:1-6,22-24

Related Texts: Matthew 1:1-6; Hebrews 11:31; James 2:25

JUST a THOUGHT

If God is willing to use a prostitute to help others, don't you think He can use you to do great things as well?

done ☐

CATCH THIS

This story of how God wanted Israel to attack Jericho reminds us that God's plans are often different from ours.

Imagine the Israelites' military headquarters. The trained soldiers were reviewing their plan on how to attack and conquer Jericho. Then their leader, Joshua, tells them to march around the city, play their trumpets, and shout so the city walls will fall down. Can you imagine the soldiers' response? "Yeah, right, Joshua. That will never work." His plan would have seemed ridiculous if God wasn't in control.

When God is in charge of your life, you may find His plans are different from yours. Next time you're faced with a problem, ask God to reveal His plan to you. It's amazing how God accomplishes His plan. And don't be surprised if His plan doesn't happen as you thought it would. Go grab your trumpet and get ready for God to work!

The Israelites Conquer Jericho

Now the gates of Jericho were tightly shut because the people were afraid of the Israelites. No one was allowed to go in or out. But the LORD said to Joshua, "I have given you Jericho, its king, and all its mighty warriors. Your entire army is to march around the city once a day for six days. Seven priests will walk ahead of the Ark, each carrying a ram's horn. On the seventh day you are to march around the city seven times, with the priests blowing the horns. When you hear the priests give one long blast on the horns, have all the people give a mighty shout. Then the walls of the city will collapse, and the people can charge straight into the city."...

When the people heard the sound of the horns, they shouted as loud as they could. Suddenly, the walls of Jericho collapsed, and the Israelites charged straight into the city from every side and captured it. They completely destroyed everything in it—men and women, young and old, cattle, sheep, donkeys—everything....

So Joshua spared Rahab the prostitute and her relatives who were with her in the house, because she had hidden the spies Joshua sent to Jericho. And she lives among the Israelites to this day.

Joshua 6:1-5,20-21,25

Related Texts: Numbers 10:1-10; Judges 7:1-22; Matthew 1:1-6

done ☐

JULY 9

Joshua Conquers the Land of Canaan

As the LORD had commanded his servant Moses, so Moses commanded Joshua. And Joshua did as he was told, carefully obeying all of the LORD's instructions to Moses.

So Joshua conquered the entire region—the hill country, the Negev, the land of Goshen, the western foothills, the Jordan Valley, and the mountains and lowlands of Israel. The Israelite territory now extended all the way from Mount Halak, which leads up to Seir, to Baal-gad at the foot of Mount Hermon in the valley of Lebanon. Joshua killed all the kings of those territories, waging war for a long time to accomplish this. No one in this region made peace with the Israelites except the Hivites of Gibeon. All the others were defeated. For the LORD hardened their hearts and caused them to fight the Israelites instead of asking for peace. So they were completely and mercilessly destroyed, as the LORD had commanded Moses. . . .

So Joshua took control of the entire land, just as the LORD had instructed Moses. He gave it to the people of Israel as their special possession, dividing the land among the tribes. So the land finally had rest from war.

Joshua 11:15-20,23

Related Texts: Deuteronomy 7; 9:1-6; 18:9-14; 20:16-18; Joshua 7–10

Give it a try

The Israelites went through a lot of pain, suffering, wandering, and disobedience before reaching the Promised Land. God proved himself faithful by fulfilling His promise to the Israelites. He brought them into their inheritance!

God is faithful! Does God's faithfulness mean anything to you? If yes, what does it mean? Can God rely on your faithfulness?

done ☐

CATCH THIS

Before Joshua's death he repeatedly challenged the Israelites to turn from their idols and love God. Doesn't it seem crazy that after all God had done for the Israelites they still worshiped idols and other gods?

When we take a look at ourselves, we see we're a lot like the Israelites. God has done a lot for us. He sent Jesus to die in our place. What more could He do? And yet we are unfaithful when we turn our backs on Him and make other "gods" higher priorities. We can point to the Israelites and say, "How could you be so stupid?" Unfortunately, they probably could make the same comments about our unfaithfulness.

Don't allow the day to end without taking a reflective journey of your faith and your commitment to God. God has proven himself to be faithful over and over. Can you say the same thing the Israelites eventually said: "We choose the Lord"? If so, let God know right away.

Joshua's Farewell Address

"So honor the LORD and serve him wholeheartedly. Put away forever the idols your ancestors worshiped when they lived beyond the Euphrates River and in Egypt. Serve the LORD alone. But if you are unwilling to serve the LORD, then choose today whom you will serve. Would you prefer the gods your ancestors served beyond the Euphrates? Or will it be the gods of the Amorites in whose land you now live? But as for me and my family, we will serve the LORD."

The people replied, "We would never forsake the LORD and worship other gods. For the LORD our God is the one who rescued us and our ancestors from slavery in the land of Egypt. He performed mighty miracles before our very eyes. As we traveled through the wilderness among our enemies, he preserved us. It was the LORD who drove out the Amorites and the other nations living here in the land. So we, too, will serve the LORD, for he alone is our God."

Then Joshua said to the people, "You are not able to serve the LORD, for he is a holy and jealous God. He will not forgive your rebellion and sins. If you forsake the LORD and serve other gods, he will turn against you and destroy you, even though he has been so good to you."

But the people answered Joshua, saying, "No, we are determined to serve the LORD!"

Joshua 24:14-21

Related Texts: Exodus 24:3-8; Leviticus 26; Romans 6; Hebrews 3–4

done ☐

THE DAYS OF THE JUDGES

And the Israelites served the LORD throughout the lifetime of Joshua and the leaders who outlived him—those who had seen all the great things the LORD had done for Israel.

Then Joshua son of Nun, the servant of the LORD, died at the age of 110. They buried him in the land he had inherited, at Timnath-serah in the hill country of Ephraim, north of Mount Gaash.

After that generation died, another generation grew up who did not acknowledge the LORD or remember the mighty things he had done for Israel. Then the Israelites did what was evil in the LORD's sight and worshiped the images of Baal. . . .

This made the LORD burn with anger against Israel, so he handed them over to marauders who stole their possessions. He sold them to their enemies all around, and they were no longer able to resist them. . . .

Then the LORD raised up judges to rescue the Israelites from their enemies. . . .

Whenever the LORD placed a judge over Israel, he was with that judge and rescued the people from their enemies throughout the judge's lifetime. For the LORD took pity on his people, who were burdened by oppression and suffering. But when the judge died, the people returned to their corrupt ways, behaving worse than those who had lived before them. They followed other gods, worshiping and bowing down to them. And they refused to give up their evil practices and stubborn ways.

Judges 2:7-11,14,16,18-19

Related Texts: Deuteronomy 4:1-10; 11:18-25; Judges 2:19-3:31; Psalm 78:1-6; Ephesians 2:1-10

What's it Mean?

Judges during Old Testament times were very different from our present-day court judges. Old Testament judges were leaders that God appointed after the Israelites occupied the Promised Land. They helped create laws, judged disputes, and provided spiritual and military leadership.

Even though the Israelites had a designated person to act as judge, God was and is the ultimate and only qualified Judge. It's written in James 4:12: "God alone, who made the law, can rightly judge among us. He alone has the power to save or to destroy. So what right do you have to condemn your neighbor?"

Don't play judge today and see if it makes any difference in your life. It's best to let God be the one to judge others.

You won't miss a thing if you stop judging.

done ☐

Personality Plus

Deborah

Deborah was a woman judge who is best known for leading a victorious battle over Sisera. Prior to this battle she was confident God had already planned and prepared the victory. When she told one of her military leaders to begin the battle, he requested her presence by saying, "I'll go, but only if you go with me!" Deborah's faith in God gave her the confidence to say: "Now is the time for action! The Lord leads on! He has already delivered Sisera into your hand!" Deborah is another example of someone who possessed faithfulness and confidence that God is who He claims to be.

How can you be more confident that God will provide?

Deborah: Prophetess and Judge

After Ehud's death, the Israelites again did what was evil in the LORD's sight. So the LORD handed them over to King Jabin of Hazor, a Canaanite king. The commander of his army was Sisera, who lived in Harosheth-haggoyim. Sisera, who had nine hundred iron chariots, ruthlessly oppressed the Israelites for twenty years. Then the Israelites cried out to the LORD for help.

Deborah, the wife of Lappidoth, was a prophet who had become a judge in Israel. She would hold court under the Palm of Deborah, which stood between Ramah and Bethel in the hill country of Ephraim, and the Israelites came to her to settle their disputes. One day she sent for Barak son of Abinoam, who lived in Kedesh in the land of Naphtali. She said to him, "This is what the LORD, the God of Israel, commands you: Assemble ten thousand warriors from the tribes of Naphtali and Zebulun at Mount Tabor. I will lure Sisera, commander of Jabin's army, along with his chariots and warriors, to the Kishon River. There I will give you victory over him."

Barak told her, "I will go, but only if you go with me!"

"Very well," she replied, "I will go with you. But since you have made this choice, you will receive no honor. For the LORD's victory over Sisera will be at the hands of a woman."

Judges 4:1-9a

Related Texts: Exodus 15:19-21; Judges 5:1-12; 2 Kings 22:11-20; 2 Chronicles 34:19-28; Luke 2:21-38

done ☐

Jael Kills the Canaanite General

Then Deborah said to Barak, "Get ready! Today the LORD will give you victory over Sisera, for the LORD is marching ahead of you." So Barak led his ten thousand warriors down the slopes of Mount Tabor into battle. When Barak attacked, the LORD threw Sisera and all his charioteers and warriors into a panic. Then Sisera leaped down from his chariot and escaped on foot. Barak chased the enemy and their chariots all the way to Harosheth-haggoyim, killing all of Sisera's warriors. Not a single one was left alive.

Meanwhile, Sisera ran to the tent of Jael, the wife of Heber the Kenite, because Heber's family was on friendly terms with King Jabin of Hazor. Jael went out to meet Sisera and said to him, "Come into my tent, sir. Come in. Don't be afraid." So he went into her tent, and she covered him with a blanket.

"Please give me some water," he said. "I'm thirsty." So she gave him some milk to drink and covered him again.

"Stand at the door of the tent," he told her. "If anybody comes and asks you if there is anyone here, say no."

But when Sisera fell asleep from exhaustion, Jael quietly crept up to him with a hammer and tent peg. Then she drove the tent peg through his temple and into the ground, and so he died.

Judges 4:14-21

Related Texts: Judges 3:12-30; 5:13-31; 1 Samuel 12:8-11; Hebrews 11:32-34

Weird or What?

Even though the Israelites had several different judges, they experienced the same events with each judge. These events can be seen in five stages:

Stage 1: SIN—when the Israelites left God and returned to worship idols.

Stage 2: OPPRESSION—because of their sin, God allowed surrounding nations to rule over the Israelites.

Stage 3: REPENT—because of the oppression and pain, the Israelites would repent and turn back to God.

Stage 4: SAVED—after they repented, God would provide a judge to save them from the ruling nations.

Stage 5: PEACE—then there was a time of peace when the Israelites would worship God and stay out of trouble.

But before long the cycle would start again with SIN.

Do you have any destructive cycles that begin with sin? If so, is there anyone who can help you break that cycle?

done ☐

14 JULY

CHECK IT OUT

When an angel appeared to Samson's mother and told her she was going to have a special son, it wasn't the last time God used an angel to announce a coming birth. Hundreds of years later an angel told the virgin Mary she was going to have a child unlike anyone the world had ever seen. God used Mary to bring His Son into this world.

Check out Luke 1:30-32: "Don't be frightened, Mary," the angel told her, "for God has decided to bless you! You will become pregnant and have a son, and you are to name him Jesus. He will be very great and will be called the Son of the Most High. And the Lord God will give him the throne of his ancestor David."

Our world hasn't been the same since that historic moment. There's a big difference between Samson and Jesus. One was only a man; the other, a God-man. Take a minute to thank God for entering the world just as you did—because He did; He came as a human and understands everything about you!

The Birth of Samson the Strongman

Again the Israelites did what was evil in the LORD's sight, so the LORD handed them over to the Philistines, who kept them in subjection for forty years.

In those days, a man named Manoah from the tribe of Dan lived in the town of Zorah. His wife was unable to become pregnant, and they had no children. The angel of the LORD appeared to Manoah's wife and said, "Even though you have been unable to have children, you will soon become pregnant and give birth to a son. You must not drink wine or any other alcoholic drink or eat any forbidden food. You will become pregnant and give birth to a son, and his hair must never be cut. For he will be dedicated to God as a Nazirite from birth. He will rescue Israel from the Philistines."...

When her son was born, they named him Samson. And the LORD blessed him as he grew up. And in Mahaneh-dan, which is located between the towns of Zorah and Eshtaol, the Spirit of the LORD began to take hold of him....

Samson was Israel's judge for twenty years, while the Philistines ruled the land.

Judges 13:1-5,24-25; 15:20

Related Texts: Genesis 25:21-24; Numbers 6:1-21; Judges 14-15; Luke 1

done ☐

Samson and Delilah

Later Samson fell in love with a woman named Delilah, who lived in the valley of Sorek. The leaders of the Philistines went to her and said, "Find out from Samson what makes him so strong and how he can be overpowered and tied up securely. Then each of us will give you eleven hundred pieces of silver."

So Delilah said to Samson, "Please tell me what makes you so strong and what it would take to tie you up securely."

Samson replied, "If I am tied up with seven new bowstrings that have not yet been dried, I will be as weak as anyone else."

So the Philistine leaders brought Delilah seven new bowstrings, and she tied Samson up with them. She had hidden some men in one of the rooms of her house, and she cried out, "Samson! The Philistines have come to capture you!" But Samson snapped the bowstrings as if they were string that had been burned in a fire. So the secret of his strength was not discovered.

Judges 16:4-9

Related Texts: Judges 14–15; Proverbs 5; 6:20–7:27; 31:1-3; 2 Timothy 2:20-23

Personality Plus

Samson

Samson is known for being a man with great strength and unique abilities. Why God chose to bless his strength by the length of his hair is a mystery. But God works in strange ways.

As you read today and will read tomorrow, Samson hung around and confided in the wrong person. Delilah broke his trust; and Samson lost his hair, his strength, and his leadership.

Samson's life can provide us a learning example. God gave him many gifts with a potential for great things. But Samson made bad decisions and aligned himself with the wrong people. Think about who you hang around today and what kind of influence they have on your life. Are they keeping you from using God's gift in your life?

done ☐

If you love me...

CATCH THIS

After reading about Delilah's manipulation, it sure doesn't seem as though the tactics have changed very much over a few thousand years. Today her line is still famous: "If you love me you'll..." What seems to be an obvious and manipulating line has caused a lot of pain over the years.

Unfortunately, the line may "win" for the manipulator, but the person who gives in usually loses. Samson lost "big time." You will too if you feel pressured to do something you don't want to do. If you hear this, "If you really love me you'll... have sex with me... steal for me... lie for me... et cetera," beware! True love for another person doesn't take selfish advantage. If someone really loves you, he or she will respect and honor your feelings. Being used is no fun.

Evaluate your relationships. Are you being used? Are you using anyone? What can you do to put a stop to it today?

The Philistines Blind Samson

Then Delilah pouted, "How can you say you love me when you don't confide in me? You've made fun of me three times now, and you still haven't told me what makes you so strong!" So day after day she nagged him until he couldn't stand it any longer.

Finally, Samson told her his secret. "My hair has never been cut," he confessed, "for I was dedicated to God as a Nazirite from birth. If my head were shaved, my strength would leave me, and I would become as weak as anyone else."

Delilah realized he had finally told her the truth, so she sent for the Philistine leaders. "Come back one more time," she said, "for he has told me everything." So the Philistine leaders returned and brought the money with them. Delilah lulled Samson to sleep with his head in her lap, and she called in a man to shave off his hair, making his capture certain. And his strength left him. Then she cried out, "Samson! The Philistines have come to capture you!"

When he woke up, he thought, "I will do as before and shake myself free." But he didn't realize the LORD had left him.

So the Philistines captured him and gouged out his eyes. They took him to Gaza, where he was bound with bronze chains and made to grind grain in the prison. But before long his hair began to grow back.

Judges 16:15-21

Related Texts: Numbers 6:2-21; 30:1-2; Proverbs 11:13; 20:19; Ecclesiastes 5:4-6; Luke 12:47-48

done ☐

Samson's Revenge

The Philistine leaders held a great festival, offering sacrifices and praising their god, Dagon. They said, "Our god has given us victory over our enemy Samson!"...

Half drunk by now, the people demanded, "Bring out Samson so he can perform for us!" So he was brought from the prison and made to stand at the center of the temple, between the two pillars supporting the roof. Samson said to the servant who was leading him by the hand, "Place my hands against the two pillars. I want to rest against them." The temple was completely filled with people. All the Philistine leaders were there, and there were about three thousand on the roof who were watching Samson and making fun of him.

Then Samson prayed to the LORD, "Sovereign LORD, remember me again. O God, please strengthen me one more time so that I may pay back the Philistines for the loss of my eyes." Then Samson put his hands on the center pillars of the temple and pushed against them with all his might. "Let me die with the Philistines," he prayed. And the temple crashed down on the Philistine leaders and all the people. So he killed more people when he died than he had during his entire lifetime.

Judges 16:23,25-30

Related Texts: Psalm 3; Isaiah 1:24; Jeremiah 5:7-9,29; 9:9; Hebrews 11:32-34

Weird or What?

Samson is written about in the Bible more than any of the other judges, but he was the least likely of all judges to be morally qualified for his leadership position. Also he was the only judge who didn't bring the Israelites any lasting relief from their oppressed condition.

So why does Samson get so much attention? It's not known why you know more about Samson than you do Judge Ibzan, but it's good to know God uses people who don't have it all together. Does that sound like you?

You're not perfect either, but God can still do great things in and through your life.

Naomi and Ruth: Love and Loyalty

JUST a THOUGHT

"Be on the lookout for God's reward in your life. He rewards faithfulness to himself and to His creations (others).

In the days when the judges ruled in Israel, a man from Bethlehem in Judah left the country because of a severe famine. He took his wife and two sons and went to live in the country of Moab. The man's name was Elimelech, and his wife was Naomi. Their two sons were Mahlon and Kilion. They were Ephrathites from Bethlehem in the land of Judah. During their stay in Moab, Elimelech died and Naomi was left with her two sons. The two sons married Moabite women. One married a woman named Orpah, and the other a woman named Ruth. But about ten years later, both Mahlon and Kilion died. This left Naomi alone, without her husband or sons.

Then Naomi heard in Moab that the LORD had blessed his people in Judah by giving them good crops again. So Naomi and her daughters-in-law got ready to leave Moab to return to her homeland. With her two daughters-in-law she set out from the place where she had been living, and they took the road that would lead them back to Judah.

But on the way, Naomi said to her two daughters-in-law, "Go back to your mothers' homes instead of coming with me. And may the LORD reward you for your kindness to your husbands and to me. May the LORD bless you with the security of another marriage." Then she kissed them good-bye, and they all broke down and wept. . . .

But Ruth replied, "Don't ask me to leave you and turn back. I will go wherever you go and live wherever you live. Your people will be my people, and your God will be my God. I will die where you die and will be buried there. May the Lord punish me severely if I allow anything but death to separate us!". . .

So Naomi returned from Moab, accompanied by her daughter-in-law Ruth, the young Moabite woman. They arrived in Bethlehem at the beginning of the barley harvest. *Ruth 1:1-9,16-17,22*

Related Texts: 2 Samuel 3:14-16; Proverbs 20:6; Song of Songs 8:6-7; 1 Corinthians 13

 done ☐

Ruth Meets Boaz

Now there was a wealthy and influential man in Bethlehem named Boaz, who was a relative of Naomi's husband, Elimelech. One day Ruth said to Naomi, "Let me go out into the fields to gather leftover grain behind anyone who will let me do it." And Naomi said, "All right, my daughter, go ahead." So Ruth went out to gather grain behind the harvesters. And as it happened, she found herself working in a field that belonged to Boaz, the relative of her father-in-law, Elimelech. . . .

Boaz went over and said to Ruth, "Listen, my daughter. Stay right here with us when you gather grain; don't go to any other fields. Stay right behind the women working in my field. . . .

Ruth fell at his feet and thanked him warmly. "Why are you being so kind to me?" she asked. "I am only a foreigner."

"Yes, I know," Boaz replied. "But I also know about the love and kindness you have shown your mother-in-law since the death of your husband. I have heard how you left your father and mother and your own land to live here among complete strangers. May the LORD, the God of Israel, under whose wings you have come to take refuge, reward you fully."

Ruth 2:1-3,8,10-12

Related Texts: Leviticus 25:25-27,49-50; Psalm 91; Jeremiah 32:6-14

Weird or What?

Gleaning was the act of gathering food left from a harvest.

Gleaners would follow the field workers and pick up dropped or leftover food. It was a law that the poor and visiting travelers could glean the fallen food or grain from a field. God always wanted provisions made for those who were less fortunate or didn't have the availability to own or buy.

God has given you many gifts and abilities that you could share with people in need. How can you distribute some of your excess to those who are not as fortunate as you?

done ☐

Personality Plus

Ruth

As you can tell by your reading, Ruth was a true friend. She was unselfish and deeply committed to Naomi. She obviously loved Naomi and enjoyed her company. Their relationship is a great example of what friendship means.

As you read about Ruth and Naomi, you might think about your relationships and the commitments you and your friends make to one another. Is there strength beyond the fun you have? Would pain devastate your relationship?

Take an inventory of your friendships and see what you need from a friend and how you can be a better friend.

Ruth Proposes Marriage to Boaz

One day Naomi said to Ruth, "My daughter, it's time that I found a permanent home for you, so that you will be provided for. Boaz is a close relative of ours, and he's been very kind by letting you gather grain with his workers. Tonight he will be winnowing barley at the threshing floor. Now do as I tell you—take a bath and put on perfume and dress in your nicest clothes. Then go to the threshing floor, but don't let Boaz see you until he has finished his meal. Be sure to notice where he lies down; then go and uncover his feet and lie down there. He will tell you what to do."...

After Boaz had finished his meal and was in good spirits, he lay down beside the heap of grain and went to sleep. Then Ruth came quietly, uncovered his feet, and lay down. Around midnight, Boaz suddenly woke up and turned over. He was surprised to find a woman lying at his feet! "Who are you?" he demanded.

"I am your servant Ruth," she replied. "Spread the corner of your covering over me, for you are my family redeemer."

"The Lord bless you, my daughter!" Boaz exclaimed. "You are showing more family loyalty now than ever by not running after a younger man, whether rich or poor. Now don't worry about a thing, my daughter. I will do what is necessary, for everyone in town knows you are an honorable woman."

Ruth 3:1-4,7-11

Related Texts: Genesis 38:8-10; Deuteronomy 25:5-10; Hebrews 13:4

done ☐

Ruth Marries Boaz

Then Boaz said to the leaders and to the crowd standing around, "You are witnesses that today I have bought from Naomi all the property of Elimelech, Kilion, and Mahlon. And with the land I have acquired Ruth, the Moabite widow of Mahlon, to be my wife. This way she can have a son to carry on the family name of her dead husband and to inherit the family property here in his hometown. You are all witnesses today."

Then the leaders and all the people standing there replied, "We are witnesses! May the LORD make the woman who is now coming into your home like Rachel and Leah, from whom all the nation of Israel descended! May you be great in Ephrathah and famous in Bethlehem. And may the LORD give you descendants by this young woman who will be like those of our ancestor Perez, the son of Tamar and Judah."

So Boaz married Ruth and took her home to live with him. When he slept with her, the LORD enabled her to become pregnant, and she gave birth to a son. And the women of the town said to Naomi, "Praise the Lord who has given you a family redeemer today! May he be famous in Israel. May this child restore your youth and care for you in your old age. For he is the son of your daughter-in-law who loves you so much and who has been better to you than seven sons!"

Ruth 4:9-15

Related Texts: Genesis 29:31–30:4; 38; Micah 5:2; Matthew 1:1-6

Give it a try

Ruth was a woman who expressed kindness. This quality of kindness is rare in today's world. List three specific acts of kindness you can do today to make a difference in someone's life.

1.
2.
3.

done ☐

In OTHER Words

Eternal life

Eternal life is life beyond our bodies. It is timeless and has no beginning and no end. God is eternal. God created the earth and human beings, both of which had a beginning and will have an end.

Eternal life is the life with God after ours ends. This life is promised to those who, by faith, believe Jesus' death paid for their sins and made them right with God. Those made right will have eternal life, while the unrighteous will have eternal punishment. Basically, eternal life is longer than you could ever imagine. The question for those who don't believe isn't How long is eternal? but Doesn't eternal life in heaven sound a lot better than eternal life in hell?

What do you say?

I Am: The Bread of Life

They replied, "You must show us a miraculous sign if you want us to believe in you. What will you do for us? After all, our ancestors ate manna while they journeyed through the wilderness! As the Scriptures say, 'Moses gave them bread from heaven to eat.' "

Jesus said, "I assure you, Moses didn't give them bread from heaven. My Father did. And now he offers you the true bread from heaven. The true bread of God is the one who comes down from heaven and gives life to the world."

"Sir," they said, "give us that bread every day of our lives."

Jesus replied, "I am the bread of life. No one who comes to me will ever be hungry again. Those who believe in me will never thirst. But you haven't believed in me even though you have seen me. However, those the Father has given me will come to me, and I will never reject them. For I have come down from heaven to do the will of God who sent me, not to do what I want. And this is the will of God, that I should not lose even one of all those he has given me, but that I should raise them to eternal life at the last day. For it is my Father's will that all who see his Son and believe in him should have eternal life—that I should raise them at the last day."

John 6:30-40

Related Texts: Deuteronomy 8:2; Proverbs 30:7-9; John 6:25-59; 1 Corinthians 10:16-17; Revelation 2:17

done ☐

I Am: The Light of the World

Jesus said to the people, "I am the light of the world. If you follow me, you won't be stumbling through the darkness, because you will have the light that leads to life."...

As Jesus was walking along, he saw a man who had been blind from birth. "Teacher," his disciples asked him, "why was this man born blind? Was it a result of his own sins or those of his parents?"

"It was not because of his sins or his parents' sins," Jesus answered. "He was born blind so the power of God could be seen in him. All of us must quickly carry out the tasks assigned us by the one who sent me, because there is little time left before the night falls and all work comes to an end. But while I am still here in the world, I am the light of the world."

Then he spit on the ground, made mud with the saliva, and smoothed the mud over the blind man's eyes. He told him, "Go and wash in the pool of Siloam" (Siloam means Sent). So the man went and washed, and came back seeing!...

Life itself was in him, and this life gives light to everyone. The light shines through the darkness, and the darkness can never extinguish it.

John 8:12; 9:1-7; 1:4-5

Related Texts: Psalm 27:1; John 1:1-14; 3:19-22; 12:44-46; 1 John 1:1-7; Revelation 21:2-27

JUST a THOUGHT

Don't be blind to what God can do in and through your life. Here's a good principle to remember: You do the possible with faith that God will do the impossible.

done ☐

One Minute Memory

The thief's purpose is to steal and kill and destroy. My purpose is to give life in all its fullness.

John 10:10

I Am: The Gate for the Sheep

"I assure you, anyone who sneaks over the wall of a sheepfold, rather than going through the gate, must surely be a thief and a robber! For a shepherd enters through the gate. The gatekeeper opens the gate for him, and the sheep hear his voice and come to him. He calls his own sheep by name and leads them out. After he has gathered his own flock, he walks ahead of them, and they follow him because they recognize his voice. They won't follow a stranger; they will run from him because they don't recognize his voice."

Those who heard Jesus use this illustration didn't understand what he meant, so he explained it to them. "I assure you, I am the gate for the sheep," he said. "All others who came before me were thieves and robbers. But the true sheep did not listen to them. Yes, I am the gate. Those who come in through me will be saved. Wherever they go, they will find green pastures. The thief's purpose is to steal and kill and destroy. My purpose is to give life in all its fullness."

John 10:1-10

Related Texts: Psalm 118:17-21; Matthew 7:13-14; 25:1-13; Luke 13:23-29; John 14

done ☐

I Am: The Good Shepherd

"I am the good shepherd. The good shepherd lays down his life for the sheep. A hired hand will run when he sees a wolf coming. He will leave the sheep because they aren't his and he isn't their shepherd. And so the wolf attacks them and scatters the flock. The hired hand runs away because he is merely hired and has no real concern for the sheep.

"I am the good shepherd; I know my own sheep, and they know me, just as my Father knows me and I know the Father. And I lay down my life for the sheep. I have other sheep, too, that are not in this sheepfold. I must bring them also, and they will listen to my voice; and there will be one flock with one shepherd.

"The Father loves me because I lay down my life that I may have it back again. No one can take my life from me. I lay down my life voluntarily. For I have the right to lay it down when I want to and also the power to take it again. For my Father has given me this command."

John 10:11-18

He personally carried away our sins in his own body on the cross so we can be dead to sin and live for what is right. You have been healed by his wounds! Once you were wandering like lost sheep. But now you have turned to your Shepherd, the Guardian of your souls.

1 Peter 2:24-25

Related Texts: Psalm 23; Isaiah 40:10-11; Zechariah 11:4-17; Matthew 25:31-46; Luke 15:3-7; Hebrews 13:20-21

Weird or What?

There are over eighty animals mentioned throughout the Bible.

Sheep appear more frequently than any other animal, over seven hundred times.

Sheep are not smart animals. Have you ever seen one doing tricks in a circus? Probably not. They are helpless animals in need of a shepherd to lead them to water and food. We are a lot like sheep. Sometimes we're dumb and get into trouble. We also have a need for a shepherd. That's why Jesus described himself as the "Good Shepherd." He takes care of His sheep... that means ewe... which isn't baaaad news.

You're a whole lot smarter than sheep if you follow the Shepherd today.

What's it Mean?

In today's reading you'll see the word Messiah. People in Old Testament times believed that God would send Israel a deliverer who would rule as king, restore the divided kingdom, and explain God's plan. This person would be called the Messiah.

Today, Christians accept Jesus as God's Son and the promised Messiah. But during Jesus' time, people didn't believe He fit the prophesied description of the Messiah. Jesus was charged with blasphemy, rejected by the Jewish leaders, and hung on a cross.

One of the main differences between present-day Jews and Christians is that many Jewish people still don't believe Jesus was the Messiah. They are still waiting for a Messiah. How about you? What are you waiting for? Do you believe Jesus was who He claimed to be? God's Son? The Messiah?

I AM: THE RESURRECTION AND THE LIFE

A man named Lazarus was sick. He lived in Bethany with his sisters, Mary and Martha. This is the Mary who poured the expensive perfume on the Lord's feet and wiped them with her hair. Her brother, Lazarus, was sick. So the two sisters sent a message to Jesus telling him, "Lord, the one you love is very sick."

But when Jesus heard about it he said, "Lazarus's sickness will not end in death. No, it is for the glory of God. I, the Son of God, will receive glory from this."...

When Jesus arrived at Bethany, he was told that Lazarus had already been in his grave for four days....

Martha said to Jesus, "Lord, if you had been here, my brother would not have died. But even now I know that God will give you whatever you ask."

Jesus told her, "Your brother will rise again."

"Yes," Martha said, "when everyone else rises, on resurrection day."

Jesus told her, "I am the resurrection and the life. Those who believe in me, even though they die like everyone else, will live again. They are given eternal life for believing in me and will never perish. Do you believe this, Martha?"

"Yes, Lord," she told him. "I have always believed you are the Messiah, the Son of God, the one who has come into the world from God."...

Then Jesus shouted, "Lazarus, come out!" And Lazarus came out, bound in graveclothes, his face wrapped in a headcloth. Jesus told them, "Unwrap him and let him go!"

John 11:1-4,17,21-27,43-44

Related Texts: Deuteronomy 32:39; John 5:19-26; Romans 5-6; 2 Timothy 1:8-10; 1 John 1:1-3

done ☐

I Am: The Way and the Truth and the Life

"Don't be troubled. You trust God, now trust in me. There are many rooms in my Father's home, and I am going to prepare a place for you. If this were not so, I would tell you plainly. When everything is ready, I will come and get you, so that you will always be with me where I am. And you know where I am going and how to get there."

"No, we don't know, Lord," Thomas said. "We haven't any idea where you are going, so how can we know the way?"

Jesus told him, "I am the way, the truth, and the life. No one can come to the Father except through me. If you had known who I am, then you would have known who my Father is. From now on you know him and have seen him!"

Philip said, "Lord, show us the Father and we will be satisfied."

Jesus replied, "Philip, don't you even yet know who I am, even after all the time I have been with you? Anyone who has seen me has seen the Father! So why are you asking to see him?"

John 14:1-9

Related Texts: Psalm 96; John 1:1-18; 3:13-16; Acts 4:12; Hebrews 10:19-22

One Minute Memory

I am the way, the truth, and the life. No one can come to the Father except through me.

John 14:6

done ☐

BIG TIMe WoRd

OBEY

This book is filled with incredible examples of people who obeyed God. The Israelites, as unfaithful as they were, were God's special nation because Abraham obeyed God. Biblical heroes, like Abraham, weren't perfect, but they obeyed.

God loves obedience. Obedience helps us to live according to God's plans. God is delighted when we choose to obey him. Obeying God is more than knowing the Bible; it's living every day by faith that God is ultimately in control and knows what's best for your life. Try pleasing God today by obeying one of His instructions.

I Am: The True Vine

"I am the true vine, and my Father is the gardener. He cuts off every branch that doesn't produce fruit, and he prunes the branches that do bear fruit so they will produce even more. You have already been pruned for greater fruitfulness by the message I have given you. Remain in me, and I will remain in you. For a branch cannot produce fruit if it is severed from the vine, and you cannot be fruitful apart from me.

"Yes, I am the vine; you are the branches. Those who remain in me, and I in them, will produce much fruit. For apart from me you can do nothing. Anyone who parts from me is thrown away like a useless branch and withers. Such branches are gathered into a pile to be burned. But if you stay joined to me and my words remain in you, you may ask any request you like, and it will be granted! My true disciples produce much fruit. This brings great glory to my Father.

"I have loved you even as the Father has loved me. Remain in my love. When you obey me, you remain in my love, just as I obey my Father and remain in his love. I have told you this so that you will be filled with my joy. Yes, your joy will overflow!"

John 15:1-11

Related Texts: Psalm 80:8-19; Isaiah 5:1-7; 27:2-6; Luke 6:43-45; Galatians 5:22-23; Colossians 1:3-12

done ☐

Hannah Prays for a Son

There was a man named Elkanah who lived in Ramah in the hill country of Ephraim. He was the son of Jeroham and grandson of Elihu, from the family of Tohu and the clan of Zuph. Elkanah had two wives, Hannah and Peninnah. Peninnah had children, while Hannah did not.

Each year Elkanah and his family would travel to Shiloh to worship and sacrifice to the LORD Almighty at the Tabernacle. The priests of the LORD at that time were the two sons of Eli—Hophni and Phinehas. On the day Elkanah presented his sacrifice, he would give portions of the sacrifice to Peninnah and each of her children. But he gave Hannah a special portion because he loved her very much, even though the LORD had given her no children. But Peninnah made fun of Hannah because the LORD had closed her womb. . . .

Once when they were at Shiloh, Hannah went over to the Tabernacle after supper to pray to the LORD. Eli the priest was sitting at his customary place beside the entrance. Hannah was in deep anguish, crying bitterly as she prayed to the LORD. And she made this vow: "O LORD Almighty, if you will look down upon my sorrow and answer my prayer and give me a son, then I will give him back to you. He will be yours for his entire lifetime, and as a sign that he has been dedicated to the LORD, his hair will never be cut."

1 Samuel 1:1-6,9a-11

Related Texts: Genesis 11:29-30; 25:21; 29:31; Psalm 113:9; Isaiah 54:1; Luke 1:4-22; 23:28-30; Hebrews 11:11

Give it a try

Hannah asked God for something that seemed impossible. Write one prayer request that might seem impossible for God to answer. Let God know the desires within your heart.

It seems impossible, but, God, please...

done ☐

30 JULY

Samuel: Hannah's Firstborn

The entire family got up early the next morning and went to worship the LORD once more. Then they returned home to Ramah. When Elkanah slept with Hannah, the Lord remembered her request, and in due time she gave birth to a son. She named him Samuel, for she said, "I asked the LORD for him."

The next year Elkanah, Peninnah, and their children went on their annual trip to offer a sacrifice to the LORD. But Hannah did not go. She told her husband, "Wait until the baby is weaned. Then I will take him to the Tabernacle and leave him there with the LORD permanently."...

"Stay here for now, and may the LORD help you keep your promise." So she stayed home and nursed the baby.

When the child was weaned, Hannah took him to the Tabernacle in Shiloh. They brought along a three-year-old bull for the sacrifice and half a bushel of flour and some wine. After sacrificing the bull, they took the child to Eli. "Sir, do you remember me?" Hannah asked. "I am the woman who stood here several years ago praying to the LORD. I asked the LORD to give me this child, and he has given me my request. Now I am giving him to the LORD, and he will belong to the LORD his whole life." And they worshiped the LORD there.

1 Samuel 1:19-22,23b-28

Related Texts: Genesis 8:1; 19:29; 30:22; Exodus 2:24; Luke 1:23-45; Acts 10:25-31; Revelation 16:19; 18:5

Give it a try

It's not uncommon for us to ask God for something and then not thank Him for answering our prayers. Hannah expressed her thankfulness by giving Samuel back to God for His service.

If any of your prayers have been answered, thank God for hearing your prayers and responding. Express your thanksgiving in a letter to God.

Dear God:

Love,

done ☐

Samuel: Prophet and Judge

Now the sons of Eli were scoundrels who had no respect for the LORD. . . .

Now Samuel, though only a boy, was the LORD's helper. He wore a linen tunic just like that of a priest. Each year his mother made a small coat for him and brought it to him when she came with her husband for the sacrifice. Before they returned home, Eli would bless Elkanah and his wife and say, "May the LORD give you other children to take the place of this one she gave to the LORD." And the LORD gave Hannah three sons and two daughters. Meanwhile, Samuel grew up in the presence of the LORD. . . .

As Samuel grew up, the LORD was with him, and everything Samuel said was wise and helpful. All the people of Israel from one end of the land to the other knew that Samuel was confirmed as a prophet of the LORD. The LORD continued to appear at Shiloh and gave messages to Samuel there at the Tabernacle. And Samuel's words went out to all the people of Israel. . . .

Samuel continued as Israel's judge for the rest of his life. Each year he traveled around, setting up his court first at Bethel, then at Gilgal, and then at Mizpah. He judged the people of Israel at each of these places. Then he would return to his home at Ramah, and he would hear cases there, too. And Samuel built an altar to the LORD at Ramah.

1 Samuel 2:12,18-21; 3:19-21; 7:15-17

Related Texts: Genesis 4:25-26; Deuteronomy 18:15-19; Joshua 21:45; Luke 1:13-17

JUST a THOUGHT

You're never too young to love God and grow up in His ways.

done ☐

August

This book... is the best gift God has given to man... But for it we could not know right from wrong.

Abraham Lincoln
(1809–1865)
United States President

Israel Asks for a King

As Samuel grew old, he appointed his sons to be judges over Israel. Joel and Abijah, his oldest sons, held court in Beersheba. But they were not like their father, for they were greedy for money. They accepted bribes and perverted justice.

Finally, the leaders of Israel met at Ramah to discuss the matter with Samuel. "Look," they told him, "you are now old, and your sons are not like you. Give us a king like all the other nations have."

Samuel was very upset with their request and went to the LORD for advice. "Do as they say," the LORD replied, "for it is me they are rejecting, not you. They don't want me to be their king any longer. Ever since I brought them from Egypt they have continually forsaken me and followed other gods. And now they are giving you the same treatment. Do as they ask, but solemnly warn them about how a king will treat them."

So Samuel passed on the LORD's warning to the people....

But the people refused to listen to Samuel's warning. "Even so, we still want a king," they said. "We want to be like the nations around us. Our king will govern us and lead us into battle."

So Samuel told the LORD what the people had said, and the LORD replied, "Do as they say, and give them a king."

1 Samuel 8:1-10,19-22a

Related Texts: Deuteronomy 17:14-20; 1 Samuel 8:11-18; Isaiah 9:6; Jeremiah 10:1-10; 1 Timothy 1:17

BIG TIME WORD

GREED

Throughout the Bible we see greed hurting people and keeping them from godliness. Greed takes our hearts away from God and puts our eyes, thoughts, and desires on the object of the greed. If we are greedy for money, we will think more about money and how to get it than we will think about God.

We can replace greed with confidence that God has a plan for our lives and will provide for us. Right now, identify the object of your greed. Realize how worthless it's going to be when you're with God. The object of your greed will eventually burn. No matter how great it is, **it's not worth taking your eyes off God.**

done ☐

Personality Plus

Samuel

Samuel was the last of the judges of Israel and the first of the prophets. His birth was a gift from God to Hannah, who asked Him for a child. Samuel's name actually means "asked of God."

As a young child, Samuel was in God's presence. It was obvious God wanted to use him in great ways, and He used Eli the priest to help Samuel learn God's standards for living.

It's good to see an example of God preparing a child to do His work. Allow Samuel to remind you that you're never too young for God to begin working in your life. Spend a minute and ask God to send the right person (like Eli) to train and help you grow stronger in your faith.

Saul: The First King of Israel

Later Samuel called all the people of Israel to meet before the LORD at Mizpah. And he gave them this message from the LORD, the God of Israel: "I brought you from Egypt and rescued you from the Egyptians and from all of the nations that were oppressing you. But though I have done so much for you, you have rejected me and said, 'We want a king instead!' Now, therefore, present yourselves before the LORD by tribes and clans."

So Samuel called the tribal leaders together before the LORD, and the tribe of Benjamin was chosen. Then he brought each family of the tribe of Benjamin before the LORD, and the family of the Matrites was chosen. And finally Saul son of Kish was chosen from among them. But when they looked for him, he had disappeared! So they asked the LORD, "Where is he?"

And the LORD replied, "He is hiding among the baggage." So they found him and brought him out, and he stood head and shoulders above anyone else.

Then Samuel said to all the people, "This is the man the LORD has chosen as your king. No one in all Israel is his equal!"

And all the people shouted, "Long live the king!"

Then Samuel told the people what the rights and duties of a king were. He wrote them down on a scroll and placed it before the LORD. Then Samuel sent the people home again.

1 Samuel 10:17-25

Related Texts: Deuteronomy 17:14-20; 1 Samuel 9:1-10:16; 11-14; John 12:12-15

done ☐

The Lord Rejects Saul as King

One day Samuel said to Saul, "I anointed you king of Israel because the LORD told me to. Now listen to this message from the LORD! This is what the LORD Almighty says: 'I have decided to settle accounts with the nation of Amalek for opposing Israel when they came from Egypt. Now go and completely destroy the entire Amalekite nation—men, women, children, babies, cattle, sheep, camels, and donkeys.' " ...

Then Saul slaughtered the Amalekites from Havilah all the way to Shur, east of Egypt. . . .

Saul and his men spared Agag's life and kept the best of the sheep and cattle, the fat calves and lambs—everything, in fact, that appealed to them. They destroyed only what was worthless or of poor quality.

Then the LORD said to Samuel, "I am sorry that I ever made Saul king, for he has not been loyal to me and has again refused to obey me." . . . .

When Samuel finally found him, Saul greeted him cheerfully. "May the LORD bless you," he said. "I have carried out the LORD's command!" . . . .

But Samuel replied, "What is more pleasing to the LORD: your burnt offerings and sacrifices or your obedience to his voice? Obedience is far better than sacrifice. Listening to him is much better than offering the fat of rams. Rebellion is as bad as the sin of witchcraft, and stubbornness is as bad as worshiping idols. So because you have rejected the word of the LORD, he has rejected you from being king."

1 Samuel 15:1-3a,7,9-11a,13,22-23

Related Texts: Exodus 17:8-16; Deuteronomy 25:17-19; Micah 6:6-8; Luke 16:10-13

CATCH THIS

God has placed a higher level of moral responsibility on Christian leaders. Don't misunderstand. God wants all His followers to live right and follow Him, but He wants His leaders to set godly examples. God doesn't expect leaders to be perfect; He knows better. But leaders are watched by those who follow.

Saul, who was chosen to be king and leader, made God angry because he disobeyed God and lied to Samuel. These are not the qualities expressed by godly leaders. A strong leader will set his heart to obey and please God.

The good news of God's love is confusing to others if Christian leaders aren't living godly lives. If you are a leader in your youth group or church, be reminded that you are modeling Christianity. Whether or not you like it, people judge Christianity by its leaders. Christianity needs you to be a faithful leader today.

You're not too young to be serving God.

done ☐

Samuel Anoints David as King

One Minute Memory

People judge by outward appearance, but the LORD looks at a person's thoughts and intentions.

1 Samuel 16:7b

Finally, the LORD said to Samuel, "You have mourned long enough for Saul. I have rejected him as king of Israel. Now fill your horn with olive oil and go to Bethlehem. Find a man named Jesse who lives there, for I have selected one of his sons to be my new king."...

When they arrived, Samuel took one look at Eliab and thought, "Surely this is the LORD's anointed!" But the LORD said to Samuel, "Don't judge by his appearance or height, for I have rejected him. The LORD doesn't make decisions the way you do! People judge by outward appearance, but the LORD looks at a person's thoughts and intentions."...

Next Jesse summoned Shammah, but Samuel said, "Neither is this the one the LORD has chosen." In the same way all seven of Jesse's sons were presented to Samuel. But Samuel said to Jesse, "The LORD has not chosen any of these." Then Samuel asked, "Are these all the sons you have?"

"There is still the youngest," Jesse replied. "But he's out in the fields watching the sheep."

"Send for him at once," Samuel said. "We will not sit down to eat until he arrives."

So Jesse sent for him. He was ruddy and handsome, with pleasant eyes. And the LORD said, "This is the one; anoint him."

So as David stood there among his brothers, Samuel took the olive oil he had brought and poured it on David's head. And the Spirit of the LORD came mightily upon him from that day on. Then Samuel returned to Ramah.

1 Samuel 16:1,6-7,9-13

Related Texts: Psalm 78:70-72; Matthew 5:8; 12:33-35; Luke 6:43-45; Acts 13:21-23

done ☐

AUGUST 5

Goliath Challenges the Armies of Israel

The Philistines now mustered their army for battle and camped between Socoh in Judah and Azekah at Ephes-dammim. Saul countered by gathering his troops near the valley of Elah. So the Philistines and Israelites faced each other on opposite hills, with the valley between them.

Then Goliath, a Philistine champion from Gath, came out of the Philistine ranks to face the forces of Israel. He was a giant of a man, measuring over nine feet tall! He wore a bronze helmet and a coat of mail that weighed 125 pounds. He also wore bronze leggings, and he slung a bronze javelin over his back. The shaft of his spear was as heavy and thick as a weaver's beam, tipped with an iron spearhead that weighed fifteen pounds. An armor bearer walked ahead of him carrying a huge shield.

Goliath stood and shouted across to the Israelites, "Do you need a whole army to settle this? Choose someone to fight for you, and I will represent the Philistines. We will settle this dispute in single combat! If your man is able to kill me, then we will be your slaves. But if I kill him, you will be our slaves! I defy the armies of Israel! Send me a man who will fight with me!" When Saul and the Israelites heard this, they were terrified and deeply shaken.

1 Samuel 17:1-11

Related Texts: Numbers 13:26-33; Deuteronomy 11:22-25; Psalm 15; Proverbs 14:27; 15:33; 29:25

Weird or What?

The **armor** that **Goliath** wore **weighed more** than **David's entire body.** David's victory over the giant is just another example of how huge obstacles can be overcome when God is involved.

6 AUGUST

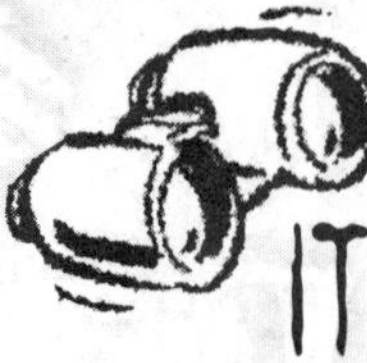

CHECK IT OUT

A lot of people want to tell students they are the "church of tomorrow." They believe God will use you when you're older. That's not true. You're the church of today, and God can use you now! God never gives a command to follow Him tomorrow or when you reach a specific age. God has used young people in the past, like David, and He will continue to use them. Check out what Paul told young Timothy in 1 Timothy 4:12: "Don't let anyone think less of you because you are young. Be an example to all believers in what you teach, in the way you live, in your love, your faith, and your purity."

Your age may be a problem for some, but not for God.

Thank Him for your age and ask Him to do something great with your life today.

David Accepts Goliath's Challenge

"Don't worry about a thing," David told Saul. "I'll go fight this Philistine!"

"Don't be ridiculous!" Saul replied. "There is no way you can go against this Philistine. You are only a boy, and he has been in the army since he was a boy!"

But David persisted. "I have been taking care of my father's sheep," he said. "When a lion or a bear comes to steal a lamb from the flock, I go after it with a club and take the lamb from its mouth. If the animal turns on me, I catch it by the jaw and club it to death. I have done this to both lions and bears, and I'll do it to this pagan Philistine, too, for he has defied the armies of the living God! The LORD who saved me from the claws of the lion and the bear will save me from this Philistine!"

Saul finally consented. "All right, go ahead," he said. "And may the LORD be with you!"...

He picked up five smooth stones from a stream and put them in his shepherd's bag. Then, armed only with his shepherd's staff and sling, he started across to fight Goliath.

1 Samuel 17:32-37,40

Related Texts: Psalms 31:11-18; 97:10; 144; Ephesians 6:10-18; 1 Timothy 4:12

done ☐

David Kills Goliath

Goliath walked out toward David with his shield bearer ahead of him, sneering in contempt at this ruddy-faced boy. "Am I a dog," he roared at David, "that you come at me with a stick?" And he cursed David by the names of his gods. . . .

David shouted in reply, "You come to me with sword, spear, and javelin, but I come to you in the name of the LORD Almighty—the God of the armies of Israel, whom you have defied. Today the LORD will conquer you, and I will kill you and cut off your head. And then I will give the dead bodies of your men to the birds and wild animals, and the whole world will know that there is a God in Israel! And everyone will know that the LORD does not need weapons to rescue his people. It is his battle, not ours. The LORD will give you to us!"

As Goliath moved closer to attack, David quickly ran out to meet him. Reaching into his shepherd's bag and taking out a stone, he hurled it from his sling and hit the Philistine in the forehead. The stone sank in, and Goliath stumbled and fell face downward to the ground.

1 Samuel 17:41-43,45-49

Related Texts: 2 Samuel 21:15-22; Psalm 27; Hebrews 11:32-34

JUST a THOUGHT

A little stone with big faith can conquer a big giant with a little god.

done ☐

Personality Plus

Jonathan

Jonathan was loyal to God and to his friends. His friendship with David is one of the great models for friendship found within the Bible. Jonathan's ultimate loyalty started with God. Because of his strong relationship with God, Jonathan was able to gain God's wisdom when he was caught in a terrible spot between his father and David.

Jonathan is a strong example for us to follow. He was an unselfish and true friend. Friends like Jonathan are difficult to find. If you have a friend who isn't selfish and is loyal to your relationship, make sure you go out of your way to express your appreciation today.

Friendships like this are definitely worth keeping!

Saul Becomes Jealous of David

After David had finished talking with Saul, he met Jonathan, the king's son. There was an immediate bond of love between them, and they became the best of friends. From that day on Saul kept David with him at the palace and wouldn't let him return home. And Jonathan made a special vow to be David's friend, and he sealed the pact by giving him his robe, tunic, sword, bow, and belt.

Whatever Saul asked David to do, David did it successfully. So Saul made him a commander in his army, an appointment that was applauded by the fighting men and officers alike. But something happened when the victorious Israelite army was returning home after David had killed Goliath. Women came out from all the towns along the way to celebrate and to cheer for King Saul, and they sang and danced for joy with tambourines and cymbals. This was their song:

"Saul has killed his thousands,
and David his ten thousands!"

This made Saul very angry. "What's this?" he said. "They credit David with ten thousands and me with only thousands. Next they'll be making him their king!" So from that time on Saul kept a jealous eye on David.

1 Samuel 18:1-9

Related Texts: Proverbs 27:4; Acts 5:12-19; 7:9-10; Romans 13:12-14; 2 Corinthians 11:2; Galatians 5:19-20

done ☐

Saul Tries to Kill David

Saul now urged his servants and his son Jonathan to assassinate David. But Jonathan, because of his close friendship with David, told him what his father was planning. "Tomorrow morning," he warned him, "you must find a hiding place out in the fields. I'll ask my father to go out there with me, and I'll talk to him about you. Then I'll tell you everything I can find out."

The next morning Jonathan spoke with his father about David, saying many good things about him. "Please don't sin against David," Jonathan pleaded. "He's never done anything to harm you. He has always helped you in any way he could. Have you forgotten about the time he risked his life to kill the Philistine giant and how the LORD brought a great victory to Israel as a result? You were certainly happy about it then. Why should you murder an innocent man like David? There is no reason for it at all!"

So Saul listened to Jonathan and vowed, "As surely as the LORD lives, David will not be killed." Afterward Jonathan called David and told him what had happened. Then he took David to see Saul, and everything was as it had been before....

But one day as Saul was sitting at home, the tormenting spirit from the LORD suddenly came upon him again. As David played his harp for the king, Saul hurled his spear at David in an attempt to kill him. But David dodged out of the way and escaped into the night, leaving the spear stuck in the wall.

1 Samuel 19:1-7,9-10

Related Texts: 1 Samuel 19-30; Psalms 52; 54; 57; 59; James 1:13-15

Give it a try

List three qualities you look for in a friend. Next to each of the qualities, come up with an action plan of how you can improve those qualities, in your own life. Be specific about what you need to do and when you're going to start working on them. If you expect those qualities in others, you should have them in your own life as well.

1.
2.
3.

done ☐

JUST a THOUGHT

In Saul's situation his disobedience resulted in a quick death. What are the consequences of disobedience in your life?

The Death of Saul and His Sons

Now the Philistines attacked Israel, forcing the Israelites to flee. Many were slaughtered on the slopes of Mount Gilboa. The Philistines closed in on Saul and his sons, and they killed three of his sons—Jonathan, Abinadab, and Malkishua. The fighting grew very fierce around Saul, and the Philistine archers caught up with him and wounded him severely. Saul groaned to his armor bearer, "Take your sword and run me through before these pagan Philistines come and humiliate me." But his armor bearer was afraid and would not do it. So Saul took his own sword and fell on it. When his armor bearer realized that Saul was dead, he fell on his own sword and died. So Saul and his three sons died there together, bringing his dynasty to an end.

When the Israelites in the Jezreel Valley saw that their army had been routed and that Saul and his sons were dead, they abandoned their towns and fled. So the Philistines moved in and occupied their towns. …

So Saul died because he was unfaithful to the LORD. He failed to obey the LORD's command, and he even consulted a medium instead of asking the LORD for guidance. So the LORD killed him and turned his kingdom over to David son of Jesse.

1 Chronicles 10:1-7,13-1

Related Texts: 1 Samuel 28; 30-31; 2 Samuel 1; 16:15-17:23; Matthew 27:1-5; Acts 16:22-28

done ☐

THE LORD MAKES A COVENANT WITH DAVID

When the LORD had brought peace to the land and King David was settled in his palace, David summoned Nathan the prophet. "Look!" David said. "Here I am living in this beautiful cedar palace, but the Ark of God is out in a tent!"

Nathan replied, "Go ahead and do what you have in mind, for the LORD is with you."

But that same night the LORD said to Nathan,. . .

"Now go and say to my servant David, 'This is what the Lord Almighty says: I chose you to lead my people Israel when you were just a shepherd boy, tending your sheep out in the pasture. I have been with you wherever you have gone, and I have destroyed all your enemies. Now I will make your name famous throughout the earth!. . . And I will keep you safe from all your enemies.

" 'And now the LORD declares that he will build a house for you—a dynasty of kings! For when you die, I will raise up one of your descendants, and I will make his kingdom strong. He is the one who will build a house—a temple—for my name. And I will establish the throne of his kingdom forever. I will be his father, and he will be my son. If he sins, I will use other nations to punish him. But my unfailing love will not be taken from him as I took it from Saul, whom I removed before you. Your dynasty and your kingdom will continue for all time before me, and your throne will be secure forever.' "

2 Samuel 7:1-4,8-9,11b-16

Related Texts: 1 Chronicles 17; Psalms 2; 89; Jeremiah 33:14-26; Romans 1:1-4

What's it Mean?

In today's reading we see God promising great things through David's family. This is one of the prophesies that addresses the birth of Jesus. God promised that a great king would be born through David's family who will live forever and build an eternal kingdom.

The Bible has recorded this specific prophecy through several different prophets and time periods. Hundreds of years later, God used Mary, who was from the family of David, to give birth to Jesus and fulfill this prophecy.

God's plan has worked out and will continue to work out as He intended. If you haven't done so already, take a minute to thank God for His plan and let Him know you want to be a part of the eternal kingdom. He has room for you!

done ☐

12 AUGUST

The Lord Is My Shepherd

The LORD is my shepherd;
I have everything I need.
He lets me rest in green meadows;
he leads me beside peaceful streams.
He renews my strength.
He guides me along right paths,
bringing honor to his name.
Even when I walk
through the dark valley of death,
I will not be afraid,
for you are close beside me.
Your rod and your staff
protect and comfort me.
You prepare a feast for me
in the presence of my enemies.
You welcome me as a guest,
anointing my head with oil.
My cup overflows with blessings.
Surely your goodness and unfailing love will pursue me
all the days of my life,
and I will live in the house of the LORD forever.

Psalm 23:1-6

"I am the good shepherd. The good shepherd lays down his life for the sheep."

John 10:11

Related Texts: Isaiah 40:10-11; Micah 5:2-5; Hebrews 13:20-21; 1 Peter 2:21-25; Revelation 7:15-17

Give it a try

Rewrite and paraphrase Psalm 23 in your own words. Personalize this psalm by using specific examples of how God is your Shepherd.

done ☐

David Commits Adultery with Bathsheba

The following spring, the time of year when kings go to war, David sent Joab and the Israelite army to destroy the Ammonites. In the process they laid siege to the city of Rabbah. But David stayed behind in Jerusalem.

Late one afternoon David got out of bed after taking a nap and went for a stroll on the roof of the palace. As he looked out over the city, he noticed a woman of unusual beauty taking a bath. He sent someone to find out who she was, and he was told, "She is Bathsheba, the daughter of Eliam and the wife of Uriah the Hittite." Then David sent for her; and when she came to the palace, he slept with her. (She had just completed the purification rites after having her menstrual period.) Then she returned home. Later, when Bathsheba discovered that she was pregnant, she sent a message to inform David.

So David sent word to Joab: "Send me Uriah the Hittite." When Uriah arrived, David asked him how Joab and the army were getting along and how the war was progressing. Then he told Uriah, "Go on home and relax." David even sent a gift to Uriah after he had left the palace. But Uriah wouldn't go home. He stayed that night at the palace entrance with some of the king's other servants.

2 Samuel 11:1-9

Related Texts: Deuteronomy 5:18; Job 31:1; Psalm 119:9-16; Proverbs 5-6; 1 Corinthians 6:9-11

CATCH THIS

David was tempted when he saw Bathsheba bathing. This temptation was not a sin. David's sin was acting upon his temptation. He sinned again when he attempted to cover up his first sin. Basically, he blew it!

It's not uncommon for us to be sexually tempted. Sex is everywhere, and it is tempting! But we have something in common with David. We can control our sexual urges. Even though David didn't control his, he could have. God knows we will be tempted, so He created us with self-control.

David was a great king, but he should have left the roof and run from his temptation. The devil uses temptation to take our eyes off God and put them on things that are pleasing to us and not to God.

Today, be thinking of the tempting situations you need to run from. And remember, God has given you the strength to have control over any temptation.

done ☐

JUST a THOUGHT

Another **way** to identify **sin** is "the wrong **use** of a right thing."

David Arranges Uriah's Death

So the next morning David wrote a letter to Joab and gave it to Uriah to deliver. The letter instructed Joab, "Station Uriah on the front lines where the battle is fiercest. Then pull back so that he will be killed." So Joab assigned Uriah to a spot close to the city wall where he knew the enemy's strongest men were fighting. And Uriah was killed along with several other Israelite soldiers.

When Bathsheba heard that her husband was dead, she mourned for him. When the period of mourning was over, David sent for her and brought her to the palace, and she became one of his wives. Then she gave birth to a son. But the LORD was very displeased with what David had done.

2 Samuel 11:14-17, 26-27

Then David confessed to Nathan, "I have sinned against the LORD."

Nathan replied, "Yes, but the LORD has forgiven you, and you won't die for this sin. But you have given the enemies of the LORD great opportunity to despise and blaspheme him, so your child will die."

2 Samuel 12:13-14

For the wages of sin is death, but the free gift of God is eternal life through Christ Jesus our Lord.

Romans 6:23

Related Texts: Numbers 32:23; 2 Samuel 12:15-25; Proverbs 26:27; Matthew 1:1-6; Hebrews 13:4

done ☐

AUGUST 15

David's Prayer of Repentance

Written after Nathan the prophet had come to inform David of God's judgment against him because of his adultery with Bathsheba and his murder of Uriah, her husband.

Have mercy on me, O God,
because of your unfailing love.
Because of your great compassion,
blot out the stain of my sins.
Wash me clean from my guilt.
Purify me from my sin.
For I recognize my shameful deeds—
they haunt me day and night.
Against you, and you alone, have I sinned;
I have done what is evil in your sight.
You will be proved right in what you say,
and your judgment against me is just.
For I was born a sinner—
yes, from the moment my mother conceived me.
But you desire honesty from the heart,
so you can teach me to be wise in my inmost being.
Purify me from my sins, and I will be clean;
wash me, and I will be whiter than snow.
Oh, give me back my joy again;
you have broken me—
now let me rejoice.
Don't keep looking at my sins.
Remove the stain of my guilt.
Create in me a clean heart, O God.
Renew a right spirit within me.
Do not banish me from your presence,
and don't take your Holy Spirit from me.
Restore to me again the joy of your salvation,
and make me willing to obey you.
Then I will teach your ways to sinners,
and they will return to you.

Psalm 51:1-13

Related Texts: 2 Samuel 12; Psalm 32; Isaiah 40:28-31; Habakkuk 3:2; Titus 3:3-7

Give it a try

After reading David's prayer of forgiveness, write God a letter asking Him to create in you a new and clean heart.

done ☐

One Minute Memory

Seek his will in all you do, and he will direct your **paths.**

Proverbs 3:6

David Appoints Solomon as King

As the time of King David's death approached, he gave this charge to his son Solomon: "I am going where everyone on earth must someday go. Take courage and be a man. Observe the requirements of the LORD your God and follow all his ways. Keep each of the laws, commands, regulations, and stipulations written in the law of Moses so that you will be successful in all you do and wherever you go. If you do this, then the LORD will keep the promise he made to me: 'If your descendants live as they should and follow me faithfully with all their heart and soul, one of them will always sit on the throne of Israel.' "

1 Kings 2:1-4

So Solomon took the throne of the LORD in place of his father, David, and he prospered greatly, and all Israel obeyed him. All the royal officials, the army commanders, and the sons of King David pledged their loyalty to King Solomon. And the LORD exalted Solomon so the entire nation of Israel stood in awe of him, and he gave Solomon even greater wealth and honor than his father.

1 Chronicles 29:23-25

Seek his will in all you do, and he will direct your paths.

Proverbs 3:6

Related Texts: 2 Samuel 7; 1 Kings 1; 1 Chronicles 17: 23-29; Matthew 1:1-6; Luke 12:22-31

done ☐

Solomon Asks for Wisdom

That night the LORD appeared to Solomon in a dream, and God said, "What do you want? Ask, and I will give it to you!"

Solomon replied..."O LORD my God, now you have made me king instead of my father, David, but I am like a little child who doesn't know his way around. And here I am among your own chosen people, a nation so great they are too numerous to count! Give me an understanding mind so that I can govern your people well and know the difference between right and wrong. For who by himself is able to govern this great nation of yours?"

The LORD was pleased with Solomon's reply and was glad that he had asked for wisdom. So God replied, "Because you have asked for wisdom in governing my people and have not asked for a long life or riches for yourself or the death of your enemies—I will give you what you asked for! I will give you a wise and understanding mind such as no one else has ever had or ever will have! And I will also give you what you did not ask for—riches and honor! No other king in all the world will be compared to you for the rest of your life! And if you follow me and obey my commands as your father, David, did, I will give you a long life."

1 Kings 3:5-14

Related Texts: 1 Kings 3:16-28; 2 Chronicles 1:1-13; Proverbs 1-4; 8:10-21; James 1:5-8

BIG TIME WORD

WISDOM

Wisdom has nothing to do with your grade point average or your achievement test scores. Wisdom comes from God. Another biblical word used for wisdom is understanding. Solomon asked God for an understanding mind so he could know the difference between right and wrong (1 Kings 3:9). This understanding is one of the essential elements of wisdom.

If you DON'T have wisdom, you'll...

- struggle between knowing right from wrong
- follow the crowd rather than lead
- be confused about what to do in and with your life
- be unsure of God's plan for your life
- conform to others' standards

Ask God to give you His wisdom for the decisions you need to make today.

done ☐

Weird or What?

The Wisdom of Solomon

Did you know Solomon was a multimillionaire? The Bible tells us that he received $250,000,000 worth of gold each year from the kings of Arabia. He also sold horses and exotic goods as well as copper and bronze that were manufactured in his mines. He would be considered a very wealthy person in today's economy, so there's no question he was one of the richest men alive. But with all his wealth and fame, Solomon still asked God for wisdom. He knew money couldn't buy what God offered.

Try to live today without concern over your financial situation and

ask God for the things money can't buy.

The people of Judah and Israel were as numerous as the sand on the seashore. They were very contented, with plenty to eat and drink. King Solomon ruled all the kingdoms from the Euphrates River to the land of the Philistines, as far south as the border of Egypt. The conquered peoples of those lands sent tribute money to Solomon and continued to serve him throughout his lifetime. . . .

God gave Solomon great wisdom and understanding, and knowledge too vast to be measured. In fact, his wisdom exceeded that of all the wise men of the East and the wise men of Egypt. He was wiser than anyone else, including Ethan the Ezrahite and Heman, Calcol, and Darda—the sons of Mahol. His fame spread throughout all the surrounding nations. He composed some 3,000 proverbs and wrote 1,005 songs. He could speak with authority about all kinds of plants, from the great cedar of Lebanon to the tiny hyssop that grows from cracks in a wall. He could also speak about animals, birds, reptiles, and fish. And kings from every nation sent their ambassadors to listen to the wisdom of Solomon.

1 Kings 4:20-21,29-34

Related Texts: 1 Kings 10:1-13; Psalm 72; Proverbs 13:10; 16:16; 23:23; Matthew 12:38-42

done ☐

The Proverbs of Solomon

These are the proverbs of Solomon, David's son, king of Israel.

The purpose of these proverbs is to teach people wisdom and discipline, and to help them understand wise sayings. Through these proverbs, people will receive instruction in discipline, good conduct, and doing what is right, just, and fair. These proverbs will make the simpleminded clever. They will give knowledge and purpose to young people.

Let those who are wise listen to these proverbs and become even wiser. And let those who understand receive guidance by exploring the depth of meaning in these proverbs, parables, wise sayings, and riddles.

Fear of the LORD is the beginning of knowledge. Only fools despise wisdom and discipline.

Proverbs 1:1-7

As the crowd pressed in on Jesus, he said, "These are evil times, and this evil generation keeps asking me to show them a miraculous sign. But the only sign I will give them is the sign of the prophet Jonah. What happened to him was a sign to the people of Nineveh that God had sent him. What happens to me will be a sign that God has sent me, the Son of Man, to these people.

"The queen of Sheba will rise up against this generation on judgment day and condemn it, because she came from a distant land to hear the wisdom of Solomon. And now someone greater than Solomon is here—and you refuse to listen to him."

Luke 11:29-31

Related Texts: 2 Chronicles 9:1-12; Proverbs 10:1; 25:1; Song of Songs 1–8; Jonah 3; 1 Corinthians 12:1-11

Personality Plus

Solomon

Solomon was the son of David and Bathsheba. He followed his family line and became king of Israel. He had great wealth, wisdom, and respect. But he also had problems, as any other person does. Though he appeared to "have it all," he made some bad decisions by marrying ungodly women and allowing them to weaken his commitment to God.

We all lack wisdom at times and must be ready to pay the consequences.

Try reading through the Proverbs and see if you can find any advice that could have helped Solomon with his relationships.

done ☐

In OTHER Words

Parable

A parable was usually a story or a verbal illustration. Jesus didn't have the technology of using a slide-show or a video presentation to make His message more clear, so He told parables.

They're great parables, and if you don't know any, you might read the good Samaritan (Luke 10:30-37), the lost coin (Luke 15:8-10), or the ten virgins (Matt. 25:1-13). There are several more; check them out and **allow God's Word to take root in your life so you'll never forget His incredible message.**

Parables of Jesus: The Sower

One day Jesus told this story to a large crowd that had gathered from many towns to hear him: "A farmer went out to plant some seed. As he scattered it across his field, some seed fell on a footpath, where it was stepped on, and the birds came and ate it. Other seed fell on shallow soil with underlying rock. This seed began to grow, but soon it withered and died for lack of moisture. Other seed fell among thorns that shot up and choked out the tender blades. Still other seed fell on fertile soil. This seed grew and produced a crop one hundred times as much as had been planted." When he had said this, he called out, "Anyone who is willing to hear should listen and understand!"

His disciples asked him what the story meant. He replied, "You have been permitted to understand the secrets of the Kingdom of God. But I am using these stories to conceal everything about it from outsiders, so that the Scriptures might be fulfilled:

'They see what I do,
but they don't really see;
they hear what I say,
but they don't understand.'"

Luke 8:4-10

Related Texts: Psalm 126; Proverbs 11:18-21; Hosea 10:12-13; Matthew 13:1-17; Mark 4:1-12

done ☐

Parables of Jesus: The Sower Explained

"This is the meaning of the story: The seed is God's message. The seed that fell on the hard path represents those who hear the message, but then the Devil comes and steals it away and prevents them from believing and being saved. The rocky soil represents those who hear the message with joy. But like young plants in such soil, their roots don't go very deep. They believe for a while, but they wilt when the hot winds of testing blow. The thorny ground represents those who hear and accept the message, but all too quickly the message is crowded out by the cares and riches and pleasures of this life. And so they never grow into maturity. But the good soil represents honest, good-hearted people who hear God's message, cling to it, and steadily produce a huge harvest.

"No one would light a lamp and then cover it up or put it under a bed. No, lamps are mounted in the open, where they can be seen by those entering the house. For everything that is hidden or secret will eventually be brought to light and made plain to all. So be sure to pay attention to what you hear. To those who are open to my teaching, more understanding will be given. But to those who are not listening, even what they think they have will be taken away from them."

Luke 8:11-18

Related Texts: Proverbs 11:30; Matthew 13:18-23; Mark 4:13-25; John 15:1-17; Galatians 6:7-10

In OTHER Words

Good News

Good is simply defined. News also is a simple word that might be translated as "information." When these two words are used together ("Good News"), they refer to what we know as the Bible. The writers of the New Testament books referred to God's Word as "Scriptures" or "Good News."

The Bible is God's love letter to us. As you know, this book in your hands is filled with sections of the Good News, but it isn't the complete Bible. If you don't have a Bible, ask a friend, parent, or pastor to help get you one.* The Good News is one of the ways God chooses to speak to us. Open it, read it, and begin to see what God wants for your life. It's a lot like what you've been reading in this book, only more; and in this case, more is better.

*Look in the back of this book for a list of some good student Bibles.

done ☐

Parables of Jesus: The Kingdom

Here is another illustration Jesus used: "The Kingdom of Heaven is like a mustard seed planted in a field. It is the smallest of all seeds, but it becomes the largest of garden plants and grows into a tree where birds can come and find shelter in its branches."

Jesus also used this illustration: "The Kingdom of Heaven is like yeast used by a woman making bread. Even though she used a large amount of flour, the yeast permeated every part of the dough."...

"The Kingdom of Heaven is like a treasure that a man discovered hidden in a field. In his excitement, he hid it again and sold everything he owned to get enough money to buy the field—and to get the treasure, too!

"Again, the Kingdom of Heaven is like a pearl merchant on the lookout for choice pearls. When he discovered a pearl of great value, he sold everything he owned and bought it!

"Again, the Kingdom of Heaven is like a fishing net that is thrown into the water and gathers fish of every kind. When the net is full, they drag it up onto the shore, sit down, sort the good fish into crates, and throw the bad ones away. That is the way it will be at the end of the world. The angels will come and separate the wicked people from the godly, throwing the wicked into the fire. There will be weeping and gnashing of teeth."

Matthew 13:31-33,44-50

Related Texts: Psalm 45:6; Mark 1:1-15; 4:30-32; Luke 13:18-19

Give it a try

After reading today's selection, write what you believe heaven will be like.

____

____

____

done ☐

Parables of Jesus: Lost and Found

Tax collectors and other notorious sinners often came to listen to Jesus teach. This made the Pharisees and teachers of religious law complain that he was associating with such despicable people—even eating with them!

So Jesus used this illustration: If you had one hundred sheep, and one of them strayed away and was lost in the wilderness, wouldn't you leave the ninety-nine others to go and search for the lost one until you found it? And then you would joyfully carry it home on your shoulders. When you arrived, you would call together your friends and neighbors to rejoice with you because your lost sheep was found. In the same way, heaven will be happier over one lost sinner who returns to God than over ninety-nine others who are righteous and haven't strayed away!

"Or suppose a woman has ten valuable silver coins and loses one. Won't she light a lamp and look in every corner of the house and sweep every nook and cranny until she finds it? And when she finds it, she will call in her friends and neighbors to rejoice with her because she has found her lost coin. In the same way, there is joy in the presence of God's angels when even one sinner repents."

Luke 15:1-10

Related Texts: Psalm 119:169-176; Matthew 18:12-14; Luke 9:22-26; 19:1-10

JUST a THOUGHT

The sheep could return to the flock, the coin could be found, and you could return to the Father; and He would welcome you home with open arms.

done ☐

What's it Mean?

The son goes his own way, blows all he was given, and then returns to his father's home with the hope of simply being hired for a job.

The father accepts him back, not as an employee but as his son.

This parable is an incredible story of God's love for us. When we go our own way and turn our backs on God, He is waiting to welcome us home. When we return home, God doesn't accept us as sinners, but He forgives us and brings us in as His sons or daughters. Wow, what an awesome God!

Right now, write in your notebook or on the palm of your hand something that will remind you of this truth all day—God loves you as His child.

PARABLES OF JESUS: THE PRODIGAL SON, PART 1

To illustrate the point further, Jesus told them this story: "A man had two sons. The younger son told his father, 'I want my share of your estate now, instead of waiting until you die.' So his father agreed to divide his wealth between his sons.

"A few days later this younger son packed all his belongings and took a trip to a distant land, and there he wasted all his money on wild living. About the time his money ran out, a great famine swept over the land, and he began to starve. He persuaded a local farmer to hire him to feed his pigs. The boy became so hungry that even the pods he was feeding the pigs looked good to him. But no one gave him anything.

"When he finally came to his senses, he said to himself, 'At home even the hired men have food enough to spare, and here I am, dying of hunger! I will go home to my father and say, "Father, I have sinned against both heaven and you, and I am no longer worthy of being called your son. Please take me on as a hired man." '

"So he returned home to his father. And while he was still a long distance away, his father saw him coming. Filled with love and compassion, he ran to his son, embraced him, and kissed him. His son said to him, 'Father, I have sinned against both heaven and you, and I am no longer worthy of being called your son.'"

Luke 15:11-21

Related Texts: 2 Chronicles 7:13-14; Proverbs 17:6,21; Hosea 6:1-3; Acts 3:19-20

done ☐

Parables of Jesus: The Prodigal Son, Part 2

"But his father said to the servants, 'Quick! Bring the finest robe in the house and put it on him. Get a ring for his finger, and sandals for his feet. And kill the calf we have been fattening in the pen. We must celebrate with a feast, for this son of mine was dead and has now returned to life. He was lost, but now he is found.' So the party began.

"Meanwhile, the older son was in the fields working. When he returned home, he heard music and dancing in the house, and he asked one of the servants what was going on. 'Your brother is back,' he was told, 'and your father has killed the calf we were fattening and has prepared a great feast. We are celebrating because of his safe return.'

"The older brother was angry and wouldn't go in. His father came out and begged him, but he replied, 'All these years I've worked hard for you and never once refused to do a single thing you told me to. And in all that time you never gave me even one young goat for a feast with my friends. Yet when this son of yours comes back after squandering your money on prostitutes, you celebrate by killing the finest calf we have.'

"His father said to him, 'Look, dear son, you and I are very close, and everything I have is yours. We had to celebrate this happy day. For your brother was dead and has come back to life! He was lost, but now he is found!' "

Luke 15:22-32

Related Texts: Isaiah 55:6-7; Matthew 18:12-14; Colossians 1:1-14; 1 Peter 2:24-25

JUST a THOUGHT

If you're **away** from **God** and in need of a **real party,** return to Him and He'll **give you** a celebration you'll **never** forget.

done ☐

What's it Mean?

Do you remember reading or hearing about the tabernacle? The tabernacle was a portable place of worship that traveled with the Israelites during their years prior to entering the Promised Land. The temple that Solomon built was like the tabernacle except that it wasn't portable. The temple was a meeting place between God and His people where worship and sacrifice took place.

This temple was not built to house or contain God. Solomon said: "Why, even the highest heavens cannot contain you. How much less this Temple I have built!" (1 Kings 8:27).

Today, God is building a "holy temple" in the lives of His followers.

If you're a follower, what condition is your temple in?

SOLOMON BUILDS THE TEMPLE

King Hiram of Tyre had always been a loyal friend of David, so when he learned that David's son Solomon was the new king of Israel, Hiram sent ambassadors to congratulate him. Then Solomon sent this message back to Hiram:

"You know that my father, David, was not able to build a Temple to honor the name of the LORD his God because of the many wars he waged with surrounding nations. He could not build until the LORD gave him victory over all his enemies. But now the LORD my God has given me peace on every side, and I have no enemies and all is well.

"So I am planning to build a Temple to honor the name of the LORD my God, just as he instructed my father that I should do. For the LORD told him, 'Your son, whom I will place on your throne, will build the Temple to honor my name.' Now please command that cedars from Lebanon be cut for me. Let my men work alongside yours, and I will pay your men whatever wages you ask. As you know, there is no one among us who can cut timber like you Sidonians!"

When Hiram received Solomon's message, he was very pleased and said, "Praise the LORD for giving David a wise son to be king of the great nation of Israel."

1 Kings 5:1-7

Related Texts: 1 Kings 5–9; 2 Chronicles 2–8; Psalm 127; Matthew 12:1-6; John 2:13-21; Ephesians 2:11-22

done ☐

The Wisdom of the Teacher

I, the Teacher, was king of Israel, and I lived in Jerusalem. I devoted myself to search for understanding and to explore by wisdom everything being done in the world. I soon discovered that God has dealt a tragic existence to the human race. Everything under the sun is meaningless, like chasing the wind.

Ecclesiastes 1:12-14

There is a time for everything,
  a season for every activity under heaven.
A time to be born and a time to die.
  A time to plant and a time to harvest.
A time to kill and a time to heal.
  A time to tear down and a time to rebuild.
A time to cry and a time to laugh.
  A time to grieve and a time to dance.
A time to scatter stones and a time to gather stones.
  A time to embrace and a time to turn away.
A time to search and a time to lose.
  A time to keep and a time to throw away.
A time to tear and a time to mend.
  A time to be quiet and a time to speak up.
A time to love and a time to hate.
  A time for war and a time for peace.

Ecclesiastes 3:1-8

Related Texts: Ecclesiastes 1:1-11; Galatians 4:4-5; 6:8-9; 1 Timothy 2:3-6; 1 Peter 5:5-6

CHECK IT OUT

Time has become a precious possession in today's world. We are a time-conscious generation. We all have the same amount of time—twenty-four hours a day. And God is in complete control of all time. He began the world in His timing, and He will return to take over the world in His timing. Because God is God, He knew exactly when to send Jesus to the world. Check out Galatians 4:4-5: "But when the right time came, God sent his Son, born of a woman, subject to the law, so that he could adopt us as his very own children."

Take a minute to give God your time. Ask Him to direct how you spend it today.

done ☐

One Minute Memory

A person **standing alone** can be **attacked and defeated,** but **two** can **stand back-to-back** and **conquer.** **Three are even better,** for a triple-braided cord is **not easily broken.** *Ecclesiastes 4:12*

The Teacher's Proverbs and Conclusion

Two people can accomplish more than twice as much as one; they get a better return for their labor. If one person falls, the other can reach out and help. But people who are alone when they fall are in real trouble. And on a cold night, two under the same blanket can gain warmth from each other. But how can one be warm alone? A person standing alone can be attacked and defeated, but two can stand back-to-back and conquer. Three are even better, for a triple-braided cord is not easily broken.

Ecclesiastes 4:9-12

Because the Teacher was wise, he taught the people everything he knew. He collected proverbs and classified them. Indeed, the Teacher taught the plain truth, and he did so in an interesting way.

A wise teacher's words spur students to action and emphasize important truths. The collected sayings of the wise are like guidance from a shepherd.

But, my child, be warned: There is no end of opinions ready to be expressed. Studying them can go on forever and become very exhausting!

Here is my final conclusion: Fear God and obey his commands, for this is the duty of every person. God will judge us for everything we do, including every secret thing, whether good or bad.

Ecclesiastes 12:9-14

Related Texts: 1 Samuel 20:24-42; Psalm 37; Proverbs 17:17; 27:6,10; 1 Corinthians 4:5; Revelation 20:11-15

done ☐

The Sins of Solomon

Now King Solomon loved many foreign women. Besides Pharaoh's daughter, he married women from Moab, Ammon, Edom, Sidon, and from among the Hittites. The LORD had clearly instructed his people not to intermarry with those nations, because the women they married would lead them to worship their gods. Yet Solomon insisted on loving them anyway. . . .

And sure enough, they led his heart away from the LORD. In Solomon's old age, they turned his heart to worship their gods instead of trusting only in the LORD his God, as his father, David, had done. . . .

The LORD was very angry with Solomon, for his heart had turned away from the LORD, the God of Israel, who had appeared to him twice. He had warned Solomon specifically about worshiping other gods, but Solomon did not listen to the LORD's command. So now the LORD said to him, "Since you have not kept my covenant and have disobeyed my laws, I will surely tear the kingdom away from you and give it to one of your servants. But for the sake of your father, David, I will not do this while you are still alive. I will take the kingdom away from your son. And even so, I will let him be king of one tribe, for the sake of my servant David and for the sake of Jerusalem, my chosen city."

1 Kings 11:1-2, 3b-4, 9-13

Related Texts: Deuteronomy 7; Ezra 9–10; Nehemiah 13:23-27; 1 Corinthians 7:39; 2 Corinthians 6:14-16

Weird or What?

It seems weird that Solomon could be so wise and yet make such dumb mistakes. The law forbade kings to have multiple wives and prohibited taking wives from other nations. Solomon married foreign women to be "politically correct" and gain other nations' loyalty. This move turned out to be unwise and led Solomon to be disloyal to God.

We can learn from Solomon's mistake. It is better to please God first and then others rather than the other way around.

Take note and be wise today.

CATCH THIS

Rehoboam didn't take the advice of the older men. No one knows how history would have been different if he had. Instead, he followed the advice of the younger men, and the results split the nation in half.

One of the most attractive qualities of a person is his or her ability to take advice from others. When we are open to advice, we communicate humility and leadership.

If you have the opportunity to get advice, take it. Evaluate the advice against the Bible before making your decisions. If you can get older people to give advice, take it even quicker. Why? Because your peers or friends may have a tendency to tell you what you want to hear, which isn't advice but confirmation.

It's wise to realize that many people are quick to give advice but slow to take it. Try turning that around in your own life—be slow to give it and quick to take it.

The Kingdom Divides

Solomon ruled in Jerusalem over all Israel for forty years. When Solomon died, he was buried in the city of his father, David. Then his son Rehoboam became the next king.

1 Kings 11:42-43

Rehoboam went to Shechem, where all Israel had gathered to make him king. When Jeroboam son of Nebat heard of Solomon's death, he returned from Egypt, for he had fled to Egypt to escape from King Solomon. The leaders of Israel sent for Jeroboam, and the whole assembly of Israel went to speak with Rehoboam. "Your father was a hard master," they said. "Lighten the harsh labor demands and heavy taxes that your father imposed on us. Then we will be your loyal subjects."...

Three days later, Jeroboam and all the people returned to hear Rehoboam's decision, just as the king had requested. But Rehoboam spoke harshly to them, for he rejected the advice of the older counselors and followed the counsel of his younger advisers. He told the people, "My father was harsh on you, but I'll be even harsher! My father used whips on you, but I'll use scorpions!"...

When all Israel realized that the king had rejected their request, they shouted, "Down with David and his dynasty! We have no share in Jesse's son! Let's go home, Israel! Look out for your own house, O David!" So the people of Israel returned home. But Rehoboam continued to rule over the Israelites who lived in the towns of Judah....

When the people of Israel learned of Jeroboam's return from Egypt, they called an assembly and made him king over all Israel. So only the tribe of Judah remained loyal to the family of David.

1 Kings 12:1-4,12-14,16-17,20

Related Texts: 1 Kings 11:26-40; 2 Chronicles 9:29-10:19; Proverbs 15:1

done ☐

THE SINS OF JEROBOAM

Jeroboam then built up the city of Shechem in the hill country of Ephraim, and it became his capital. Later he went and built up the town of Peniel. Jeroboam thought to himself, "Unless I am careful, the kingdom will return to the dynasty of David. When they go to Jerusalem to offer sacrifices at the Temple of the LORD, they will again give their allegiance to King Rehoboam of Judah. They will kill me and make him their king instead."

So on the advice of his counselors, the king made two gold calves. He said to the people, "It is too much trouble for you to worship in Jerusalem. O Israel, these are the gods who brought you out of Egypt!"

He placed these calf idols at the southern and northern ends of Israel—in Bethel and in Dan. This became a great sin, for the people worshiped them, traveling even as far as Dan.

Jeroboam built shrines at the pagan high places and ordained priests from the rank and file of the people—those who were not from the priestly tribe of Levi.

1 Kings 12:25-31

This became a great sin and resulted in the destruction of Jeroboam's kingdom and the death of all his family.

1 Kings 13:34

Related Texts: Exodus 32; 2 Kings 10:16-31; 23:1-15; 2 Chronicles 11:14-16; Acts 17:15-31; 1 Corinthians 6:9-10

What's it Mean?

For over one hundred years three kings ruled the Israelites: Saul, David, and Solomon. When Solomon died, his son, Rehoboam, became king. Immediately, he started a national rebellion because he promised to increase the Israelites' pain. His peers told him: "This is what you should tell those complainers... 'If you think (my father) was hard on you, just wait and see what I'll be like!'" (1 Kings 12:10) When the Israelites heard those words, ten of the twelve kingdoms revolted and formed a new nation. The new nation became the Northern Kingdom, called Israel. King Rehoboam maintained control of the southern nation, which was called Judah.

The Northern Kingdom had a new king named Jeroboam. He was worse than Rehoboam because he tried to replace God with two golden calves.

You should take hope when you see how God patiently cared for the Israelites even after they continually messed up. Pray a prayer of thanksgiving today, thanking God for His patience with you.

done ☐

September

The Bible is Alive; it speaks to me.

Martin Luther
(1483–1546)
German Theologian and Reformer

Elijah Confronts King Ahab

Ahab son of Omri began to rule over Israel in the thirty-eighth year of King Asa's reign in Judah. He reigned in Samaria twenty-two years. But Ahab did what was evil in the LORD's sight, even more than any of the kings before him. And as though it were not enough to live like Jeroboam, he married Jezebel, the daughter of King Ethbaal of the Sidonians, and he began to worship Baal. First he built a temple and an altar for Baal in Samaria. Then he set up an Asherah pole. He did more to arouse the anger of the LORD, the God of Israel, than any of the other kings of Israel before him.

1 Kings 16:29-33

Now Elijah, who was from Tishbe in Gilead, told King Ahab, "As surely as the LORD, the God of Israel, lives—the God whom I worship and serve—there will be no dew or rain during the next few years unless I give the word!"

Then the LORD said to Elijah, "Go to the east and hide by Kerith Brook at a place east of where it enters the Jordan River. Drink from the brook and eat what the ravens bring you, for I have commanded them to bring you food."

So Elijah did as the LORD had told him and camped beside Kerith Brook. The ravens brought him bread and meat each morning and evening, and he drank from the brook.

1 Kings 17:1-6

At times I might shut up the heavens so that no rain falls, or I might command locusts to devour your crops, or I might send plagues among you. Then if my people who are called by my name will humble themselves and pray and seek my face and turn from their wicked ways, I will hear from heaven and will forgive their sins and heal their land.

2 Chronicles 7:13-14

Related Texts: Deuteronomy 11:16-17; Mark 6:14-15; Luke 1:11-17; 9:7-8; James 5:17-18

In OTHER Words

King

The reign of kings replaced Israel's period of judges. God was slow to give the Israelites a king because He wanted to be the king of the Israelites. Only He could be a totally wise and just king. The Israelites wanted to be ruled by a king just as the surrounding nations were. Because the Israelites wanted to be like other nations, they rejected God as their true King.

Many people want to be like others so much that they reject God's ways and go the ways of their friends. Have you rejected God so you can be like others?

Ask God to show you His way and try to honor Him as King of your life.

done ☐

Weird or What?

Elijah called on God to consume an idol with fire because He was known as a God of fire. For example, a cherub with a flaming sword guarded the Garden of Eden; a burning bush spoke to Moses; Isaiah saw a throne with "fiery" beings flying around when he was taken into God's presence.

The author of Hebrews calls God a "consuming fire" (see 12:29). Fire is a purifier.

In heaven our bodies will be purified because of Jesus. Are you ready to be tested by God's fire?

Elijah Challenges the Prophets of Baal

After many months passed, in the third year of the drought, the LORD said to Elijah, "Go and present yourself to King Ahab. Tell him that I will soon send rain!"...

"So it's you, is it—Israel's troublemaker?" Ahab asked when he saw him.

"I have made no trouble for Israel," Elijah replied. "You and your family are the troublemakers, for you have refused to obey the commands of the LORD and have worshiped the images of Baal instead. Now bring all the people of Israel to Mount Carmel, with all 450 prophets of Baal and the 400 prophets of Asherah, who are supported by Jezebel."

So Ahab summoned all the people and the prophets to Mount Carmel. Then Elijah stood in front of them and said, "How long are you going to waver between two opinions? If the LORD is God, follow him! But if Baal is God, then follow him!" But the people were completely silent.

Then Elijah said to them, "I am the only prophet of the LORD who is left, but Baal has 450 prophets. Now bring two bulls. The prophets of Baal may choose whichever one they wish and cut it into pieces and lay it on the wood of their altar, but without setting fire to it. I will prepare the other bull and lay it on the wood on the altar, but not set fire to it. Then call on the name of your god, and I will call on the name of the LORD. The god who answers by setting fire to the wood is the true God!" And all the people agreed.

1 Kings 18:1,17-24

Related Texts: Deuteronomy 12:28-31; 32:36-39; Mark 8:27-29; Luke 9:28-36; James 5:14-18

done ☐

SEPTEMBER 3

The Lord Defeats Baal

Then Elijah said to the prophets of Baal, "You go first, for there are many of you. Choose one of the bulls and prepare it and call on the name of your god. But do not set fire to the wood."

So they prepared one of the bulls and placed it on the altar. Then they called on the name of Baal all morning, shouting, "O Baal, answer us!" But there was no reply of any kind. Then they danced wildly around the altar they had made. . . .

They raved all afternoon until the time of the evening sacrifice, but still there was no reply, no voice, no answer. . . .

At the customary time for offering the evening sacrifice, Elijah the prophet walked up to the altar and prayed, "O LORD, God of Abraham, Isaac, and Jacob, prove today that you are God in Israel and that I am your servant. Prove that I have done all this at your command. O LORD, answer me! Answer me so these people will know that you, O LORD, are God and that you have brought them back to yourself."

Immediately the fire of the LORD flashed down from heaven and burned up the young bull, the wood, the stones, and the dust. It even licked up all the water in the ditch! And when the people saw it, they fell on their faces and cried out, "The LORD is God! The LORD is God!"

Then Elijah commanded, "Seize all the prophets of Baal. Don't let a single one escape!" So the people seized them all, and Elijah took them down to the Kishon Valley and killed them there.

1 Kings 18:25-26,29,36-40

Related Texts: Deuteronomy 13; 17:2-5; 18:18-22; 1 Kings 21-22; 2 Kings 9:30–10:28; Philippians 2:5-11

Personality Plus

Elijah

Elijah was the most famous of prophets. God used him in mighty ways. As you read today, you learned how he showed others that idols were no match for God.

Although Elijah was a great prophet, he did get tired and frustrated while working for God. He became depressed because he didn't believe people were responding to his message. During this "down time," God reminded Elijah that He is God and big enough to understand Elijah's discouragement and care for his prophetic ministry.

Doing ministry can get tiring. But BEING God's person will help you survive the DOING. Be God's person today and allow Him to give you the strength to do His work.

done ☐

4 SEPTEMBER

Jonah Disobeys the Lord

The LORD gave this message to Jonah son of Amittai: "Get up and go to the great city of Nineveh! Announce my judgment against it because I have seen how wicked its people are."

But Jonah got up and went in the opposite direction in order to get away from the LORD. He went down to the seacoast, to the port of Joppa, where he found a ship leaving for Tarshish. He bought a ticket and went on board, hoping that by going away to the west he could escape from the LORD.

But as the ship was sailing along, suddenly the LORD flung a powerful wind over the sea, causing a violent storm that threatened to send them to the bottom. Fearing for their lives, the desperate sailors shouted to their gods for help and threw the cargo overboard to lighten the ship. . . .

Then the crew cast lots to see which of them had offended the gods and caused the terrible storm. When they did this, Jonah lost the toss. . . .

And since the storm was getting worse all the time, they asked him, "What should we do to you to stop this storm?"

"Throw me into the sea," Jonah said, "and it will become calm again. For I know that this terrible storm is all my fault."...

Then the sailors picked Jonah up and threw him into the raging sea, and the storm stopped at once! The sailors were awestruck by the LORD's great power, and they offered him a sacrifice and vowed to serve him.

Now the LORD had arranged for a great fish to swallow Jonah. And Jonah was inside the fish for three days and three nights.

Jonah 1:1-5a,7,11-12,15-17

Related Texts: 2 Kings 14:25; Matthew 12:38-41; 16:1-4; Luke 11:29-32

Give it a try

Below you will find three ways we are often like Jonah:

1. We run from good things.
2. We think we can hide from God.
3. We keep truth from people.

Write a few thoughts about how one of these three statements most relates to your life.

done ☐

Jonah Prays from the Belly of a Fish

Then Jonah prayed to the LORD his God from inside the fish. He said, "I cried out to the LORD in my great trouble, and he answered me. I called to you from the world of the dead, and LORD, you heard me! You threw me into the ocean depths, and I sank down to the heart of the sea. I was buried beneath your wild and stormy waves. Then I said, 'O LORD, you have driven me from your presence. How will I ever again see your holy Temple?'

"I sank beneath the waves, and death was very near. The waters closed in around me, and seaweed wrapped itself around my head. I sank down to the very roots of the mountains. I was locked out of life and imprisoned in the land of the dead. But you, O LORD my God, have snatched me from the yawning jaws of death!

"When I had lost all hope, I turned my thoughts once more to the LORD. And my earnest prayer went out to you in your holy Temple. Those who worship false gods turn their backs on all God's mercies. But I will offer sacrifices to you with songs of praise, and I will fulfill all my vows. For my salvation comes from the LORD alone."

Then the LORD ordered the fish to spit up Jonah on the beach, and it did.

Jonah 2

Related Texts: 2 Kings 17:13-15; Psalms 42; 69; Isaiah 44:9-20; Acts 27

One Minute Memory

I will never worship anyone but you! For how can I thank you enough for all you have done? I will surely fulfill my promises. For my deliverance comes from the Lord alone.

Jonah 2:9

done ☐

CATCH THIS

God has proven Himself to be a God of second chances, forgiveness, and grace. The Ninevites turned from their evil ways, and God spared them from destruction. Then they were thankful people!

God also has promised not to destroy Christians. If you are a Christian, this is good news! God is worthy of your praise and worship.

Today, thank God for his unconditional love for you and spend some time identifying an area of your life that needs to be changed. God graciously gives second chances, but **He prefers our obedience.**

The Lord Relents from Sending Disaster

Then the LORD spoke to Jonah a second time: "Get up and go to the great city of Nineveh, and deliver the message of judgment I have given you."

This time Jonah obeyed the LORD's command and went to Nineveh, a city so large that it took three days to see it all. On the day Jonah entered the city, he shouted to the crowds: "Forty days from now Nineveh will be destroyed!" The people of Nineveh believed God's message, and from the greatest to the least, they decided to go without food and wear sackcloth to show their sorrow.

When the king of Nineveh heard what Jonah was saying, he stepped down from his throne and took off his royal robes. He dressed himself in sackcloth and sat on a heap of ashes. Then the king and his nobles sent this decree throughout the city: "No one, not even the animals, may eat or drink anything at all. Everyone is required to wear sackcloth and pray earnestly to God. Everyone must turn from their evil ways and stop all their violence. Who can tell? Perhaps even yet God will have pity on us and hold back his fierce anger from destroying us."

When God saw that they had put a stop to their evil ways, he had mercy on them and didn't carry out the destruction he had threatened.

Jonah 3

Related Texts: Exodus 32:1-14; Jeremiah 18:1-11; Joel 2:12-14; Luke 11:29-32

done ☐

SEPTEMBER 7

Joel Calls Israel to Repent

That is why the LORD says, "Turn to me now, while there is time! Give me your hearts. Come with fasting, weeping, and mourning. Don't tear your clothing in your grief; instead, tear your hearts." Return to the LORD your God, for he is gracious and merciful. He is not easily angered. He is filled with kindness and is eager not to punish you. Who knows? Perhaps even yet he will give you a reprieve, sending you a blessing instead of this terrible curse. Perhaps he will give you so much that you will be able to offer grain and wine to the LORD your God as before!

"Blow the trumpet in Jerusalem! Announce a time of fasting; call the people together for a solemn meeting. Bring everyone—the elders, the children, and even the babies. Call the bridegroom from his quarters and the bride from her private room. The priests, who minister in the LORD's presence, will stand between the people and the altar, weeping. Let them pray, "Spare your people, LORD! They belong to you, so don't let them become an object of mockery. Don't let their name become a proverb of unbelieving foreigners who say, 'Where is the God of Israel? He must be helpless!' "

Then the LORD will pity his people and be indignant for the honor of his land!

Joel 2:12-18

Related Texts: Exodus 34:1-7; Deuteronomy 10:16; Jonah 3; James 4:6-8

CHECK IT OUT

Today's reading describes Joel's calling for Judah to repent from her sinfulness. Prior to Joel's calling, God sent His judgment on the people of Judah in the form of locust or grasshoppers. Millions of locusts invaded them, darkened the skies, and devastated the land.

In Revelation 9:3,7 there is a similar image used to turn people from God: "Then locusts came from the smoke and descended on the earth, and they were given power to sting like scorpions. They were told not to hurt the grass or plants or trees but to attack all the people who did not have the seal on their foreheads. . . . The locusts looked like horses armed for battle."

There's no reason to be scared if you are a Christian. The enemy can use locusts, anteaters, or wild boars; but the blood of Jesus will protect you from the enemy's tricks. Thank God for that truth today.

done ☐

In OTHER Words

"Says the Lord your God."

Amos finished his prophecy with the key words "says the Lord your God." These words were his guarantee that his spoken vision would be fulfilled by the God of creation, the God of Abraham, the God of Moses, etc. He wanted the people to know that his prophetic words weren't his own words but God's words and vision for His chosen people.

The Bible you read isn't filled with words of men. The Bible is filled with God's words. These words are life-changing because they're from the Lord your God.

Read these words, learn from them, memorize them, and you'll never be the same.

Amos: Judgment and Hope

"I, the Sovereign LORD, am watching this sinful nation of Israel, and I will uproot it and scatter its people across the earth. Yet I have promised that I will never completely destroy the family of Israel," says the LORD. . . . But all the sinners will die by the sword—all those who say, 'Nothing bad will happen to us.'

"In that day I will restore the fallen kingdom of David. It is now like a house in ruins, but I will rebuild its walls and restore its former glory. And Israel will possess what is left of Edom and all the nations I have called to be mine. I, the LORD, have spoken, and I will do these things.

"The time will come," says the LORD, "when the grain and grapes will grow faster than they can be harvested. Then the terraced vineyards on the hills of Israel will drip with sweet wine! I will bring my exiled people of Israel back from distant lands, and they will rebuild their ruined cities and live in them again. They will plant vineyards and gardens; they will eat their crops and drink their wine. I will firmly plant them there in the land I have given them," says the LORD your God. "Then they will never be uprooted again."

Amos 9:8,10-15

Related Texts: 2 Samuel 7; Isaiah 55; Acts 15:1-21; Romans 9-11

done ☐

Hosea: The Lord's Anger and Compassion

"When Israel was a child, I loved him as a son, and I called my son out of Egypt. But the more I called to him, the more he rebelled, offering sacrifices to the images of Baal and burning incense to idols. It was I who taught Israel how to walk, leading him along by the hand. But he doesn't know or even care that it was I who took care of him. I led Israel along with my ropes of kindness and love. I lifted the yoke from his neck, and I myself stooped to feed him.

"But since my people refuse to return to me, they will go back to Egypt and will be forced to serve Assyria. . . .

"Oh, how can I give you up, Israel? How can I let you go? How can I destroy you like Admah and Zeboiim? My heart is torn within me, and my compassion overflows. No, I will not punish you as much as my burning anger tells me to. I will not completely destroy Israel, for I am God and not a mere mortal. I am the Holy One living among you, and I will not come to destroy.

"For someday the people will follow the LORD. I will roar like a lion, and my people will return trembling from the west. Like a flock of birds, they will come from Egypt. Flying like doves, they will return from Assyria. And I will bring them home again," says the LORD.

Hosea 11:1-5,8-11

Related Texts: Genesis 19:1-29; Deuteronomy 29:18-23; Zechariah 10:6-12; 2 Peter 3:8-15

JUST a THOUGHT

Today's reading and the parable of the prodigal son are similar because they both reveal to us the loving Father-heart of God.

done ☐

CATCH THIS

God spoke, and His people didn't hear. He repeated miracles, and the people didn't know what they meant. God continually revealed Himself to the Israelites, and yet they continued to worship idols instead of worshiping Him. People reacted the same way when Jesus entered the world's scene hundreds of years later. Jesus spoke, and some people didn't respond.

You may run into a similar reaction when you're trying to reach your friends for God. You may show them Christian love, invite them to church, help them with problems, and provide them examples of God's love; and they still may not respond. If this happens, realize you're in good company—it happened to God AND to Jesus.

It is important to understand that you can't make decisions for your friends. They all make their own decisions. A Christian's responsibility is to be an example of God's love and remain faithful. Do the possible today and allow God to do the impossible with your friends.

Isaiah Sees the Lord

In the year King Uzziah died, I saw the LORD. He was sitting on a lofty throne, and the train of his robe filled the Temple. Hovering around him were mighty seraphim, each with six wings. With two wings they covered their faces, with two they covered their feet, and with the remaining two they flew. In a great chorus they sang, "Holy, holy, holy is the LORD Almighty! The whole earth is filled with his glory!"...

Then I said, "My destruction is sealed, for I am a sinful man and a member of a sinful race. Yet I have seen the King, the LORD Almighty!"

Then one of the seraphim flew over to the altar, and he picked up a burning coal with a pair of tongs. He touched my lips with it and said, "See, this coal has touched your lips. Now your guilt is removed, and your sins are forgiven."

Then I heard the LORD asking, "Whom should I send as a messenger to my people? Who will go for us?"

And I said, "LORD, I'll go! Send me."

And he said, "Yes, go. But tell my people this: 'You will hear my words, but you will not understand. You will see what I do, but you will not perceive its meaning.' Harden the hearts of these people. Close their ears, and shut their eyes. That way, they will not see with their eyes, hear with their ears, understand with their hearts, and turn to me for healing."

Isaiah 6:1-3,5-10

Related Texts: Exodus 3:1-6; 33:15-23; Job 19:25-27; Matthew 5:8; 13:10-17; John 12:37-41; Revelation 4

done ☐

MICAH: THE SINS OF ISRAEL

The LORD gave these messages to Micah of Moresheth during the years when Jotham, Ahaz, and Hezekiah were kings of Judah. The messages concerned both Samaria and Jerusalem, and they came to Micah in the form of visions.

Attention! Let all the people of the world listen! The Sovereign LORD has made accusations against you; the LORD speaks from his holy Temple.

Look! The LORD is coming! He leaves his throne in heaven and comes to earth, walking on the high places. They melt beneath his feet and flow into the valleys like wax in a fire, like water pouring down a hill.

And why is this happening? Because of the sins and rebellion of Israel and Judah. Who is to blame for Israel's rebellion? Samaria, its capital city! Where is the center of idolatry in Judah? In Jerusalem, its capital!

"So I, the LORD, will make the city of Samaria a heap of rubble. Her streets will be plowed up for planting vineyards. I will roll the stones of her walls down into the valley below, exposing all her foundations. All her carved images will be smashed to pieces. All her sacred treasures will be burned up. These things were bought with the money earned by her prostitution, and they will now be carried away to pay prostitutes elsewhere."

Micah 1:1-7

Related Texts: Deuteronomy 5:6-10; Judges 10:11-16; Psalms 68:1-3; 97; Jeremiah 26; Acts 1:1-8

What's it Mean?

Samaria was the capital of the Northern Kingdom. The leaders of this kingdom led people away from God and into idol worship. All the people of Judah were going to pay for their leader's mistakes. God sent Elijah, Elisha, and Amos in an attempt to get them to turn from their idols. But there was no change. Then Micah came along and prophesied their future destruction as God's judgment for their unfaithfulness.

One famous verse in Micah reminds the Israelites what God wants from them: "to be fair, just, merciful, and to walk humbly with your God." These words are a good reminder for us today.

Circle one of these words and try to work on it in your life (fair, just, merciful, walk humbly with God).

done ☐

BIG TIMe WoRd

STUBBORN

What's the first thing that comes to your mind when someone says, "Don't be so stubborn"? Do you get defensive? angry? Being stubborn usually is a negative quality displayed by a selfish person who is unwilling to move from a strongly held position or belief. A stubborn person rarely compromises.

If you're known to be stubborn, try changing a negative into a positive and become "stubborn" for God. Being stubborn for God means you won't compromise your beliefs, and you won't give in to the distractions that can turn your thoughts, actions, and focus from God.

Israel Goes into Exile

Finally, in the ninth year of King Hoshea's reign, Samaria fell, and the people of Israel were exiled to Assyria. They were settled in colonies in Halah, along the banks of the Habor River in Gozan, and among the cities of the Medes.

This disaster came upon the nation of Israel because the people worshiped other gods, sinning against the LORD their God, who had brought them safely out of their slavery in Egypt. They had imitated the practices of the pagan nations the Lord had driven from the land before them, as well as the practices the kings of Israel had introduced. The people of Israel had also secretly done many things that were not pleasing to the LORD their God. They built pagan shrines for themselves in all their towns, from the smallest outpost to the largest walled city. They set up sacred pillars and Asherah poles at the top of every hill and under every green tree. They burned incense at the shrines, just like the nations the LORD had driven from the land ahead of them. So the people of Israel had done many evil things, arousing the LORD's anger. Yes, they worshiped idols, despite the LORD's specific and repeated warnings. Again and again the LORD had sent his prophets and seers to warn both Israel and Judah: "Turn from all your evil ways. Obey my commands and laws, which are contained in the whole law that I commanded your ancestors and which I gave you through my servants the prophets."

But the Israelites would not listen. They were as stubborn as their ancestors and refused to believe in the LORD their God.

2 Kings 17:6-14

Related Texts: Deuteronomy 28:14-68; 2 Kings 15:16-20; Acts 7:51-53

done ☐

Israel Goes into Exile

He removed the pagan shrines, smashed the sacred pillars, and knocked down the Asherah poles. He broke up the bronze serpent that Moses had made, because the people of Israel had begun to worship it by burning incense to it. The bronze serpent was called Nehushtan.

Hezekiah trusted in the LORD, the God of Israel. There was never another king like him in the land of Judah, either before or after his time. He remained faithful to the LORD in everything, and he carefully obeyed all the commands the LORD had given Moses. So the LORD was with him, and Hezekiah was successful in everything he did. He revolted against the king of Assyria and refused to pay him tribute. He also conquered the Philistines as far distant as Gaza and its territory, from their smallest outpost to their largest walled city.

During the fourth year of Hezekiah's reign, which was the seventh year of King Hoshea's reign in Israel, King Shalmaneser of Assyria attacked Israel and began a siege on the city of Samaria. Three years later, during the sixth year of King Hezekiah's reign and the ninth year of King Hoshea's reign in Israel, Samaria fell.

2 Kings 18:4-10

Related Texts: Numbers 21:1-9; Deuteronomy 28:1-14; 2 Chronicles 29-31; Proverbs 25:1; Matthew 1:1-10

CATCH THIS

King Hezekiah is a rare example of someone who followed God during a time of sin and rebellion. Today's reading explains that God blessed King Hezekiah because he obeyed God. God was with him, and he prospered in everything he did. Those are great results for following God!

If you follow God, you should stand out as being unique. Following God doesn't mean you will prosper financially, but it does mean you will have a relationship with God that causes you to live a different life.

The Bible tells us that those who don't follow God live in the darkness, and those who do walk in the light. Following God won't mean you'll have an easy or perfect life, but being in God's light will make life worth living; you will experience His rewards for all eternity.

done ☐

JUST a THOUGHT

Prayers of trouble need to be followed by prayers of praise.

The Lord Delivers Judah from Assyria

In the fourteenth year of King Hezekiah's reign, King Sennacherib of Assyria came to attack the fortified cities of Judah and conquered them.

2 Kings 18:13

And Hezekiah prayed this prayer before the LORD: "O LORD, God of Israel, you are enthroned between the mighty cherubim! You alone are God of all the kingdoms of the earth. You alone created the heavens and the earth. Listen to me, O LORD, and hear! Open your eyes, O LORD, and see! Listen to Sennacherib's words of defiance against the living God.

"It is true, LORD, that the kings of Assyria have destroyed all these nations, just as the message says. And they have thrown the gods of these nations into the fire and burned them. But of course the Assyrians could destroy them! They were not gods at all—only idols of wood and stone shaped by human hands. Now, O LORD our God, rescue us from his power; then all the kingdoms of the earth will know that you alone, O LORD, are God."

Then Isaiah son of Amoz sent this message to Hezekiah: "This is what the LORD, the God of Israel, says: I have heard your prayer about King Sennacherib of Assyria.

That night the angel of the LORD went out to the Assyrian camp and killed 185,000 Assyrian troops. When the surviving Assyrians woke up the next morning, they found corpses everywhere. Then King Sennacherib of Assyria broke camp and returned to his own land. He went home to his capital of Nineveh and stayed there.

2 Kings 19:15-20,35-36

Related Texts: 2 Kings 19-20; 2 Chronicles 32; Isaiah 36-39; Acts 12

done ☐

Nahum: God's Vengeance on Assyria

The LORD is a jealous God, filled with vengeance and wrath. He takes revenge on all who oppose him and furiously destroys his enemies! The LORD is slow to get angry, but his power is great, and he never lets the guilty go unpunished. He displays his power in the whirlwind and the storm. The billowing clouds are the dust beneath his feet. . . .

Who can stand before his fierce anger? Who can survive his burning fury? His rage blazes forth like fire, and the mountains crumble to dust in his presence.

The LORD is good. When trouble comes, he is a strong refuge. And he knows everyone who trusts in him. But he sweeps away his enemies in an overwhelming flood. He pursues his foes into the darkness of night.

Why are you scheming against the LORD? He will destroy you with one blow; he won't need to strike twice!

Nahum 1:2-3,6-9

O Assyrian king, your princes lie dead in the dust. Your people are scattered across the mountains. There is no longer a shepherd to gather them together. There is no healing for your wound; your injury is fatal. All who hear of your destruction will clap their hands for joy. Where can anyone be found who has not suffered from your cruelty?

Nahum 3:18-19

Related Texts: Exodus 34:1-7; Jonah; John 3:31-36; Romans 1:18-19; Ephesians 5:5-6

CHECK IT OUT

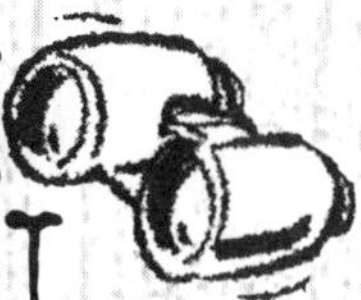

In many Old Testament passages we have seen God's anger and disappointment directed at both individuals and nations. In the New Testament, God's anger is aimed at those who push away God's truth. Check out Romans 1:18-20: "But God shows his anger from heaven against all sinful, wicked people who push the truth away from themselves. For the truth about God is known to them instinctively. God has put this knowledge in their hearts. From the time the world was created, people have seen the earth and sky and all that God made. They can clearly see his invisible qualities—his eternal power and divine nature. So they have no excuse whatsoever for not knowing God (when standing before God at Judgment Day)."

We can avoid God's anger by following the truth He has revealed to us. If you know the truth, the truth will set you free from God's anger.

done ☐

Zephaniah: Jerusalem's Correction

How terrible it will be for rebellious, polluted Jerusalem, the city of violence and crime. It proudly refuses to listen even to the voice of the LORD. No one can tell it anything; it refuses all correction. It does not trust in the LORD or draw near to its God.

Its leaders are like roaring lions hunting for their victims—out for everything they can get. Its judges are like ravenous wolves at evening time, who by dawn have left no trace of their prey. Its prophets are arrogant liars seeking their own gain. Its priests defile the Temple by disobeying God's laws. But the LORD is still there in the city, and he does no wrong. Day by day his justice is more evident, but no one takes notice—the wicked know no shame. . . .

Sing, O daughter of Zion; shout aloud, O Israel! Be glad and rejoice with all your heart, O daughter of Jerusalem! For the LORD will remove his hand of judgment and will disperse the armies of your enemy. And the LORD himself, the King of Israel, will live among you! At last your troubles will be over, and you will fear disaster no more.

On that day the announcement to Jerusalem will be, "Cheer up, Zion! Don't be afraid! For the LORD your God has arrived to live among you. He is a mighty savior. He will rejoice over you with great gladness. With his love, he will calm all your fears. He will exult over you by singing a happy song."

Zephaniah 3:1-5,14-17

Related Texts: Psalms 25; 34:1-5; Isaiah 40; Romans 10:9-11

One Minute Memory

For the **LORD** your God **has arrived** to **live among you.** He is a mighty **savior.** He **will rejoice over you** with great **gladness.** With his love, **he will calm all your fears.** He will exult over **you** by **singing a happy song.** *Zephaniah 3:17*

done ☐

The Call of Jeremiah: Part 1

These are the words of Jeremiah son of Hilkiah, one of the priests from Anathoth, a town in the land of Benjamin. The LORD first gave messages to Jeremiah during the thirteenth year of King Josiah's reign in Judah. He continued to give messages throughout the reign of Josiah's son, King Jehoiakim, until the eleventh year of King Zedekiah's reign in Judah. In August of that year, the people of Jerusalem were taken away as captives.

The LORD gave me a message. He said, "I knew you before I formed you in your mother's womb. Before you were born I set you apart and appointed you as my spokesman to the world."

"O Sovereign LORD," I said, "I can't speak for you! I'm too young!"

"Don't say that," the LORD replied, "for you must go wherever I send you and say whatever I tell you. And don't be afraid of the people, for I will be with you and take care of you. I, the LORD, have spoken!"

Then the LORD touched my mouth and said, "See, I have put my words in your mouth! Today I appoint you to stand up against nations and kingdoms. You are to uproot some and tear them down, to destroy and overthrow them. You are to build others up and plant them."

Jeremiah 1:1-10

Related Texts: Psalm 136; Isaiah 6; Luke 1:13-16; 1 Timothy 4:12

CATCH THIS

When God wants to use someone, He doesn't respond to excuses such as those Jeremiah used: "I can't do that! I'm far too young! I'm only a youth!" Jeremiah may not have felt qualified because he lacked training and experience. But that didn't matter to God. God overruled his excuses and let him know that His authority and presence didn't depend on Jeremiah's training or experience. God was present in the prophet's life.

Excuses don't limit God when He wants to get hold of our life. So get rid of your excuses and prepare yourself to be used by God. Preparing yourself means being open to God and faithful to living the Christian life. If you have any excuses, go ahead and list them, share them with a friend or youth pastor, and then throw them away. Remember, it's not you anyway—it's God working in you.

done ☐

JUST a THOUGHT

Where **God** leads, He will provide for your needs!

The Call of Jeremiah: Part 2

Then the LORD spoke to me again and asked, "What do you see now?"

And I replied, "I see a pot of boiling water, tipping from the north."

"Yes," the LORD said, "for terror from the north will boil out on the people of this land. Listen! I am calling the armies of the kingdoms of the north to come to Jerusalem. They will set their thrones at the gates of the city. They will attack its walls and all the other towns of Judah. I will pronounce judgment on my people for all their evil—for deserting me and worshiping other gods. Yes, they worship idols that they themselves have made!

"Get up and get dressed. Go out, and tell them whatever I tell you to say. Do not be afraid of them, or I will make you look foolish in front of them. For see, today I have made you immune to their attacks. You are strong like a fortified city that cannot be captured, like an iron pillar or a bronze wall. None of the kings, officials, priests, or people of Judah will be able to stand against you. They will try, but they will fail. For I am with you, and I will take care of you. I, the LORD, have spoken!"

Jeremiah 1:13-19

Related Texts: Deuteronomy 28; Joshua 1; Ezekiel 11; 24; 33:1-20; 1 John 5:3-4

done ☐

Jeremiah Is Saved by Micah's Prophecy

This message came to Jeremiah from the LORD early in the reign of Jehoiakim son of Josiah, king of Judah. . . .

"Say to them, 'This is what the LORD says: If you will not listen to me and obey the law I have given you, and if you will not listen to my servants, the prophets—for I sent them again and again to warn you, but you would not listen to them—then I will destroy this Temple as I destroyed Shiloh, the place where the Tabernacle was located. And I will make Jerusalem an object of cursing in every nation on earth.' ". . .

The priests, the prophets, and all the people listened to Jeremiah as he spoke in front of the LORD's Temple. But when Jeremiah had finished his message, saying everything the LORD had told him to say, the priests and prophets and all the people at the Temple mobbed him. "Kill him!" they shouted. . . .

Then some of the wise old men stood and spoke to the people there. They said, "Think back to the days when Micah of Moresheth prophesied during the reign of King Hezekiah of Judah. He told the people of Judah, 'This is what the LORD Almighty says: Mount Zion will be plowed like an open field; Jerusalem will be reduced to rubble! A great forest will grow on the hilltop, where the Temple now stands.' But did King Hezekiah and the people kill him for saying this? No, they turned from their sins and worshiped the LORD. They begged him to have mercy on them. Then the LORD held back the terrible disaster he had pronounced against them. If we kill Jeremiah, who knows what will happen to us?"

Jeremiah 26:1,4-6,7-8,17-19

Related Texts: Jeremiah 18:1-11; 19:1–20:2; 38:1-13; Lamentations 3:52-57; Micah 3:9-12; Matthew 16:13-14

Although being a prophet was a "big-time" responsibility, holding that job had nothing to do with who the parents were. Being a king or priest was a hereditary position, which parents passed down the family line. Prophets were different because they came from all different backgrounds and life experiences. They had a special calling from God.

Again and again we see the Bible filled with ordinary people doing extraordinary things. Let that be an encouragement to you today. And be reminded that if you're a Christian, you're part of an incredible family line and eternal life is passed on to you from Jesus.

done ☐

JUDAH GOES INTO EXILE

Zedekiah was twenty-one years old when he became king, and he reigned in Jerusalem eleven years. He did what was evil in the sight of the LORD his God, and he refused to humble himself in the presence of the prophet Jeremiah, who spoke for the LORD. . . .

The LORD, the God of their ancestors, repeatedly sent his prophets to warn them, for he had compassion on his people and his Temple. But the people mocked these messengers of God and despised their words. They scoffed at the prophets until the LORD's anger could no longer be restrained and there was no remedy.

So the LORD brought the king of Babylon against them. The Babylonians killed Judah's young men, even chasing after them into the Temple. They had no pity on the people, killing both young and old, men and women, healthy and sick. God handed them all over to Nebuchadnezzar. The king also took home to Babylon all the utensils, large and small, used in the Temple of God, and the treasures from both the LORD's Temple and the royal palace. He also took with him all the royal princes. Then his army set fire to the Temple of God, broke down the walls of Jerusalem, burned all the palaces, and completely destroyed everything of value. The few who survived were taken away to Babylon, and they became servants to the king and his sons until the kingdom of Persia came to power. So the message of the LORD spoken through Jeremiah was fulfilled. The land finally enjoyed its Sabbath rest, lying desolate for seventy years, just as the prophet had said.

2 Chronicles 36:11-12,15-21

Related Texts: Leviticus 26:1-43; 2 Kings 20:12-18; 25; Isaiah 39; Jeremiah 25; 38; 52; Matthew 1:1-17

What's it Mean?

Jeremiah had warned the Israelites that their temple would be destroyed. Today's reading describes this destruction that was the result of their sin, for they had taken God out of their temple. God tried to show great compassion to the Israelites by warning them through the prophets. But the Babylonian enemy showed no compassion at all and even killed them in the temple itself. God's presence had left the temple. The Babylonians burned the temple and plundered its treasures.

Your church building allows people to gather for worship, but God doesn't live in your church. The Bible informs us that Christians are God's temple because His presence lives in people. Are you doing anything to your body or life that might be destroying God's temple? If so, what can you do today to stop the destruction?

done ☐

Lament over Fallen Jerusalem

Jerusalem's streets, once bustling with people, are now silent. Like a widow broken with grief, she sits alone in her mourning. Once the queen of nations, she is now a slave.

She sobs through the night; tears stream down her cheeks. Among all her lovers, there is no one left to help her. All her friends have betrayed her; they are now her enemies.

Lamentations 1:1-2

I cry out, "My splendor is gone! Everything I had hoped for from the LORD is lost!"

The thought of my suffering and homelessness is bitter beyond words. I will never forget this awful time, as I grieve over my loss. Yet I still dare to hope when I remember this:

The unfailing love of the LORD never ends! By his mercies we have been kept from complete destruction. Great is his faithfulness; his mercies begin afresh each day. I say to myself, "The LORD is my inheritance; therefore, I will hope in him!"

The LORD is wonderfully good to those who wait for him and seek him. So it is good to wait quietly for salvation from the LORD.

Lamentations 3:18-26

Related Texts: Psalm 137; Ezekiel 19; 24; Matthew 23:33-39

One Minute Memory

The **Lord** is wonderfully good to those who wait for him and **seek him.**

Lamentations 3:25

done ☐

CHECK IT OUT

Obadiah describes God's punishment on Edom for helping Babylon invade and conquer Israel. He prophesied that God would destroy the Edomites because of their actions.

In many places throughout the Bible it has been prophesied that God will punish and destroy all those who have not repented of their sin. Check out Peter's description of what this future will look like: "But the day of the Lord will come as unexpectedly as a thief. Then the heavens will pass away with a terrible noise, and everything in them will disappear in fire, and the earth and everything on it will be exposed to judgment....You should look forward to that day and hurry it along—the day when God will set the heavens on fire and the elements will melt away in the flames" (2 Pet. 3:10,12).

It's good advice to be on God's side. God is compassionate and slow to anger, but his final judgment against the godless will be severe. Read the rest of 2 Peter 3 and see how you are called to prepare yourself.

The Lord Promises Vengeance on Babylon

Look at the proud! They trust in themselves, and their lives are crooked; but the righteous will live by their faith. Wealth is treacherous, and the arrogant are never at rest. They range far and wide, with their mouths opened as wide as death, but they are never satisfied. In their greed they have gathered up many nations and peoples. But the time is coming when all their captives will taunt them, saying, "You thieves! At last justice has caught up with you! Now you will get what you deserve for your oppression and extortion!"

Habakkuk 2:4-6

I trembled inside when I heard all this; my lips quivered with fear. My legs gave way beneath me, and I shook in terror. I will wait quietly for the coming day when disaster will strike the people who invade us. Even though the fig trees have no blossoms, and there are no grapes on the vine; even though the olive crop fails, and the fields lie empty and barren; even though the flocks die in the fields, and the cattle barns are empty, yet I will rejoice in the LORD! I will be joyful in the God of my salvation. The Sovereign LORD is my strength! He will make me as surefooted as a deer and bring me safely over the mountains.

Habakkuk 3:16-19

Related Texts: Genesis 9:5-6; 12:1-3; Romans 1:16-17; Galatians 3:8-14; Hebrews 10:32-39

Obadiah: The Day of the Lord

At that time not a single wise person will be left in the whole land of Edom!" says the LORD. "For on the mountains of Edom I will destroy everyone who has wisdom and understanding.

"And why? Because of the violence you did to your close relatives in Israel. Now you will be destroyed completely and filled with shame forever. For you deserted your relatives in Israel during their time of greatest need. You stood aloof, refusing to lift a finger to help when foreign invaders carried off their wealth and cast lots to divide up Jerusalem. You acted as though you were one of Israel's enemies.

"You shouldn't have done this! You shouldn't have gloated when they exiled your relatives to distant lands. You shouldn't have rejoiced because they were suffering such misfortune. You shouldn't have crowed over them as they suffered these disasters.

"The day is near when I, the LORD, will judge the godless nations! As you have done to Israel, so it will be done to you. All your evil deeds will fall back on your own heads. Just as you swallowed up my people on my holy mountain, so you and the surrounding nations will swallow the punishment I pour out on you. Yes, you nations will drink and stagger and disappear from history, as though you had never even existed.

"But Jerusalem will become a refuge for those who escape; it will be a holy place. And the people of Israel will come back to reclaim their inheritance."

Obadiah 8,10-12,15-17

Related Texts: Isaiah 13; Joel 3; 2 Peter 3

Obadiah is the shortest of the thirty-nine Old Testament books. In only twenty-one verses the prophet Obadiah expressed nothing but bad news. His words were directed at the Edomites, who rejoiced at the destruction of Jerusalem. The Edomites were a neighboring nation who were always opposing the Israelites.

God loved the Israelites, His chosen children, and promised to deal forcefully with the nations that went against them. As a Christian, you are one of God's children. He will protect you—count on it.

EZEKIEL SEES THE RESTORATION OF ISRAEL

The LORD took hold of me, and I was carried away by the Spirit of the LORD to a valley filled with bones. He led me around among the old, dry bones that covered the valley floor. . . .

Then he said to me, "Speak to these bones and say, 'Dry bones, listen to the word of the LORD! This is what the Sovereign LORD says: Look! I am going to breathe into you and make you live again! I will put flesh and muscles on you and cover you with skin. I will put breath into you, and you will come to life. Then you will know that I am the LORD.' "

So I spoke these words, just as he told me. Suddenly as I spoke, there was a rattling noise all across the valley. The bones of each body came together and attached themselves as they had been before. . . .

Then he said to me, "Speak to the winds and say: 'This is what the Sovereign LORD says: Come, O breath, from the four winds! Breathe into these dead bodies so that they may live again.' "

So I spoke as he commanded me, and the wind entered the bodies, and they began to breathe. They all came to life and stood up on their feet—a great army of them.

Then he said to me, "Son of man, these bones represent the people of Israel. They are saying, 'We have become old, dry bones—all hope is gone.' Now give them this message from the Sovereign LORD: O my people, I will open your graves of exile and cause you to rise again. Then I will bring you back to the land of Israel. . . . I will put my Spirit in you, and you will live and return home to your own land. Then you will know that I am the LORD. You will see that I have done everything just as I promised. I, the LORD, have spoken!"

Ezekiel 37:1-2a,4-7,9-12,14

Related Texts: Deuteronomy 30:1-10; Psalm 80; Isaiah 40; Ezekiel 36; Acts 17:24-25; 2 Thessalonians 2:7-8

What's it Mean?

Ezekiel's vision is an example of something that only God could accomplish. The scattered bones refer to the nation of Israel, who seemed to be spiritually dead and hopeless. Only God could restore this nation. It was God's promise!

Today there are nations, churches, and people who are spiritually dead and hopeless. Like the nation of Israel, only God can restore them. Our responsibility is to pray for them. If your church or youth group is a graveyard of scattered bones, you should pray that God would breathe life into it. It may appear hopeless, but it's not impossible for God. Begin praying today for those "dead bones" that only God can raise up.

 done ☐

The Writing on the Wall

A number of years later, King Belshazzar gave a great feast for a thousand of his nobles and drank wine with them. While Belshazzar was drinking, he gave orders to bring in the gold and silver cups that his predecessor, Nebuchadnezzar, had taken from the Temple in Jerusalem, so that he and his nobles, his wives, and his concubines might drink from them. . . . They drank toasts from them to honor their idols made of gold, silver, bronze, iron, wood, and stone.

At that very moment they saw the fingers of a human hand writing on the plaster wall of the king's palace, near the lampstand. The king himself saw the hand as it wrote, and his face turned pale with fear. Such terror gripped him that his knees knocked together and his legs gave way beneath him. . . .

But when the queen mother heard what was happening, she hurried to the banquet hall. She said to Belshazzar, "Long live the king! Don't be so pale and afraid about this. There is a man in your kingdom who has within him the spirit of the holy gods. During Nebuchadnezzar's reign, this man was found to have insight, understanding, and wisdom as though he himself were a god. Your predecessor, King Nebuchadnezzar, made him chief over all the magicians, enchanters, astrologers, and fortune-tellers of Babylon. This man Daniel, whom the king named Belteshazzar, has a sharp mind and is filled with divine knowledge and understanding. He can interpret dreams, explain riddles, and solve difficult problems. Call for Daniel, and he will tell you what the writing means."

Daniel 5:1-2,4-6,10-12

Related Texts: Genesis 41; Daniel 1-4; Joel 2:28-32; Acts 2:1-21

Personality Plus

Daniel

Daniel was born in Israel but was taken captive in 605 B.C. by the Babylonians. He became a servant of the Babylonian king, Nebuchadnezzar. In an attempt to brainwash and take away Daniel's identity, he was given the name Belteshazzar. But Daniel had an unwavering, deep-rooted faith in God. Because of this faith, God granted him gifts of exceptional wisdom and understanding.

As you read about Daniel, you'll see his godliness expressed in his courage.

done ☐

JUST a THOUGHT

It's much easier to keep your mouth closed and your hand open for gifts than it is to reject rewards and speak against the wickedness of the gift giver!

Daniel Interprets the Writing

So Daniel was brought in before the king. The king asked him, "Are you Daniel, who was exiled from Judah by my predecessor, King Nebuchadnezzar? . . . I am told that you can give interpretations and solve difficult problems. If you can read these words and tell me their meaning, you will be clothed in purple robes of royal honor, and you will wear a gold chain around your neck. You will become the third highest ruler in the kingdom."

Daniel answered the king, "Keep your gifts or give them to someone else, but I will tell you what the writing means. . . . For you have defied the LORD of heaven and have had these cups from his Temple brought before you. You and your nobles and your wives and concubines have been drinking wine from them while praising gods of silver, gold, bronze, iron, wood, and stone—gods that neither see nor hear nor know anything at all. But you have not honored the God who gives you the breath of life and controls your destiny! So God has sent this hand to write a message.

"This is the message that was written: Mene, Mene, Tekel, Parsin. This is what these words mean:

Mene means 'numbered'—God has numbered the days of your reign and has brought it to an end.

Tekel means 'weighed'—you have been weighed on the balances and have failed the test.

Parsin means 'divided'—your kingdom has been divided and given to the Medes and Persians." . . .

That very night Belshazzar, the Babylonian king, was killed. And Darius the Mede took over the kingdom at the age of sixty-two.

Daniel 5:13,16-17,23-28,30-31

Related Texts: Isaiah 47; Daniel 4; Matthew 24:14-22; 1 Corinthians 12

 done ☐

Cyrus Sends Israel Home

In the first year of King Cyrus of Persia, the LORD fulfilled Jeremiah's prophecy by stirring the heart of Cyrus to put this proclamation into writing and to send it throughout his kingdom:

"This is what King Cyrus of Persia says: The LORD, the God of heaven, has given me all the kingdoms of the earth. He has appointed me to build him a Temple at Jerusalem in the land of Judah. All of you who are his people may return to Jerusalem in Judah to rebuild this Temple of the LORD, the God of Israel, who lives in Jerusalem. And may your God be with you! Those who live in any place where Jewish survivors are found should contribute toward their expenses by supplying them with silver and gold, supplies for the journey, and livestock, as well as a freewill offering for the Temple of God in Jerusalem."

Then God stirred the hearts of the priests and Levites and the leaders of the tribes of Judah and Benjamin to return to Jerusalem to rebuild the Temple of the LORD. And all their neighbors assisted by giving them vessels of silver and gold, supplies for the journey, and livestock. They gave them many choice gifts in addition to all the freewill offerings.

King Cyrus himself brought out the valuable items which King Nebuchadnezzar had taken from the LORD's Temple in Jerusalem and had placed in the temple of his own gods.

Ezra 1:1-7

Related Texts: 2 Chronicles 36:22-23; Jeremiah 25:11-12; 29:10-14

BIG TIMe WoRd

CONTRIBUTE

In the rebuilding of the temple, the Israelites needed to help out with the workload or contribute to the finances.

When we think of contributing, we usually think of donating money to church or to a worthy organization. But you can contribute more than your money. In addition to money, God can use your skills and your time. Numerous ministries outside the church need your contribution to help build and rebuild their ministries.

Make a contribution today! Your contribution may not seem like much to you, but it may be a treasure to another.

done ☐

28 SEPTEMBER

Haggai: Rebuild the Temple!

"This is what the LORD Almighty says: The people are saying, 'The time has not yet come to rebuild the LORD's house—the Temple.' "

So the LORD sent this message through the prophet Haggai: "Why are you living in luxurious houses while my house lies in ruins?. . .

"This is what the LORD Almighty says: Consider how things are going for you! Now go up into the hills, bring down timber, and rebuild my house. Then I will take pleasure in it and be honored, says the LORD. You hoped for rich harvests, but they were poor. And when you brought your harvest home, I blew it away. Why? Because my house lies in ruins, says the LORD Almighty, while you are all busy building your own fine houses. That is why the heavens have withheld the dew and the earth has withheld its crops. I have called for a drought on your fields and hills—a drought to wither the grain and grapes and olives and all your other crops, a drought to starve both you and your cattle and to ruin everything you have worked so hard to get."

Then Zerubbabel son of Shealtiel, Jeshua son of Jehozadak, the high priest, and the whole remnant of God's people obeyed the message from the LORD their God. It had been delivered by the prophet Haggai, whom the LORD their God had sent, and the people worshiped the LORD in earnest

Haggai 1:2-4,7-12

Related Texts: Haggai 2; Zechariah 1-6; 1 Corinthians 3:9-17; 2 Corinthians 6:14-16; Ephesians 2:11-22

Give it a try

God withheld His blessing from the people because of their selfish hearts. What are two things in your life that cause you to have a selfish heart?

1.

2.

Today, ask God to work on the selfish areas in your life.

done ☐

Zechariah Encourages the Exiles

Then on February 15 of the second year of King Darius's reign, the LORD sent another message to the prophet Zechariah son of Berekiah and grandson of Iddo. Zechariah said:

In a vision during the night, I saw a man sitting on a red horse that was standing among some myrtle trees in a small valley. Behind him were red, brown, and white horses, each with its own rider. . . .

Then the other riders reported to the angel of the LORD, who was standing among the myrtle trees, "We have patrolled the earth, and the whole earth is at peace."

Upon hearing this, the angel of the LORD prayed this prayer: "O LORD Almighty, for seventy years now you have been angry with Jerusalem and the towns of Judah. How long will it be until you again show mercy to them?" And the LORD spoke kind and comforting words to the angel who talked with me.

Then the angel said to me, "Shout this message for all to hear: 'This is what the LORD Almighty says: My love for Jerusalem and Mount Zion is passionate and strong. But I am very angry with the other nations that enjoy peace and security. I was only a little angry with my people, but the nations punished them far beyond my intentions.

" 'Therefore, this is what the LORD says: I have returned to show mercy to Jerusalem. My Temple will be rebuilt, says the LORD Almighty, and plans will be made for the reconstruction of Jerusalem.' Say this also: 'This is what the LORD Almighty says: The towns of Israel will again overflow with prosperity, and the LORD will again comfort Zion and choose Jerusalem as his own.' "

Zechariah 1:7-8,11-17

Related Texts: Isaiah 40:1-2; Zechariah 1-6; 1 Corinthians 14:3; 2 Corinthians 1:3-7

CHECK IT OUT

The Israelites suffered great pain and defeat. Although God directed His anger toward the nations that beat up the Israelites, He also expressed compassion for the Israelites' pain.

In the New Testament we read that God expresses compassion for suffering Christians. Check out 2 Corinthians 1:3-4: "All praise to the God and Father of our Lord Jesus Christ. He is the source of every mercy and the God who comforts us. He comforts us in all our troubles so that we can comfort others. When others are troubled, we will be able to give them the same comfort God has given us."

Rest in the promise that God continues to give encouragement and support to those in need.

done ☐

JUST a THOUGHT

Discouragement and fear are two tactics the devil uses to stop God's work. Don't let them get in your way.

The Exiles Rebuild the Temple

The enemies of Judah and Benjamin heard that the exiles were rebuilding a Temple to the LORD, the God of Israel. So they approached Zerubbabel and the other leaders and said, "Let us build with you, for we worship your God just as you do. We have sacrificed to him ever since King Esarhaddon of Assyria brought us here."

But Zerubbabel, Jeshua, and the other leaders of Israel replied, "You may have no part in this work, for we have nothing in common. We alone will build the Temple for the LORD, the God of Israel, just as King Cyrus of Persia commanded us."

Then the local residents tried to discourage and frighten the people of Judah to keep them from their work. They bribed agents to work against them and to frustrate their aims. This went on during the entire reign of King Cyrus of Persia and lasted until King Darius of Persia took the throne.

Ezra 4:1-5

Tattenai, governor of the province west of the Euphrates River, and Shethar-bozenai and their colleagues complied at once with the command of King Darius. So the Jewish leaders continued their work, and they were greatly encouraged by the preaching of the prophets Haggai and Zechariah son of Iddo. The Temple was finally finished, as had been commanded by the God of Israel and decreed by Cyrus, Darius, and Artaxerxes, the kings of Persia. The Temple was completed on March 12, during the sixth year of King Darius's reign.

Ezra 6:13-15

Related Texts: Ezra 3-6; Ezekiel 40-48; Haggai 1-2; John 2:13-21

done ☐

october

I feel that a comprehensive study of the **Bible** is a **liberal** education for anyone. Nearly **all** the great **men** of **our** country have been **well versed** in the teachings of the Bible.

Franklin D. Roosevelt
(1882–1945)
United States President

OCTOBER 1

Nehemiah Prays for the Exiles

These are the memoirs of Nehemiah son of Hacaliah.

In late autumn of the twentieth year of King Artaxerxes' reign, I was at the fortress of Susa. Hanani, one of my brothers, came to visit me with some other men who had just arrived from Judah. I asked them about the Jews who had survived the captivity and about how things were going in Jerusalem. They said to me, "Things are not going well for those who returned to the province of Judah. They are in great trouble and disgrace. The wall of Jerusalem has been torn down, and the gates have been burned."

When I heard this, I sat down and wept. In fact, for days I mourned, fasted, and prayed to the God of heaven. Then I said, "O LORD, God of heaven, the great and awesome God who keeps his covenant of unfailing love with those who love him and obey his commands, listen to my prayer! Look down and see me praying night and day for your people Israel. I confess that we have sinned against you. Yes, even my own family and I have sinned! We have sinned terribly by not obeying the commands, laws, and regulations that you gave us through your servant Moses.

"Please remember what you told your servant Moses: 'If you sin, I will scatter you among the nations. But if you return to me and obey my commands, even if you are exiled to the ends of the earth, I will bring you back to the place I have chosen for my name to be honored.' "

Nehemiah 1:1-9

Related Texts: Leviticus 26:14-46; Deuteronomy 7:6-15; 28:15-68; Daniel 9:1-19; James 5:13-16

Personality Plus

Nehemiah

Nehemiah is an example of a great leader. He had to provide the necessary leadership to rebuild the wall of Jerusalem. This was no easy job! He faced one obstacle after another. But his vision, courage, and faith were much stronger than any of the problems that came his way.

Nehemiah's prayer life is one leadership quality worth studying. He knew his strongest defense against the enemy was to be on his knees and in conversation with God.

Check out Nehemiah, copy his characteristics, begin praying about everything, and ask God to bless your leadership.

done ☐

2 OCTOBER

CHECK IT OUT

Being a Christian isn't easy. Trying to follow God and keeping His Commandments will bring opposition, frustration, and trials. But Jesus understands these struggles and reminds Christians that problems are only temporary. Check out the good news in John 16:33: "I have told you all this so that you may have peace in me. Here on earth you will have many trials and sorrows. But take heart, because I have overcome the world."

This is a great verse to remember when you're struggling. Pain is temporary. Trials will clear up. Problems will pass away. Christians will have an eternity to rejoice and celebrate because Jesus has overcome the world.

Praise Him today.

The Exiles Rebuild Jerusalem's Wall

At last the wall was completed to half its original height around the entire city, for the people had worked very hard. But when Sanballat and Tobiah and the Arabs, Ammonites, and Ashdodites heard that the work was going ahead and that the gaps in the wall were being repaired, they became furious. They all made plans to come and fight against Jerusalem and to bring about confusion there. But we prayed to our God and guarded the city day and night to protect ourselves. . . .

But from then on, only half my men worked while the other half stood guard with spears, shields, bows, and coats of mail. The officers stationed themselves behind the people of Judah who were building the wall. The common laborers carried on their work with one hand supporting their load and one hand holding a weapon. All the builders had a sword belted to their side.

Nehemiah 4:6-9,16-18a

So on October 2 the wall was finally finished—just fifty-two days after we had begun. When our enemies and the surrounding nations heard about it, they were frightened and humiliated. They realized that this work had been done with the help of our God.

Nehemiah 6:15-16

Related Texts: Nehemiah 2–6; Psalms 27; 51:18-19; 127:1; John 16:33; 1 John 4:4

Pray for the Peace of Jerusalem

I was glad when they said to me,
"Let us go to the house of the LORD."
And now we are standing here
inside your gates, O Jerusalem.
Jerusalem is a well-built city,
knit together as a single unit.
All the people of Israel—the LORD's people—
make their pilgrimage here.
They come to give thanks to the name of the LORD as the law requires.
Here stand the thrones where judgment is given,
the thrones of the dynasty of David.
Pray for the peace of Jerusalem.
May all who love this city prosper.
O Jerusalem, may there be peace within your walls
and prosperity in your palaces.
For the sake of my family and friends, I will say,
"Peace be with you."
For the sake of the house of the LORD our God,
I will seek what is best for you, O Jerusalem.

Psalm 122

Related Texts: Psalm 85; Zechariah 9:9-17; Luke 13:34-35; Ephesians 2:11-22

BIG TIME WORD

PEACE

Peace is an important word for Christians. Those without a relationship with God really can't understand or experience the peace God offers. This peace comes from being in harmony with God and with other people and brings a confidence that doesn't worry. It's a peace that can't be quenched. God used Jesus to bring this type of peace into the world. Those who rejected Jesus rejected His peace.

If you're a Christian and you don't feel peace, then talk to someone who can provide you wise counsel and help you experience this peace. It's worth the risk of asking someone for help—go for it today!

done ☐

Personality Plus

Ezra

Ezra was a priest known for his diligent study of the Scriptures. While in Babylonian captivity, he took advantage of a negative situation and made it positive for himself as well as for the Israelites. Ezra's work strengthened the Israelites' faith and helped them keep focused on God.

How much work would it take for you to become a man or woman of God who knows the Scriptures can spiritually influence others?

Try putting together an action plan on how you might become this type of person.

Ezra Reads the Law to the Exiles

Ezra the priest brought the scroll of the law before the assembly, which included the men and women and all the children old enough to understand. He faced the square just inside the Water Gate from early morning until noon and read aloud to everyone who could understand. All the people paid close attention to the Book of the Law. . . .

Ezra stood on the platform in full view of all the people. When they saw him open the book, they all rose to their feet.

Then Ezra praised the LORD, the great God, and all the people chanted, "Amen! Amen!" as they lifted their hands toward heaven. Then they bowed down and worshiped the LORD with their faces to the ground.

Now the Levites—Jeshua, Bani, Sherebiah, Jamin, Akkub, Shabbethai, Hodiah, Maaseiah, Kelita, Azariah, Jozabad, Hanan, and Pelaiah—instructed the people who were standing there. They read from the Book of the Law of God and clearly explained the meaning of what was being read, helping the people understand each passage. Then Nehemiah the governor, Ezra the priest and scribe, and the Levites who were interpreting for the people said to them, "Don't weep on such a day as this! For today is a sacred day before the LORD your God." All the people had been weeping as they listened to the words of the law.

And Nehemiah continued, "Go and celebrate with a feast of choice foods and sweet drinks, and share gifts of food with people who have nothing prepared. This is a sacred day before our LORD. Don't be dejected and sad, for the joy of the LORD is your strength!"

Nehemiah 8:2-3,5-10

Related Texts: Deuteronomy 16:13-15; Ezra 6:19-22; Isaiah 58; Matthew 13:18-23; Acts 17:10-11

done ☐

OCTOBER 5

Persia Needs a New Queen

This happened in the days of King Xerxes, who reigned over 127 provinces stretching from India to Ethiopia. At that time he ruled his empire from his throne at the fortress of Susa. In the third year of his reign, he gave a banquet for all his princes and officials. He invited all the military officers of Media and Persia, as well as the noblemen and provincial officials. . . .

On the seventh day of the feast, when King Xerxes was half drunk with wine, he told Mehuman, Biztha, Harbona, Bigtha, Abagtha, Zethar, and Carcas, the seven eunuchs who attended him, to bring Queen Vashti to him with the royal crown on her head. He wanted all the men to gaze on her beauty, for she was a very beautiful woman. But when they conveyed the king's order to Queen Vashti, she refused to come. This made the king furious, and he burned with anger. . . .

Memucan answered the king and his princes, "Queen Vashti has wronged not only the king but also every official and citizen throughout your empire. . . . So if it please the king, we suggest that you issue a written decree, a law of the Persians and Medes that cannot be revoked. It should order that Queen Vashti be forever banished from your presence and that you choose another queen more worthy than she. When this decree is published throughout your vast empire, husbands everywhere, whatever their rank, will receive proper respect from their wives!"

Esther 1:1-3,10-12,16,19-20

Related Texts: Ezra 4:1-6; Proverbs 31:1-9; Daniel 9:1-2; 1 Corinthians 6:9-10

done ☐

The name of God is not mentioned in the entire Book of Esther.

Nevertheless, the book's 167 verses definitely show the hand of God working in people's lives. The Book of Esther is a story of God's love for the Israelites and His protection for them.

God is always loving and protecting—even when you're not aware of it. Today, look for ways God is working in your life that you normally wouldn't notice.

His work doesn't stop even when His name isn't mentioned.

6 OCTOBER

Personality Plus

Esther

Esther was a Jewish orphan raised in Persia by her uncle Mordecai. She became the queen of Persia when the previous queen refused to appear at a banquet hosted by her husband. Her absence offended the king, and he chose Esther to replace her.

As queen, Esther kept her Jewish identity a secret even though she remained faithful to the Jewish people by stopping a madman from destroying the Jewish race.

Over and over we see God using unlikely people like Esther to do great things. Sometimes God uses men; other times He uses women. You never know when He's going to use you.

Prepare yourself to be used by God today.

Esther Becomes Queen of Persia

Now at the fortress of Susa there was a certain Jew named Mordecai son of Jair. He was from the tribe of Benjamin and was a descendant of Kish and Shimei. His family had been exiled from Jerusalem to Babylon by King Nebuchadnezzar, along with King Jehoiachin of Judah and many others. This man had a beautiful and lovely young cousin, Hadassah, who was also called Esther. When her father and mother had died, Mordecai adopted her into his family and raised her as his own daughter. As a result of the king's decree, Esther, along with many other young women, was brought to the king's harem at the fortress of Susa and placed in Hegai's care. Hegai was very impressed with Esther and treated her kindly. He quickly ordered a special menu for her and provided her with beauty treatments. He also assigned her seven maids specially chosen from the king's palace, and he moved her and her maids into the best place in the harem.

Esther had not told anyone of her nationality and family background, for Mordecai had told her not to. Every day Mordecai would take a walk near the courtyard of the harem to ask about Esther and to find out what was happening to her. . . .

The king loved her more than any of the other young women. He was so delighted with her that he set the royal crown on her head and declared her queen instead of Vashti.

Esther 2:5-11,17

Related Texts: Genesis 39; 41; Nehemiah 1:1-11; 1 Peter 3:1-6

done ☐

HAMAN PLOTS TO KILL THE JEWS

Some time later, King Xerxes promoted Haman son of Hammedatha the Agagite to prime minister, making him the most powerful official in the empire next to the king himself. All the king's officials would bow down before Haman to show him respect whenever he passed by, for so the king had commanded. But Mordecai refused to bow down or show him respect. . . .

When Haman saw that Mordecai would not bow down or show him respect, he was filled with rage. So he decided it was not enough to lay hands on Mordecai alone. Since he had learned that Mordecai was a Jew, he decided to destroy all the Jews throughout the entire empire of Xerxes. . . .

Then Haman approached King Xerxes and said, "There is a certain race of people scattered through all the provinces of your empire. Their laws are different from those of any other nation, and they refuse to obey even the laws of the king. So it is not in the king's interest to let them live. If it please Your Majesty, issue a decree that they be destroyed, and I will give 375 tons of silver to the government administrators so they can put it into the royal treasury."

The king agreed, confirming his decision by removing his signet ring from his finger and giving it to Haman son of Hammedatha the Agagite—the enemy of the Jews. "Keep the money," the king told Haman, "but go ahead and do as you like with these people."

Esther 3:1-2,5-6,8-11

Related Texts: Genesis 12:1-3; Deuteronomy 30:1-7; Esther 4–6; Psalm 44:1-8; Daniel 3; 6; Romans 9-11

What's it Mean?

Haman was a madman full of pride who became outraged when Mordecai didn't bow to him. Rather than confronting Mordecai with his anger, he made an oath to kill the entire race of Jewish people. But God thwarted his plans and used Esther to save the Jewish people. Haman was then killed as a result of his evil plans.

Throughout thousands of years, Haman has been followed by others who have expressed rage and hatred by committing crimes on innocent victims. We need to pray daily for these angry people and do whatever we can do to stamp out hatred. Today, ask God to give you a sensitive heart that mourns over hatred.

Walk in love today and be an example for others to follow.

done ☐

JUST a THOUGHT

"When a situation seems hopeless, remind yourself of God's power and ask Him to turn things around. He has done it before and can do it again.

Haman's Downfall

So the king and Haman went to Queen Esther's banquet. And while they were drinking wine that day, the king again asked her, "Tell me what you want, Queen Esther. What is your request? I will give it to you, even if it is half the kingdom!"

And so Queen Esther replied, "If Your Majesty is pleased with me and wants to grant my request, my petition is that my life and the lives of my people will be spared. For my people and I have been sold to those who would kill, slaughter, and annihilate us. If we had only been sold as slaves, I could remain quiet, for that would have been a matter too trivial to warrant disturbing the king."

"Who would do such a thing?" King Xerxes demanded. "Who would dare touch you?"

Esther replied, "This wicked Haman is our enemy." Haman grew pale with fright before the king and queen. . . .

Then Harbona, one of the king's eunuchs, said, "Haman has set up a gallows that stands seventy-five feet tall in his own courtyard. He intended to use it to hang Mordecai, the man who saved the king from assassination."

"Then hang Haman on it!" the king ordered. So they hanged Haman on the gallows he had set up for Mordecai, and the king's anger was pacified.

Esther 7:1-6,9-10

Related Texts: Deuteronomy 23:3-5; Esther 8–10; Joel 3:1-8; Obadiah 15; Revelation 19:11–20:10

done ☐

OCTOBER 9

Malachi: Messenger of the Covenant

"Look! I am sending my messenger, and he will prepare the way before me. Then the LORD you are seeking will suddenly come to his Temple. The messenger of the covenant, whom you look for so eagerly, is surely coming," says the LORD Almighty. "But who will be able to endure it when he comes? Who will be able to stand and face him when he appears? For he will be like a blazing fire that refines metal or like a strong soap that whitens clothes. He will sit and judge like a refiner of silver, watching closely as the dross is burned away. He will purify the Levites, refining them like gold or silver, so that they may once again offer acceptable sacrifices to the LORD. Then once more the LORD will accept the offerings brought to him by the people of Judah and Jerusalem, as he did in former times."

Malachi 3:1-4

The LORD Almighty says, "The day of judgment is coming, burning like a furnace. The arrogant and the wicked will be burned up like straw on that day. They will be consumed like a tree—roots and all.

"But for you who fear my name, the Sun of Righteousness will rise with healing in his wings. And you will go free, leaping with joy like calves let out to pasture. On the day when I act, you will tread upon the wicked as if they were dust under your feet," says the LORD Almighty. . . .

"Look, I am sending you the prophet Elijah before the great and dreadful day of the LORD arrives. His preaching will turn the hearts of parents to their children, and the hearts of children to their parents. Otherwise I will come and strike the land with a curse."

Malachi 4:1-3,5-6

Related Texts: Isaiah 60; Luke 1:1-17; Matthew 3:1-12; 17:10-13

Weird or What?

Malachi is the last of the Old Testament prophets.

We know nothing about the person of Malachi. All we have are his written words. But by these words we can sense his dynamic love for God and a strong faith in God's plan.

What would your words tell the world about your love and faith in God?

done ☐

10 OCTOBER

CHECK IT OUT

To "be commissioned" means "to receive the authority, permission, and support to be sent out." Churches throughout the country commission missionaries, with prayer and other types of support, to serve God in foreign nations.

In Matthew 28:19-20, Jesus commissions His followers by saying: "Therefore, go and make disciples of all the nations, baptizing them in the name of the Father and the Son and the Holy Spirit. Teach these new disciples to obey all the commands I have given you. And be sure of this: I am with you always, even to the end of the age."

Today, pray for a missionary you know. Also ask God how you might be commissioned to make disciples in your "nation" (school, neighborhood, church, etc.).

The Promise of Jesus' Coming

And now the LORD speaks—he who formed me in my mother's womb to be his servant, who commissioned me to bring his people of Israel back to him. The LORD has honored me, and my God has given me strength. He says, "You will do more than restore the people of Israel to me. I will make you a light to the Gentiles, and you will bring my salvation to the ends of the earth."

Isaiah 49:5-6

But you, O Bethlehem Ephrathah, are only a small village in Judah. Yet a ruler of Israel will come from you, one whose origins are from the distant past. The people of Israel will be abandoned to their enemies until the time when the woman in labor gives birth to her son. Then at last his fellow countrymen will return from exile to their own land. And he will stand to lead his flock with the LORD's strength, in the majesty of the name of the LORD his God. Then his people will live there undisturbed, for he will be highly honored all around the world. And he will be the source of our peace.

When the Assyrians invade our land and break through our defenses, we will appoint seven rulers to watch over us, eight princes to lead us.

Micah 5:2-5

Related Texts: Genesis 35:14-19; Ruth 4:10-17; 1 Samuel 17:12; Matthew 2:1-6

done ☐

Jesus: Son of God, Son of Man

As my vision continued that night, I saw someone who looked like a man coming with the clouds of heaven. He approached the Ancient One and was led into his presence. He was given authority, honor, and royal power over all the nations of the world, so that people of every race and nation and language would obey him. His rule is eternal—it will never end. His kingdom will never be destroyed.

Daniel 7:13-14

Long ago God spoke many times and in many ways to our ancestors through the prophets. But now in these final days, he has spoken to us through his Son. God promised everything to the Son as an inheritance, and through the Son he made the universe and everything in it. The Son reflects God's own glory, and everything about him represents God exactly. He sustains the universe by the mighty power of his command. After he died to cleanse us from the stain of sin, he sat down in the place of honor at the right hand of the majestic God of heaven.

This shows that God's Son is far greater than the angels, just as the name God gave him is far greater than their names. For God never said to any angel what he said to Jesus:

"You are my Son.
Today I have become your Father."

And again God said,

"I will be his Father,
and he will be my Son."

Hebrews 1:1-5

Related Texts: 2 Samuel 7:14; 1 Chronicles 17:13; Psalm 2:7; Matthew 23:63-64; Mark 14:61-62; Luke 22:67-70; John 1:32-34

One Minute Memory

The Son of God reflects God's own glory, and everything about him represents God exactly.

Hebrews 1:3a

done ☐

In OTHER Words

Holy Spirit

The Holy Spirit is the name for God's Spirit who lives within Christians. When Jesus left the earth, God gave Christians the Holy Spirit to guide them. The Bible reveals the Holy Spirit as having an identity that is one or equal with God the Father and God the Son. The Holy Spirit is also given different names within the Bible: Holy Ghost, Helper, Counselor, and Comforter.

The Holy Spirit's role is to direct Christians, comfort them, convict them of sin, help them understand and obey God's will, and speak to God on their behalf.

Today, pray that the Holy Spirit would be evident in your life.

Jesus Christ Is Born

Now this is how Jesus the Messiah was born. His mother, Mary, was engaged to be married to Joseph. But while she was still a virgin, she became pregnant by the Holy Spirit. Joseph, her fiancé, being a just man, decided to break the engagement quietly, so as not to disgrace her publicly.

As he considered this, he fell asleep, and an angel of the Lord appeared to him in a dream. "Joseph, son of David," the angel said, "do not be afraid to go ahead with your marriage to Mary. For the child within her has been conceived by the Holy Spirit. And she will have a son, and you are to name him Jesus, for he will save his people from their sins." All of this happened to fulfill the LORD's message through his prophet:

"Look! The virgin will conceive a child!
She will give birth to a son,
and he will be called Immanuel
(meaning, God is with us)."

When Joseph woke up, he did what the angel of the Lord commanded. He brought Mary home to be his wife, but she remained a virgin until her son was born. And Joseph named him Jesus.

Matthew 1:18-25

Related Texts: Isaiah 7:14; Matthew 2; Luke 1–2; John 4:1-42

done ☐

OCTOBER 13

The Boy Jesus in the Temple

Every year Jesus' parents went to Jerusalem for the Passover festival. When Jesus was twelve years old, they attended the festival as usual. After the celebration was over, they started home to Nazareth, but Jesus stayed behind in Jerusalem. His parents didn't miss him at first, because they assumed he was with friends among the other travelers. But when he didn't show up that evening, they started to look for him among their relatives and friends. When they couldn't find him, they went back to Jerusalem to search for him there. Three days later they finally discovered him. He was in the Temple, sitting among the religious teachers, discussing deep questions with them. And all who heard him were amazed at his understanding and his answers.

His parents didn't know what to think. "Son!" his mother said to him. "Why have you done this to us? Your father and I have been frantic, searching for you everywhere."

"But why did you need to search?" he asked. "You should have known that I would be in my Father's house." But they didn't understand what he meant.

Then he returned to Nazareth with them and was obedient to them; and his mother stored all these things in her heart. So Jesus grew both in height and in wisdom, and he was loved by God and by all who knew him.

Luke 2:41-52

Related Texts: 1 Samuel 2:21,26; Psalms 26:8; 27:4; 65; Matthew 2:13-23; John 2:13-17; 2 Corinthians 4:18–5:4

The Bible is God's complete instruction manual to the world. But it's interesting that God gives us very little information about Jesus' teenage years. For some reason God doesn't reveal much about Jesus from His birth until His public ministry, which began when He was approximately thirty years old. We assume that Jesus grew up like most Jewish boys except that He was also 100 percent God.

done ☐

Jesus Is Baptized

Here begins the Good News about Jesus the Messiah, the Son of God.

In the book of the prophet Isaiah, God said,

"Look, I am sending my messenger before
you,
and he will prepare your way.
He is a voice shouting in the wilderness:
'Prepare a pathway for the Lord's coming!
Make a straight road for him!' "

This messenger was John the Baptist. He lived in the wilderness and was preaching that people should be baptized to show that they had turned from their sins and turned to God to be forgiven. People from Jerusalem and from all over Judea traveled out into the wilderness to see and hear John. And when they confessed their sins, he baptized them in the Jordan River. His clothes were woven from camel hair, and he wore a leather belt; his food was locusts and wild honey. He announced: "Someone is coming soon who is far greater than I am—so much greater that I am not even worthy to be his slave. I baptize you with water, but he will baptize you with the Holy Spirit!"

One day Jesus came from Nazareth in Galilee, and he was baptized by John in the Jordan River. And when Jesus came up out of the water, he saw the heavens split open and the Holy Spirit descending like a dove on him. And a voice came from heaven saying, "You are my beloved Son, and I am fully pleased with you."

Mark 1:1-11

Related Texts: Isaiah 40:3; Malachi 3:1; Matthew 3; Luke 3; John 1:19-34

In OTHER Words

Baptism

"Baptism" can be defined as "an outward act that represents an inward decision." Baptism follows a faith decision and shouts to the world, "I'm a Christian!" Baptism without this faith is merely a bath.

In baptism, when the person is dunked under water, it is symbolic of the person dying to the world and being buried. Then the rising up from the water symbolizes a resurrection to a new beginning and a new life in Jesus. The old nature of sin is buried in water, while the new person (in Jesus) is risen to a new life.

If you haven't been baptized, you might want to ask about it so you can show the world your commitment to Jesus.

done ☐

Jesus Is Tempted by the Devil

Then Jesus was led out into the wilderness by the Holy Spirit to be tempted there by the Devil. For forty days and forty nights he ate nothing and became very hungry. Then the Devil came and said to him, "If you are the Son of God, change these stones into loaves of bread."

But Jesus told him, "No! The Scriptures say,

'People need more than bread for their life;
they must feed on every word of God.' "

Then the Devil took him to Jerusalem, to the highest point of the Temple, and said, "If you are the Son of God, jump off! For the Scriptures say,

'He orders his angels to protect you.
And they will hold you with their hands
to keep you from striking your foot on a stone.' "

Jesus responded, "The Scriptures also say, 'Do not test the Lord your God.' "

Next the Devil took him to the peak of a very high mountain and showed him the nations of the world and all their glory. "I will give it all to you," he said, "if you will only kneel down and worship me."

"Get out of here, Satan," Jesus told him. "For the Scriptures say,

'You must worship the Lord your God;
serve only him.' "

Then the Devil went away, and angels came and cared for Jesus.

Matthew 4:1-11

Related Texts: Deuteronomy 6:13,16; 8:3; Psalm 91:11-12; Mark 1:12-13; Luke 4:1-13

CATCH THIS

Jesus wasn't tempted so God could reward His victory over Satan with two thumbs up and a pat on the back for a job well done. Jesus was tempted for our own good. Because He went through temptations as a human, He completely understands our humanity and temptations.

Jesus used the same weapons to fight off temptation that are available to us today. He used the Scriptures, the power of the Holy Spirit, and prayer to defeat Satan. We can use those same tools today—Scripture, the Holy Spirit, and prayer.

Praise God today because He understands everything you are going through. He cares about you! That should be enough good news to give you hope for another week.

done ☐

JUST a THOUGHT

If you like to party, you can be **assured** that **God** is throwing **one** that will **never** end!

Jesus' First Miracle

The next day Jesus' mother was a guest at a wedding celebration in the village of Cana in Galilee. Jesus and his disciples were also invited to the celebration. The wine supply ran out during the festivities, so Jesus' mother spoke to him about the problem. "They have no more wine," she told him.

"How does that concern you and me?" Jesus asked. "My time has not yet come."

But his mother told the servants, "Do whatever he tells you."

Six stone waterpots were standing there. . . . Jesus told the servants, "Fill the jars with water." When the jars had been filled to the brim, he said, "Dip some out and take it to the master of ceremonies." So they followed his instructions.

When the master of ceremonies tasted the water that was now wine, not knowing where it had come from (though, of course, the servants knew), he called the bridegroom over. "Usually a host serves the best wine first," he said. "Then, when everyone is full and doesn't care, he brings out the less expensive wines. But you have kept the best until now!"

This miraculous sign at Cana in Galilee was Jesus' first display of his glory. And his disciples believed in him.

John 2:1-6a,7-11

And I suppose that if all the other things Jesus did were written down, the whole world could not contain the books.

John 21:25

Related Texts: Isaiah 55; Joel 3:16-18; Amos 9:11-15; John 20:30-31

done ☐

You Must Be Born Again

After dark one evening, a Jewish religious leader named Nicodemus, a Pharisee, came to speak with Jesus. "Teacher," he said, "we all know that God has sent you to teach us. Your miraculous signs are proof enough that God is with you."

Jesus replied, "I assure you, unless you are born again, you can never see the Kingdom of God."

"What do you mean?" exclaimed Nicodemus. "How can an old man go back into his mother's womb and be born again?"

Jesus replied, "The truth is, no one can enter the Kingdom of God without being born of water and the Spirit." . . .

"What do you mean?" Nicodemus asked.

Jesus replied, "You are a respected Jewish teacher, and yet you don't understand these things? . . . But if you don't even believe me when I tell you about things that happen here on earth, how can you possibly believe if I tell you what is going on in heaven? For only I, the Son of Man, have come to earth and will return to heaven again. And as Moses lifted up the bronze snake on a pole in the wilderness, so I, the Son of Man, must be lifted up on a pole, so that everyone who believes in me will have eternal life.

"For God so loved the world that he gave his only Son, so that everyone who believes in him will not perish but have eternal life."

John 3:1-5,9-10,12-16

Related Texts: Numbers 21:1-9; John 1:1-13; 1 Peter 1; 1 John 2:28-29; 3:1-10; 4:7-8; 5

One Minute Memory

Unless you are **born again**, you can **never** see the Kingdom of God.

John 3:3

done ☐

18 OCTOBER

Jesus Calls His First Disciples

One day as Jesus was preaching on the shore of the Sea of Galilee, great crowds pressed in on him to listen to the word of God. He noticed two empty boats at the water's edge, for the fishermen had left them and were washing their nets. Stepping into one of the boats, Jesus asked Simon, its owner, to push it out into the water. So he sat in the boat and taught the crowds from there.

When he had finished speaking, he said to Simon, "Now go out where it is deeper and let down your nets, and you will catch many fish."

"Master," Simon replied, "we worked hard all last night and didn't catch a thing. But if you say so, we'll try again." And this time their nets were so full they began to tear! A shout for help brought their partners in the other boat, and soon both boats were filled with fish and on the verge of sinking.

When Simon Peter realized what had happened, he fell to his knees before Jesus and said, "Oh, Lord, please leave me—I'm too much of a sinner to be around you." For he was awestruck by the size of their catch, as were the others with him. His partners, James and John, the sons of Zebedee, were also amazed.

Jesus replied to Simon, "Don't be afraid! From now on you'll be fishing for people!" And as soon as they landed, they left everything and followed Jesus.

Luke 5:1-11

Related Texts: Psalm 51:1-13; Matthew 4:18-22; Mark 1:16-20; John 1:35-51

Give it a try

If Jesus came to you today and asked you to drop everything and leave everyone to follow Him, how would you respond? Write your answer below.

done ☐

HEALING ILLNESS; FORGIVING SIN

One day while Jesus was teaching, some Pharisees and teachers of religious law were sitting nearby. (It seemed that these men showed up from every village in all Galilee and Judea, as well as from Jerusalem.) And the Lord's healing power was strongly with Jesus. Some men came carrying a paralyzed man on a sleeping mat. They tried to push through the crowd to Jesus, but they couldn't reach him. So they went up to the roof, took off some tiles, and lowered the sick man down into the crowd, still on his mat, right in front of Jesus. Seeing their faith, Jesus said to the man, "Son, your sins are forgiven."

"Who does this man think he is?" the Pharisees and teachers of religious law said to each other. "This is blasphemy! Who but God can forgive sins?"

Jesus knew what they were thinking, so he asked them, "Why do you think this is blasphemy? Is it easier to say, 'Your sins are forgiven' or 'Get up and walk'? I will prove that I, the Son of Man, have the authority on earth to forgive sins." Then Jesus turned to the paralyzed man and said, "Stand up, take your mat, and go on home, because you are healed!"

And immediately, as everyone watched, the man jumped to his feet, picked up his mat, and went home praising God. Everyone was gripped with great wonder and awe. And they praised God, saying over and over again, "We have seen amazing things today."

Luke 5:17-26

Related Texts: Psalm 25:1-11; Micah 7:18; Matthew 9:1-8; Mark 2:1-12

What's it Mean?

Teachers of the Law saw Jesus' act as blasphemous because they believed only God could forgive sin. They didn't accept Jesus' claim to be God's Son, so His words and actions were unacceptable to them.

Although the teachers didn't believe, they did observe Jesus heal a man they knew to be paralyzed. It's likely this experience left them confused and frustrated and fueled their feelings of hatred toward Jesus.

Jesus didn't forgive the leaders because they wouldn't admit they were wrong. Do you have any areas of your life today where you need forgiveness? **Ask God to forgive you and cleanse you from anything that is keeping you from being healed.**

done ☐

20 OCTOBER

Jesus Controls Storms and Spirits

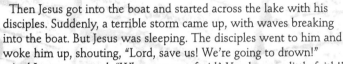

Then Jesus got into the boat and started across the lake with his disciples. Suddenly, a terrible storm came up, with waves breaking into the boat. But Jesus was sleeping. The disciples went to him and woke him up, shouting, "Lord, save us! We're going to drown!"

And Jesus answered, "Why are you afraid? You have so little faith!" Then he stood up and rebuked the wind and waves, and suddenly all was calm. The disciples just sat there in awe. "Who is this?" they asked themselves. "Even the wind and waves obey him!"

When Jesus arrived on the other side of the lake in the land of the Gadarenes, two men who were possessed by demons met him. They lived in a cemetery and were so dangerous that no one could go through that area. They began screaming at him, "Why are you bothering us, Son of God? You have no right to torture us before God's appointed time!" A large herd of pigs was feeding in the distance, so the demons begged, "If you cast us out, send us into that herd of pigs."

"All right, go!" Jesus commanded them. So the demons came out of the men and entered the pigs, and the whole herd plunged down the steep hillside into the lake and drowned in the water.

Matthew 8:23-32

Related Texts: Deuteronomy 14:8; Isaiah 65:1-4; Mark 4:35–5:20; Luke 8:22-39

Give it a try

What are some of the "storms" in your life that make you fearful?

1.
2.
3.

Spend a minute and talk to God about your fears.

done ☐

Faith and Healing

As Jesus was saying this, the leader of a synagogue came and knelt down before him. "My daughter has just died," he said, "but you can bring her back to life again if you just come and lay your hand upon her."

As Jesus and the disciples were going to the official's home, a woman who had had a hemorrhage for twelve years came up behind him. She touched the fringe of his robe, for she thought, "If I can just touch his robe, I will be healed."

Jesus turned around and said to her, "Daughter, be encouraged! Your faith has made you well." And the woman was healed at that moment.

When Jesus arrived at the official's home, he noticed the noisy crowds and heard the funeral music. He said, "Go away, for the girl isn't dead; she's only asleep." But the crowd laughed at him. When the crowd was finally outside, Jesus went in and took the girl by the hand, and she stood up! The report of this miracle swept through the entire countryside.

Matthew 9:18-26

Are any among you suffering? They should keep on praying about it. And those who have reason to be thankful should continually sing praises to the Lord.

Are any among you sick? They should call for the elders of the church and have them pray over them, anointing them with oil in the name of the Lord. And their prayer offered in faith will heal the sick, and the Lord will make them well. And anyone who has committed sins will be forgiven.

Confess your sins to each other and pray for each other so that you may be healed. The earnest prayer of a righteous person has great power and wonderful results. *James 5:13-16*

Related Texts: Habakkuk 2:4; Matthew 9:27-30; Mark 5:21-43; Luke 7:1-10,36-50; 8:22-25,40-56; 17:11-19; 18:35-43

CATCH THIS

Jesus isn't walking the earth today performing miracles. But that doesn't mean miracles aren't happening on a daily basis. God's miraculous healing power hasn't stopped!

Today, healing happens in many different ways. One type of healing involves YOU if you're a Christian. A verse from today's reading states that healing can come from sharing with another person. Here it is again: "Admit your faults to one another and pray for each other so that you may be healed."

There's something powerful about confessing your faults or sins to another person. Confession, followed up by prayer, is one way in which God heals. If you are suffering with anger or hatred toward a person or situation, try sharing your pain and confessing your feelings to another Christian. Pray together and allow God to do the rest. God wants you to live life to its fullest, and unconfessed pain doesn't allow us to live abundantly. Find someone today who can share in your pain.

done ☐

22 OCTOBER

Personality Plus

Satan

Satan was God's right-hand angel, whose glory and power was overshadowed only by God himself. Satan was big time! He ruled over the angels as well as overseeing all the music. His downfall came when he desired to have the same power as God. This act of pride got him thrown out of heaven.

Today, Satan is intent on demolishing God's kingdom and followers. Satan is effective in this plot because his methods are discreet. He destroys Christians with temptation, guilt, fear, and doubt. He'd love to see you live a life that doesn't reflect godliness. Watch out for the subtle ways he will try to take your eyes off God. He's not a fairy-tale character; he's for real! Don't let him have any part of you!

Jesus Responds to Lack of Faith

When Jesus returned to the house where he was staying, the crowds began to gather again, and soon he and his disciples couldn't even find time to eat. When his family heard what was happening, they tried to take him home with them. "He's out of his mind," they said.

But the teachers of religious law who had arrived from Jerusalem said, "He's possessed by Satan, the prince of demons. That's where he gets the power to cast out demons."

Jesus called them over and said to them by way of illustration, "How can Satan cast out Satan? A kingdom at war with itself will collapse. A home divided against itself is doomed. And if Satan is fighting against himself, how can he stand? He would never survive. Let me illustrate this. You can't enter a strong man's house and rob him without first tying him up. Only then can his house be robbed!

"I assure you that any sin can be forgiven, including blasphemy; but anyone who blasphemes against the Holy Spirit will never be forgiven. It is an eternal sin." He told them this because they were saying he had an evil spirit.

Mark 3:20-30

Related Texts: Exodus 22:28; Psalm 106:1-37; Matthew 12:22-37; 13:53-58; Mark 6:1-6; Luke 11:14-23; 12:10

done ☐

Jesus Feeds Five Thousand

Jesus soon saw a great crowd of people climbing the hill, looking for him. Turning to Philip, he asked, "Philip, where can we buy bread to feed all these people?" He was testing Philip, for he already knew what he was going to do.

Philip replied, "It would take a small fortune to feed them!"

Then Andrew, Simon Peter's brother, spoke up. "There's a young boy here with five barley loaves and two fish. But what good is that with this huge crowd?"

"Tell everyone to sit down," Jesus ordered. So all of them—the men alone numbered five thousand—sat down on the grassy slopes. Then Jesus took the loaves, gave thanks to God, and passed them out to the people. Afterward he did the same with the fish. And they all ate until they were full. "Now gather the leftovers," Jesus told his disciples, "so that nothing is wasted." There were only five barley loaves to start with, but twelve baskets were filled with the pieces of bread the people did not eat!

When the people saw this miraculous sign, they exclaimed, "Surely, he is the Prophet we have been expecting!"

John 6:5-14

Related Texts: Deuteronomy 8:2-3; Matthew 14:13-21; Mark 6:32-44; Luke 9:10-17

JUST A THOUGHT

A little faith left in the hands of God can turn into big results.

done ☐

24 OCTOBER

Who Is Jesus?

When Jesus came to the region of Caesarea Philippi, he asked his disciples, "Who do people say that the Son of Man is?"

"Well," they replied, "some say John the Baptist, some say Elijah, and others say Jeremiah or one of the other prophets."

Then he asked them, "Who do you say I am?"

Simon Peter answered, "You are the Messiah, the Son of the living God."

Jesus replied, "You are blessed, Simon son of John, because my Father in heaven has revealed this to you. You did not learn this from any human being. Now I say to you that you are Peter, and upon this rock I will build my church, and all the powers of hell will not conquer it. And I will give you the keys of the Kingdom of Heaven. Whatever you lock on earth will be locked in heaven, and whatever you open on earth will be opened in heaven." Then he sternly warned them not to tell anyone that he was the Messiah.

From then on Jesus began to tell his disciples plainly that he had to go to Jerusalem, and he told them what would happen to him there. He would suffer at the hands of the leaders and the leading priests and the teachers of religious law. He would be killed, and he would be raised on the third day.

Matthew 16:13-21

Related Texts: Isaiah 52:14-15; Mark 8:27-33; Luke 9:18-22; John 6:67-71

Give it a try

How would you answer this question? "Who do you think I (Jesus) am?" Write a brief description of what you know about Jesus.

done ☐

The Transfiguration

Six days later Jesus took Peter, James, and John to the top of a mountain. No one else was there. As the men watched, Jesus' appearance changed, and his clothing became dazzling white, far whiter than any earthly process could ever make it. Then Elijah and Moses appeared and began talking with Jesus.

"Teacher, this is wonderful!" Peter exclaimed. "We will make three shrines—one for you, one for Moses, and one for Elijah." He didn't really know what to say, for they were all terribly afraid.

Then a cloud came over them, and a voice from the cloud said, "This is my beloved Son. Listen to him." Suddenly they looked around, and Moses and Elijah were gone, and only Jesus was with them. As they descended the mountainside, he told them not to tell anyone what they had seen until he, the Son of Man, had risen from the dead. So they kept it to themselves, but they often asked each other what he meant by "rising from the dead."

Mark 9:2-10

So the Word became human and lived here on earth among us. He was full of unfailing love and faithfulness. And we have seen his glory, the glory of the only Son of the Father.

John 1:14

Related Texts: Exodus 40:33-35; Matthew 17:1-9; Luke 9:28-36; Romans 16:25-27; 1 Timothy 1:17; Jude 24-25

One Minute Memory

So the **Word** became **human** and **lived** here on earth **among us**. He was full of **unfailing love** and **faithfulness**. And we have seen his **glory**, the **glory** of the **only Son of the Father**. *John 1:14*

CATCH THIS

Chances are high you won't have the need or the opportunity to physically move a mountain. When Jesus used this illustration, He wasn't referring to the finer points of landscaping but to a vital truth having to do with our faith. Jesus wanted His followers to know that all things are possible with faith. By using the example of the mustard seed, Jesus was emphasizing littleness. This means we don't need A LOT of faith to see God do incredible things. With just a little faith, we will be able to move the mountains of difficulty facing us.

Faith is believing that God is God and that He's **TOTALLY** in control.

If you believe this to be true, ask God to help you move a mountain in your life and perform the impossible. Remember, it doesn't take a lot of faith—just a little.

Small Faith—Large Results

When they arrived at the foot of the mountain, a huge crowd was waiting for them. A man came and knelt before Jesus and said, "Lord, have mercy on my son, because he has seizures and suffers terribly. He often falls into the fire or into the water. So I brought him to your disciples, but they couldn't heal him."

Jesus replied, "You stubborn, faithless people! How long must I be with you until you believe? How long must I put up with you? Bring the boy to me." Then Jesus rebuked the demon in the boy, and it left him. From that moment the boy was well.

Afterward the disciples asked Jesus privately, "Why couldn't we cast out that demon?"

"You didn't have enough faith," Jesus told them. "I assure you, even if you had faith as small as a mustard seed you could say to this mountain, 'Move from here to there,' and it would move. Nothing would be impossible."

Matthew 17:14-20

"The truth is, anyone who believes in me will do the same works I have done, and even greater works, because I am going to be with the Father. You can ask for anything in my name, and I will do it, because the work of the Son brings glory to the Father."

John 14:12-13

Related Texts: 1 Samuel 16:14-23; Mark 9:14-32; Luke 9:37-45; Romans 4:18-21; 11:1-23; Hebrews 3:16-19

 done ☐

Jesus Teaches His Disciples to Pray

Once when Jesus had been out praying, one of his disciples came to him as he finished and said, "Lord, teach us to pray, just as John taught his disciples."

He said, "This is how you should pray:

"Father, may your name be honored.
May your Kingdom come soon.
Give us our food day by day.
And forgive us our sins—
just as we forgive those who have sinned against us.
And don't let us yield to temptation."

Then, teaching them more about prayer, he used this illustration: "Suppose you went to a friend's house at midnight, wanting to borrow three loaves of bread. You would say to him, 'A friend of mine has just arrived for a visit, and I have nothing for him to eat.' He would call out from his bedroom, 'Don't bother me. The door is locked for the night, and we are all in bed. I can't help you this time.' But I tell you this—though he won't do it as a friend, if you keep knocking long enough, he will get up and give you what you want so his reputation won't be damaged.

"And so I tell you, keep on asking, and you will be given what you ask for. Keep on looking, and you will find. Keep on knocking, and the door will be opened. For everyone who asks, receives. Everyone who seeks, finds. And the door is opened to everyone who knocks."

Luke 11:1-10

Related Texts: Psalm 89:19-29; Isaiah 9:6-7; Matthew 6:6-13; 7:7-11; Revelation 3:14-22

One Minute Memory

He said, "This is how you should pray:
**"Father, may your name be honored.
May your Kingdom come soon.
Give us our food day by day.
And forgive us our sins—
just as we forgive those who have sinned against us.
And don't let us yield to temptation."**

Luke 11:2-4

done ☐

BIG TIMe WoRd

CHILDREN

We can learn a lot from children.

Jesus knew this and referred to them as examples that we should follow for life.

Look at the following four words that begin with the letters L.I.F.E. and try to think of ways you can be more childlike (not childish) in your faith.

Laughter
Imagination
Faith
Enthusiasm

Ask God to help you possess these childlike qualities today!

Jesus Welcomes Little Children

Then there was an argument among them as to which of them would be the greatest. But Jesus knew their thoughts, so he brought a little child to his side. Then he said to them, "Anyone who welcomes a little child like this on my behalf welcomes me, and anyone who welcomes me welcomes my Father who sent me. Whoever is the least among you is the greatest."

Luke 9:46-48

One day some parents brought their children to Jesus so he could touch them and bless them, but the disciples told them not to bother him. But when Jesus saw what was happening, he was very displeased with his disciples. He said to them, "Let the children come to me. Don't stop them! For the Kingdom of God belongs to such as these. I assure you, anyone who doesn't have their kind of faith will never get into the Kingdom of God." Then he took the children into his arms and placed his hands on their heads and blessed them.

Mark 10:13-16

Then Jesus was filled with the joy of the Holy Spirit and said, "O Father, Lord of heaven and earth, thank you for hiding the truth from those who think themselves so wise and clever, and for revealing it to the childlike. Yes, Father, it pleased you to do it this way.

"My Father has given me authority over everything. No one really knows the Son except the Father, and no one really knows the Father except the Son and those to whom the Son chooses to reveal him."

Luke 10:21-22

Related Texts: Psalm 127:3-5; Matthew 18:1-14; 19:13-15; Mark 9:33-37; Luke 18:15-17

done ☐

JESUS HEALS ON THE SABBATH

One Sabbath day as Jesus was teaching in a synagogue, he saw a woman who had been crippled by an evil spirit. She had been bent double for eighteen years and was unable to stand up straight. When Jesus saw her, he called her over and said, "Woman, you are healed of your sickness!" Then he touched her, and instantly she could stand straight. How she praised and thanked God!

But the leader in charge of the synagogue was indignant that Jesus had healed her on the Sabbath day. "There are six days of the week for working," he said to the crowd. "Come on those days to be healed, not on the Sabbath."

But the Lord replied, "You hypocrite! You work on the Sabbath day! Don't you untie your ox or your donkey from their stalls on the Sabbath and lead them out for water? Wasn't it necessary for me, even on the Sabbath day, to free this dear woman from the bondage in which Satan has held her for eighteen years?" This shamed his enemies. And all the people rejoiced at the wonderful things he did.

Luke 13:10-17

Related Texts: Exodus 20:8-11; Matthew 12:1-14; Mark 2:23–3:6; Luke 6:1-11; 14:1-6; John 5:1-18

What's it Mean?

The leader accusing Jesus of healing on the Sabbath cared more about the Law being broken than he did about the woman. Jesus rebuked this man by calling him a hypocrite for not seeing beyond the Sabbath rules to the needs of a hurting woman. The religious leader would rather the woman suffer or return to the synagogue another day before he would break the Sabbath rule.

Don't wait for good timing to ask for a **miracle. Right now God is waiting for your words.** He's equipped to heal if it's in His plan. **It sure can't hurt to ask!**

done ☐

BIG TIMe WoRd

DIVORCE

Divorce is devastating! If your parents aren't divorced, that's good news. Most likely you know a friend who is experiencing the pain of divorce. It isn't easy to live with the pain, loss, guilt, and frustration that goes along with being separated from two people you love the most.

God hates divorce and knows the deep pain it brings. If you have been affected by divorce, ask God to comfort you. Your pain won't quickly disappear, but be assured that you aren't alone, and you don't have to go through it alone. If your parents aren't divorced, pray for the strength of their marriage and ask God to provide you an opportunity to care for a friend hurt by divorce.

Jesus Teaches on Divorce and Celibacy

Some Pharisees came and tried to trap him with this question: "Should a man be allowed to divorce his wife for any reason?"

"Haven't you read the Scriptures?" Jesus replied. "They record that from the beginning 'God made them male and female.' And he said, 'This explains why a man leaves his father and mother and is joined to his wife, and the two are united into one.' Since they are no longer two but one, let no one separate them, for God has joined them together."

"Then why did Moses say a man could merely write an official letter of divorce and send her away?" they asked.

Jesus replied, "Moses permitted divorce as a concession to your hard-hearted wickedness, but it was not what God had originally intended. And I tell you this, a man who divorces his wife and marries another commits adultery—unless his wife has been unfaithful."

Jesus' disciples then said to him, "Then it is better not to marry!"

"Not everyone can accept this statement," Jesus said. "Only those whom God helps. Some are born as eunuchs, some have been made that way by others, and some choose not to marry for the sake of the Kingdom of Heaven. Let anyone who can, accept this statement."

Matthew 19:3-12

Related Texts: Deuteronomy 24:1-4; Mark 10:2-12; 1 Corinthians 7:10-13

 done ☐

Treasure in Heaven

Once a religious leader asked Jesus this question: "Good teacher, what should I do to get eternal life?"

"Why do you call me good?" Jesus asked him. "Only God is truly good. But as for your question, you know the commandments: 'Do not commit adultery. Do not murder. Do not steal. Do not testify falsely. Honor your father and mother.' "

The man replied, "I've obeyed all these commandments since I was a child."

"There is still one thing you lack," Jesus said. "Sell all you have and give the money to the poor, and you will have treasure in heaven. Then come, follow me." But when the man heard this, he became sad because he was very rich.

Jesus watched him go and then said to his disciples, "How hard it is for rich people to get into the Kingdom of God! It is easier for a camel to go through the eye of a needle than for a rich person to enter the Kingdom of God!"

Those who heard this said, "Then who in the world can be saved?"

He replied, "What is impossible from a human perspective is possible with God."

Peter said, "We have left our homes and followed you."

"Yes," Jesus replied, "and I assure you, everyone who has given up house or wife or brothers or parents or children, for the sake of the Kingdom of God, will be repaid many times over in this life, as well as receiving eternal life in the world to come."

Luke 18:18-30

Related Texts: Exodus 20:12-16; Deuteronomy 5:16-20; Matthew 19:16-30; Mark 10:17-31; 1 Corinthians 13:3

Just a Thought

Wealth and happiness don't always go together. Wealthy people who don't know God are spiritually bankrupt. Don't allow yourself to love money more than you love God.

done ☐

November

Give me a used **Bible** and I will, I think, **be able** to tell you about a **man** by the **places** that are edged with the **dirt** of **seeking fingers.**

John Steinbeck
(1902–1968)
American Novelist

Jesus Visits a Sinner

Jesus entered Jericho and made his way through the town. There was a man there named Zacchaeus. He was one of the most influential Jews in the Roman tax-collecting business, and he had become very rich. He tried to get a look at Jesus, but he was too short to see over the crowds. So he ran ahead and climbed a sycamore tree beside the road, so he could watch from there.

When Jesus came by, he looked up at Zacchaeus and called him by name. "Zacchaeus!" he said. "Quick, come down! For I must be a guest in your home today."

Zacchaeus quickly climbed down and took Jesus to his house in great excitement and joy. But the crowds were displeased. "He has gone to be the guest of a notorious sinner," they grumbled.

Meanwhile, Zacchaeus stood there and said to the Lord, "I will give half my wealth to the poor, Lord, and if I have overcharged people on their taxes, I will give them back four times as much!"

Jesus responded, "Salvation has come to this home today, for this man has shown himself to be a son of Abraham. And I, the Son of Man, have come to seek and save those like him who are lost."

Luke 19:1-10

And just as it is destined that each person dies only once and after that comes judgment, so also Christ died only once as a sacrifice to take away the sins of many people. He will come again but not to deal with our sins again. This time he will bring salvation to all those who are eagerly waiting for him.

Hebrews 9:27-28

Related Texts: Ezekiel 34:7-16; Mark 2:14-17; Luke 7:36-47

BIG TIME WORD

INFLUENTIAL

Our world has established an unwritten standard by which many people measure themselves. This standard usually includes money, popularity, possessions, and career positions. People who try to fit into these categories often see themselves as influential and enjoy being noticed for what they have.

The Bible's standard for being influential is completely different from the world's. Jesus told His disciples that influential people are servants, and if they wanted to be influential (or great), they needed to serve others.

Try living by God's standards and discover ways you can influence someone today by serving.

done ☐

Jesus Anointed for Burial

Six days before the Passover ceremonies began, Jesus arrived in Bethany, the home of Lazarus—the man he had raised from the dead. A dinner was prepared in Jesus' honor. Martha served, and Lazarus sat at the table with him. Then Mary took a twelve-ounce jar of expensive perfume made from essence of nard, and she anointed Jesus' feet with it and wiped his feet with her hair. And the house was filled with fragrance.

But Judas Iscariot, one of his disciples—the one who would betray him—said, "That perfume was worth a small fortune. It should have been sold and the money given to the poor." Not that he cared for the poor—he was a thief who was in charge of the disciples' funds, and he often took some for his own use.

Jesus replied, "Leave her alone. She did it in preparation for my burial. You will always have the poor among you, but I will not be here with you much longer."

When all the people heard of Jesus' arrival, they flocked to see him and also to see Lazarus, the man Jesus had raised from the dead. Then the leading priests decided to kill Lazarus, too, for it was because of him that many of the people had deserted them and believed in Jesus.

John 12:1-11

Related Texts: Psalm 16:9-11; Matthew 26:6-13; Mark 14:3-9; Luke 7:36-50; John 11

In OTHER Words

Disciple

The twelve men Jesus chose to be with Him on a regular basis are called disciples. The word "disciple" comes from a root word meaning "to learn." A disciple developed a special relationship with a rabbi and learned from his teachings. Today, "disciple" refers to someone learning from another Christian.

Do you know a leader or teacher who is more knowledgeable than you? Can you become that person's disciple and learn more about God's ways? This relationship can be a great investment of your time as long as you remember to **put your faith in GOD and not in the other person.**

done ☐

The Triumphal Entry

As they came to the towns of Bethphage and Bethany, on the Mount of Olives, he sent two disciples ahead. "Go into that village over there," he told them, "and as you enter it, you will see a colt tied there that has never been ridden. Untie it and bring it here. If anyone asks what you are doing, just say, 'The Lord needs it.' "

So they went and found the colt, just as Jesus had said. And sure enough, as they were untying it, the owners asked them, "Why are you untying our colt?"

And the disciples simply replied, "The Lord needs it." So they brought the colt to Jesus and threw their garments over it for him to ride on.

Then the crowds spread out their coats on the road ahead of Jesus. As they reached the place where the road started down from the Mount of Olives, all of his followers began to shout and sing as they walked along, praising God for all the wonderful miracles they had seen.

"Bless the King who comes in the name of
the Lord!
Peace in heaven and glory in highest
heaven!"

But some of the Pharisees among the crowd said, "Teacher, rebuke your followers for saying things like that!"

He replied, "If they kept quiet, the stones along the road would burst into cheers!"

Luke 19:29-40

Related Texts: Psalm 118; Matthew 21:1-9; Mark 11:1-10; John 12:12-19

CHECK IT OUT

Jesus entered Jerusalem as the Messiah to the world. His arrival had been prophesied for hundreds of years, but the Jewish people did not recognize Him as their Messiah and Savior. Check out the prophecy in Psalm 118:22-26: "The stone rejected by the builders has now become the cornerstone. This is the Lord's doing, and it is marvelous to see. This is the day the Lord has made. We will rejoice and be glad in it. Please, Lord, please save us. Please, Lord, please give us success. Bless the one who comes in the name of the Lord. We bless you from the house of the Lord."

It has also been foretold that Jesus will return to earth. This is called the second coming. Again, some will reject this truth. Don't allow yourself to miss the signs of His return.

done ☐

THE PARABLE OF THE VINEYARD

Now Jesus turned to the people again and told them this story: "A man planted a vineyard, leased it out to tenant farmers, and moved to another country to live for several years. At grape-picking time, he sent one of his servants to collect his share of the crop. But the farmers attacked the servant, beat him up, and sent him back empty-handed. So the owner sent another servant, but the same thing happened; he was beaten up and treated shamefully, and he went away empty-handed. A third man was sent and the same thing happened. He, too, was wounded and chased away.

" 'What will I do?' the owner asked himself. 'I know! I'll send my cherished son. Surely they will respect him.'

"But when the farmers saw his son, they said to each other, 'Here comes the heir to this estate. Let's kill him and get the estate for ourselves!' So they dragged him out of the vineyard and murdered him.

"What do you suppose the owner of the vineyard will do to those farmers?" Jesus asked. "I'll tell you—he will come and kill them all and lease the vineyard to others."

"But God forbid that such a thing should ever happen," his listeners protested.

Jesus looked at them and said, "Then what do the Scriptures mean?

'The stone rejected by the builders
has now become the cornerstone.'

"All who stumble over that stone will be broken to pieces, and it will crush anyone on whom it falls."

Luke 20:9-18

Related Texts: Psalm 118; Matthew 21:33-46; Mark 12:1-12

What's it Mean?

Jesus didn't answer when He was questioned about where He got His authority to drive out merchants from the Temple. Instead, He told them the parable found in today's reading.

This parable illustrates that some people will reject Jesus as God's Son. This rejection will result in their destruction. The message of this parable leaves no room for a compromising position with one's faith. Jesus will either save you or judge you. There are no other options.

Let God know that you have no compromise in your faith and are prepared for His return.

done ☐

The Last Supper

Then Judas Iscariot, one of the twelve disciples, went to the leading priests and asked, "How much will you pay me to betray Jesus to you?" And they gave him thirty pieces of silver. From that time on, Judas began looking for the right time and place to betray Jesus.

On the first day of the Festival of Unleavened Bread, the disciples came to Jesus and asked, "Where do you want us to prepare the Passover supper?"

"As you go into the city," he told them, "you will see a certain man. Tell him, 'The Teacher says, My time has come, and I will eat the Passover meal with my disciples at your house.' " So the disciples did as Jesus told them and prepared the Passover supper there.

When it was evening, Jesus sat down at the table with the twelve disciples. While they were eating, he said, "The truth is, one of you will betray me."

Greatly distressed, one by one they began to ask him, "I'm not the one, am I, Lord?"

He replied, "One of you who is eating with me now will betray me. For I, the Son of Man, must die, as the Scriptures declared long ago. But how terrible it will be for my betrayer. Far better for him if he had never been born!"

Judas, the one who would betray him, also asked, "Teacher, I'm not the one, am I?"

And Jesus told him, "You have said it yourself."

Matthew 26:14-25

Related Texts: Psalm 41:9; Proverbs 11:13; Mark 14:10-25; Luke 22:3-23; John 13–17

BIG TIME WORD

BETRAYAL

Quality relationships are built on trust. Betrayal breaks this trust and makes the relationship difficult to repair. Restoration isn't impossible, but it's always difficult to forget an act of betrayal.

Humans are known to betray other people and even to betray God, but God has promised not to betray His people. For thousands of years He has kept His promises, and He's not about to change His ways. This is good news! **Thank God for this truth and think about how you can keep betrayal out of your life.**

done ☐

CATCH THIS

Peter said, "I will never desert you no matter what the others do!" Since that day, thousands of Christians have spoken those same words at youth retreats or revivals. They say this boldly because they made a decision to get their act together and follow Jesus. They stood up or raised their hands, indicating they'd do whatever it takes to live the Christian life with excitement and intensity. But after the retreat is over and the warm fuzzies have worn off, it's usually back to normal Christian living, which translates into very little time, if any, for God. Does this describe you?

Maintaining a vibrant faith takes work. Actually, it's a lot like a marriage. Imagine being married to someone you didn't talk to or spend time with. That marriage would dry up. The same is true in your "marriage" with God; that relationship needs time. Go ahead and make bold statements like Peter, but be ready to put time into your relationship with God.

Faithless Friends

"All of you will desert me," Jesus told them. "For the Scriptures say,

'God will strike the Shepherd,
    and the sheep will be scattered.'

"But after I am raised from the dead, I will go ahead of you to Galilee and meet you there."

Peter said to him, "Even if everyone else deserts you, I never will."

"Peter," Jesus replied, "the truth is, this very night, before the rooster crows twice, you will deny me three times."

"No!" Peter insisted. "Not even if I have to die with you! I will never deny you!" And all the others vowed the same.

And they came to an olive grove called Gethsemane, and Jesus said, "Sit here while I go and pray." He took Peter, James, and John with him, and he began to be filled with horror and deep distress. He told them, "My soul is crushed with grief to the point of death. Stay here and watch with me."

He went on a little farther and fell face down on the ground. He prayed that, if it were possible, the awful hour awaiting him might pass him by. "Abba, Father," he said, "everything is possible for you. Please take this cup of suffering away from me. Yet I want your will, not mine."

Then he returned and found the disciples asleep. "Simon!" he said to Peter. "Are you asleep? Couldn't you stay awake and watch with me even one hour? Keep alert and pray. Otherwise temptation will overpower you. For though the spirit is willing enough, the body is weak."

Mark 14:27-38

Related Texts: Zechariah 13:7; Mark 14:26-42; Luke 22:31-46; John 13:36-38

done ☐

NOVEMBER 7

Betrayal and Denial

But even as he said this, a mob approached, led by Judas, one of his twelve disciples. Judas walked over to Jesus and greeted him with a kiss. But Jesus said, "Judas, how can you betray me, the Son of Man, with a kiss?"...

So they arrested him and led him to the high priest's residence, and Peter was following far behind. The guards lit a fire in the courtyard and sat around it, and Peter joined them there. A servant girl noticed him in the firelight and began staring at him. Finally she said, "This man was one of Jesus' followers!"

Peter denied it. "Woman," he said, "I don't even know the man!"

After a while someone else looked at him and said, "You must be one of them!"

"No, man, I'm not!" Peter replied.

About an hour later someone else insisted, "This must be one of Jesus' disciples because he is a Galilean, too."

But Peter said, "Man, I don't know what you are talking about." And as soon as he said these words, the rooster crowed. At that moment the Lord turned and looked at Peter. Then Peter remembered that the Lord had said, "Before the rooster crows tomorrow morning, you will deny me three times." And Peter left the courtyard, crying bitterly.

Luke 22:47-48,54-62

Related Texts: Psalm 42; Matthew 26:47-56,69-75; Mark 14:43-53, 66-72; John 18:2-12,25-27

Personality Plus

Peter

Peter was one of Jesus' most enthusiastic and committed followers. He was the first disciple and one of the closest to Jesus.

Although Peter denied Jesus when He was arrested, he later turned around and became very outspoken about Jesus' work. In the Book of Acts we see Peter as an instrumental figure in starting the early church that we are a part of today. Jesus renamed Peter as "the rock." Although he had his faults, he did become a solid Rock and a foundational person.

You might want to rename yourself "lucky" because of all God has done for you.

done ☐

JUST a THOUGHT

"Jesus could withstand the abuses of others because He had already surrendered to the will of God. He knew God was with Him no matter what people said or did. How about you?

Jesus Is Sentenced to Death

Inside, the leading priests and the entire high council were trying to find witnesses who would testify against Jesus, so they could put him to death. But their efforts were in vain. Many false witnesses spoke against him, but they contradicted each other. Finally, some men stood up to testify against him with this lie: "We heard him say, 'I will destroy this Temple made with human hands, and in three days I will build another, made without human hands.' " But even then they didn't get their stories straight!

Then the high priest stood up before the others and asked Jesus, "Well, aren't you going to answer these charges? What do you have to say for yourself?" Jesus made no reply. Then the high priest asked him, "Are you the Messiah, the Son of the blessed God?"

Jesus said, "I am, and you will see me, the Son of Man, sitting at God's right hand in the place of power and coming back on the clouds of heaven."

Then the high priest tore his clothing to show his horror and said, "Why do we need other witnesses? You have all heard his blasphemy. What is your verdict?" And they all condemned him to death.

Then some of them began to spit at him, and they blindfolded him and hit his face with their fists. "Who hit you that time, you prophet?" they jeered. And even the guards were hitting him as they led him away.

Mark 14:55-65

Related Texts: Exodus 20:16; Daniel 7:13-14; Matthew 26:59-67; Mark 14:55-65; Luke 23:63-71; John 18:19-24

done ☐

JESUS IS CRUCIFIED

Two others, both criminals, were led out to be executed with him. Finally, they came to a place called The Skull. All three were crucified there—Jesus on the center cross, and the two criminals on either side.

Jesus said, "Father, forgive these people, because they don't know what they are doing." And the soldiers gambled for his clothes by throwing dice.

The crowd watched, and the leaders laughed and scoffed. "He saved others," they said, "let him save himself if he is really God's Chosen One, the Messiah."...

One of the criminals hanging beside him scoffed, "So you're the Messiah, are you? Prove it by saving yourself—and us, too, while you're at it!"

But the other criminal protested, "Don't you fear God even when you are dying? We deserve to die for our evil deeds, but this man hasn't done anything wrong." Then he said, "Jesus, remember me when you come into your Kingdom."

And Jesus replied, "I assure you, today you will be with me in paradise."

By this time it was noon, and darkness fell across the whole land until three o'clock. The light from the sun was gone. And suddenly, the thick veil hanging in the Temple was torn apart. Then Jesus shouted, "Father, I entrust my spirit into your hands!" And with those words he breathed his last.

When the captain of the Roman soldiers handling the executions saw what had happened, he praised God and said, "Surely this man was innocent."

Luke 23:32-35,39-47

Related Texts: Psalm 22; Matthew 27; Mark 15; Luke 23; John 18:28–19:42

What's it Mean?

"Grace" is defined as **"undeserved favor."** God expresses this grace even though we don't deserve it and can do nothing to earn it. Jesus expressed grace to one of the criminals hanging on a cross beside His. The crucifixion scene was chaotic. People were yelling at Jesus; He was under unbelievable physical pain, and yet He still had compassion for the criminal.

Imagine yourself as a criminal being charged with sin. Now imagine yourself receiving God's love despite your sins. It's easy to imagine because it's real.

Tell someone today about God's grace and how much He loves you.

done ☐

JUST a THOUGHT

If you don't believe in the resurrection of Jesus, your faith is worth nothing. If Jesus didn't rise from the grave, He'd still be dead, and so would your faith. Any questions? (See 1 Cor. 15:17.)

The Resurrection

Early Sunday morning, while it was still dark, Mary Magdalene came to the tomb and found that the stone had been rolled away from the entrance. She ran and found Simon Peter and the other disciple, the one whom Jesus loved. She said, "They have taken the Lord's body out of the tomb, and I don't know where they have put him!"

Peter and the other disciple ran to the tomb to see. The other disciple outran Peter and got there first. He stooped and looked in and saw the linen cloth lying there, but he didn't go in. Then Simon Peter arrived and went inside. He also noticed the linen wrappings lying there, while the cloth that had covered Jesus' head was folded up and lying to the side. Then the other disciple also went in, and he saw and believed—for until then they hadn't realized that the Scriptures said he would rise from the dead. . . .

She glanced over her shoulder and saw someone standing behind her. It was Jesus, but she didn't recognize him. "Why are you crying?" Jesus asked her. "Who are you looking for?"

She thought he was the gardener. "Sir," she said, "if you have taken him away, tell me where you have put him, and I will go and get him."

That evening, on the first day of the week, the disciples were meeting behind locked doors because they were afraid of the Jewish leaders. Suddenly, Jesus was standing there among them! "Peace be with you," he said. As he spoke, he held out his hands for them to see, and he showed them his side. They were filled with joy when they saw their Lord!

John 20:1-9,19-20

Related Texts: Psalm 16:9-11; Isaiah 53:9-12; Matthew 28; Mark 16; Luke 24; John 20-21

done ☐

THE RESURRECTION

Don't let anyone lead you astray with empty philosophy and high-sounding nonsense that come from human thinking and from the evil powers of this world, and not from Christ. For in Christ the fullness of God lives in a human body, and you are complete through your union with Christ. He is the Lord over every ruler and authority in the universe.

When you came to Christ, you were "circumcised," but not by a physical procedure. It was a spiritual procedure—the cutting away of your sinful nature. For you were buried with Christ when you were baptized. And with him you were raised to a new life because you trusted the mighty power of God, who raised Christ from the dead.

You were dead because of your sins and because your sinful nature was not yet cut away. Then God made you alive with Christ. He forgave all our sins. He canceled the record that contained the charges against us. He took it and destroyed it by nailing it to Christ's cross. In this way, God disarmed the evil rulers and authorities. He shamed them publicly by his victory over them on the cross of Christ.

Colossians 2:8-15

Related Texts: Isaiah 1:11-14; Acts 2:22-36; Romans 6:1-11; 1 Corinthians 15:12-58

What's it Mean?

If you are a Christian, you can rejoice over the fact that your "old nature" passed away when you gave your life to Jesus.

The Bible informs us that the old nature represents your sinful life BEFORE coming to Jesus. Imagine the word "old" having negative images: dusty, bad, smelly, rotten, and ragged.

The new nature represents light, life, alive, eternal. These are great words! Jesus' death conquered the old and put it to death. What's that mean to you today?

You don't have to live life plagued by the past—that's old—you're new!

Congratulations!

done ☐

Jesus Returns to the Father

Dear Theophilus:

In my first book I told you about everything Jesus began to do and teach until the day he ascended to heaven after giving his chosen apostles further instructions from the Holy Spirit. During the forty days after his crucifixion, he appeared to the apostles from time to time and proved to them in many ways that he was actually alive. On these occasions he talked to them about the Kingdom of God.

In one of these meetings as he was eating a meal with them, he told them, "Do not leave Jerusalem until the Father sends you what he promised. Remember, I have told you about this before. John baptized with water, but in just a few days you will be baptized with the Holy Spirit."

When the apostles were with Jesus, they kept asking him, "Lord, are you going to free Israel now and restore our kingdom?"

"The Father sets those dates," he replied, "and they are not for you to know. But when the Holy Spirit has come upon you, you will receive power and will tell people about me everywhere—in Jerusalem, throughout Judea, in Samaria, and to the ends of the earth."

It was not long after he said this that he was taken up into the sky while they were watching, and he disappeared into a cloud. As they were straining their eyes to see him, two white-robed men suddenly stood there among them. They said, "Men of Galilee, why are you standing here staring at the sky? Jesus has been taken away from you into heaven. And someday, just as you saw him go, he will return!"

Acts 1:1-11

Related Texts: 1 Chronicles 16:8,23-31; Psalms 67; 72; Isaiah 45:22-23; 49:6; Luke 24:50-53

One Minute Memory

But when the **Holy Spirit** has come upon you, **you will receive power** and will tell people about me everywhere—in **Jerusalem**, throughout **Judea**, in **Samaria**, and to the **ends of the earth.**

Acts 1:8

done ☐

The Gift of the Holy Spirit

On the day of Pentecost, seven weeks after Jesus' resurrection, the believers were meeting together in one place. Suddenly, there was a sound from heaven like the roaring of a mighty windstorm in the skies above them, and it filled the house where they were meeting. Then, what looked like flames or tongues of fire appeared and settled on each of them. And everyone present was filled with the Holy Spirit and began speaking in other languages, as the Holy Spirit gave them this ability.

Godly Jews from many nations were living in Jerusalem at that time. When they heard this sound, they came running to see what it was all about, and they were bewildered to hear their own languages being spoken by the believers.

They were beside themselves with wonder. "How can this be?" they exclaimed. "These people are all from Galilee, and yet we hear them speaking the languages of the lands where we were born! Here we are—Parthians, Medes, Elamites, people from Mesopotamia, Judea, Cappadocia, Pontus, the province of Asia, Phrygia, Pamphylia, Egypt, and the areas of Libya toward Cyrene, visitors from Rome (both Jews and converts to Judaism), Cretans, and Arabians. And we all hear these people speaking in our own languages about the wonderful things God has done!" They stood there amazed and perplexed. "What can this mean?" they asked each other. But others in the crowd were mocking. "They're drunk, that's all!" they said.

Acts 2:1-13

Related Texts: Leviticus 23:4-16; Matthew 3:1-12; John 14:15-26; 15:26-27; 16:12-15

In OTHER Words

Speaking in languages

Today, this act of speaking in unknown languages is called "speaking in tongues" and is listed among the spiritual gifts in 1 Corinthians 12. This particular spiritual gift comes with an instruction; if you speak in tongues in public, you need to be with someone who has the spiritual gift of interpretation. Interpretation allows others to understand the language and be built up or ministered to.

Not all Christians speak in tongues. We can ask God for this gift, but the Bible does not say it's the most important gift. Check them all out and ask God to show you what spiritual gifts He has given you.

done ☐

JUST a THOUGHT

God knew the code word to break the lock of Satan's death grip; it was spelled J.E.S.U.S.

Peter's First Sermon

Then Peter stepped forward with the eleven other apostles and shouted to the crowd, "Listen carefully, all of you, fellow Jews and residents of Jerusalem! Make no mistake about this. Some of you are saying these people are drunk. It isn't true! It's much too early for that. People don't get drunk by nine o'clock in the morning. No, what you see this morning was predicted centuries ago by the prophet Joel:

'In the last days, God said,
I will pour out my Spirit upon all people.
Your sons and daughters will prophesy,
your young men will see visions,
and your old men will dream dreams.
In those days I will pour out my Spirit upon
all my servants, men and women alike,
and they will prophesy. . . .
And anyone who calls on the name of the Lord
will be saved.'

"People of Israel, listen! God publicly endorsed Jesus of Nazareth by doing wonderful miracles, wonders, and signs through him, as you well know. But you followed God's prearranged plan. With the help of lawless Gentiles, you nailed him to the cross and murdered him. However, God released him from the horrors of death and raised him back to life again, for death could not keep him in its grip. . . .

"Each of you must turn from your sins and turn to God, and be baptized in the name of Jesus Christ for the forgiveness of your sins. Then you will receive the gift of the Holy Spirit."

Acts 2:14-18,21-24,38

Related Texts: Ezekiel 36:16-28; 39:21-29; Joel 2:28-32; Romans 10:1-13

done ☐

PETER HEALS A CRIPPLED BEGGAR

Peter and John went to the Temple one afternoon to take part in the three o'clock prayer service. As they approached the Temple, a man lame from birth was being carried in. Each day he was put beside the Temple gate, the one called the Beautiful Gate, so he could beg from the people going into the Temple. When he saw Peter and John about to enter, he asked them for some money.

Peter and John looked at him intently, and Peter said, "Look at us!" The lame man looked at them eagerly, expecting a gift. But Peter said, "I don't have any money for you. But I'll give you what I have. In the name of Jesus Christ of Nazareth, get up and walk!"

Then Peter took the lame man by the right hand and helped him up. And as he did, the man's feet and anklebones were healed and strengthened. He jumped up, stood on his feet, and began to walk! Then, walking, leaping, and praising God, he went into the Temple with them.

All the people saw him walking and heard him praising God. When they realized he was the lame beggar they had seen so often at the Beautiful Gate, they were absolutely astounded!

Acts 3:1-10

While Peter and John were speaking to the people, the leading priests, the captain of the Temple guard, and some of the Sadducees came over to them. They were very disturbed that Peter and John were claiming, on the authority of Jesus, that there is a resurrection of the dead. They arrested them and, since it was already evening, jailed them until morning. But many of the people who heard their message believed it, so that the number of believers totaled about five thousand men, not counting women and children.

Acts 4:1-4

Related Texts: Jeremiah 37:15; 38:6; Matthew 15:29-31; 21:1-16; John 5; 14:12-14

What's it Mean?

Peter and John preached the message that Jesus was alive and had risen from the dead. Jesus' resurrection made it possible for them to heal the beggar.

The people who were mad at Peter and John's preaching are the same people who forced the crucifixion of Jesus. They saw the five thousand new believers respond to the message. They were afraid that word of the healing and salvation would spread throughout the country.

Events like these make up the beginning of the church. The early chapters of Acts record the beginning days of the early church. These events took place almost two thousand years ago, and yet people are still being added to the kingdom day by day... even today!

Can you do anything to help the message of the resurrected Jesus get out today?

done ☐

16 NOVEMBER

CATCH THIS

The Council knew that Peter and John had no formal educational training, and yet they were amazed at their teaching and actions. Years earlier Jesus had also surprised the Jewish leaders by His teaching and actions. They said, "How can he (Jesus) know so much when he's never been to our schools?" Jesus handed down this wisdom to His disciples, and they carried on the Good News.

Ask God to give you godly wisdom so you too can amaze others at God's Good News.

Obey God Before People

The members of the council were amazed when they saw the boldness of Peter and John, for they could see that they were ordinary men who had had no special training. They also recognized them as men who had been with Jesus. But since the man who had been healed was standing right there among them, the council had nothing to say. So they sent Peter and John out of the council chamber and conferred among themselves.

"What should we do with these men?" they asked each other. "We can't deny they have done a miraculous sign, and everybody in Jerusalem knows about it. But perhaps we can stop them from spreading their propaganda. We'll warn them not to speak to anyone in Jesus' name again." So they called the apostles back in and told them never again to speak or teach about Jesus.

But Peter and John replied, "Do you think God wants us to obey you rather than him? We cannot stop telling about the wonderful things we have seen and heard."

The council then threatened them further, but they finally let them go because they didn't know how to punish them without starting a riot. For everyone was praising God for this miraculous sign—the healing of a man who had been lame for more than forty years.

As soon as they were freed, Peter and John found the other believers and told them what the leading priests and elders had said.

Acts 4:13-23

Related Texts: Jeremiah 20:9; Matthew 5:10-12; Acts 5:17-42

done ☐

Stephen Is Martyred for His Testimony

God's message was preached in ever-widening circles. The number of believers greatly increased in Jerusalem, and many of the Jewish priests were converted, too.

Stephen, a man full of God's grace and power, performed amazing miracles and signs among the people. But one day some men from the Synagogue of Freed Slaves, as it was called, started to debate with him. They were Jews from Cyrene, Alexandria, Cilicia, and the province of Asia. None of them was able to stand against the wisdom and Spirit by which Stephen spoke.

So they persuaded some men to lie about Stephen, saying, "We heard him blaspheme Moses, and even God." Naturally, this roused the crowds, the elders, and the teachers of religious law. So they arrested Stephen and brought him before the high council.

Acts 6:7-12

But Stephen, full of the Holy Spirit, gazed steadily upward into heaven and saw the glory of God, and he saw Jesus standing in the place of honor at God's right hand. And he told them, "Look, I see the heavens opened and the Son of Man standing in the place of honor at God's right hand!"

Then they put their hands over their ears, and drowning out his voice with their shouts, they rushed at him. They dragged him out of the city and began to stone him. The official witnesses took off their coats and laid them at the feet of a young man named Saul.

And as they stoned him, Stephen prayed, "Lord Jesus, receive my spirit." And he fell to his knees, shouting, "Lord, don't charge them with this sin!" And with that, he died.

Acts 7:55-60

Related Texts: Leviticus 24:10-16; Mark 13:9-13; John 16:1-4; Acts 7:1-54; 8:1-4

Give it a try

Stephen was wrongly accused. Has this ever happened to you? After reading Stephen's response, is there anything you can learn from him in case you're ever wrongly accused of something? Write out a blueprint for how you would handle it.

done ☐

JUST a THOUGHT

Will God have to knock you to the ground and blind you to fulfill His plan? It seems much easier to give Him your heart and save yourself the unnecessary pain.

Saul Meets Jesus

A great wave of persecution began that day, sweeping over the church in Jerusalem, and all the believers except the apostles fled into Judea and Samaria. (Some godly people came and buried Stephen with loud weeping.) Saul was going everywhere to devastate the church. He went from house to house, dragging out both men and women to throw them into jail.

But the believers who had fled Jerusalem went everywhere preaching the Good News about Jesus.

Acts 8:1b-4

Meanwhile, Saul was uttering threats with every breath. He was eager to destroy the Lord's followers, so he went to the high priest. He requested letters addressed to the synagogues in Damascus, asking their cooperation in the arrest of any followers of the Way he found there. He wanted to bring them—both men and women—back to Jerusalem in chains.

As he was nearing Damascus on this mission, a brilliant light from heaven suddenly beamed down upon him! He fell to the ground and heard a voice saying to him, "Saul! Saul! Why are you persecuting me?"

"Who are you, sir?" Saul asked.

And the voice replied, "I am Jesus, the one you are persecuting! Now get up and go into the city, and you will be told what you are to do."

The men with Saul stood speechless with surprise, for they heard the sound of someone's voice, but they saw no one! As Saul picked himself up off the ground, he found that he was blind. So his companions led him by the hand to Damascus. He remained there blind for three days. And all that time he went without food and water.

Acts 9:1-9

Related Texts: Daniel 8:26-27; Luke 1:18-20; Acts 22:1-21; 26:1-29

done ☐

Saul Begins to Preach about Jesus

Now there was a believer in Damascus named Ananias. The Lord spoke to him in a vision, calling, "Ananias!"

"Yes, Lord!" he replied.

The Lord said, "Go over to Straight Street, to the house of Judas. When you arrive, ask for Saul of Tarsus. He is praying to me right now. I have shown him a vision of a man named Ananias coming in and laying his hands on him so that he can see again."

"But Lord," exclaimed Ananias, "I've heard about the terrible things this man has done to the believers in Jerusalem! And we hear that he is authorized by the leading priests to arrest every believer in Damascus."

But the Lord said, "Go and do what I say. For Saul is my chosen instrument to take my message to the Gentiles and to kings, as well as to the people of Israel."...

So Ananias went and found Saul. He laid his hands on him and said, "Brother Saul, the Lord Jesus, who appeared to you on the road, has sent me so that you may get your sight back and be filled with the Holy Spirit." Instantly something like scales fell from Saul's eyes, and he regained his sight. Then he got up and was baptized. Afterward he ate some food and was strengthened.

Saul stayed with the believers in Damascus for a few days. And immediately he began preaching about Jesus in the synagogues, saying, "He is indeed the Son of God!"

Acts 9:10-15,17-20

Related Texts: Genesis 20; Numbers 12; 1 Corinthians 15:1-11; Galatians 1:11-24

Personality Plus

Paul

The Paul you read about today is about to have his life changed. He started off with a zealous anti-Jesus crusade and ended his life as one of the true heros of the Christian faith.

After Paul's conversion he helped build up the early church by announcing the news about salvation through Jesus. Through his many years of traveling and preaching, Paul started several churches. He wrote letters to these churches to instruct them on Christian living. These letters became books in the New Testament.

One of Paul's instructions directed his followers to follow him as he followed Jesus. Paul was worthy of following because he was sold out for Jesus. Read Paul's letters, follow his teaching, and allow him to become a hero to you.

done ☐

20 NOVEMBER

Personality Plus

Barnabas

Though Barnabas never wrote a book in the Bible, he was known for his tremendous encouragement to Paul and John—who, together, wrote over half the New Testament. Barnabas was an important figure in the development of the early church because he empowered others through his encouragement and support. The name Barnabas actually means "son of encouragement." He lived up to his name!

It's tough to encourage others. Being an encourager takes confidence in oneself and God's ability to use you. It's much easier to be critical! Criticism doesn't take much time or thought. But encouragement is life changing. You'll be able to see the results if you replace criticism with encouragement. Try to live up to the name: "son or daughter of encouragement."

The First Missionary Journey

One day as these men were worshiping the Lord and fasting, the Holy Spirit said, "Dedicate Barnabas and Saul for the special work I have for them." So after more fasting and prayer, the men laid their hands on them and sent them on their way.

Sent out by the Holy Spirit, Saul and Barnabas went down to the seaport of Seleucia and then sailed for the island of Cyprus. There, in the town of Salamis, they went to the Jewish synagogues and preached the word of God. . . .

Afterward they preached from town to town across the entire island until finally they reached Paphos, where they met a Jewish sorcerer, a false prophet named Bar-Jesus. He had attached himself to the governor, Sergius Paulus, a man of considerable insight and understanding. The governor invited Barnabas and Saul to visit him, for he wanted to hear the word of God. But Elymas, the sorcerer (as his name means in Greek), interfered and urged the governor to pay no attention to what Saul and Barnabas said. He was trying to turn the governor away from the Christian faith.

Then Saul, also known as Paul, filled with the Holy Spirit, looked the sorcerer in the eye and said, "You son of the Devil, full of every sort of trickery and villainy, enemy of all that is good, will you never stop perverting the true ways of the Lord? And now the Lord has laid his hand of punishment upon you, and you will be stricken awhile with blindness." Instantly mist and darkness fell upon him, and he began wandering around begging for someone to take his hand and lead him. When the governor saw what had happened, he believed and was astonished at what he learned about the Lord.

Acts 13:2-5a,6-12

Related Texts: Numbers 27:22-23; Deuteronomy 34:9; Matthew 19:13-15; Luke 4:40; Acts 6:1-6; 8:5-25; 1 Timothy 4:11-14

done ☐

Paul and Barnabas among the Gentiles

While they were at Lystra, Paul and Barnabas came upon a man with crippled feet. He had been that way from birth, so he had never walked. He was listening as Paul preached, and Paul noticed him and realized he had faith to be healed. So Paul called to him in a loud voice, "Stand up!" And the man jumped to his feet and started walking. . . .

Now some Jews arrived from Antioch and Iconium and turned the crowds into a murderous mob. They stoned Paul and dragged him out of the city, apparently dead. But as the believers stood around him, he got up and went back into the city. The next day he left with Barnabas for Derbe.

After preaching the Good News in Derbe and making many disciples, Paul and Barnabas returned again to Lystra, Iconium, and Antioch of Pisidia, where they strengthened the believers. They encouraged them to continue in the faith, reminding them that they must enter into the Kingdom of God through many tribulations. Paul and Barnabas also appointed elders in every church and prayed for them with fasting, turning them over to the care of the Lord, in whom they had come to trust. . . .

Finally, they returned by ship to Antioch of Syria, where their journey had begun and where they had been committed to the grace of God for the work they had now completed. Upon arriving in Antioch, they called the church together and reported about their trip, telling all that God had done and how he had opened the door of faith to the Gentiles too. And they stayed there with the believers in Antioch for a long time. *Acts 14:8-10,19-23,26-28*

Related Texts: Exodus 17:1-4; Numbers 14:1-10; 1 Samuel 30:6; John 8:31-59; Acts 7:52-60; 14:1-7; Romans 1:1-17; Ephesians 2:11-22

BIG TIMe WoRd

GROW

"Grow" is an important word because growth is one of the important Christian goals. Growth is a reflection of what's taking place in our relationship with God. If we're growing in this relationship, it will be evident in our lives and our actions.

Are you growing? Are you moving toward becoming more mature in your faith? What steps do you need to take in your spiritual life to ensure you're moving ahead and growing?

Growth is like learning to drive—no one can do it for you.

done ☐

In Everything Give Thanks

One Minute Memory

Always be joyful. Keep on praying. No matter what happens, always be thankful, for this is God's will for you who belong to Christ Jesus.

1 Thessalonians 5:16–18

Give thanks to the LORD and proclaim
his greatness.
Let the whole world know what he has
done.
Sing to him; yes, sing his praises.
Tell everyone about his miracles.

1 Chronicles 16:8-9

Come, let us sing to the LORD!
Let us give a joyous shout to the rock of
our salvation!
Let us come before him with thanksgiving.
Let us sing him psalms of praise.
For the LORD is a great God,
the great King above all gods.
He owns the depths of the earth,
and even the mightiest mountains are his.
The sea belongs to him, for he made it.
His hands formed the dry land, too.
Come, let us worship and bow down.
Let us kneel before the LORD our maker,
for he is our God.
We are the people he watches over,
the sheep under his care.
Oh, that you would listen to his voice
today!

Psalm 95:1-7

Always be joyful. Keep on praying. No matter what happens, always be thankful, for this is God's will for you who belong to Christ Jesus.

1 Thessalonians 5:16-18

Related Texts: Nehemiah 12:27-43; Psalms 77; 135:1-7; 148; Luke 22:14-19

done ☐

NOVEMBER 23

Give Thanks for God's Provision

Give thanks to the LORD, for he is good!
His faithful love endures forever.
Has the LORD redeemed you? Then speak out!
Tell others he has saved you from your enemies.
For he has gathered the exiles from many lands,
from east and west, from north and south.
Some wandered in the desert,
lost and homeless.
Hungry and thirsty,
they nearly died.
"LORD, help!" they cried in their trouble,
and he rescued them from their distress.
He led them straight to safety,
to a city where they could live.
Let them praise the LORD for his great love
and for all his wonderful deeds to them.
For he satisfies the thirsty
and fills the hungry with good things. . . .
Let them praise the LORD for his great love
and for all his wonderful deeds to them.
Let them offer sacrifices of thanksgiving
and sing joyfully about his glorious acts.

Psalm 107:1-9,21-22

Related Texts: 2 Chronicles 20:14-26; Psalms 104; 118; 145; Matthew 6:25-34

Give it a try

List five things you're thankful for today:

1.

2.

3.

If you did this exercise every day, your attitude and life would change dramatically. It's hard to be depressed when you're continually thankful.

done ☐

24 NOVEMBER

In OTHER Words

Body

Imagine a body without a head. Now, imagine Jesus as the head of the body. Imagine yourself as one dot along with millions of others that make up and fill in the body. The body refers to the church body, and Jesus is the head of this body. Christians who make up this body receive their life support from Jesus—who is the head over everything.

Although we have never met, as believers we are part of the same body. We are also Jesus' living body and represent Jesus and His work to the world. To maintain a healthy body we must be connected to the Head. Today, find someone who is part of the body and see how you work together as parts of the church body.

Give Thanks to God among His People

Shout with joy to the LORD, O earth!
  Worship the LORD with gladness.
  Come before him, singing with joy.
Acknowledge that the LORD is God!
  He made us, and we are his.
  We are his people, the sheep of his
    pasture.
Enter his gates with thanksgiving;
  go into his courts with praise.
  Give thanks to him and bless his name.
For the LORD is good.
  His unfailing love continues forever,
  and his faithfulness continues to each
    generation.

Psalm 100

And let the peace that comes from Christ rule in your hearts. For as members of one body you are all called to live in peace. And always be thankful.

Let the words of Christ, in all their richness, live in your hearts and make you wise. Use his words to teach and counsel each other. Sing psalms and hymns and spiritual songs to God with thankful hearts. And whatever you do or say, let it be as a representative of the Lord Jesus, all the while giving thanks through him to God the Father.

Colossians 3:15-17

Related Texts: 2 Chronicles 6:41; Psalms 65; 84; 96; Ephesians 5:18-20; 3 John 11

done ☐

NOVEMBER 25

Give Thanks to God for His Enduring Love

Give thanks to the LORD, for he is good!
His faithful love endures forever.
Give thanks to the God of gods.
His faithful love endures forever.
Give thanks to the Lord of lords.
His faithful love endures forever.

Psalm 136:1-3

We always pray for you, and we give thanks to God the Father of our Lord Jesus Christ, for we have heard that you trust in Christ Jesus and that you love all of God's people. You do this because you are looking forward to the joys of heaven—as you have been ever since you first heard the truth of the Good News. This same Good News that came to you is going out all over the world. It is changing lives everywhere, just as it changed yours that very first day you heard and understood the truth about God's great kindness to sinners.

Colossians 1:3-6

I always thank God when I pray for you, Philemon, because I keep hearing of your trust in the Lord Jesus and your love for all of God's people. You are generous because of your faith. And I am praying that you will really put your generosity to work, for in so doing you will come to an understanding of all the good things we can do for Christ. I myself have gained much joy and comfort from your love, my brother, because your kindness has so often refreshed the hearts of God's people.

Philemon 1:4-7

Related Texts: 1 Chronicles 16:34-36; 2 Chronicles 5-7; Psalms 118:1-4; 136:4-26; 2 Corinthians 9:10-15

In some of Paul's writings he expresses a deep, heartfelt thankfulness. The Greek word for "heart" literally means "bowel." You can understand why many biblical translators have changed the word from bowel to heart. In Greek thought (the language of Paul's writings) the bowels were referred to as the center of affection. It wouldn't sound very good if we still used BOWEL instead of HEART. Imagine this: "The Thanksgiving dinner was great, Mom. I mean that compliment from the bottom of my bowels!"

No matter what word you choose to use, express your thankfulness to God today for creating hearts, bowels, and everything else.

done ☐

CATCH THIS

The fitness craze is everywhere! We have placed a superficial importance on looking good and getting in shape. Millions of dollars are spent each year by those in desperate search of physical fitness.

Unfortunately, billions of pounds of exercise equipment rests unused in garages. The money to buy the equipment was available, but the discipline to use it wasn't. Discouragement sets in, and people give up. It's tough to get back into shape—especially as you get older.

The Bible instructs us that spiritual fitness is a much more important goal. Your physical body will eventually decay and rot away, but your spiritual body will last forever. Spiritual fitness requires discipline and hard work. If you're not in spiritual shape, get started on a training program that works for you. If you're spiritually fit, keep growing and don't allow your faith to get flabby.

Receive God's Good Gifts with Thanksgiving

Now the Holy Spirit tells us clearly that in the last times some will turn away from what we believe; they will follow lying spirits and teachings that come from demons. These teachers are hypocrites and liars. They pretend to be religious, but their consciences are dead.

They will say it is wrong to be married and wrong to eat certain foods. But God created those foods to be eaten with thanksgiving by people who know and believe the truth. Since everything God created is good, we should not reject any of it. We may receive it gladly, with thankful hearts. For we know it is made holy by the word of God and prayer.

If you explain this to the brothers and sisters, you will be doing your duty as a worthy servant of Christ Jesus, one who is fed by the message of faith and the true teaching you have followed. Do not waste time arguing over godless ideas and old wives' tales. Spend your time and energy in training yourself for spiritual fitness. Physical exercise has some value, but spiritual exercise is much more important, for it promises a reward in both this life and the next. This is true, and everyone should accept it. We work hard and suffer much in order that people will believe the truth, for our hope is in the living God, who is the Savior of all people, and particularly of those who believe.

Teach these things and insist that everyone learn them.

1 Timothy 4:1-11

Related Texts: 1 Chronicles 16:4-14; Romans 8:18-28; 14; 1 Corinthians 10

done ☐

GIVE THANKS TO GOD IN HEAVEN

And instantly I was in the Spirit, and I saw a throne in heaven and someone sitting on it! The one sitting on the throne was as brilliant as gemstones—jasper and carnelian. And the glow of an emerald circled his throne like a rainbow. Twenty-four thrones surrounded him, and twenty-four elders sat on them. They were all clothed in white and had gold crowns on their heads. And from the throne came flashes of lightning and the rumble of thunder. And in front of the throne were seven lampstands with burning flames. They are the seven spirits of God. In front of the throne was a shiny sea of glass, sparkling like crystal.

In the center and around the throne were four living beings, each covered with eyes, front and back. . . . Each of these living beings had six wings, and their wings were covered with eyes, inside and out. Day after day and night after night they keep on saying,

"Holy, holy, holy is the Lord God
Almighty—
the one who always was, who is, and
who is still to come."

Whenever the living beings give glory and honor and thanks to the one sitting on the throne, the one who lives forever and ever, the twenty-four elders fall down and worship the one who lives forever and ever. And they lay their crowns before the throne and say,

"You are worthy, O Lord our God,
to receive glory and honor and power.
For you created everything,
and it is for your pleasure that they exist
and were created."

Revelation 4:2-6,8-11

Related Texts: Exodus 24:1-11; Isaiah 6; Psalms 103:20-22; 148; Mark 10:17-18

What's it Mean?

The Book of Revelation is John's vision describing what the end times will be like. The visions and scenes described in this book have been interpreted many different ways by thousands of scholars. If you struggle to understand the Book of Revelation, you're not alone. The Big Picture is that Jesus is revealed as King and wins the final battle over Satan. That's definitely worth reading about.

You'll have eternity to praise and thank God for this victory, but why don't you get a head start and praise Him today.

done ☐

Let Everything Praise the Lord!

One Minute Memory

Don't drink too much wine,
for many **evils** lie along that
path; **be filled** instead with the
Holy Spirit and **controlled**
by him.

Ephesians 5:18

Praise the LORD!
Praise God in his heavenly dwelling;
praise him in his mighty heaven!
Praise him for his mighty works;
praise his unequaled greatness!
Praise him with a blast of the trumpet;
praise him with the lyre and harp!
Praise him with the tambourine and dancing;
praise him with stringed instruments and flutes!
Praise him with a clash of cymbals;
praise him with loud clanging cymbals.
Let everything that lives sing praises to the LORD!
Praise the LORD!

Psalm 150

Don't be drunk with wine, because that will ruin your life. Instead, let the Holy Spirit fill and control you. Then you will sing psalms and hymns and spiritual songs among yourselves, making music to the Lord in your hearts. And you will always give thanks for everything to God the Father in the name of our Lord Jesus Christ.

Ephesians 5:18-20

Related Texts: Exodus 15:1-21; 1 Chronicles 15-16; Colossians 3:16-17

done ☐

NOVEMBER 29

Jews and Gentiles Are One in Christ

God did not reveal it to previous generations, but now he has revealed it by the Holy Spirit to his holy apostles and prophets.

And this is the secret plan: The Gentiles have an equal share with the Jews in all the riches inherited by God's children. Both groups have believed the Good News, and both are part of the same body and enjoy together the promise of blessings through Christ Jesus. By God's special favor and mighty power, I have been given the wonderful privilege of serving him by spreading this Good News.

Just think! Though I did nothing to deserve it, and though I am the least deserving Christian there is, I was chosen for this special joy of telling the Gentiles about the endless treasures available to them in Christ. I was chosen to explain to everyone this plan that God, the Creator of all things, had kept secret from the beginning.

God's purpose was to show his wisdom in all its rich variety to all the rulers and authorities in the heavenly realms. They will see this when Jews and Gentiles are joined together in his church. This was his plan from all eternity, and it has now been carried out through Christ Jesus our Lord.

Because of Christ and our faith in him, we can now come fearlessly into God's presence, assured of his glad welcome.

Ephesians 3:5-12

Related Texts: Isaiah 49:1-6; Acts 15; Galatians 3:25-29; Ephesians 2:11-22

CHECK IT OUT

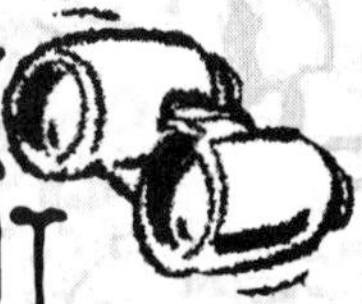

Today's reading provides a message that many Christians need to hear. Differences should never separate us from other Christians. We are one in Jesus whether we are thin, tall, squatty, large, colored, uncolored, transparent, ear pierced, nose pierced—it doesn't matter. We are one in Jesus!

Paul explains this truth in Galatians 3:28-29: "There is no longer Jew or Gentile, slave or free, male or female. For you are all Christians—you are one in Christ Jesus. And now that you belong to Christ, you are the true children of Abraham. You are his heirs, and now all the promises God gave to him belong to you."

Celebrate this truth today with a Christian who is different from you by telling him or her you're related.

done ☐

Weird or What?

Spiritual Gifts

In the New Testament there are four different passages that discuss and describe spiritual gifts. It's interesting that none of these passages have the exact same list of gifts. Some believe that the lists weren't intended to be all-inclusive, and others debate that the ones listed are the only spiritual gifts available. Regardless of whether there are nine spiritual gifts or seventeen, we do know that God has assigned each of us with specific gifts to build up the body of Jesus. Read through the spiritual gift passages* and begin to discover how God has specially gifted you.

*Also read Romans 12:3-8; 1 Corinthians 12:28-30; Ephesians 4:7-12; 1 Peter 4:10-11

And now, dear brothers and sisters, I will write about the special abilities the Holy Spirit gives to each of us, for I must correct your misunderstandings about them. . . .

Now there are different kinds of spiritual gifts, but it is the same Holy Spirit who is the source of them all. There are different kinds of service in the church, but it is the same Lord we are serving. There are different ways God works in our lives, but it is the same God who does the work through all of us. A spiritual gift is given to each of us as a means of helping the entire church.

To one person the Spirit gives the ability to give wise advice; to another he gives the gift of special knowledge. The Spirit gives special faith to another, and to someone else he gives the power to heal the sick. He gives one person the power to perform miracles, and to another the ability to prophesy. He gives someone else the ability to know whether it is really the Spirit of God or another spirit that is speaking. Still another person is given the ability to speak in unknown languages, and another is given the ability to interpret what is being said. It is the one and only Holy Spirit who distributes these gifts. He alone decides which gift each person should have.

1 Corinthians 12:1,4-11

Related Texts: Exodus 31:1-6; 35:30–36:2; Romans 12:1-8; 1 Corinthians 13–14; Ephesians 4:1-16; Hebrews 2:1-4; 1 Peter 4:7-11

done ☐

It is impossible to rightly govern the world without God and the Bible.

George Washington
(1732–1799)
United States President

December

DECEMBER 1

Future Hope, Future Reward

For we know that when this earthly tent we live in is taken down—when we die and leave these bodies—we will have a home in heaven, an eternal body made for us by God himself and not by human hands. We grow weary in our present bodies, and we long for the day when we will put on our heavenly bodies like new clothing. For we will not be spirits without bodies, but we will put on new heavenly bodies. Our dying bodies make us groan and sigh, but it's not that we want to die and have no bodies at all. We want to slip into our new bodies so that these dying bodies will be swallowed up by everlasting life. God himself has prepared us for this, and as a guarantee he has given us his Holy Spirit.

So we are always confident, even though we know that as long as we live in these bodies we are not at home with the Lord. That is why we live by believing and not by seeing. Yes, we are fully confident, and we would rather be away from these bodies, for then we will be at home with the Lord. So our aim is to please him always, whether we are here in this body or away from this body. For we must all stand before Christ to be judged. We will each receive whatever we deserve for the good or evil we have done in our bodies.

2 Corinthians 5:1-10

Related Texts: Ecclesiastes 12; John 11:20-27; Romans 14:1-13; Philippians 1:20-26; 1 Corinthians 15:35-54

CHECK IT OUT

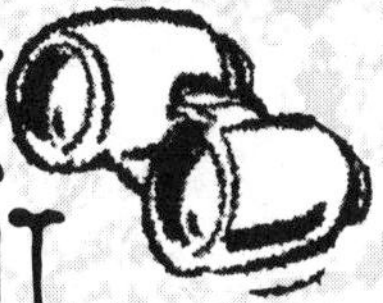

To a Christian, a future of living with God in heaven is good news. We can view death as a move up or a victory. Paul expressed this by describing the tension between his desire to live in pain on earth and spread the gospel and his desire to be with God in heaven. Check out Philippians 1:21: "For to me, living is for Christ, and dying is even better."

There is hope for you! What God has planned for Christians can't be matched by your greatest day on earth.

But while you are on this earth, it's best to live with celebration in your heart and a joyful eye to your future in God's presence.

done ☐

Sealed for Salvation

Long ago, even before he made the world, God loved us and chose us in Christ to be holy and without fault in his eyes. His unchanging plan has always been to adopt us into his own family by bringing us to himself through Jesus Christ. And this gave him great pleasure.

So we praise God for the wonderful kindness he has poured out on us because we belong to his dearly loved Son. He is so rich in kindness that he purchased our freedom through the blood of his Son, and our sins are forgiven. He has showered his kindness on us, along with all wisdom and understanding.

God's secret plan has now been revealed to us; it is a plan centered on Christ, designed long ago according to his good pleasure. And this is his plan: At the right time he will bring everything together under the authority of Christ—everything in heaven and on earth. Furthermore, because of Christ, we have received an inheritance from God, for he chose us from the beginning, and all things happen just as he decided long ago. God's purpose was that we who were the first to trust in Christ should praise our glorious God. And now you also have heard the truth, the Good News that God saves you. And when you believed in Christ, he identified you as his own by giving you the Holy Spirit, whom he promised long ago. The Spirit is God's guarantee that he will give us everything he promised and that he has purchased us to be his own people. This is just one more reason for us to praise our glorious God.

Ephesians 1:4-14

Related Texts: Psalm 113; Romans 8:29-39; Ephesians 2:4-10; Revelation 3:5; 13:8; 17:8; 20:15

Give it a try

Christians have been "sealed" with God by the Holy Spirit. How does that make you feel right now?

done ☐

Humility and Glory

Is there any encouragement from belonging to Christ? Any comfort from his love? Any fellowship together in the Spirit? Are your hearts tender and sympathetic? Then make me truly happy by agreeing wholeheartedly with each other, loving one another, and working together with one heart and purpose.

Don't be selfish; don't live to make a good impression on others. Be humble, thinking of others as better than yourself. Don't think only about your own affairs, but be interested in others, too, and what they are doing.

Your attitude should be the same that Christ Jesus had. Though he was God, he did not demand and cling to his rights as God. He made himself nothing; he took the humble position of a slave and appeared in human form. And in human form he obediently humbled himself even further by dying a criminal's death on a cross. Because of this, God raised him up to the heights of heaven and gave him a name that is above every other name, so that at the name of Jesus every knee will bow, in heaven and on earth and under the earth, and every tongue will confess that Jesus Christ is Lord, to the glory of God the Father.

Philippians 2:1-11

Related Texts: Isaiah 45:22-25; John 13:1-15; Romans 14:11-12; 1 Corinthians 15:20-28; Philippians 2:19-21; 1 Peter 5:5-6

BIG TIMe WoRd

ATTITUDE

Having a positive attitude is vital in today's world. People are attracted to those with quality attitudes. Christians are typically known for having good attitudes because the Holy Spirit resides in them. The Spirit's indwelling allows Christians to live with confidence that God is in control.

When your attitude is positive, people notice that something is different. They can see the security of your peace and joy. Is your attitude one that people notice? If not, what needs to be done to improve it? If it is noticed, congratulations! You are in a minority of positive people.

done ☐

One Minute Memory

Forgetting the past and **looking forward** to what lies **ahead**, I **strain** to reach the **end of the race** and **receive the prize** for which **God**, through **Christ**, is **calling us up to heaven.**

Philippians 3:13b–14

To Know Christ

Yet I could have confidence in myself if anyone could. If others have reason for confidence in their own efforts, I have even more! For I was circumcised when I was eight days old, having been born into a pure-blooded Jewish family that is a branch of the tribe of Benjamin. So I am a real Jew if there ever was one! What's more, I was a member of the Pharisees, who demand the strictest obedience to the Jewish law. . . .

I once thought all these things were so very important, but now I consider them worthless because of what Christ has done. Yes, everything else is worthless when compared with the priceless gain of knowing Christ Jesus my Lord. I have discarded everything else, counting it all as garbage, so that I may have Christ and become one with him. I no longer count on my own goodness or my ability to obey God's law, but I trust Christ to save me. For God's way of making us right with himself depends on faith. . . .

No, dear brothers and sisters, I am still not all I should be, but I am focusing all my energies on this one thing: Forgetting the past and looking forward to what lies ahead, I strain to reach the end of the race and receive the prize for which God, through Christ Jesus, is calling us up to heaven.

Philippians 3:4-5,7-9,13-14

Related Texts: Psalm 18:30-33; Matthew 5:43-48; Mark 8:34-37; Acts 22:1-21; Colossians 1:24; Hebrews 12:1-3

done ☐

The Supremacy of Christ

Christ is the visible image of the invisible God. He existed before God made anything at all and is supreme over all creation. Christ is the one through whom God created everything in heaven and earth. He made the things we can see and the things we can't see—kings, kingdoms, rulers, and authorities. Everything has been created through him and for him. He existed before everything else began, and he holds all creation together.

Christ is the head of the church, which is his body. He is the first of all who will rise from the dead, so he is first in everything. For God in all his fullness was pleased to live in Christ, and by him God reconciled everything to himself. He made peace with everything in heaven and on earth by means of his blood on the cross. This includes you who were once so far away from God. You were his enemies, separated from him by your evil thoughts and actions, yet now he has brought you back as his friends. He has done this through his death on the cross in his own human body. As a result, he has brought you into the very presence of God, and you are holy and blameless as you stand before him without a single fault. But you must continue to believe this truth and stand in it firmly. Don't drift away from the assurance you received when you heard the Good News. The Good News has been preached all over the world, and I, Paul, have been appointed by God to proclaim it.

Colossians 1:15-23

Related Texts: Genesis 1:26; John 1:1-18; Romans 5:9-11; 2 Corinthians 5:17-21; Colossians 2:9-10; Hebrews 1:1-3

done ☐

JUST a THOUGHT

If anyone asks you what God is like, open your Bible and have him check out Jesus—He's the exact likeness of God.

6 DECEMBER

BIG TIMe WoRd

SORROW

Sorrow is an appropriate emotion to express at the death of a loved one. God created you with the ability to cry and show compassion. If your sorrow is because of the death of a Christian, your tears can eventually become tears of hope. You can rest in the truth that death to a Christian is entrance into God's presence and eternal home.

As a Christian, you have nothing to fear about your future. If you live by faith that your future is sealed, you can live with assurance. That's a great way to live!

Try it.

Meeting the Lord in the Air

And now, brothers and sisters, I want you to know what will happen to the Christians who have died so you will not be full of sorrow like people who have no hope. For since we believe that Jesus died and was raised to life again, we also believe that when Jesus comes, God will bring back with Jesus all the Christians who have died.

I can tell you this directly from the Lord: We who are still living when the Lord returns will not rise to meet him ahead of those who are in their graves. For the Lord himself will come down from heaven with a commanding shout, with the call of the archangel, and with the trumpet call of God. First, all the Christians who have died will rise from their graves. Then, together with them, we who are still alive and remain on the earth will be caught up in the clouds to meet the Lord in the air and remain with him forever. So comfort and encourage each other with these words.

1 Thessalonians 4:13-18

I really don't need to write to you about how and when all this will happen, dear brothers and sisters. For you know quite well that the day of the Lord will come unexpectedly, like a thief in the night. When people are saying, "All is well; everything is peaceful and secure," then disaster will fall upon them as suddenly as a woman's birth pains begin when her child is about to be born. And there will be no escape.

But you aren't in the dark about these things, dear brothers and sisters, and you won't be surprised when the day of the Lord comes like a thief.

1 Thessalonians 5:1-4

Related Texts: Daniel 12:1-3; Matthew 24; 2 Peter 3; Revelation 3:1-6

done ☐

WORK IS GOOD

And now, dear brothers and sisters, we give you this command with the authority of our Lord Jesus Christ: Stay away from any Christian who lives in idleness and doesn't follow the tradition of hard work we gave you. For you know that you ought to follow our example. We were never lazy when we were with you. We never accepted food from anyone without paying for it. We worked hard day and night so that we would not be a burden to any of you. It wasn't that we didn't have the right to ask you to feed us, but we wanted to give you an example to follow. Even while we were with you, we gave you this rule: "Whoever does not work should not eat."

Yet we hear that some of you are living idle lives, refusing to work and wasting time meddling in other people's business. In the name of the Lord Jesus Christ, we appeal to such people—no, we command them: Settle down and get to work. Earn your own living. And I say to the rest of you, dear brothers and sisters, never get tired of doing good.

Take note of those who refuse to obey what we say in this letter. Stay away from them so they will be ashamed. Don't think of them as enemies, but speak to them as you would to a Christian who needs to be warned.

2 Thessalonians 3:6-15

Related Texts: Genesis 1:26-30; 2:15; 1 Corinthians 9; 2 Corinthians 12:12-18; 1 Thessalonians 2:1-12

What's it Mean?

In today's passage we see an example of biblical church discipline. Paul had taught that Jesus was going to return. The people in the church believed this and used it as an excuse to stop working. Some people even began to sponge food and money from others. They wasted their time by gossiping and getting involved in other people's business. Paul was telling them to get busy and begin working.

Work is an important part of your development. Some students don't take their jobs seriously because the jobs aren't what they want for a career. No matter what kind of job you have, try to do your best to honor God with your positive attitude and hard work. Your job will provide you many opportunities to tell coworkers about your love for God. Earn their respect first by living right and working hard.

done ☐

CATCH THIS

Do you know someone who loves to argue? Some people actually enjoy creating and maintaining tension. But arguing just to argue usually results in wasted chatter. No real purpose is ever served with empty arguments.

Some Christians love to argue about the Bible. They know a lot of biblical answers and enjoy debating non-Christians with their knowledge.

Unfortunately, very few people enter into a relationship with God during an argument. People are usually defensive and less open while arguing—even if what they hear is the truth.

Learn as much as you can about the Bible so you can talk rationally but reserve arguing for another topic. If you replace your arguments with love, you'll find people more responsive to the truth. Love works—even if you don't have all the right Bible answers. Keep learning and replace arguing with love.

Godliness and Contentment

Some false teachers may deny these things, but these are the sound, wholesome teachings of the Lord Jesus Christ, and they are the foundation for a godly life. Anyone who teaches anything different is both conceited and ignorant. Such a person has an unhealthy desire to quibble over the meaning of words. This stirs up arguments ending in jealousy, fighting, slander, and evil suspicions. These people always cause trouble. Their minds are corrupt, and they don't tell the truth. To them religion is just a way to get rich.

Yet true religion with contentment is great wealth. After all, we didn't bring anything with us when we came into the world, and we certainly cannot carry anything with us when we die. So if we have enough food and clothing, let us be content. . . .

Tell those who are rich in this world not to be proud and not to trust in their money, which will soon be gone. But their trust should be in the living God, who richly gives us all we need for our enjoyment. Tell them to use their money to do good. They should be rich in good works and should give generously to those in need, always being ready to share with others whatever God has given them. By doing this they will be storing up their treasure as a good foundation for the future so that they may take hold of real life.

1 Timothy 6:3-8,17-19

Related Texts: Psalm 112:4; Proverbs 11:24-26; 14:31; 19:17; 22:9; 28:8; Luke 12:13-34; 16:1-15; Philippians 4:10-14

done ☐

The Profit of the Scriptures

One Minute Memory

All Scripture is **inspired** by **God** and is **useful** to **teach us** what is **true** and to make us **realize** what is **wrong** in **our lives.** It **straightens us out** and **teaches us to do** what is **right.**

2 Timothy 3:16

But you know what I teach, Timothy, and how I live, and what my purpose in life is. You know my faith and how long I have suffered. You know my love and my patient endurance. You know how much persecution and suffering I have endured. You know all about how I was persecuted in Antioch, Iconium, and Lystra—but the Lord delivered me from all of it. Yes, and everyone who wants to live a godly life in Christ Jesus will suffer persecution. But evil people and impostors will flourish. They will go on deceiving others, and they themselves will be deceived.

But you must remain faithful to the things you have been taught. You know they are true, for you know you can trust those who taught you. You have been taught the holy Scriptures from childhood, and they have given you the wisdom to receive the salvation that comes by trusting in Christ Jesus. All Scripture is inspired by God and is useful to teach us what is true and to make us realize what is wrong in our lives. It straightens us out and teaches us to do what is right. It is God's way of preparing us in every way, fully equipped for every good thing God wants us to do.

2 Timothy 3:10-17

Related Texts: Isaiah 40:6-8; Matthew 5:10-12; Acts 14; 2 Corinthians 4; 12:1-10; 1 Peter 1:23-2:3

done ☐

Jesus: Our High Priest

Weird or What?

During Old Testament times the high priest would present sacrifices to atone for people's sins. It's interesting to note that in the New Testament, Jesus is referred to as our great High Priest. His one sacrifice was totally sufficient for all of us to be forgiven forever.

As a Christian you now have direct access to God and don't need a high priest to go before you.

Take advantage of that direct access and thank God for the ultimate sacrifice of Jesus.

That is why we have a great High Priest who has gone to heaven, Jesus the Son of God. Let us cling to him and never stop trusting him. This High Priest of ours understands our weaknesses, for he faced all of the same temptations we do, yet he did not sin. So let us come boldly to the throne of our gracious God. There we will receive his mercy, and we will find grace to help us when we need it.

Hebrews 4:14-16

While Jesus was here on earth, he offered prayers and pleadings, with a loud cry and tears, to the one who could deliver him out of death. And God heard his prayers because of his reverence for God. So even though Jesus was God's Son, he learned obedience from the things he suffered. In this way, God qualified him as a perfect High Priest, and he became the source of eternal salvation for all those who obey him. And God designated him to be a High Priest in the line of Melchizedek.

Hebrews 5:7-10

Therefore, it was necessary for Jesus to be in every respect like us, his brothers and sisters, so that he could be our merciful and faithful High Priest before God. He then could offer a sacrifice that would take away the sins of the people. Since he himself has gone through suffering and temptation, he is able to help us when we are being tempted.

Hebrews 2:17-18

Related Texts: Genesis 14:18-20; Psalm 110; Matthew 4:1-11

done ☐

Heroes of Faith: Part 1

What is faith? It is the confident assurance that what we hope for is going to happen. It is the evidence of things we cannot yet see. God gave his approval to people in days of old because of their faith.

By faith we understand that the entire universe was formed at God's command, that what we now see did not come from anything that can be seen.

It was by faith that Abel brought a more acceptable offering to God than Cain did. God accepted Abel's offering to show that he was a righteous man. And although Abel is long dead, he still speaks to us because of his faith.

It was by faith that Enoch was taken up to heaven without dying—"suddenly he disappeared because God took him." But before he was taken up, he was approved as pleasing to God. So, you see, it is impossible to please God without faith. Anyone who wants to come to him must believe that there is a God and that he rewards those who sincerely seek him.

It was by faith that Noah built an ark to save his family from the flood. He obeyed God, who warned him about something that had never happened before. By his faith he condemned the rest of the world and was made right in God's sight.

It was by faith that Abraham obeyed when God called him to leave home and go to another land that God would give him as his inheritance. He went without knowing where he was going.

Hebrews 11:1-8

Related Texts: Genesis 1; 4:1-16; 5:23-24; 6–8; 12; Jude 14-15

Give it a try

Write a definition of faith:

____

____

____

Share what you wrote with someone who is more knowledgeable than you regarding Christianity. Discuss your definition.

done ☐

12 DECEMBER

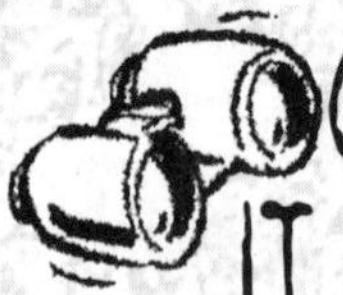

CHECK IT OUT

Yesterday you came up with your own definition of faith. Today look at how Jesus responded to His followers' questions about the amount of faith they needed. Check out Matthew 17:20: "I assure you, even if you had faith as small as a mustard seed you could say to this mountain, 'Move from here to there,' and it would move. Nothing would be impossible."

Jesus didn't emphasize the amount of faith needed but stressed that true faith, even in its smallest form, can do great things.

Ask God to help you strengthen your faith today.

Heroes of Faith: Part 2

It was by faith that Sarah together with Abraham was able to have a child, even though they were too old and Sarah was barren. Abraham believed that God would keep his promise. And so a whole nation came from this one man, Abraham, who was too old to have any children—a nation with so many people that, like the stars of the sky and the sand on the seashore, there is no way to count them. . . .

It was by faith that Abraham offered Isaac as a sacrifice when God was testing him. Abraham, who had received God's promises, was ready to sacrifice his only son, Isaac, though God had promised him, "Isaac is the son through whom your descendants will be counted." Abraham assumed that if Isaac died, God was able to bring him back to life again. And in a sense, Abraham did receive his son back from the dead. . . .

It was by faith that Moses, when he grew up, refused to be treated as the son of Pharaoh's daughter. He chose to share the oppression of God's people instead of enjoying the fleeting pleasures of sin. He thought it was better to suffer for the sake of the Messiah than to own the treasures of Egypt, for he was looking ahead to the great reward that God would give him. It was by faith that Moses left the land of Egypt. He was not afraid of the king. Moses kept right on going because he kept his eyes on the one who is invisible. . . .

All of these people we have mentioned received God's approval because of their faith, yet none of them received all that God had promised. For God had far better things in mind for us that would also benefit them, for they can't receive the prize at the end of the race until we finish the race.

Hebrews 11:11-12,17-19,24-27,39-40

Related Texts: Genesis 21-22; Exodus 2–3; Hebrews 10:36-39

done ☐

Wisdom in Trials

Dear brothers and sisters, whenever trouble comes your way, let it be an opportunity for joy. For when your faith is tested, your endurance has a chance to grow. So let it grow, for when your endurance is fully developed, you will be strong in character and ready for anything.

If you need wisdom—if you want to know what God wants you to do—ask him, and he will gladly tell you. He will not resent your asking. But when you ask him, be sure that you really expect him to answer, for a doubtful mind is as unsettled as a wave of the sea that is driven and tossed by the wind. People like that should not expect to receive anything from the Lord. They can't make up their minds. They waver back and forth in everything they do. . . .

God blesses the people who patiently endure testing. Afterward they will receive the crown of life that God has promised to those who love him. And remember, no one who wants to do wrong should ever say, "God is tempting me." God is never tempted to do wrong, and he never tempts anyone else either. Temptation comes from the lure of our own evil desires. These evil desires lead to evil actions, and evil actions lead to death.

James 1:2-8,12-15

Related Texts: Job 1–42; Matthew 6:9-13; 21:18-22; 1 Corinthians 10:12-13

CATCH THIS

One of the many confusions regarding the Christian faith has to do with God and temptation. Many Christians believe God tempts us in order to test our response and measure our faith. Today's passage explains this isn't true. God doesn't tempt us! God provides a way for us to escape temptation because He doesn't want us to sin.

When you're tempted, realize it's not God doing the tempting. Run from temptation and don't allow the temptation to know where you're going. Better yet, think through potentially tempting situations before they happen. As you think about them, plan your escape route so that when temptations do come along you'll know exactly what to do. With an escape plan, the temptations can become an opportunity to run to God for strength.

done ☐

CHECK IT OUT

Words can hurt!

Almost everyone has been hurt by someone's damaging words directed at them. If you haven't, consider yourself lucky but expect it to happen sooner or later.

Jesus said that the words that come from our mouths are a reflection of what's in our hearts. Check out Matthew 12:35: "A good person produces good words from a good heart, and an evil person produces evil words from an evil heart."

Try using good words today. Think about the power behind the words you use. Your words can either heal or hurt.

Choose healing words today.

Controlling the Tongue

Those who control their tongues can also control themselves in every other way. We can make a large horse turn around and go wherever we want by means of a small bit in its mouth. And a tiny rudder makes a huge ship turn wherever the pilot wants it to go, even though the winds are strong. So also, the tongue is a small thing, but what enormous damage it can do. A tiny spark can set a great forest on fire. And the tongue is a flame of fire. It is full of wickedness that can ruin your whole life. It can turn the entire course of your life into a blazing flame of destruction, for it is set on fire by hell itself.

People can tame all kinds of animals and birds and reptiles and fish, but no one can tame the tongue. It is an uncontrollable evil, full of deadly poison. Sometimes it praises our Lord and Father, and sometimes it breaks out into curses against those who have been made in the image of God. And so blessing and cursing come pouring out of the same mouth. Surely, my brothers and sisters, this is not right! Does a spring of water bubble out with both fresh water and bitter water? Can you pick olives from a fig tree or figs from a grapevine? No, and you can't draw fresh water from a salty pool.

James 3:2b-12

Related Texts: Psalm 12; Proverbs 6:16-19; 10:18-21,31-32; 12:17-19,22

done ☐

The Promise of Salvation

All honor to the God and Father of our Lord Jesus Christ, for it is by his boundless mercy that God has given us the privilege of being born again. Now we live with a wonderful expectation because Jesus Christ rose again from the dead. For God has reserved a priceless inheritance for his children. It is kept in heaven for you, pure and undefiled, beyond the reach of change and decay. And God, in his mighty power, will protect you until you receive this salvation, because you are trusting him. It will be revealed on the last day for all to see. So be truly glad! There is wonderful joy ahead, even though it is necessary for you to endure many trials for a while. . . .

You love him even though you have never seen him. Though you do not see him, you trust him; and even now you are happy with a glorious, inexpressible joy. Your reward for trusting him will be the salvation of your souls.

This salvation was something the prophets wanted to know more about. . . .

They were told that these things would not happen during their lifetime, but many years later, during yours. And now this Good News has been announced by those who preached to you in the power of the Holy Spirit sent from heaven. It is all so wonderful that even the angels are eagerly watching these things happen.

1 Peter 1:3-6,8-10a,12

Related Texts: Isaiah 52:13–53:12; Zechariah 13:7-9; Hebrews 1–2; James 1

JUST a THOUGHT

When you put your faith in Jesus, you not only receive a heavenly birth but also a promise for eternity and God's strength to keep you until then.

done ☐

BIG TIMe WoRd

HATRED

Unfortunately, our world has a lot of hatred floating around. Hatred displays itself in many different ways. When anger isn't processed or dealt with in a godly manner, it usually leads to resentment and then to hatred. This hatred usually shows itself in some form of rebellion or rage.

Hatred is the opposite of peace. If you choose hatred, you'll slowly destroy yourself and will eventually fall to pieces. But if you refuse hatred, you'll experience God's peace.

What's your choice? Peace or Pieces?

Living Stones and the Cornerstone

So get rid of all malicious behavior and deceit. Don't just pretend to be good! Be done with hypocrisy and jealousy and backstabbing. You must crave pure spiritual milk so that you can grow into the fullness of your salvation. Cry out for this nourishment as a baby cries for milk, now that you have had a taste of the Lord's kindness.

Come to Christ, who is the living cornerstone of God's temple. He was rejected by the people, but he is precious to God who chose him.

And now God is building you, as living stones, into his spiritual temple. What's more, you are God's holy priests, who offer the spiritual sacrifices that please him because of Jesus Christ. As the Scriptures express it,

"I am placing a stone in Jerusalem,
 a chosen cornerstone,
and anyone who believes in him
 will never be disappointed.". . .

But you are not like that, for you are a chosen people. You are a kingdom of priests, God's holy nation, his very own possession. This is so you can show others the goodness of God, for he called you out of the darkness into his wonderful light.

"Once you were not a people;
 now you are the people of God.
Once you received none of God's mercy;
 now you have received his mercy."

1 Peter 2:1-6,9-10

Related Texts: Psalms 34; 118:22-29; Isaiah 28:16-17; Matthew 16:13-19; Luke 20:9-19; Hebrews 5:11-14

done ☐

THE MORNING STAR

For we were not making up clever stories when we told you about the power of our Lord Jesus Christ and his coming again. We have seen his majestic splendor with our own eyes. And he received honor and glory from God the Father when God's glorious, majestic voice called down from heaven, "This is my beloved Son; I am fully pleased with him." We ourselves heard the voice when we were there with him on the holy mountain.

Because of that, we have even greater confidence in the message proclaimed by the prophets. Pay close attention to what they wrote, for their words are like a light shining in a dark place—until the day Christ appears and his brilliant light shines in your hearts. Above all, you must understand that no prophecy in Scripture ever came from the prophets themselves or because they wanted to prophesy. It was the Holy Spirit who moved the prophets to speak from God.

2 Peter 1:16-21

Your word is a lamp for my feet
and a light for my path.

Psalm 119:105

"I, Jesus, have sent my angel to give you this message for the churches. I am both the source of David and the heir to his throne. I am the bright morning star."

Revelation 22:16

Related Texts: Jeremiah 26; Amos 3:1-8; Isaiah 61; Mark 9:2-9; Luke 1:1-4

What's it Mean?

Peter had an incredible experience at the mount of transfiguration. But this experience couldn't replace his love and convictions for the Scriptures. Peter instructs Christians to trust the Scriptures more than experience.

Living by God's Word will provide light and guide us in the darkness. Although the Bible is filled with human words, it was God who inspired the writers with the right words to use. God "spoke" or "breathed" those words into life. They are God's words and are as reliable as God himself.

When God's words are hidden in your heart, you can't help but be different—it's guaranteed!

done ☐

Love one another

CATCH THIS

The greatest gift of all is God's love to us expressed through Jesus' death in our place. That's love! The Bible is another example of God's love.

Jesus expressed this when He wrapped up all the commandments by using "love" three times. He said to LOVE God with all of our heart, soul, and mind and to LOVE our neighbors as we LOVE ourselves. This love will not only change your life but will also show others you are a follower of God. This is especially true if you can love others without any expectations of them. Try loving regardless of how others act or treat you. This type of love isn't easy to express, but if you can do it, you'll find yourself loving just as

God loves you.

Love One Another

My dear children, I am writing this to you so that you will not sin. But if you do sin, there is someone to plead for you before the Father. He is Jesus Christ, the one who pleases God completely. He is the sacrifice for our sins. He takes away not only our sins but the sins of all the world.

And how can we be sure that we belong to him? By obeying his commandments. If someone says, "I belong to God," but doesn't obey God's commandments, that person is a liar and does not live in the truth. But those who obey God's word really do love him. That is the way to know whether or not we live in him. Those who say they live in God should live their lives as Christ did.

Dear friends, I am not writing a new commandment, for it is an old one you have always had, right from the beginning. This commandment—to love one another—is the same message you heard before. Yet it is also new. This commandment is true in Christ and is true among you, because the darkness is disappearing and the true light is already shining.

1 John 2:1-8

"So now I am giving you a new commandment: Love each other. Just as I have loved you, you should love each other. Your love for one another will prove to the world that you are my disciples."

John 13:34-35

Related Texts: 1 Kings 8:46-51; Psalm 119:9-11; John 14:15; Hebrews 2:17-18; 4:14-16; 7–9; 1 John 3:11-24

done ☐

The Love of the Father

Stop loving this evil world and all that it offers you, for when you love the world, you show that you do not have the love of the Father in you. For the world offers only the lust for physical pleasure, the lust for everything we see, and pride in our possessions. These are not from the Father. They are from this evil world. And this world is fading away, along with everything it craves. But if you do the will of God, you will live forever.

1 John 2:15-17

See how very much our heavenly Father loves us, for he allows us to be called his children, and we really are! But the people who belong to this world don't know God, so they don't understand that we are his children.

1 John 3:1

Everyone who believes that Jesus is the Christ is a child of God. And everyone who loves the Father loves his children, too. We know we love God's children if we love God and obey his commandments. Loving God means keeping his commandments, and really, that isn't difficult. For every child of God defeats this evil world by trusting Christ to give the victory. And the ones who win this battle against the world are the ones who believe that Jesus is the Son of God.

1 John 5:1-5

Related Texts: Deuteronomy 30:11-16; John 15:17-25; 1 John 4:7-21

One Minute Memory

Everyone who believes that Jesus is the Christ is a child of God. And everyone who loves the Father loves his children, too.

1 John 5:1

done ☐

Personality Plus

Anti-Christ

The word "anti-Christ" appears only five times in the New Testament, but the theme of an anti-Christ person is woven throughout the Old Testament prophecies. The word "anti" means "in place of" or "against." The Bible describes the Antichrist as someone who will try to exalt himself and be worshiped. The Antichrist will be given power or directed by Satan and try to lead people against God during the end times.

One of God's responsibilities is to take care of history. One of our responsibilities is to remain faithful to God. A strong faith in God will replace your fears with the security that the Antichrist will have no power over you.

Antichrists

Dear children, the last hour is here. You have heard that the Antichrist is coming, and already many such antichrists have appeared. From this we know that the end of the world has come. These people left our churches because they never really belonged with us; otherwise they would have stayed with us. When they left us, it proved that they do not belong with us. . . . And who is the great liar? The one who says that Jesus is not the Christ. Such people are antichrists, for they have denied the Father and the Son. Anyone who denies the Son doesn't have the Father either. But anyone who confesses the Son has the Father also.

1 John 2:18-19,22-23

Many deceivers have gone out into the world. They do not believe that Jesus Christ came to earth in a real body. Such a person is a deceiver and an antichrist. Watch out, so that you do not lose the prize for which we have been working so hard. Be diligent so that you will receive your full reward. For if you wander beyond the teaching of Christ, you will not have fellowship with God. But if you continue in the teaching of Christ, you will have fellowship with both the Father and the Son.

If someone comes to your meeting and does not teach the truth about Christ, don't invite him into your house or encourage him in any way. Anyone who encourages him becomes a partner in his evil work.

2 John 7-11

Related Texts: Proverbs 13:5; Isaiah 44:24-25; Jeremiah 14:14-15; 2 Timothy 3; 2 Peter 2-3

done ☐

The Salvation We Share

But now I find that I must write about something else, urging you to defend the truth of the Good News. God gave this unchanging truth once for all time to his holy people. I say this because some godless people have wormed their way in among you, saying that God's forgiveness allows us to live immoral lives. The fate of such people was determined long ago, for they have turned against our only Master and Lord, Jesus Christ. . . .

But you, my dear friends, must remember what the apostles of our Lord Jesus Christ told you, that in the last times there would be scoffers whose purpose in life is to enjoy themselves in every evil way imaginable. Now they are here, and they are the ones who are creating divisions among you. They live by natural instinct because they do not have God's Spirit living in them. . . .

Live in such a way that God's love can bless you as you wait for the eternal life that our Lord Jesus Christ in his mercy is going to give you. Show mercy to those whose faith is wavering. Rescue others by snatching them from the flames of judgment. There are still others to whom you need to show mercy, but be careful that you aren't contaminated by their sins.

And now, all glory to God, who is able to keep you from stumbling, and who will bring you into his glorious presence innocent of sin and with great joy. All glory to him, who alone is God our Savior, through Jesus Christ our Lord. Yes, glory, majesty, power, and authority belong to him, in the beginning, now, and forevermore. Amen.

Jude 3b-4,17-19,21-25

Related Texts: Amos 4:11; Zechariah 3; Acts 20:28-31; 2 Peter 3; 1 Timothy 4:1-6

In OTHER Words

godless teachers

The problem addressed in the Book of Jude is still a problem today. There are still godless teachers who are trying to pervert or add to the Bible. We need to watch out for these men and women because their teaching can be seductive and subtle. False teachers can creep into the church like worms and lead good people in the wrong direction.

One way to identify these teachers is to observe how they live their lives. If you are following someone's teachings, you need to ask yourself, "Does he practice what he teaches? Does she hate what is evil?"

Do what it takes to remain in God's love, and you'll be protected from the ungodly.

done ☐

What's it Mean?

This psalm is a great example of how futile it is to try to rebel against God. God laughs at our plans when we go against His plans.

If you are searching for true freedom, you will never find it in rebellion. Freedom is found in submission, which is the flip side of rebellion. Submission to God is giving everything you are into everything God is. Submission leads to freedom.

Don't you think that if God was capable of planning the coming of Jesus, He could also plan your life?

Trust in His wisdom and be a part of His eternal plan.

THE LORD'S ANOINTED KING

Why do the nations rage?
  Why do the people waste their time with
  futile plans?
The kings of the earth prepare for battle;
  the rulers plot together against the Lord
  and against his anointed one.
"Let us break their chains," they cry,
  "and free ourselves from this slavery."
But the one who rules in heaven laughs.
  The Lord scoffs at them.
Then in anger he rebukes them,
  terrifying them with his fierce fury.
For the Lord declares, "I have placed my chosen king on the throne
  in Jerusalem, my holy city."
The king proclaims the LORD's decree:
"The LORD said to me, 'You are my son.
  Today I have become your Father.
Only ask, and I will give you the nations as your inheritance,
  the ends of the earth as your possession.
You will break them with an iron rod
  and smash them like clay pots.' "
Now then, you kings, act wisely!
  Be warned, you rulers of the earth!
Serve the Lord with reverent fear,
  and rejoice with trembling.
Submit to God's royal son, or he will become angry,
  and you will be destroyed in the midst of your pursuits—
  for his anger can flare up in an instant.
But what joy for all who find protection in him!

Psalm 2

Related Texts: 2 Samuel 7; 1 Chronicles 17; Mark 1:1-11; Revelation 2:18-29

done ☐

David's Son and Lord

The LORD said to my Lord,
"Sit in honor at my right hand
until I humble your enemies,
making them a footstool under your feet."
The LORD will extend your powerful dominion from Jerusalem;
you will rule over your enemies.
In that day of battle,
your people will serve you willingly.
Arrayed in holy garments,
your vigor will be renewed each day like the morning dew.
The LORD has taken an oath and will not break his vow:
"You are a priest forever in the line of Melchizedek."
The Lord stands at your right hand to protect you.
He will strike down many kings in the day of his anger.
He will punish the nations
and fill them with their dead;
he will shatter heads
over the whole earth.
But he himself will be refreshed from brooks along the way.
He will be victorious.

Psalm 110

Another difference is that there were many priests under the old system. When one priest died, another had to take his place. But Jesus remains a priest forever; his priesthood will never end. Therefore he is able, once and forever, to save everyone who comes to God through him. He lives forever to plead with God on their behalf.

He is the kind of high priest we need because he is holy and blameless, unstained by sin. He has now been set apart from sinners, and he has been given the highest place of honor in heaven.

Hebrews 7:23-26

Related Texts: Genesis 14:18-20; Matthew 22:41-46; Hebrews 5:1-10; 7

done ☐

JUST a THOUGHT

If you have Jesus, you have all you need... forever. He has taken care of every-thing!

24 DECEMBER

Christ Is Born

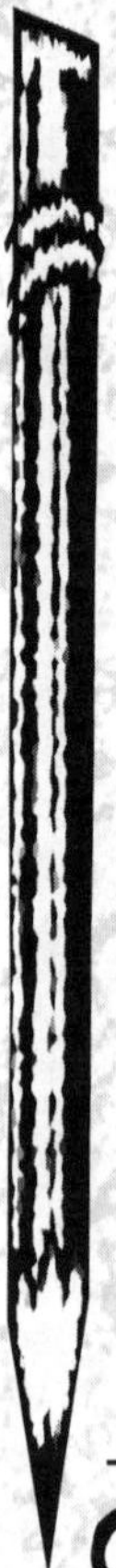

And because Joseph was a descendant of King David, he had to go to Bethlehem in Judea, David's ancient home. He traveled there from the village of Nazareth in Galilee. He took with him Mary, his fiancée, who was obviously pregnant by this time.

And while they were there, the time came for her baby to be born. She gave birth to her first child, a son. She wrapped him snugly in strips of cloth and laid him in a manger, because there was no room for them in the village inn.

That night some shepherds were in the fields outside the village, guarding their flocks of sheep. Suddenly, an angel of the Lord appeared among them, and the radiance of the Lord's glory surrounded them. They were terribly frightened, but the angel reassured them. "Don't be afraid!" he said. "I bring you good news of great joy for everyone! The Savior—yes, the Messiah, the Lord—has been born tonight in Bethlehem, the city of David! And this is how you will recognize him: You will find a baby lying in a manger, wrapped snugly in strips of cloth!"

Suddenly, the angel was joined by a vast host of others—the armies of heaven—praising God:

"Glory to God in the highest heaven,
    and peace on earth to all whom God favors."

Luke 2:4-14

Related Texts: 2 Samuel 7:8-17; Psalm 89:20-37; Isaiah 9:6-7; Matthew 1:18-25; Luke 1–2

Give it a try

Tomorrow we celebrate the birth of Jesus. If you could write Jesus a birthday letter, what would you write?

done ☐

DECEMBER 25

The Gifts of the Magi

Jesus was born in the town of Bethlehem in Judea, during the reign of King Herod. About that time some wise men from eastern lands arrived in Jerusalem, asking, "Where is the newborn king of the Jews? We have seen his star as it arose, and we have come to worship him."

Herod was deeply disturbed by their question, as was all of Jerusalem. He called a meeting of the leading priests and teachers of religious law. "Where did the prophets say the Messiah would be born?" he asked them.
"In Bethlehem," they said, "for this is what the prophet wrote:

"O Bethlehem of Judah,
you are not just a lowly village in Judah,
for a ruler will come from you
who will be the shepherd for my
people Israel.'"

Then Herod sent a private message to the wise men, asking them to come see him. At this meeting he learned the exact time when they first saw the star. Then he told them, "Go to Bethlehem and search carefully for the child. And when you find him, come back and tell me so that I can go and worship him, too!"

After this interview the wise men went their way. Once again the star appeared to them, guiding them to Bethlehem. It went ahead of them and stopped over the place where the child was. When they saw the star, they were filled with joy! They entered the house where the child and his mother, Mary, were, and they fell down before him and worshiped him. Then they opened their treasure chests and gave him gifts of gold, frankincense, and myrrh. But when it was time to leave, they went home another way, because God had warned them in a dream not to return to Herod.

Matthew 2:1-12

Related Texts: Exodus 30:22-33; Micah 5:2-5; Mark 15:16-24; Luke 1–2; John 12:1-7; Hebrews 13:15-21

Personality Plus

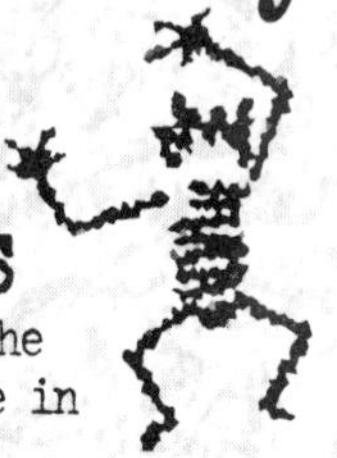

Jesus

Jesus is the key figure in the New Testament and the prophesied Messiah of the Old Testament. Although we know very little about Jesus' life prior to His public ministry, we do know Jesus is God's Son, He's the living example of the invisible God, He lived a perfect life, He was fully human and fully God, He died for our sins, He rose from the dead three days later, and He promised to return to earth someday. It may not seem like a lot of information, but it's enough to make it possible for you to live forever.

Today, much of the world celebrates Jesus' birth. But someday the entire world will bow and be judged according to their faith. Today is a special day, but it's not a real holiday unless Jesus is a part of your life. Merry Christmas!

done ☐

26 DECEMBER

Weird or What?

No one knows the time of Jesus' return and the establishment of a new heaven.

But there are several prophecies concerning the last days, some of which include: widespread violence, the rejection of God's Word, the rise of false prophets and Antichrists, abnormal sexual activity, intense demonic activity, extreme materialism, increase of wars, and political and religious uproar in the Holy Land.

These aren't all of the signs but a few to get you thinking. Many of these signs are already present in our world.

Find someone who can help you better understand the end times.

New Heavens and a New Earth

"Look! I am creating new heavens and a new earth—so wonderful that no one will even think about the old ones anymore. Be glad; rejoice forever in my creation! And look! I will create Jerusalem as a place of happiness. Her people will be a source of joy. I will rejoice in Jerusalem and delight in my people. And the sound of weeping and crying will be heard no more.

"No longer will babies die when only a few days old. No longer will adults die before they have lived a full life. No longer will people be considered old at one hundred! Only sinners will die that young!. . . They will not work in vain, and their children will not be doomed to misfortune. For they are people blessed by the LORD, and their children, too, will be blessed. I will answer them before they even call to me. While they are still talking to me about their needs, I will go ahead and answer their prayers! The wolf and lamb will feed together. The lion will eat straw like the ox. Poisonous snakes will strike no more. In those days, no one will be hurt or destroyed on my holy mountain. I, the LORD, have spoken!"

Isaiah 65:17-20,23-25

Related Texts: Genesis 3:1-14; Isaiah 66:22-24; 2 Peter 3:1-14; Revelation 21:1-5

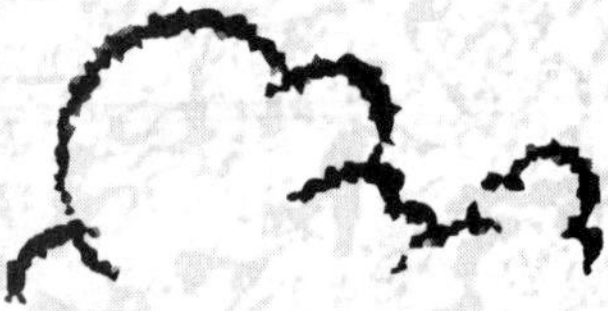

Ezekiel Sees the Glory Return to Jerusalem

After this, the man brought me back around to the east gateway. Suddenly, the glory of the God of Israel appeared from the east. The sound of his coming was like the roar of rushing waters, and the whole landscape shone with his glory. This vision was just like the others I had seen, first by the Kebar River and then when he came to destroy Jerusalem. And I fell down before him with my face in the dust. And the glory of the LORD came into the Temple through the east gateway.

Then the Spirit took me up and brought me into the inner courtyard, and the glory of the LORD filled the Temple. And I heard someone speaking to me from within the Temple. (The man who had been measuring was still standing beside me.) And the LORD said to me, "Son of man, this is the place of my throne and the place where I will rest my feet. I will remain here forever, living among the people of Israel. They and their kings will not defile my holy name any longer by their adulterous worship of other gods or by raising monuments in honor of their dead kings. They put their idol altars right next to mine with only a wall between them and me. They defiled my holy name by such wickedness, so I consumed them in my anger. Now let them put away their idols and the sacred pillars erected to honor their kings, and I will live among them forever."

Ezekiel 43:1-9

Related Texts: Ezekiel 1; 3; 8–11; Zechariah 14; Revelation 21:1-4

In OTHER Words

Jerusalem

Jerusalem is a city that is continually mentioned in both the Old and New Testaments. During biblical times this popular city was both the capital of Israel and its center for worship. The temple, which was the Israelites' symbol for their faith, was built in Jerusalem; each succeeding temple (after it was destroyed) was always rebuilt on its original site. Also, the majority of Jesus' ministry took place in Jerusalem as well as the events surrounding the beginning of the church.

Much of the prophetic literature (including today's reading) uses the city of Jerusalem or a Jerusalem-like setting as the place of Jesus' return and rule. If you're ready for His return, it won't matter when or where—so be ready!

done ☐

28 DECEMBER

Personality Plus

John

John was one of Jesus' first disciples and formed the "inner group" with Peter and James. John was more than a fisherman who turned author; he was an intelligent man who educated himself with Jewish teachings.

He received the nickname "son of thunder" and is often described as being scrappy and ambitious. He's also known as the disciple whom Jesus loved. John's life is really an expression of what Jesus did with people. Jesus was able to take a self-centered fisherman and turn him into the man of love we see from his writings.

Read John's Gospel if you want a better picture of Jesus' life on earth.

His Face Was Like the Sun

I am John, your brother. In Jesus we are partners in suffering and in the Kingdom and in patient endurance. I was exiled to the island of Patmos for preaching the word of God and speaking about Jesus. It was the Lord's Day, and I was worshiping in the Spirit. Suddenly, I heard a loud voice behind me, a voice that sounded like a trumpet blast. It said, "Write down what you see, and send it to the seven churches: Ephesus, Smyrna, Pergamum, Thyatira, Sardis, Philadelphia, and Laodicea."

When I turned to see who was speaking to me, I saw seven gold lampstands. And standing in the middle of the lampstands was the Son of Man. He was wearing a long robe with a gold sash across his chest. His head and his hair were white like wool, as white as snow. And his eyes were bright like flames of fire. His feet were as bright as bronze refined in a furnace, and his voice thundered like mighty ocean waves. He held seven stars in his right hand, and a sharp two-edged sword came from his mouth. And his face was as bright as the sun in all its brilliance.

When I saw him, I fell at his feet as dead. But he laid his right hand on me and said, "Don't be afraid! I am the First and the Last. I am the living one who died. Look, I am alive forever and ever! And I hold the keys of death and the grave. Write down what you have seen—both the things that are now happening and the things that will happen later."

Revelation 1:9-19

Related Texts: Psalm 149; Daniel 7; 2 Timothy 3; Hebrews 4:12-13; Revelation 2–11; 19:11-21

done ☐

The Saints and the Serpent

Then I saw an angel come down from heaven with the key to the bottomless pit and a heavy chain in his hand. He seized the dragon—that old serpent, the Devil, Satan—and bound him in chains for a thousand years. The angel threw him into the bottomless pit, which he then shut and locked so Satan could not deceive the nations anymore until the thousand years were finished. Afterward he would be released again for a little while.

Then I saw thrones, and the people sitting on them had been given the authority to judge. And I saw the souls of those who had been beheaded for their testimony about Jesus, for proclaiming the word of God. And I saw the souls of those who had not worshiped the beast or his statue, nor accepted his mark on their forehead or their hands. They came to life again, and they reigned with Christ for a thousand years. This is the first resurrection. (The rest of the dead did not come back to life until the thousand years had ended.) Blessed and holy are those who share in the first resurrection. For them the second death holds no power, but they will be priests of God and of Christ and will reign with him a thousand years.

When the thousand years end, Satan will be let out of his prison. He will go out to deceive the nations from every corner of the earth, which are called Gog and Magog. He will gather them together for battle—a mighty host, as numberless as sand along the shore. And I saw them as they went up on the broad plain of the earth and surrounded God's people and the beloved city. But fire from heaven came down on the attacking armies and consumed them.

Then the Devil, who betrayed them, was thrown into the lake of fire that burns with sulfur, joining the beast and the false prophet. There they will be tormented day and night forever and ever.

Revelation 20:1-10

Related Texts: Genesis 3:1–15; Ezekiel 38–39; 1 Corinthians 6:1-3; Revelation 12–13; 17–19

JUST a THOUGHT

The Book of Revelation is no fairy tale! Satan is real, and God defeats him. It's tough to understand and certainly takes faith to believe, but God's Word gives you enough light to know that a life without Jesus isn't worth eternity in hell—ouch!

done ☐

Judgment Day

One Minute Memory

He will **remove all** of their **sorrows,** and there will be **no more death** or **sorrow** or **crying** or **pain.** For the old world and its **evils** are gone **forever.**

Revelation 21:4

And I saw a great white throne, and I saw the one who was sitting on it. The earth and sky fled from his presence, but they found no place to hide. I saw the dead, both great and small, standing before God's throne. And the books were opened, including the Book of Life. And the dead were judged according to the things written in the books, according to what they had done. The sea gave up the dead in it, and death and the grave gave up the dead in them. They were all judged according to their deeds. And death and the grave were thrown into the lake of fire. This is the second death—the lake of fire. And anyone whose name was not found recorded in the Book of Life was thrown into the lake of fire.

Revelation 20:11-15

Then I saw a new heaven and a new earth, for the old heaven and the old earth had disappeared. And the sea was also gone. And I saw the holy city, the new Jerusalem, coming down from God out of heaven like a beautiful bride prepared for her husband.

I heard a loud shout from the throne, saying, "Look, the home of God is now among his people! He will live with them, and they will be his people. God himself will be with them. He will remove all of their sorrows, and there will be no more death or sorrow or crying or pain. For the old world and its evils are gone forever."

Revelation 21:1-4

Related Texts: Isaiah 65:17-25; 66:22-24; Daniel 12:1-3; John 1:14-18; 2 Peter 3:1-14

done ☐

DECEMBER 31

Jesus Is Coming Soon!

Then the angel said to me, "These words are trustworthy and true: 'The Lord God, who tells his prophets what the future holds, has sent his angel to tell you what will happen soon.'"

"Look, I am coming soon! Blessed are those who obey the prophecy written in this scroll." . . .

"See, I am coming soon, and my reward is with me, to repay all according to their deeds. I am the Alpha and the Omega, the First and the Last, the Beginning and the End."

Blessed are those who wash their robes so they can enter through the gates of the city and eat the fruit from the tree of life. Outside the city are the dogs—the sorcerers, the sexually immoral, the murderers, the idol worshipers, and all who love to live a lie.

"I, Jesus, have sent my angel to give you this message for the churches. I am both the source of David and the heir to his throne. I am the bright morning star."

The Spirit and the bride say, "Come." Let each one who hears them say, "Come." Let the thirsty ones come—anyone who wants to. Let them come and drink the water of life without charge. . . .

He who is the faithful witness to all these things says, "Yes, I am coming soon!" Amen! Come, Lord Jesus!

The grace of the Lord Jesus be with you all.

Revelation 22:6-7,12-17,20-21

Related Texts: Psalms 1; 37; Matthew 16:24-27; Luke 12:35-40; 1 Thessalonians 4:13-5:11; Revelation 1:1-3

JUST a THOUGHT

Begin your year right by committing your faith to Jesus and remaining faithful this entire year (and until His return). A year of walking with Jesus is a great year!

done ☐

topical index

N

O

P

Q

R